DATE DUE

TEXTBOOK OF TRANSPERSONAL PSYCHIATRY AND PSYCHOLOGY

TEXTBOOK OF TRANSPERSONAL PSYCHIATRY AND PSYCHOLOGY

EDITED BY
BRUCE W. SCOTTON,
ALLAN B. CHINEN, AND
JOHN R. BATTISTA

BasicBooks
A Division of HarperCollins*Publishers*

Library of Congress Cataloging-in-Publication Data

Scotton, Bruce W.
    Textbook of transpersonal psychiatry and psychology / Bruce W. Scotton, Allan B. Chinen, and John R. Battista.
        p.   cm.
    Includes bibliographical references and index.
    ISBN 0-465-09530-5
    1. Transpersonal psychotherapy.   2. Transpersonal psychology.
I. Chinen, Allan B., 1952– .   II. Battista, John R. (John Robert), 1946– .
III. Title.
RC489.T75S37   1996
616.89—dc20   95–43397
                                                                CIP

96 97 98 99 ❖/HC 9 8 7 6 5 4 3 2 1

This book is dedicated to Jerry Garcia,
a wounded healer who made the realm of the spirit a
palpable experience for several generations, and
Miles Vich, who launched so many of us.

CONTENTS

CONTRIBUTORS

JOHN R. BATTISTA, M.D., M.A. Private practice of psychiatry in New Milford, Connecticut, and author in the fields of consciousness studies and personality theory.

SEYMOUR BOORSTEIN, M.D. Certified Psychoanalyst, Associate Clinical Professor of Psychiatry, University of California, San Francisco, and author in the field of transpersonal psychiatry.

SYLVIA BOORSTEIN, Ph.D. Cofounding teacher at Spirit Rock Meditation Center in Woodacre, California, and private psychotherapy practice in Kentfield, California.

GARY BRAVO, M.D. Staff Psychiatrist, Sonoma County Mental Health Hospital, researcher and author in the field of psychedelics.

ALLAN B. CHINEN, M.D. Associate Clinical Professor of Psychiatry, University of California, San Francisco, and author of numerous works on the transpersonal dimensions of midlife and aging.

ARTHUR J. DEIKMAN, M.D. Clinical Professor of Psychiatry, University of California, San Francisco, and author of numerous works on transpersonal themes.

DONNA DRYER, M.D. Associate Professor of Psychiatry, University of Maryland, and one of the very few researchers currently permitted to work with psychedelic substances by the U.S. government.

MARK EPSTEIN, M.D. Private practice in New York City, author and editor of works on Buddhism and psychiatry.

WILLIAM W. FOOTE, M.D. Private practice in San Francisco specializing in paranormal, metaphysical, and spiritual experiences and lecturer on similar topics.

BRUCE GREYSON, M.D. Professor of Psychiatric Medicine, University of Virginia Health Sciences Center and editor, *Journal of Near-Death Studies*.

CHARLES GROB, M.D. Director of Child and Adolescent Psychiatry, Harbor–UCLA Medical Center, researcher and author in the field of psychedelics.

JOHN F. HIATT, M.D. Associate Professor of Psychiatry, University of California, San Francisco and Director, Transpersonal Clinic, San Francisco Veterans Administration Medical Center.

THE REVEREND DWIGHT H. JUDY, M.Th., Ph.D. Director of Program and Administration at Oakwood Spiritual Life Center, Syracuse, Indiana, and president of the Association for Transpersonal Psychology.

RONALD W. JUE, Ph.D. Private practice in southern California and past president of the Association for Transpersonal Psychology.

KATHRYN J. LEE, M.D. Private practice of psychiatry in San Francisco and staff psychiatrist, Sunset–Parkside Community Mental Health Clinic.

FRANCIS G. LU, M.D. Clinical Professor of Psychiatry, University of California, San Francisco, and Director, Asian Task Force, American Psychiatric Association.

DAVID LUKOFF, Ph.D. Professor of Psychology, Saybrook Institute, San Francisco, California, and staff psychologist, San Francisco Veterans Administration Medical Center.

LARRY G. PETERS, Ph.D. (anthropology), M.A. (psychology). Co-director, Program in Marriage and Family Therapy, California Graduate Institute, Los Angeles, and private practice.

DONALD F. SANDNER, M.D. Certified Jungian analyst in private practice in San Francisco and Corte Madera, California, and author in the fields of Jungian psychology and Native American culture.

RABBI ZALMAN M. SCHACHTER-SHALOMI. Lecturer and author of works on the Kabbalah and Jewish mysticism; Sufi sheik.

BRUCE W. SCOTTON, M.D. Associate Clinical Professor of Psychiatry, University of California, San Francisco, and certified Jungian analyst and psychiatrist in private practice.

PATRICIA L. SPEIER, M.D. Associate Director, Child and Adolescent Outpatient Service, Langley Porter Psychiatric Institute, University of California, San Francisco.

CHARLES T. TART, Ph.D. Professor Emeritus of Psychology, University of California at Davis and internationally known author and researcher in the areas of altered states of consciousness and parapsychology.

EUGENE TAYLOR, Ph.D. Lecturer in Psychiatry, Harvard Medical School and author of works on the history of psychiatry and psychology.

ROBERT TURNER, M.D. Associate Clinical Professor of Psychiatry, University of California, San Francisco, and psychiatrist and transpersonal psychotherapist in private practice.

FRANCES VAUGHAN, Ph.D. Private practice of psychology in Mill Valley, California, member of the clinical faculty of the University of California Medical School at Irvine, and transpersonal author.

BRUCE S. VICTOR, M.D. Director, Clinical Psychopharmacology, California Pacific Medical Center in San Francisco and lecturer and author.

ROGER WALSH, M.D., Ph.D. Professor of Psychiatry, Philosophy, and Anthropology at the University of California at Irvine and award-winning author in the field of consciousness and its relationship to other disciplines.

RICHARD YENSEN, Ph.D. Founder and Director of Orenda Institute, Baltimore, Maryland, and one of the very few researchers currently permitted to work with psychedelic substances by the U.S. government.

ACKNOWLEDGMENTS

Dr. Scotton would like to thank the following people and organizations: The C. G. Jung Institute of San Francisco and Millie Fortier, Ph.D.; the Residency Training Program in Psychiatry, University of California, San Francisco and Enoch Callaway, M.D., for extending grants to support parts of this work. Thanks also to M. Robert Harris, M.D., for supporting the view that travel to study other cultures had to do with psychiatry; Robert Michels, M.D., and Stuart Yudofsky, M.D., for helping cement his interest in psychiatry; Roger Walsh, M.D., Ph.D., for groundwork in getting this material out to the world; Jaichima and Vicente, Swami Atmananda, Swami Muktananda, Thaungpulu Sayadaw, Sri M. P. Pandit, Dr. Rina Sircar, Tashi Gyaltsen, and Thartang Tulku for sharing their spiritual traditions; the members of the Tuesday night Bay Area transpersonal psychiatry group from whose regular gatherings this book arose; all the authors for their essential contributions; Jo Ann Miller, Michael Mueller, Michael Wilde, and the staff at Basic Books; and June Yokell, M.F.A., for her helpful comments, support, and forbearance.

Dr. Chinen would also like to thank Seymour Boorstein for hosting the transpersonal psychiatry study group from which this textbook arose; and Miles Vich for his encouragement and advice, and for tending the field for so many years. Special thanks to the many clinicians too numerous to name or to include in this textbook who have taken personal and professional risks to develop and use transpersonal techniques in their practice.

Dr. Battista also would like to thank Justine McCabe, Ph.D., for her helpful reviews of his articles.

FOREWORD

Ken Wilber

BIOLOGICAL AND MEDICAL scientists are in the midst of intensive work on the Human Genome Project, an endeavor to map all of the genes in the entire sequence of human DNA. This spectacular project promises to revolutionize our ideas of human growth, development, disease, and medical treatment, and its completion surely will mark one of the greatest advances in human knowledge.

Not as well known but arguably more important is what might be called the Human Consciousness Project, an endeavor well under way to *map the entire spectrum of the various states of human consciousness* (including realms of the human unconscious as well). This project, involving hundreds of researchers from around the world, involves a series of multidisciplinary, multicultural, multimodal approaches that together promise an exhaustive mapping of the entire range of consciousness, the entire sequence of the "genes" of awareness, as it were.

The various attempts amply represented in the following pages are rapidly converging on a "master template" of the stages, structures, and states of consciousness available to men and women. By comparing and contrasting a variety of multicultural approaches— from Zen Buddhism to Western psychoanalysis, Vedanta Hinduism to existential phenomenology, Tundra Shamanism to altered states—the approaches together constitute a master template, that is, a spectrum of consciousness, in which each culture fills some gaps left by others.

Although many of the specifics are still being intensively researched, the overall evidence for the existence of this spectrum of consciousness is already so significant as to put it largely beyond serious dispute. The existence of these various structures and states of consciousness is based on careful experimentation and consensual validation; from such gatherings of consensual and documented data, firmly anchored in appropriate validity claims, the spectrum of consciousness is constructed. This spectrum appears to range from prepersonal to personal to transpersonal experiences, from instinctual to egoic to spiritual modes, from subconscious to self-conscious to superconscious structures, from prerational to rational to transrational states. And it is this all-inclusive spectrum of consciousness upon which transpersonal psychiatry and psychology are primarily based.

The word *transpersonal* simply means "personal plus." That is, the transpersonal orientation explicitly and carefully includes all the facets of personal psychology and psychiatry, then *adds* those deeper or higher aspects of human experience that transcend the ordinary and the average—experiences that are, in other words, "transpersonal" or "more than the personal," personal plus. Thus, in the attempt to more fully, accurately, and scientifically reflect the entire range of human experience, transpersonal psychiatry and psychology take as their starting point the entire spectrum of consciousness.

In the following chapters you will see the most important approaches to this spectrum outlined. You will also see the diverse methodologies that have evolved to address (and assess) the different dimensions of this spectrum, including empiricism, phenomenology, representational models, hermeneutical interpretations, meditative states, and so on, yet all oriented toward careful verification and justification procedures. The transpersonal orientation in all cases is geared toward consensual *evidence* that can be confirmed or rejected by a community of the adequate (the all-important fallibist criterion for genuine accumulation of knowledge).

You will see that this spectrum develops. Like all complex living systems, the spectrum of consciousness grows and evolves; it moves, in the most general sense, from subconscious to self-conscious to superconscious modes, or prepersonal to personal to transpersonal capacities. And you will see some of the more important models that have been proposed to account for this extraordinary growth and development of human consciousness. Precisely because the spectrum of consciousness develops, various "misdevelopments" can occur at any stage of the unfolding. As with any living entity, pathology can occur at any point in growth. Thus, the spectrum of consciousness is also a spectrum of different types of possible pathologies: psychotic, borderline, neurotic, cognitive, existential, spiritual. And, as you will clearly see, transpersonal psychiatry and psychology have developed a sophisticated battery of treatment modalities that address these different types of pathologies.

Because transpersonal psychiatry and psychology are dedicated to a careful and rigorous investigation into the entire spectrum of consciousness, they naturally find themselves allied with other transpersonal approaches, ranging from transpersonal ecology to transpersonal philosophy, transpersonal anthropology to transpersonal sociology. And the following pages reveal an impressive collection of essays touching on these various fields. The point, of course, is that if the entire spectrum of consciousness is accurately acknowledged and taken into account, it will dramatically alter each and every discipline it touches. And this, indeed, is part of the extraordinary interest and excitement that the transpersonal orientation has generated in numerous disciplines.

The editors of this book—Bruce Scotton, Allan Chinen, and John Battista—have done a superb job in presenting a balanced, thoughtful, and inclusive cross-section of virtually every aspect of transpersonal studies, with appropriate emphasis, of course, on the psychological and psychiatric dimensions. It is a brilliant and pioneering effort that will no doubt become an indispensable standard in the field, for which the editors deserve the highest praise. It is such remarkable inclusiveness that especially announces the transpersonal orientation. If nothing human is alien to me, then neither should it be alien to our sciences of the mind, the soul, the psyche, the possible human. How could orthodox psychology ignore, dismiss, or pathologize the further reaches of human nature? How could positivistic science reduce it all to a pile of sensory matter?

Looking deeply into our world, into ourselves, into our brethren, is there really nothing more to be found than a bunch of material atoms hurling through the void? Is there not more in heaven and earth than is dreamt of in that philosophy? Are there not depths and heights that awe and inspire, that bring us to our knees, that stun us with the beauty of the sublime, the radiance of the real, the truth and goodness of a spiritual domain that outshines our loveless ways? Are these not part of the extraordinary spectrum of human possibilities?

Transpersonal psychiatry and psychology are dedicated to the assumption that there is decidedly more than conventional approaches assume; that the spectrum of consciousness is vast indeed, that there is in fact a "personal plus." And, in addition to the undeniable importance of biological psychiatry and personal psychology, it is the nature of that plus, that depth, that height, that transpersonal psychiatry and psychology are dedicated to exploring.

PART I

Introduction

CHAPTER 1

Introduction and Definition of Transpersonal Psychiatry

BRUCE W. SCOTTON

THIS TEXTBOOK PROPOSES a fresh look at what is known about the human psyche: its functioning, development, pathology, and treatment. Although traditional psychiatry and psychology have made impressive strides in the understanding of the human mind and brain, they adhere to an unnecessarily restricted view of the psyche and its functioning, and in so doing, they refuse to follow the scientific method. Specifically, our current sciences of the psyche fail to examine the data concerning, build theories to explain, and work therapeutically with spiritual experiences and experiences of nonordinary reality. Existing research shows that such experiences often indicate higher than usual levels of functioning and that the increased ability to attain spiritual and nonordinary experience correlates with development beyond the average.[1,2] The fields of transpersonal psychiatry and psychology have evolved as a context to study and work with these experiences and levels of development.

Transpersonal, meaning beyond the personal, refers to development beyond conventional, personal, or individual levels. More specifically, *transpersonal* refers to development beyond the average, although such higher functioning turns out to be more common than previously was thought. Transpersonal development is

3

part of a continuum of human functioning or consciousness, ranging from the *prepersonal* (before the formation of a separate ego), to the *personal* (with a functioning ego), to the transpersonal (in which the ego remains available but is superseded by more inclusive frames of reference). The transpersonal schema of development extends and clarifies what is implied in the familiar biopsychosocial model: that the later stages of human development address concerns beyond those of the individual. Such thinking follows the work of Ken Wilber, William James, Carl Jung, Roberto Assagioli, Erik Erikson, and Abraham Maslow, all of whom observed that the development of human consciousness follows such a schema, first differentiating an independent, functioning ego and then transcending attachment to that ego.

Transpersonal psychiatry, therefore, is psychiatry that seeks to foster development, correct developmental arrests, and heal traumas at all levels of development, including transpersonal levels. It extends the standard biopsychosocial model of psychiatry to a biopsychosocial–spiritual one in which the later stages of human development are concerned with development beyond, or transcendent of, the individual.

The meanings of the terms *transpersonal* and *spiritual* must be (and are throughout this book) sharply differentiated from the meaning of the term *religious*. *Religious* refers to the belief system of a specific group, whose members usually gather around specific contents and contexts that contain some transpersonal elements. *Spiritual* refers to the realm of the human spirit, that part of humanity that is not limited to bodily experience. *Transpersonal experience*, in addressing all human experience beyond the ego level, includes spiritual experience but also includes embodied human experience of higher levels. An example of this intermediate transpersonal level, still embodied but beyond ego functioning, might be found in some of the practitioners of Gandhi's *satyagraha* and in Martin Luther King's civil rights workers, who were willing to nonviolently risk their lives for higher values, transcending concern with personal survival for larger goals.

The words *transpersonal* and *spiritual* refer to levels of functioning of human consciousness that are potentially available in all cultures, with widely varying content and context. An account of a mystical, ineffable experience that brought about improved functioning for the experiencer would be an account of a transpersonal experience. If that experience were enfolded in the concepts of a religion, it would also be a religious experience; however, many transpersonal experiences exist outside of any religion. Transpersonal psychiatry and psychology address that universal aspect of human consciousness that is transpersonal experience and do not propound the belief of any one religion.

Public interest in transpersonal experiences and levels of development has grown tremendously in the last few years as indicated by the publication of many books on spiritual and transpersonal topics. In 1992, the International Transpersonal Association conference in Prague entirely filled the 2,000 available slots and drew several hundred more persons on a waiting list. Attendees came from approximately 40 countries and all continents. A cover article in *Newsweek*, dated November 28, 1994, reported that 58% of all Americans felt the need to experience spiritual growth. A national poll documented that 70 to 80% of the American public were dissatisfied enough with the limited scientific model of current medical practice that they had used alternative healing practices within the last year. Numerous studies have set the incidence of mystical experience in members of the general population at 30 to 40%.[3]

The interest demonstrated by these studies points to the need for transpersonal research. Spiritual experience is widespread throughout all cultures and all times. Any survey of the greatest artists and thinkers and their best works would reveal an extremely high incidence of concern with spiritual–transpersonal issues: universal brother- and sisterhood, surpassing love, attachment to principles above self, life beyond death, the search for connection between human beings and the world, and moral and ethical virtue. Despite the universality of transpersonal experience and the implied value it is accorded in our collective judgments of what constitutes greatness in human endeavor, our current "scientific" study of the psyche fails almost entirely to deal with the transpersonal realm. The word *scientific* is set in quotation marks because, as stated earlier, such a study of the mind is by definition unscientific in that it fails to take into account, or even to report, a large body of phenomena that is not explained by the current theory: a point William James made at the turn of the century.

Despite this official neglect, a significant amount of work has been done in transpersonal research and clinical practice. In Western psychiatry and psychology, such work goes back at least as far as James' *Varieties of Religious Experience*, and it continues with Jung's insistence to Sigmund Freud of the importance of spiritual as well as sexual development and with Assagioli's development of the system he called *psychosynthesis*. The work continues to the present with impressive research on psychedelics, meditation, and near-death experiences, as well as theory building by Wilber, Roger Walsh, Stanislav Grof, Charles Tart, Michael Washburn, and others.

An important reason for the limitation of Western theories of the mind is ethnocentrism. The wisdom traditions of other cultures, particularly Hinduism and Buddhism, for centuries have contained much about higher states of consciousness and how to produce them. Only in the last few decades has science taken these traditions seriously enough to begin to research them.

Finally, related academic disciplines have added much to our knowledge about transpersonal experience. The tradition of social relativism is well into its second generation with the work of Jacques Derrida and Michel Foucault, following that of Benjamin Whorf and Edward Sapir. Sociologists have developed a key concept stating that societies construct different realities by directing and training attention to (and away from) certain aspects of experience. The field of anthropology confirms that other societies experience realities that are vastly different from our own Western scientific reality. Indigenous Australian people can use trance states to enter "dream time" and locate hidden sources of water miles away. Hindu yogis can be sealed in an airtight box and slow their respiration and heartbeat so dramatically that they can be released many hours later unharmed. Developments in physics have produced sophisticated new models of the cosmos that no longer posit a single "objective" reality but many realities according to the state of the observer.

This textbook describes a science of the mind that takes into account all these sources of data, drawing on what is already known in psychiatry and psychology, in other Western academic disciplines, and by members of other cultures. This newly enlarged psychiatry stands in relationship to the current psychiatry much as modern physics does to classical Newtonian physics: The current "classical" psychiatry is a subset of a larger system, the new transpersonal psychiatry. Like Newtonian physics, classical psychiatry derived from a specific vantage point: the logical-positivistic, scientific worldview created through participation in our cultural assumptions. Transpersonal psychiatry allows not only that other vantage points (other societies) construct equally valid realities, but also that reality can be constructed in more positive directions with adequate techniques and personal development.

Some researchers and clinicians have already made the shift to this new paradigm for the psyche. The *Textbook of Transpersonal Psy-*

chiatry and Psychology examines how the new theories and concepts are being elucidated and used in practice. It also examines the benefits as well as the risks of transpersonal treatment and of spiritual experience in general. The textbook considers how to facilitate spiritual experience and higher states of consciousness ethically, without preaching one's own path or religion.

The editors are fortunate to have chapter authors who are recognized within the field as experts in their areas. None has chosen lightly to leave the prevalent model; rather, each has decided to do so only after years of academic preparation in the standard mode. Almost all have current teaching appointments at major universities and medical centers. We hope that their years of labor will enable the reader to readily grasp this new approach.

The book begins by reviewing the history of the transpersonal model. Following that is a review of the contributions to the theory of the new discipline of various psychiatrists and psychologists: James, Freud, Jung, Maslow, Assagioli, Wilber, Grof, and the information theorists. The book surveys what is known about higher levels of human functioning within the wisdom traditions: shamanism, Native American spirituality, yoga and Hinduism, Buddhism, Kabbalah, and Christian mysticism, sources that have previously been largely ignored by traditional psychiatry and psychology. Research on transpersonal experience is reported, including studies of meditation, psychedelics, near-death experience, and parapsychology. There are also chapters on other academic disciplines that have contributed to the new science of the mind, including physics, anthropology, and philosophy.

After a theoretical beginning, the book turns to clinical information, with a section on transpersonal diagnosis and the specific pitfall of narcissism in transpersonal work. An inquiry is made into the nature of transpersonal therapeutic work, with chapters on transpersonal psychopharmacology, psychotherapy of psychotic disorders, psychotherapy of borderline and neurotic patients, and psychotherapy with religious patients. Techniques that are of particular interest or relevance to transpersonal treatment are surveyed, with chapters on visualization, breathwork, "past-lives" regression, and psychedelic therapy. The text then turns to the question of how to train theoreticians, researchers, and clinicians.

The book concludes by integrating the various sections to provide a new, broader model of the human mind and by suggesting directions for future development of the field.

NOTES

1. Goleman, D. (1988). *The meditative mind.* Los Angeles: Tarcher.
2. Wilber, K., Engler, J., & Brown, D. (1986). *Transformations of consciousness.* Boston: New Science Library.
3. Spika, B., Hood, R., & Gorsuch, R. (1985). *The psychology of religion: An empirical approach.* Englewood Cliffs, NJ: Prentice-Hall.

CHAPTER 2

The Emergence of
Transpersonal Psychiatry

ALLAN B. CHINEN

HISTORY

This chapter describes the origins of the fields of transpersonal psychiatry and psychology[1,2] and their development in relation to American culture, particularly during the turbulent decade of the 1960s.

The first documented use of the term *transpersonal* was by William James in a 1905 lecture[3,4] (see Chapter 3). In 1942, Jung's translators followed suit, using the term *transpersonal* as a gloss on the German word *ueberpersonlich;* however, transpersonal psychology and psychiatry emerged as a field distinguished from other professional domains only in the 1960s. The discipline arose from the humanistic psychology movement, often called the "third force" in psychology, which sought to counterbalance the first two forces that dominated the period, psychoanalysis and behaviorism.[5] Focusing on psychological health rather than psychopathology, humanistic psychology soon entered popular culture as the "human potential movement," characterized by encounter groups, sensitivity training, and so on.

9

In the mid-1960s, Anthony Sutich, founding editor of the *Journal of Humanistic Psychology*, began gathering like-minded individuals in his California home for informal discussions on "transhumanistic" topics: issues that seemed to go beyond humanistic psychology and the popular human potential movement.[6,7] The informal study group included Miles Vich, James Fadiman, and Harriet Francisco as regulars, but it involved many other occasional but vital participants, including Michael Murphy, cofounder of the Esalen Institute. Fueling the discussions was a dissatisfaction with the focus of humanistic psychology on the individual self. The group also sought more diverse cross-cultural approaches.[8] The meetings were remarkable not only for their wide-ranging topics, but also because Sutich, totally disabled by a chronic illness, participated from a gurney, using an overhead mirror to see the other discussants. Abraham Maslow, a pioneer in the study of "peak" experiences and psychological health, was a major guiding spirit for these early "salons." Stanislav Grof was another influence: With Maslow and Viktor Frankl, Grof suggested the use of the term *transpersonal* for the emerging field.

In 1968, a humanistic psychology interest group, including Joseph Adams, Fadiman, Francisco, Sidney Jourard, John Levy, Maslow, Sonja Margulis, Murphy, Grof, Vich, and Sutich, announced a "fourth force," which they called "transpersonal psychology" to distinguish it from its humanistic predecessor. They established a new organization, the Transpersonal Institute, and later, the Association for Transpersonal Psychology, whose purposes were to explore the relationship of spirituality and altered states of consciousness to psychology. A year later, the first issue of the *Journal of Transpersonal Psychology* was published, edited by Sutich. The *Journal's* original mission statement is noteworthy:

> The *Journal of Transpersonal Psychology* is concerned with the publication of theoretical and applied research, original contributions, *empirical* papers, articles and studies in meta-needs, ultimate values, unitive consciousness, peak experience, ecstasy, mystical experience, B-values, essence, bliss, awe, wonder, self-actualization, ultimate meaning, transcendence of the self, spirit, sacralization of everyday life, oneness, cosmic awareness, cosmic play, individual and species wide synergy, maximal interpersonal encounter, transcendental phenomena; maximal sensory awareness, responsiveness and expression; and related concepts, experiences and activities. As a statement of purpose, this formulation is to be understood as subject to *optional* individual or group inter-

pretations, either wholly or in part, with regard to the acceptance of its content as essentially naturalistic, theistic, supernaturalistic, or any other designated classification. [Emphasis in original.]

Of note in the mission statement are three major motifs: (1) a focus on issues traditionally considered religious or spiritual, for example, transcendence and ultimate meanings or values; (2) an emphasis on empirical, scientific studies; and (3) a suspension of belief in the content of the experiences, that is, "optional" interpretations about whether the phenomena are supernatural or not. In other words, transpersonal psychology was to be a reflective, scientific-minded approach to matters traditionally considered religious or spiritual.

Early contributions to the journal included Ram Dass's discussions of spirituality from a countercultural viewpoint, Charles Tart's investigations of altered states, Lawrence LeShan's reflections on the implications of modern physics, and Alyce and Elmer Green's physiological research concerning meditation and yogis. There were also important essays by Maslow, Murphy, Sutich, and Grof. Since 1975, when Vich, previously editor of the *Journal of Humanistic Psychology*, was appointed editor of the *Journal of Transpersonal Psychology (JTP)*, the latter publication has become a vital forum, bringing together the pioneers of transpersonal psychology, many of whom worked independently in widely scattered locations in highly diverse domains. For example, *JTP* brought to public attention the work of an unknown graduate student, Ken Wilber. In reflecting on the field, Vich[8] noted that clinicians were central to the transpersonal literature from the beginning, providing "tough-minded" grounding. Yet there was surprisingly little interdisciplinary rivalry, like that often seen today between psychologists and psychiatrists, reflecting the ecumenical and inclusive spirit of transpersonal investigators.

The year the *Journal of Transpersonal Psychology* was first published, the first Council Grove Conference was also held, sponsored by the Menninger Foundation. Discussion included research on biofeedback, psychedelics, meditation, and yoga. In subsequent years, many transpersonally oriented institutions were founded, including the Institute of Noetic Sciences in California, established in 1973; the International Transpersonal Psychology Association, founded by Grof, which had its first conference in 1973; the California Institute of Transpersonal Psychology, organized by Robert Frager in 1976; and the California Institute for Integral Studies, formerly the California Institute for Asian Studies, founded earlier by Frederick Spiegelberg.

Transpersonal psychology has grown steadily since its origins and now includes several graduate, degree-granting educational institutions. The rise of transpersonal psychology and psychiatry is graphically documented in scholarly publications. Published papers using the term *transpersonal*, indexed in *Psychological Abstracts*, start off with 1 instance in 1965 and 3 in 1970, rising to 6 in 1975, 11 in 1980, and 21 in 1985. Since then, the number has fluctuated in the 20s. Dissertations using the term *transpersonal* experienced a similar growth, as demonstrated by *Dissertation Abstracts*. None are indexed before 1973, when 2 such dissertations were written. In 1975, 1 was indexed; in 1980, 10; in 1985, 13; and in 1990, 16, at which level the number has stabilized. Mirroring this pattern are the numbers of members in the Association for Transpersonal Psychology, which rose steadily until arriving at a plateau in the early 1990s at approximately 3,000 members.

The leveling off of numbers of publications and membership does not appear to reflect a decline in interest but a maturation of the field. Indeed, the Menninger Clinic organized its first symposium explicitly on transpersonal psychiatry in 1992, with an unexpectedly large attendance. Increasing professional acceptance of transpersonal issues is most dramatically demonstrated by the 1994 inclusion in the American Psychiatric Association's *Diagnostic and Statistical Manual (DSM-IV)* of "psychoreligious" and "psychospiritual" problems, proposed by Francis Lu, David Lukoff, and Robert Turner (see Chapter 23). On the other hand, establishment professional publications still appear to be reluctant to publish articles that use the term *transpersonal*. As of 1993, the *American Journal of Psychiatry* had published only one such article, and the *American Psychologist*, none.

CRITICISM OF THE FIELD

The field of transpersonal psychiatry and psychology has not been without critics. On two occasions, a group of transpersonal psychologists petitioned the American Psychological Association for the formation of a formal division focused on transpersonal issues, analogous to Division 32, which focuses on humanistic psychology. The first proposal was denied, with some concerns expressed about the "unscientific" nature of transpersonal psychology. The second proposal, submitted shortly thereafter, was also denied, this time in part because of criticisms from prominent humanistic psychologists like Rollo May.[9] Since 1992, however, Division 32 on humanistic psychology has included a transpersonal track within its activities.

May criticized transpersonal psychology and psychiatry primarily for trying to "leap across" the dark side of human nature, going directly to transcendental states, and ignoring envy, suffering, guilt, and jealousy on the way. Many popular books on transpersonal topics and the so-called New Age movement do in fact stress an optimistic, upbeat view that often ignores the tragic, more sinister aspect of life. Pioneering clinicians using transpersonal techniques such as meditation also were enthusiastic and optimistic, sometimes not recognizing the contraindications and risks. But this optimism is characteristic of emerging fields in general: Early proponents of humanistic psychology were similarly enthusiastic, overlooking the dangers of marathon groups, for instance.

Albert Ellis,[10] an early pioneer in cognitive therapy, also attacked transpersonal psychology. He criticized the field for irrational belief in divine beings; elevating animals and nature to equal importance with human beings; a tendency toward dogmatism, absolutism, and fanaticism; opposition to science; and narcissistic preoccupation with the self, among other issues. Ellis did not distinguish between transpersonal psychology and psychiatry, on the one hand, and a broad range of popularized transpersonal philosophies and religions, on the other. This lack of differentiation confuses reflective, pragmatic study of transpersonal beliefs with uncritical or fervent practice of them. Ellis' objections are important, however, because they reflect a common confusion between transpersonal psychologists and "transpersonalists."

Other critics, including Eugene Taylor[11] and Kirk Schneider,[12] have raised subtler objections on the basis of issues including the reprehensible behavior of many "gurus" and spiritual leaders, which casts doubt on the value of "spiritual enlightenment"; the relation between psychotic and transcendent states; the practical importance of transpersonal psychology for human problems; and the philosophical naivete that is sometimes apparent concerning aspects of transpersonal psychology. These objections have been answered in various ways (see Chapters 7 and 23).

CULTURAL CONTEXT

The field of transpersonal psychology and psychiatry was not born in a cultural vacuum. Indeed, the discipline is very much a child of the turbulent 1960s in the United States, when political, cultural, and religious changes swept the country and later spread to Europe. Most dramatic were the political protests that began with the civil rights crusade; expanded into student opposition to the Vietnam War; and diversified later into movements for ecology, women's liberation, ethnic diversity, and gay rights. Beneath these political movements ran a strong spiritual current.[13,14,15] The civil rights movement drew its inspiration from black churches, for example, and many white congregations were active in protesting against the Vietnam War. Radical leaders such as Jerry Rubin, Michael Rossman, Lou Krupnik, Rennie Davis, and Noel McInnis also described their motivations and experiences in spiritual terms and later turned toward explicitly spiritual pursuits.

Protest went far beyond politics as the baby boom generation came of age in the 1960s. In a general rejection of modern American materialism, the "counterculture" was born, which included experimentation with marijuana and psychedelics like mescaline, peyote, and LSD. These personal explorations introduced many individuals to altered states of consciousness (see Chapter 18). Perhaps even more important to the movement was another drug, the birth control pill, which was first developed in 1955 and in wide use during the 1960s. Effective contraception made possible sexual liberation and the sensual celebration of the body. This repudiation of traditional American puritanism developed into various schools of "body work," which are active within transpersonal psychology.

From its origins, the counterculture grew rapidly. In 1967 more than 15,000 people gathered in San Francisco for a "be-in," a cultural version of the political "sit-in." In 1969 almost 500,000 people gathered at Woodstock, the legendary conclave of the new generation. Various alternative life philosophies emerged as part of the counterculture, such as Werner Erhart's est, Sylva Mind Control, and Arica Training. Many of these developments later entered mainstream society, although surveys completed in 1980 and 1981 showed that only 10 to 17% of Americans actively pursued transpersonal practices.[13,15,16] Those participants were mainly educated individuals under 35 years of age living in urban areas on the East and West Coasts.[17]

Important in the counterculture was a turn toward Eastern religions. Although scholars like Watts and Daisetz T. Suzuki had been writing since the 1950s and earlier, they became extremely popular in the 1960s, beginning with the Beatles' highly publicized interest in Hinduism. The Krishna Consciousness movement, for instance, more commonly known as the "Hare Krishna," started in 1966, when A. C. Bhaktivedanta set up his first center in New York. By 1974 there were 54 Krishna temples in the United States and Europe. Also from the Hindu tradition came Transcendental Meditation, taught by Maharishi Mahesh Yogi, which millions of Americans at one time or another tried. There were more controversial organizations, too, like the commune organized by Bagwan Rajneesh. Tibetan Buddhism arrived at about this time and rapidly became popular, with centers like the Nyingma Institute in California and the Naropa Institute in Colorado.

At the same time that Eastern religions became popular, charismatic, mystical Christianity flourished. Evangelical and Pentecostal churches experienced a sharp growth in membership, whereas traditional, "mainline" churches suffered a general decline. Christian broadcasting became enormously successful, with fundamentalist Protestants like Jerry Falwell, Jim Bakker, and Pat Robertson soliciting and receiving millions of dollars in contributions. Fundamentalist Christian groups spread rapidly on college campuses, too, beginning in 1968, with the appearance in California of the "Children of God," one of the first "Jesus-freak" movements. Within Judaism, ultraorthodox groups like the Hasidim and mystical approaches like Kabbalah enjoyed a surge of popularity and interest. Although dramatic, the interest in Eastern and mystical Western traditions remained a minority phenomenon. In 1977, of those Americans practicing a religion, 90% reported they participated in traditional religions, with the remaining 10% taking part in alternative practices such as yoga, Zen, Buddhism, or other mystical traditions.[13,15,16]

The origin of transpersonal psychology as a cultural development can be identified in the countercultural movement. Indeed, transpersonal psychology mirrors the major concerns of that era: dissatisfaction with traditional religions, a rejection of secular materialism and consumerism, a search for alternative sources of meaning in life, an emphasis on self-actualization and liberation, and experimentation with altered states of consciousness. In summing up the 1960s, a number of scholars have pointed out two basic themes that underlie the diverse political and cultural developments of the counterculture: dissent and liberation, or protest and self-actualization.[15,16,18] Both themes are clear in transpersonal psychology. Not surprisingly, popular interest in transpersonal psychology has expanded steadily. Books on transpersonal or psychospiritual issues regularly hit best-seller status, like Carlos Castenada's *Teachings of Don Juan* (1968), Ram Dass's *Be Here Now* (1971), Robert Pirsig's *Zen and the Art of Motorcycle Maintenance* (1974), *A Course in Miracles* (1978), and Shirley MacLaine's *Out on a Limb* (1983). Meanwhile, periodicals like *Common Boundary, Yoga Journal, East-West Journal, New Age Journal,* and *Shaman's Drum* provided vital forums for various transpersonal concepts and practices.

The flowering of the counterculture and its transpersonal interests can be traced to a number of basic demographic and economic factors.[13,15,16,18] First was the huge increase in the number of college-educated individuals who were familiar with psychological concepts and willing to experiment with alternative philosophies of life. This youthful generation was raised in a relatively permissive environment during childhood, which made sexual liberation and psychedelic exploration less threatening. A second factor was the unprecedented economic prosperity of the 1950s and 1960s, which allowed more individuals to explore personal growth. The rise of consumerism and its advertising, which emphasized ideal images of the self, also probably accelerated the cultural emphasis on self-actualization. Third, there was a general shift from an industrial economy focused on production and machines to a service-based economy, emphasizing human interactions. This change made psychology and personal experiences as significant as engineering and technology. Fourth, increasing travel and communication made the rapid and wide dissemination of new ideas possible. The interest in Eastern religions, in particular, was facilitated by greater contact with Asia during the American occupation of Japan and, later, the Korean and Vietnam Wars.

These factors also help explain why California was an exceptionally fertile field for transpersonal psychology. Most Californians had moved there from elsewhere, and they represented a less traditional population who were more open to new possibilities. California also enjoyed a booming economy from the 1960s until well into the 1990s, protected from the oil shocks of the 1970s because of its local oil and defense industries. Finally, the state has a large number of highly educated citizens.

The counterculture and its transpersonal interests are not new in American history. From the earliest Pilgrims to the many religious revivals of the nineteenth century, Americans have emphasized personal advancement and individual salvation. The counterculture and transpersonal psychology are therefore only the latest manifestations in a long tradition. Indeed, many specific themes in transpersonal psychology, such as an emphasis on rebirthing or altered states, fall squarely within American tradition. During periodic eighteenth- and nineteenth-century religious revivals, many individuals came forward to be "born again," often entering an ecstatic state and speaking in tongues. The Shakers and Quakers of that period prefigured the rock and rollers of the 1960s. Even the fascination with Eastern spirituality is not new. Nineteenth-century American transcendentalists, like Ralph Waldo Emerson and Henry David Thoreau, were intensely interested in Eastern religions. Moreover, both of these men espoused many of the themes that became central to the counterculture and transpersonal psychology: protesting against the government, seeking a divinity beyond traditional religion, cultivating personal growth and illumination, and respecting nature. American history is also filled with the establishment of alternative religions, particularly during the nineteenth century when the Seventh Day Adventist, Jehovah's Witness, Christian Science, and Mormon churches were founded.

If the interest in alternative spiritual viewpoints is not new in American history, what transpersonal psychology and psychiatry add is a scientific and pragmatic perspective: an emphasis on the reflective study of transcendent experiences and its practical application to healing. The scientific motif is not surprising: Transpersonal psychology emerged in California in 1980, when the state was a major science center for the United States, with more Nobel laureates and members of the National Academy of Science than any other state. Significantly, the *Journal of Transpersonal Psychology* was first published in 1969, the year that astronauts first walked on the moon. Symbolically, science took humanity on a historic step into inner and outer space: into the cosmos and into the transpersonal.

Born in the heady days of the 1960s, the field of transpersonal psychiatry and psychology very much reflects the period, as well as long-standing historical trends within American culture. By attempting to integrate pragmatic science with spirituality, however, transpersonal psychiatry and psychology represent a genuinely new development, and this may be their enduring contribution to American culture.

NOTES

1. Walsh, R. (1993). The transpersonal movement: A history and state of the art. *Journal of Transpersonal Psychology, 25,* 123–140.

2. Vich, M. (1990). The origins and growth of transpersonal psychology. *Journal of Humanistic Psychology, 30,* 47–50.

3. Vich, M. A. (1988). Some historical sources for the term "transpersonal." *Journal of Transpersonal Psychology, 20,* 107–110.

4. Valle, R. S. (1989). The emergence of transpersonal psychology. In R. S. Valle & S. Halling (Eds.), *Existential-phenomenological perspectives in psychology: The breadth of human experience* (pp. 257–268). New York: Plenum Press.

5. Sutich, A. (1968). Transpersonal psychology: An emerging force. *Journal of Humanistic Psychology, 8,* 77–78.

6. Vich, M. (1976). Anthony J. Sutich: An appreciation. *Journal of Transpersonal Psychology, 8,* 2–4.

7. Sutich, A. (1976). The emergence of the transpersonal orientation: A personal account. *Journal of Transpersonal Psychology, 8,* 5–18.

8. Vich, M. (1994). Personal communication.

9. May, R. (1986). Transpersonal or transcendental? *Humanistic Psychologist, 19,* 87–90.

10. Ellis, A., & Yeager, R. (1989). *Why some therapies don't work: The dangers of transpersonal psychology.* Buffalo, NY: Prometheus Books.

11. Taylor, E. (1992). Transpersonal psychology: Its several virtues. *Humanistic Psychologist, 20,* 285–300.

12. Schneider, K. J. (1987). The deified self: A "centaur" response to Wilber and the transpersonal movement. *Journal of Humanistic Psychology, 27,* 196–216.

13. Ferguson, M. (1980). *The Aquarian conspiracy: Personal and social transformation in the 1980s.* Los Angeles: Tarcher.

14. Bellah, R. (1976). The new consciousness and the Berkeley New Left. In C. Glock & R. Bellah (Eds.), *The new religious consciousness* (pp. 77–92). Berkeley: University of California Press.

15. Clecak, P. (1983). *America's quest for the ideal self: Dissent and fulfillment in the 60s and 70s.* New York: Oxford University Press.

16. Wuthnow, R. (1976). The new religions in social context. In C. Glock & R. Bellah (Eds.), *The new religious consciousness* (pp. 267–294). Berkeley: University of California Press.

17. Stone, D. (1976). The human potential movement. In C. Glock & R. Bellah (Eds.), *The new religious consciousness* (pp. 93–115). Berkeley: University of California Press.

18. Goldstein, T. (1988). *Waking from the dream: America in the sixties.* New York: Julian Messner.

PART II

Theory and Research

WESTERN PSYCHIATRY AND PSYCHOLOGY

CROSS-CULTURAL ROOTS

RESEARCH ON ALTERED STATES OF
CONSCIOUSNESS

OTHER WESTERN ACADEMIC DISCIPLINES

CHAPTER 3

William James and Transpersonal Psychiatry

EUGENE TAYLOR

THE AMERICAN PHILOSOPHER-PSYCHOLOGIST William James is arguably the father of modern transpersonal psychology and psychiatry. He was the first to use the term *transpersonal* in an English-language context and the first to articulate a scientific study of consciousness within the framework of evolutionary biology. He experimented with psychoactive substances to observe their effects on his own consciousness and was a pioneer in founding the field that is now called parapsychology. He helped to cultivate modern interest in dissociated states, multiple personality, and theories of the subconscious. He explored the field of comparative religion and was probably the first American psychologist to establish relationships with or to influence a number of Asian meditation teachers. He also pioneered in writing about the psychology of mystical experience.

BACKGROUND AND EARLY WORK

The eldest of five children, James was born in New York City in 1842 into a family of both wealth and privilege. His grandfather had made a fortune second only to that of the Astors and the Van

Rensselaers. Inheriting this wealth, James's father, Henry James, Sr., raised his five children while traveling throughout Europe. The education of William and his siblings thus took place in the great European museums, amidst the families of famous English and continental thinkers, through reading books, and by observing and discussing everything. The family dinner table was the scene of lively, provocative exchanges on all subjects.[1]

Henry James, Sr., developed a unique religious philosophy that greatly influenced young William. His philosophy was inspired by the works of the Scottish minister Robert Sandeman, the French sociologist Charles Fourier, and the Swedish mystic Emanuel Swedenborg.[2] Henry James, Sr., was also an intimate friend of Ralph Waldo Emerson's, who became godfather to young William. William thus inherited the Swedenborgian and transcendentalist legacy, which foreshadowed many current transpersonal theories.

James earned an M.D. from Harvard Medical School in 1869 and, after specializing in anatomy and physiology, began brain research using surgical dissection. In 1875, James taught the first course in physiological psychology to be offered at an American university. He was also a member of an informal group of botanists, chemists, neurologists, and physiologists who were Darwin's first American supporters. James's principal interest, however, was the role of consciousness in the biological evolution of the species. His primary contribution became the application of the laws of natural selection to different types of mental activity.

Much like the transpersonalists of today, James tested his ideas about consciousness through experiments with psychoactive chemicals. His younger brother Henry, who became a famous novelist, alluded to some of James's experiments performed at the age of 12. As an adult, James also experimented with nitrous oxide and peyote. He later applied the insights from his own experience to the comparative study of altered states of consciousness in *The Varieties of Religious Experience*, published in 1902.[3]

PSYCHOLOGY

During the 1870s and 1880s, James labored to bring psychology out of abstract philosophy and into physiological science. He wrote on such topics as instincts, cognition, reflexes, emotions, perception, the sensation of space, phantom limb phenomena, and the semicircular canals. His essays in psychology, meanwhile, were widely read in the United States and Europe. They were critiqued in the English professional journals and translated immediately into French.

In 1878 James agreed to write a textbook in the new experimental psychology. Instead of the 2 years he envisioned, the project took 12: The death of his father, the scope of his subject, and his belief that he was unable to write anything meaningful prolonged his effort.

During this period, James's views concerning reductionistic psychology underwent a slow but massive change. Although the psychophysical measurement of vision and hearing and simple physiological experiments in reaction time defined laboratory psychology, new evidence began pouring in from Europe proposing the existence of subconscious processes. Hypnosis soon became a respectable experimental tool in the laboratory for inducing the trance states of spiritualists and mediums and the symptoms of neuroses.

James was instrumental in helping found the American Society for Psychical Research (ASPR) in the fall of 1884. An offshoot of the American Association for the Advancement of Science with offices located in Boston's fashionable Tavern Club, the ASPR soon established experimental committees to conduct research into alleged supernatural phenomena. Their detailed investigation of trance mediums confirmed the existence of a number of subconscious processes already described by Jean Martin Charcot, Alfred Binet, Pierre Janet, and Hippolyte Bernheim in France.

James finally produced his monumental *Principles of Psychology* in 1890 to international acclaim.[4] In the work, James situated psychology within the domain of the natural sciences. His focus was on a cognitive psychology, and in this context he set forth his famous image of consciousness as a stream. Psychology was the scientific study of mental states, James declared, through which thoughts, warmed by emotion, move like a giant river.

James also advanced a pluralistic concept of the self. He distinguished between the biological self, which involved bodily perceptions; the material self, which included all the objects that an individual owned; the social self, made up of as many selves as an individual had relationships; and finally the spiritual self, that part of the inward life known only to the individual. James was keenly aware of multiple personality disorders, but he emphasized that a plurality of selves was normal.

In the end, James's *Principles of Psychology* had two distinct centers of gravity. One presumed that psychology was a positivistic science that dealt only with what could be observed about consciousness. The other held that consciousness involved many different states, including hidden dimensions, both pathological and spiritual. His classic text provides a model for today's transpersonal psychiatry.

EXCEPTIONAL MENTAL STATES

James soon abandoned the reductionistic point of view for a more dynamic one. In a series of lectures on exceptional mental states delivered before the Lowell Institute in 1896, James wrote on such topics as dreams and hypnotism, automatism, hysteria, multiple personality, demoniacal possession, witchcraft, degeneration, and genius.[5] In his talks, James reviewed the work of Pierre Janet on the nature of the subconscious, mentioning the work of Josef Breuer and Sigmund Freud as corroboration for Janet's findings. Here James followed the lead of the English psychical researcher, F. W. H. Myers, who at that time had presented the most comprehensive model of consciousness, ranging from the pathological to the transcendent.

James was receptive to non-Western conceptions of personality and consciousness, much as transpersonal authors are today. James knew Swami Vivekananda, sponsored one of his talks at Harvard, read a number of his works on Vedanta philosophy, and saw him demonstrate techniques of yoga and meditation.[6] James also knew Anagarika Dharmapala, the theosophist and Theravada Buddhist practitioner. In addition, as a member of the Theosophical Society in Boston, James supported Dharmapala's lectures on meditation at Harvard. James was also familiar with the young D. T. Suzuki, who later married one of James's Radcliffe students. Significantly, Suzuki was influenced by James's philosophy of pragmatism, which Suzuki helped introduce into Japanese philosophy and later used to interpret Zen to Western audiences.[7]

MYSTICAL EXPERIENCE

James's most important statement on the psychology of spirituality was his analysis of mystical consciousness in *The Varieties of Religious Experience* (1902), a book-length version of his Gifford Lectures at the University of Edinburgh, delivered in 1901 and 1902. In this work, James maintained three important themes. First, he argued that religion lies within the individual. By this he meant that the source of religion, first and foremost, comes from experience. James focused, therefore, on "living human documents": personal testimonies from individuals about their religious awakening. Second, James argued that exploration of the subconscious was the doorway to transforming experiences. By this he meant that any method for exposing a person to his or her own inward experience was the first step to self-exploration and that the entire range of states of consciousness was then open, "beyond the margin" of everyday waking reality. Third, James concluded that the truths of these mystical experiences could be measured only in terms of their results: by their ability to increase the moral and aesthetic quality of daily life and to improve the interactions among people. "By their fruits ye shall know them," became James's measure for testing any religious belief.

In his discussion, James emphasized the noetic quality of mystical states: that the experiences carried a sense of knowledge unplumbed by the normal intellect and that, because of their depth, they also evoked a sense of authority in the inward life of the individual. Mystical consciousness was also ineffable, James said, noting how attempts to describe such experiences had always faltered. Also, although the episodes lasted only for a short time, they characteristically commanded a complete sense of personal surrender. In a celebrated passage, James summed up his views:

> Our normal waking consciousness, rational consciousness as we call it, is but one special type of consciousness, whilst all about it, parted from it by the filmiest of screens, there lie potential forms of consciousness entirely different. We may go through life without suspecting their existence; but apply the requisite stimulus, and at a touch they are there in all their completeness, definite types of mentality which probably somewhere have their field of application and adaptation. No account of the universe in its totality can be final which leaves these other forms of consciousness quite disregarded. How to regard them is the question,—for they are so discontinuous with ordinary consciousness. Yet they may determine attitudes though they cannot furnish formulas, and open a region though they fail to give a map. At any rate, they forbid a premature closing of our accounts with reality.[8]

DEFINITION OF *TRANSPERSONAL*

James first used the term *transpersonal* in a Harvard University course syllabus in 1905.[9] When two people see the same object, he said, the object becomes "trans-personal." It was the first appearance of that word in the English language. As part of the concept of transpersonal, James suggested that psychological science was wrong in separating subject and object as if they were two separate entities. There is no such thing as an object independent of perception, he said, because all objects are always dependent on being perceived by someone. James first made this argument in his presidential address to the American Psychological Association in 1894. His title was appropriately "The Knowing of Things Together," and he developed the ideas contained therein into a sophisticated metaphysical critique of experimentalism in psychology, which he later called *radical empiricism*. James insisted on exploring raw human experience in all its manifestations.[10] It was not permissible, he argued, for psychology to restrict itself to subjects for which established methodologies were available. The legitimate purview of psychology was everything within human experience. Thus, James sought to legitimize the study of the subconscious processes, psychic phenomena, accounts of after-death communication, and nonnormative religious experiences.[11]

CONCLUSION

James was a leading figure of American intellectual ideas in the late nineteenth century: a founding father of modern psychology, a significant influence on the development of scientific psychotherapy, a leader of the international philosophical movement called pragmatism, a transition figure from transcendentalism to modernism, and a mentor to numerous influential personalities of the twentieth century (among them, W. E. B. DuBois, Helen Keller, Gertrude Stein, and Walter Lippmann, and in psychology, E. L. Thorndike, Boris Sidis, and Robert Woodworth). His works later influenced Gordon Allport, Henry A. Murray, and Gardner Murphy, among others.

Because of James's pioneering role in transpersonal research, it is instructive to consider what he might advise transpersonal psychologists and psychiatrists today.[12] I think he would ask for less experiential fervor and more philosophical sophistication with regard to the basic issues underlying the mind–body problem (see Chapters 22 and 9). Because of his strong cross-cultural interests, James would also probably recommend less indiscriminate picking and choosing from different Asian traditions to fit a preconceived transpersonal definition of spiritual consciousness.[13] Instead, he would advise transpersonal theorists to take a more systematic look at diverse religious traditions from the standpoint of how the traditions uniquely view themselves. James worked in many different disciplines, ranging from philosophy to physiology, and would probably call for more direct dialogue among transpersonal theorists and modern philosophers of science instead of the present attempts by transpersonalists to redefine science by speaking largely to popular audiences. James would likely concede, however, that transpersonal psychology opens up an extraordinarily important debate in both psychology and psychiatry about the broad range of human experiences, which our present definition of science does not easily address.

NOTES

1. Allen, G. W. (1967). *William James: A biography.* New York: Viking.

2. Habegger, A. (1994). *The father: A life of Henry James, Sr.* New York: Farrar, Straus & Giroux.

3. James, W. (1902). *The varieties of religious experience.* New York: Longmans.

4. James, W. (1890). *The principles of psychology.* 2 vols. New York: Henry Holt.

5. Taylor, E. I. (1982). *William James on exceptional mental states: The unpublished Lowell lectures of 1896.* New York: Scribner's Sons.

6. Taylor, E. I. (1986, September). Swami Vivekananda and William James. *Prabuddha Bharata: Journal of the Ramakrishna Society, Calcutta, 91,* 374–385.

7. Taylor, E. I. (1993, November). *The influence of Swedenborgian thought on American pragmatism.* Paper presented to the Swedenborg Study Group, annual meeting of the American Academy of Religion, Washington, D.C.

8. James, *Varieties of religious experience,* p. 388.

9. Vich, M. (1988). Some historical sources of the term "Transpersonal." *Journal of Transpersonal Psychology, 20,* 109.

10. Taylor, E. I., & Wozniak, R. (Eds.). (1995). *Pure experience: The response to William James.* London/Tokyo: Routledge/Thommes.

11. Taylor, E. I. (1996). *William James on consciousness beyond the margin.* Princeton: Princeton University Press.

12. Taylor, E. I. (1988). Contemporary interest in classical Eastern psychology. In A. Paranjpe, D. Ho, & R. Rieber (Eds.), *Asian contributions to psychology* (pp. 79–122). New York: Praeger.

13. Taylor, E. I. (1978). Psychology of religion and Asian studies: The William James legacy. *Journal of Transpersonal Psychology, 10,* 66–79.

CHAPTER 4

Freud's Influence on Transpersonal Psychology

MARK EPSTEIN

HOWEVER AMBIVALENT MOST contemporary practitioners of transpersonal psychology may be about Freud, it is safe to say that there would be no transpersonal psychology as we know it without Freud's influence. Freud might be considered the grandfather of the entire movement. His relationship to the field is analogous to his relationship to the psychology of women: Just as Freud pioneered the study of women's psychology but remained confused about essential aspects of it, so too did he pioneer the study of spirituality while remaining confused about its place in a healthy psyche. Although he took stands in such works as *Moses and Monotheism* and *The Future of an Illusion* that were judgmental of spiritual experience, he was deeply interested in the subject and made great contributions to it. He taught, nurtured, fought with, anticipated, and influenced most of the pioneers in the field, such as Carl Jung. Despite his involvement in trying to solve the mysteries inherent in the subject, however, he was blind to certain fundamental aspects of it. The transpersonal field is still trying to sort out where Freud's contributions begin and where his misunderstandings end.

Freud's contributions can be grouped into three categories. First, his descriptions of the oceanic feeling as the apotheosis of the religious experience have influenced the ways in which generations of psychotherapists have interpreted spirituality. His equation of this oceanic feeling with the bliss of primary narcissism, the unambivalent union of infant and mother at the breast, has served as the gold standard for psychological explanations of meditative or mystical attainments. Second, his exploration of voluntary manipulations of attention—first in hypnosis, then in free association, and finally in evenly suspended attention—prefigured later interest on the part of the therapeutic community in meditation and sensory awareness. Freud's efforts were pioneering from a transpersonal perspective in that they opened up awareness as a therapeutic tool. Third, some of Freud's most important conceptual contributions— of the pleasure principle as the source of suffering in life and his ideas of going beyond it through sublimation—echo the teachings of the Buddha and prefigure transpersonal themes.

Far from the supreme rationalist that Freud sometimes wished he could be, Freud was constantly sifting myth, dreams, religious experience, sex, and emotion for truths about the human psyche. He was consistently amazed at the unpredictable power of the human mind and entertained his analytic colleagues with stories of inexplicable psychic or telepathic phenomena that he had witnessed in his consulting room. He corresponded with a wide range of figures, some of whom were more open to mystical experiences than he was, and he always attempted to understand their experiences from the perspective of his developing theories.

THE OCEANIC FEELING

One of Freud's more mystically inclined friends and correspondents was the French poet Romain Rolland, who had become a devout follower of the Hindu gurus Ramakrishna and Vivekananda. In attempting to understand Rolland's meditative experiences, Freud put forward his own explanations in his volume of 1930 entitled *Civilization and Its Discontents*. Rolland began corresponding with Freud in 1927 shortly after the publication of Freud's *The Future of an Illusion*. As Freud described the exchange:

> I had sent him my small book that treats religion as an illusion, and he answered that he entirely agreed with my judgement upon religion, but that he was sorry I had not properly appreciated the true source of religious sentiments. This, he says, consists in a peculiar feeling, which he himself is never without, which he finds confirmed by many others, and which he may suppose is

present in millions of people. It is a feeling which he would like to call a sensation of "eternity", a feeling as of something limitless, unbounded—as it were, "oceanic". This feeling, he adds, is a purely subjective fact, not an article of faith; it brings with it no assurance of personal immortality, but it is the source of the religious energy which is seized upon by the various Churches and religious systems, directed by them into particular channels, and doubtless also exhausted by them.[1]

Freud took Rolland's description very seriously; it puzzled and intrigued him that he (Freud) was able to grasp the subjective quality of the feeling described without finding it in his own experience. As Freud described it, Rolland's views "caused me no small difficulty. I cannot discover this 'oceanic' feeling in myself."[2] Rolland's views proved something of a koan for Freud.* As he mused on their meaning, he began to explore the issue of ego boundaries and their relationship to mystical experience in a manner that prefigures much of transpersonal psychology.

"Normally," suggested Freud, "there is nothing of which we are more certain than the feeling of our self, of our own ego. This ego appears to us as something autonomous and unitary, marked off distinctly from everything else."[3] Echoing the Buddhist psychologists of whom he was altogether ignorant, Freud went on to question this view of an independent, autonomous ego. "Such an appearance is deceptive,"[4] suggested Freud, because the ego continues inwardly with no clear boundary into the unconscious entity that he named the id. He termed the ego a "kind of facade" that surrounds and obscures the unconscious but that is not really separate from it. Thus Freud used his psychoanalytic explorations to break down the intrinsic certainty of most people in the ego's inviolability, but he emphasized the *internal* direction of the ego's infinitude. For Freud, the ego was but a tiny part of an infinite unconscious that continued forever inwardly.

Yet Freud recognized that this lack of boundary with the id was not the source of Rolland's feeling of eternity. Rolland suggested a connection to the *external* world, a feeling of merger or oneness with all of creation, not a sense of the infinite depth of the unconscious. This was the state that Freud could not readily find in his own experience.

"Towards the outside," Freud suggested, "the ego seems to maintain clear and sharp lines of demarcation. There is only one

---

*A *koan* is a riddle designed to paralyze the rational, thinking mind, used in Zen meditation.

state—admittedly an unusual state, but not one that can be stigmatized as pathological—in which it does not do this."[5] Only in the state of being in love, decided Freud, does the boundary between ego and the external world melt away. "Against all the evidence of his senses, a man who is in love declares that 'I' and 'you' are one, and is prepared to behave as if it were a fact."[6] Taking this capacity of the ego to dissolve into another, Freud went back to the experience of the infant at the breast and suggested that there once existed a state of merger that predated the emergence of the self-conscious ego in which the infant was essentially dissolved in love. Freud deduced that

> originally, the ego includes everything, . . . later it separates off an external world from itself. Our present ego-feeling is, therefore, only a shrunken residue of a much more inclusive—indeed, an all-embracing—feeling which corresponded to a more intimate bond between the ego and the world around it.[7]

Rolland's experience must have resurrected this original ego feeling, Freud decided, returning him to a state reminiscent of that of the infant at the breast whose ego contained everything. He supported his argument by referring to another, unnamed friend, who had made "the most unusual experiments" with yoga and had induced regressions to "primordial states of mind."[8]

On the basis of a limited knowledge of the meditation traditions of the East, therefore, Freud came to a conception of the individual ego as extending infinitely in both internal and external directions. Each individual, he hypothesized, contains the entire universe, because each ego extends infinitely to encompass both the inner unconscious and the external world. After his correspondence with Rolland, he decided that mystical experiences had the capacity to return someone to the state of merger with the external world that characterized the infantile state. Yet Freud was apparently not entirely satisfied with this formulation; in his final recorded entry in his collected works, written in 1938, Freud apparently was still struggling with this question. In this entry, Freud wrote of mysticism as a route to exploring the *internal* dimension of the psyche. "Mysticism is the obscure self-perception of the realm outside the ego, of the id,"[9] he wrote just before his death, redirecting our attention once again from the external back to the depths of the psyche.

Freud's attempts to understand spiritual experiences are typical of psychologists both in and out of the transpersonal field. His recognition of the similarity between certain mystical experiences and early infantile experiences of unconditional love cannot simply be dismissed as reductionistic. Because the two experiences *are* similar, such mystical states can be tremendously reassuring for those with deficits in their early experiences of intimacy. Although most psychoanalysts have followed Freud's lead in seeing mystical experience in this way, transpersonal theorists have tended to ignore the ways in which mystical experiences of unity evoke primitive narcissistic cravings, focusing instead on the expansive or transcendent nature of those states. The expansive nature of the oceanic experience can clearly invigorate the self, but such states also provide the opportunity to work through early narcissistic issues in a new way. The spiritual path is ultimately about confronting one's own inherent narcissism, after all is said and done. Freud laid the foundation, however incomplete, for this understanding.

EVENLY SUSPENDED ATTENTION

Freud's major breakthrough, which he referred to over and over again in his writings, was his discovery that it is possible to suspend what he called the "critical faculty" of the thinking mind. This suspension was what made the practice of psychoanalysis possible for Freud. It was the key to both the free association of the patient and the evenly suspended attention of the therapist. It is a feat that Freud apparently taught himself without knowing that this was precisely the attentional stance that Eastern meditators had been invoking for millennia.

Freud's writings on the subject reveal the most essential quality of evenly suspended attention: its impartiality. Repeatedly admonishing psychoanalysts to "suspend ... judgement and give ... impartial attention to everything there is to observe,"[10] Freud insisted that in this state it was possible to understand phenomena of the mind in a unique fashion. Remaining interested in psychic content, he nevertheless encouraged his followers to practice a kind of beginning meditation while listening to their patients. His instructions have all the clarity of the writings of the best Buddhist teachers. In his definitive article on the subject, Freud can be appreciated in his best Zen-like form:

> The rule for the doctor may be expressed: "He should withhold all conscious influences from his capacity to attend, and give

himself over completely to his 'unconscious memory'." Or, to put it purely in terms of technique: He should simply listen, and not bother about whether he is keeping anything in mind.[11]

Freud's credo that the therapist should "simply listen, and not bother about whether he is keeping anything in mind" led him to some rather remarkable conclusions. He became convinced of a kind of unconscious, or psychic, communication between therapist and patient that he felt was the most important therapeutic tool that the therapist could offer:

> Experience soon showed that the attitude which the analytic physician could most advantageously adopt was to surrender himself to his own unconscious mental activity, in a state of evenly suspended attention, to avoid so far as possible reflection and the construction of conscious expectations, not to try to fix anything that he heard particularly in his memory, and by these means to catch the drift of the patient's unconscious with his own unconscious.[12]

As explicit as Freud was about the critical importance of evenly suspended attention, therapists have had great difficulty in practicing his advice and overcoming the tendency to relate to patients cognitively. Otto Fenichel dismissed the efforts of those who struggled to implement Freud's original recommendations by accusing them of merely floating in their unconscious and of doing "hardly any work at all."[13]

What analysts such as Fenichel failed to understand is that it is possible for a single conscious state of mind—a poised and balanced state of bare, or evenly suspended, attention—to encompass both nonverbal and rational, intellectual thought. This does not have to be an unconscious process, as Freud seemed to imply. This is one area in which transpersonal psychology may be able to give something back to psychoanalysis. The cognitive processing that Fenichel and many psychoanalysts regard so highly does not have to be sought after by the therapist; there is more than enough of it happening of its own accord. When there is something meaningful to say, it is more than apparent. More often than not, however, the intellectual activity of the therapist is a defense against experiencing the patient's being, a refusal to enter the jointly experienced not-knowing that makes discovery a real possibility.

Although Freud's picture of the state of evenly suspended attention aptly describes the meditative stance, he emphasized only the value for the therapist in catching the drift of the patient's unconscious. What he did not describe is the impact of this state of mind on the patient. The state that Freud described is necessary not just because it offers the possibility of unconscious transmission, but also because it is only in this state that the therapist's mind is not felt as an intrusion by the patient. The therapist's expectations and desires, however subtle, create a pressure against which the patient is compelled to react or with which the patient is compelled to comply. The analogy with the intrusive or ignoring parent cannot be exaggerated.

Much of the emphasis of the transpersonal psychology movement on cultivating the power of awareness has its roots not only in Eastern thought but also in Freud's pioneering experiments with therapeutic attention. Present-day therapists would not be in a position to appreciate the Eastern modes of manipulating attention were it not for Freud's pioneering efforts in that direction. To suspend the "critical faculty" is not something that most people could come to on their own, yet Freud somehow managed to create a movement based on that very phenomenon.

BEYOND THE PLEASURE PRINCIPLE

Freud's final contribution to transpersonal psychology lies in his elucidation of the pleasure principle, the cause, in his view, of much of our self-imposed misery. In his descriptions of the pleasure principle, Freud unknowingly paralleled the first two of the Buddha's Four Noble Truths, the truth of suffering and of its cause. In early life, Freud said, the state of "psychical rest" or contentment is first disturbed by the demands of internal needs for food, comfort, warmth, and so on.[14] Whatever was needed was originally provided (by the mother) magically, "in a hallucinatory manner," giving the child a feeling of omnipotence or magical control. This feeling that every need could be immediately satisfied, every sense pleasure immediately obtained, or every unpleasurable sensation immediately avoided is the foundation of what the Buddha described as our sense of pervasive unsatisfactoriness. We crave the original feeling of pleasure but cannot realize it. Although the pleasure principle is the first organizing principle of the human psyche, its persistence, according to both the Buddha and Freud, can be the source of much emotional turmoil. As Freud described it:

It was only the non-occurrence of the expected satisfaction, the disappointment experienced, that led to the abandonment of this attempt at satisfaction by means of hallucination. Instead of it, the psychical apparatus had to decide to form a conception of the real circumstances in the external world and to endeavor to make a real alteration in them. A new principle of mental functioning was thus introduced; what was presented in the mind was no longer what was agreeable but what was real, even if it happened to be disagreeable. This setting-up of the reality principle proved to be a momentous step.[15]

It was only by forsaking an exclusive reliance on the pleasure principle, Freud taught, that the higher pleasures could be achieved. It is paradoxical, but nevertheless true, that spiritual experiences depend on just this acceptance of reality.

Within both transpersonal psychology and psychoanalysis, there exists a perspective on working with reality that senses the possibility of transformation through the bringing of awareness to the very feelings of desire and dissatisfaction that are often feared or rejected. Although it is not often viewed this way, this process, which Freud called *sublimation,* is another important link between psychoanalysis and spirituality. Frustrated in our demands to make the pleasure principle operative, we can bring nonjudgmental awareness to bear on that very frustration and so begin the transformative process that is crucial to both sublimation and spiritual growth.

Freud described sublimation as the means by which "the energy of the infantile wishful impulses is not cut off but remains ready for use—the unserviceable aim of the various impulses being replaced by one that is higher, and perhaps no longer sexual."[16] Sublimation, for Freud, held out the possibility of escape from the pleasure principle, but he did not imply that the passions themselves were inherently dangerous. In his descriptions of Leonardo da Vinci's mental state, for instance, Freud described how da Vinci was able to "throw off" the positive or negative signs of love and hate and transform them into "intellectual interest." He was not "devoid of passion," insisted Freud, "he had merely converted his passion into a thirst for knowledge. . . . At the climax of a discovery,"[17] said Freud, da Vinci's emotion would come rushing forth in a kind of ecstasy.

Freud provided an alternative model in these writings for the transpersonal experience. It need not be a regression to infantile omnipotence or to the demands of the pleasure principle but could, instead, grow out of the relentless pursuit of knowledge and self-awareness that he attributed to da Vinci. By throwing off the positive and negative signs of love and hate, Freud proposed, by not grasping after the pleasant and rejecting the unpleasant, one could come to an ecstatic experience of mystical proportions. For all of his antipathy toward religion, Freud came to a place of tremendous spiritual resonance.

NOTES

1. Freud, S. (1961). Civilization and its discontents. In J. Strachey (Ed. and Trans.), *The standard edition of the complete psychological works of Sigmund Freud* (Vol. 21, p. 64). London: Hogarth Press. (Original work published 1930)

2. Ibid., p. 65.

3. Ibid., p. 66.

4. Ibid.

5. Ibid.

6. Ibid.

7. Ibid., p. 68.

8. Ibid., p. 72.

9. Freud, S. (1964). Findings, ideas, problems. In J. Strachey (Ed. and Trans.), *The standard edition of the complete psychological works of Sigmund Freud* (Vol. 23, p. 300). London: Hogarth Press. (Original work published 1938 and 1941) Thanks to Michael Eigen for making me aware of this passage.

10. Freud, S. (1955). Analysis of a phobia in a five-year-old boy. In J. Strachey (Ed. and Trans.), *The standard edition of the complete psychological works of Sigmund Freud* (Vol. 10, p. 23). London: Hogarth Press. (Original work published 1909)

11. Freud, S. (1958). Recommendations to physicians practising psychoanalysis. In J. Strachey (Ed. and Trans.), *The standard edition of the complete psychological works of Sigmund Freud* (Vol. 12, pp. 111–112). London: Hogarth Press. (Original work published 1912)

12. Freud, S. (1955). Two encyclopedia articles. In J. Strachey (Ed. and Trans.), *The standard edition of the complete psychological works of Sigmund Freud* (Vol. 18, p. 239). London: Hogarth Press. (Original work published 1923)

13. Fenichel, O. (1941). *Problems of psychoanalytic technique* (p. 5). New York: Psychoanalytic Quarterly.

14. Freud, S. (1958). Formulations on the two principles of mental functioning. In J. Strachey (Ed. and Trans.), *The standard edition of the complete psychological works of Sigmund Freud* (Vol. 12, p. 219). London: Hogarth Press. (Original work published 1911)

15. Ibid.

16. Freud, S. (1957). Five lectures on psycho-analysis. In J. Strachey (Ed. and Trans.), *The standard edition of the complete psychological works of Sigmund Freud* (Vol. 11, pp. 53–54). London: Hogarth Press. (Original work published 1910)

17. Freud, S. (1957). Leonardo da Vinci and a memory of his childhood. In J. Strachey (Ed. and Trans.), *The standard edition of the complete psychological works of Sigmund Freud* (Vol. 11, pp. 74–75). London: Hogarth Press. (Original work published 1910)

CHAPTER 5

The Contribution of C. G. Jung to Transpersonal Psychiatry

BRUCE W. SCOTTON

CARL JUNG WAS THE FIRST clinical transpersonal psychiatrist and depth psychologist. His work remains pertinent both for clinical concepts that have proved invaluable to transpersonal psychotherapy and for its attitude of personal and cultural receptivity. Jung's attempt at a spiritual approach to psychology, as both a theoretician and a clinician, has had the greatest acceptance in the academic world of any such endeavor. Jung's insistence on the importance of the life of the spirit, as shown in his 1912 work, *Psychology of the Unconscious*, was maintained at great cost to him. It was the cause of his split with Freud, who insisted that he leave out references to spiritual themes, and resulted in Jung's exile from the Freudian psychoanalytic world.[1]

Jung's work in the transpersonal realm prefigured much of what is current in the field. A brief list of Jung's contributions includes the following:

I wish to thank Donald Sandner, M.D., for assistance in the preparation of this chapter.

1. The notion that psychological development should include growth to higher levels of consciousness and continue throughout life.
2. The concept that the transcendent lies within and is available to each individual.
3. The willingness to explore the wisdom traditions of other cultures and the West for insights relevant to today's clinical work.
4. The recognition that healing and growth often result from experiences of symbolic imagery or states of consciousness that cannot be grasped by rational reduction.

Jung was among the first to study various phenomena from a psychiatric perspective, including trance channeling, yoga, Native American spirituality, African shamanism, the I Ching, alchemy, Gnosticism, and unidentified flying objects (UFOs).

BRIEF LIFE HISTORY

Carl Jung was born July 26, 1875, in Kesswil, Switzerland, the son of a philologist mother and parson father. Because of the family's Swiss–German Protestant origins and his parents' personalities, Jung apparently was largely left to his own resources from an early age. He had a particularly vivid imaginal and dream life.

From childhood, Jung's experience included the transpersonal. For example, Jung reported an episode in which he became excited about an essay topic, producing such a good essay that his teacher refused to believe he had written it himself and accused Jung of plagiarism. Although he defended himself stoutly, Jung could not convince the teacher and suffered for days. Finally, he wrote:

> There was a sudden inner silence . . . as though a breath of the great world of stars and endless space had touched me, or as if a spirit had invisibly entered the room—the spirit of one who had long been dead and yet was perpetually present in timelessness until far into the future.

This transpersonal experience gave Jung emotional release from the pain and allowed him to analyze how his and his teacher's personalities had led to the clash.[2]

In medical school at Zurich, Jung wrote his senior thesis about his cousin Helene Preiswerk's trance channeling and dissociative states. After graduation in 1902, he worked with Eugen Bleuler at the Burgholzli Hospital in Zurich. Here Jung had exposure to the deep layers of the unconscious through contact with psychotic patients. Jung was fascinated by the power of the symbolism that emerged and sought to understand its origins and meaning. In one case he listened to a patient's experience of the sun having a phallus and managed to find an ancient Egyptian picture that closely paralleled the image described by the patient. The comparison of the patient's vision and the ancient Egyptian symbol of masculine, solar power elucidated the meaning of both.

Jung was an early supporter of Freud's psychoanalytic approach to the unconscious. The two met after an exchange of letters and worked closely for 5 years. Jung became the heir apparent to leadership of the psychoanalytic movement and president of the International Psychoanalytic Society. Freud and Jung's divergent worldviews soon became apparent, however. During a visit by Jung to Vienna, the two men were discussing parapsychological phenomena when a loud crash suddenly issued from a bookcase. Jung said the experience reflected the topic of parapsychology they were discussing and furthermore predicted that the noise would be repeated. Freud dismissed both contentions, but a second crash resounded. Freud later wrote to Jung that the fact that the noises continued to recur after Jung's departure dissuaded him from attaching import to the experience.[3] Jung went on to view such experiences as examples of *synchronicity,* or "meaningful coincidences" that held important symbolism if properly attended to.

Jung's break with Freud may have started during their joint voyage to lecture in the United States at Clark University. On the way, Jung suggested they analyze one another's dreams; however, Freud was willing to analyze but not to be analyzed. The final break came with Jung's insistence on the importance of spiritual experience and Freud's unwillingness to give primary importance to any factor other than sexuality.

Following the break with Freud, Jung went through a period of self-questioning and inner search in which he gave free rein to the sort of visions and dreams he had experienced in his childhood. Some have suggested that Jung experienced a psychotic episode during this period. Jung worked extensively with his experience in much the same way he had handled that of his patients at the Burgholzli, emphasizing the healing symbolic meanings. In this period, Jung began his adult self-analysis in which he carved, painted, wrote poetry, built a stone house with his own hands, and

played in the earth making miniature dams, mountains, and villages. The latter apparently was the origin of both his therapeutic
sand-play technique, in which patients create "worlds" in a sand
tray with miniature symbolic figures and objects,[4] and his use of
active imagination; both techniques involve types of dream-reverie
that are made conscious. It was during this period that he wrote
The Transcendent Function and *The Seven Sermons of the Dead*, two
pieces that were particularly transpersonally oriented.

Jung's conversations with an inner figure named Philemon illustrate his technique of active imagination. Philemon was a "guru"
figure from Egypto-Hellenic and Gnostic sources who first
appeared in Jung's dreams. Jung would fix him in his mind as he
walked in the garden of his Bollingen retreat and wait to see what
Philemon would do or say. In time Jung held many conversations
with Philemon, receiving much guidance.[5]

Jung soon started his own analytic school in Zurich, which he
termed *analytical psychology*. He accepted Freud's work but felt it
was necessary to extend it to include development in the second
half of life, which involved spiritual questions and which Jung
termed *individuation*. He was greatly interested in comparing the
maps of individuation found in various cultures. This interest, and
his Germanic background, led him to some writings during the
Nazi era that were laudatory of the German psyche in a way that
was at best politically naive and probably constituted unconscious
anti-Semitism. On the other hand, he distanced himself from the
Nazis when their policies became clear, and some Jewish colleagues, such as James Kirsch, founder of the Jung Institute of Los
Angeles, have reported that Jung acknowledged and apologized
for his error and developed a deep understanding of Judaism.[6]

Although Jung continued his clinical work and training of analysts, in his later years he became something of an international
consultant on human development, writing some popularly accessible books such as *Man and His Symbols*. He was also interviewed
in depth by the British Broadcasting Company (BBC).

In 1944 Jung had a myocardial infarction that prompted a near-
death experience (see Chapter 29).[7] After returning to awareness of
the physical world, he continued to have spiritual visions in his
hospital bed. Although one of his priorities had been to make his
vision of humanity's spiritual life understandable and acceptable
to academic psychiatry, after his heart attack he seemed less interested in academic acceptance and more concerned about speaking
the truth as he experienced it. He finally published the transper-

sonally oriented *Seven Sermons of the Dead;* wrote *Synchronicity: An Acausal Connecting Principle, Answer to Job,* and *Mysterium Coniunctionis;* prepared a remarkably revealing memoir, *Memories, Dreams, Reflections;* and announced to his BBC interviewer when questioned about the existence of God, "I don't think, I know He exists." Jung died in 1961.

BASIC CONCEPTS OF ANALYTICAL PSYCHOLOGY

Autonomous Complexes

Two research projects led Jung to his view that semi-independent parts of the psyche exist, which he termed *autonomous feeling-toned complexes.* His observations of his cousin, Helene Preiswerk, who entered trance states, convinced him that parts of the psyche could maintain a consistent thought pattern and emotional content while remaining separate from the ego. Jung's word-association experiment revealed consistent patterns that revolved around specific content and feelings, individual to each subject. Furthermore, the subjects were unconscious of these patterns or complexes.

Jung held that complexes were organized around cores, which he called *archetypes,* psychological forms common to all people that structure the experience of the world. Archetypes, much like Plato's forms, contain the potential for many different manifestations and can never be adequately represented by any one manifestation. For example, the image and concept of *mother* derives from an archetype which includes wide cultural and individual variations yet is united by common themes that transcend culture.[8] If an individual's relationship with his or her mother is too painful over time to be assimilated by the ego, those experiences form a complex around the mother archetype. The complex serves a defensive function, fending off pain for the ego. Repetitive behavior results, however, even when it is inappropriate to the situation. The individual may treat other people as he would his mother. Complexes are replications of significant troublesome figures that recreate the troubled relationships.

Later writers have made it clear that complexes are bipolar. The mother complex mandates a child complex that is complementary.[9] As the word-association experiment showed, complexes assert themselves regularly when sensitive topics and emotions arise. The more painful the wounding experiences, the more powerful the complex and the more likely the complex is to be elicited inappropriately. Clinically, patients are found to carry with them replications of significant troublesome figures, such as the mother, and to recreate the troubled relationships. Although the type, severity, and contents of the complexes vary, their existence is universal.

This concept of the complex was adopted by the psychoanalytic world but later dropped, along with Jung himself. Recent psychoanalytic writers have rediscovered the idea under the name of *internalized object relations*. Psychedelic research has also validated the concept and resulted in two more such rediscoveries (see Chapter 8).

The idea of the complex is significant for transpersonal work because it points the way to important parts of the self that remain outside the conscious ego. When work with the complexes reaches the archetypal core, it frequently allows a first experience with the numinous (i.e., that which resonates with transcendent energy).

This progression highlights another of Jung's important contributions: that a symptom of psychopathology may lead to a healing transpersonal experience. Jung believed that each symptom both indicated pathology and pointed the way toward the resolution of that pathology. For example, a patient prone to angry outbursts who had been badly abused as a child might come to understand that angry behavior represented a need to provide security for himself and that satisfaction of that need could be pursued as zealously but not as ferociously once it was conscious. Numinous experience for such a patient would likely contain a strong sense of security.

Reconciliation of the Opposites

Closely related to the idea of the bipolar complex is Jung's emphasis on the importance of opposites in the psyche. Jung stressed that the human mind does not perceive singular qualities but that qualities always exist in relationship to their opposite. Both members of the pair of opposites are present in the patient's psyche and both sides are manifested at times. To perceive someone as cruel implies that the perceiver holds a concept of what constitutes kindness. Analytic work often consists of recognizing the tendency to identify with one member of a pair of opposites and project the other (e.g., my kindness and their cruelty) and then to allow the presence of both in one's self and others. Such one-sided identifications can be not only self-aggrandizing but also self-diminishing (e.g., my rationality and their visionary nature).

The Self

As Jung saw it, consciousness does not consist solely of the ego. Relatively early in development, consciousness becomes focused on the complexes. Ego, the most important complex with the broadest range of associated experiences and emotions, is usually the center of consciousness. Under stressful circumstances, however, other complexes become the focus of consciousness.

The Self consists simultaneously of the whole of the psyche and its core, or essence; it is the archetype of wholeness found within each human being. Jung furnished a picture of his model in *Man and His Symbols.*[10] The Self is represented as both a sphere with complexes floating on its surface like continents on the earth and as the center of the sphere, like the core of the earth. One of the major tasks of constructive analytic work in the second half of life is the development of an *ego-Self axis,* which is a broader, deeper connection between the conscious ego and the core Self. As this axis develops, the ego is not abandoned but acts more and more in the service of the Self. In this model, consciousness would be the area of the surface that is illuminated by the light of awareness falling on the surface of the sphere, as the light of the sun falls on different parts of the earth. At times the light of awareness is confined to a complex. At such times the individual is said to have been captured by a complex, and the ego is not in charge; therefore, although the ego is not always illuminated, it is the only complex with conscious access to the Self, by way of the ego–Self axis.

The Self includes the unconscious. In addition to accepting Freud's idea of the personal unconscious (aspects of one's life experience that are out of awareness), Jung described the *collective unconscious,* which he said consists of universal aspects of human experience that are not derived from personal history. The archetypes are specific contents of the collective unconscious.

Persona

The *persona* (taken from the word for the masks worn in Greek drama) covers the ego and presents one's best face to the world. The persona differs from a complex in that the persona is less autonomous and more a tool of the ego. For instance, one knows when to stifle a yawn to be polite but might choose not to stifle it if a guest overstayed his welcome. The persona in this situation is that of one who is generally polite but assertive enough to send a subtle signal of the need to retire when necessary.

Animus and Anima

Animus and *anima* make up one of the most important aspects of the psyche clinically. The *animus* is the male aspect contained within every human female, including male modes of emotion, valuation, conceptualization, and relatedness. *Anima* is the corresponding female aspect within every human male. Animus and anima frequently appear in dreams as a figure of the opposite sex that may function as a guide to other parts of the psyche. Later writers have criticized Jung's depiction of these inner representations of "the opposite" as too bound to his twentieth-century European culture and are working toward more inclusive descriptions.[11]

Shadow

The *shadow* is what Jung termed the aspects of the Self outside awareness, particularly parts that are unlike one's self-image and therefore repressed. The term, therefore, is usually used to describe negative and even evil aspects of the self. To the degree that the self-image is negative or unrealistically restricted, however, the shadow may carry positive characteristics that are ego-alien. The shadow often appears in dreams, frequently as an ominous and uncanny figure. Conscious personal experience with the shadow can aid spiritual development by leading to the reowning of projections of evil on others, followed by synthesis and growth.

Libido

Jung's concept of libido differs from Freud's and lies much closer to Henri Bergson's notion of *élan vital* and Hinduism's *prana*. Jung's libido is the basic psychophysical energy of life. It includes, but is not limited to, sexual energy: to Jung, sexual energy was only one presentation of the more universal life force. For instance, the extreme energy states that may be generated by spiritual experiences are not seen simply as misdirected sexual energy but as possibly more developed manifestations of the universal life force.

Individuation

Jung held that the psyche possesses an inherent tendency toward development throughout life, which he called a tendency toward *individuation*. Because in individuation the person "completes" ego development, working with repressed or universal potentials, it may appear as though an enhanced ego is developing. For instance, a person who has never demonstrated artistic ability may begin to do so at midlife. As individuation proceeds, however, the person begins to use her particular abilities and proclivities as tools, not for personal gain but for the benefit of the community, the world, and the spiritual realm. The individual transcends the ego in the service of the Self.

This process of ego transcendence is promoted by attention to the development of the ego–Self axis mentioned previously. The person looks for instruction and guidance from the Self, which may take the form of internal conversations as Jung had with Philemon but which are more frequently mediated by transpersonal symbols. Such symbols might be derived from the person's cultural background or may be spontaneous productions of the psyche; in any case, their importance is marked by the numinous power they carry for the perceiver. By pursuing the presentation and meaning of transpersonal symbols in her life, the person can identify both issues and levels of functioning that transcend ego concerns for her. Through the doors opened by the symbols, the ego can begin surrendering its skills and structuring capacity to the purposes of the Self. The specific content of the symbol was less important than that the symbol bring the perceiver an experience of awe, peace, or wonder: a felt sense of the transcendent. He took a particular interest in and studied the presentation of symbols such as circles, mandalas, crosses, stars, and trees across cultures. Spiritual experience, found in all times and all cultures, is a normal part of human development; its absence is evidence of a developmental arrest.

PROCESS OF ANALYSIS

A stylized view of a Jungian analysis might be as follows: The patient presents bothered by external life difficulties prompted by his major complexes. Early work focuses on the identification of the complexes, their developmental origins, and current replications in relationships and dreams. With attention to dreams, anima figures appear, and the patient works on assimilating qualities formerly assigned to the opposite sex. Shadow figures emerge in dreams, and the patient comes to trust the analyst enough to share life events that illustrate the appearance of shadowy kinds of behavior deemed unacceptable to family and culture. The patient comes to accept the existence of previously unowned parts of himself and to gain more control over them. After several years of analysis, the patient might experience or remember an experience of the numinous, quite likely through some symbol. This experience would become the basis for the development of the ego–Self axis, the facilitation of communication with the Self. As that axis is developed through pursuit of the felt sense of the transcendent, the patient develops new skills and becomes progressively more interested in connection with the community, the planet, and the realm of the spirit. Of course, it is understood that no actual case follows such a stylized course.

CROSS-CULTURAL AND MYSTICAL STUDIES

As noted previously, Jung was the first prominent psychiatrist to suggest that the psychologies of other cultures and the mystical systems of the West might contain important knowledge about the human mind. Jung neatly sidestepped the objections raised by most scientifically trained observers about unusual experiences described by non-Western and nonscientific systems by suggesting a psychological interpretation of the experiences. Jung was not interested in the objective validation of the vision of a yogi or shaman but in the subjective experience of that vision and its psychological consequences. For example, rather than dismiss alchemy as a failed attempt to turn base metals to gold, Jung suggested that the gold the alchemists sought was a psychological symbol of the developed Self. Transpersonal psychiatry aims to implement just such a psychologically informed approach to cross-cultural and mystical studies.

Jung collected and read many alchemical manuscripts, deriving information on archetypes which he found particularly important to the practice of psychoanalysis. For instance, he explored the alchemical imagery of the union of male and female principles to form a hermaphroditic syzygy (i.e., the union of opposites). Jung saw these as descriptions of the union with the animus or anima, which takes place in successful development in the second half of life.[12]

Jung lent his standing, thereby risking his reputation, to the publication of several important mystical texts in European languages. He wrote forewords or commentary to the texts of Richard Wilhelm's translations of the *I Ching* and *The Secret of the Golden Flower;* W. Y. Evans-Wentz's translations of *The Tibetan Book of the Great Liberation* and *The Tibetan Book of the Dead;* and D. T. Suzuki's *Introduction to Zen Buddhism.*[13] Jung emphasized that these mystical treatises pointed the way to levels of operation of the universe that were as yet unknown to science.

Jung was also willing to expose himself directly to the experience of other cultures rather than remaining content with analyzing them from a distance. He felt it was essential for both clinicians and theoreticians to experience the way in which other cultures and their languages structure different worlds of experience. Only with such foreign experience would the student of the mind have a chance to begin to see his or her own cultural stance and biases.[14]

Jung visited Algiers, Tunis, Uganda, and Kenya. He conferred with the elders of the people around Mt. Elgon and concluded that they used the same division of dreams as he did, discriminating between small, everyday dreams and rare, momentous, "big" dreams that might shape the course of a life. Jung's acceptance of the wisdom of other cultures was not complete. Some of his comments, when read today, clearly depict a developmental hierarchy of cultures, with European civilization at the top. Yet when Jung visited Taos pueblo in New Mexico, his meeting with the chief led him to a clear and moving vision of the decimation of other cultures brought about by whites thinking only with the head and not with the heart.

Jung's deepest immersion in another culture probably occurred with Hinduism; it also seems his most ambivalent cross-cultural connection. He presented a series of seminars on yoga to his group of analysts in Zurich and wrote several pieces on Hinduism and yoga. Again Jung led the way for Western psychiatry in recognizing the worth of this tradition, which had been largely dismissed as superstition and myth. He also felt that such paths would not work for Westerners, however, and might prove dangerous. While traveling in India, Jung avoided visiting the famed saint Sri Ramana Maharshi.[15] His own account shows Jung struggling at the absolute limit of his openness to foreign experience, and his fear of the power of such a holy man is almost palpable.[16]

CONCLUSION

As illustrated by his cross-cultural and cross-disciplinary studies, Jung saw the movements of consciousness not as primarily defensive but as amplifying the matter at hand. For him, the mind did not constantly pull up whatever subject might serve as a senseless distraction from reality; therefore, it did not require determined adherence to reason to hold to the important truths. Rather, seemingly unrelated topics could be profitably pursued. One's associations could be trusted as guides to deeper understanding of the topic at hand. Following this principle, Jung undertook the psychiatric study of previously neglected aspects of conscious experience, of mystical disciplines, and of other cultures.

The unconscious often seemed to know where unsuspected psychic gold lay. Jung's approach, rather than to attempt to gain control over the unconscious, was to try to know it and enter into continuing dialog with it. Once such a relationship was established, the unconscious could be expected to provide assistance and creativity. This principle of trust of one's own mental productions and those of other cultures may constitute Jung's greatest contribution to the study of the mind and spirit.

NOTES

1. Parenthetically, it is interesting to note that Freud's Vienna office is literally awash with dozens of images of the gods he collected from all over the ancient Western world. Juxtaposing that fact with Freud's strong conscious opposition to spiritual matters (see also *Moses and Monotheism*), one must conclude that Jung touched a highly conflicted area for Freud.

2. Jung, C. (1965). *Memories, dreams, reflections* (pp. 64–66). New York: Random House.

3. Ibid., pp. 155–156 and 361–363.

4. Brodway, K., & Signall, K., et al. (1990). *Sandplay studies: Origins, theory and practice*. Boston: Sigo Press.

5. Jung, *Memories*, pp. 182–235.

6. Kirsch, J. (1991). Carl Gustav Jung and the Jews: The real story. In A. Maidenbaum & S. Martin (Eds.), *Lingering shadows*. Boston: Shambhala.

7. Jung, *Memories*, pp. 289–296.

8. See Neumann, E. (1983). *The great mother*. Princeton, NJ: Princeton University Press.

9. See Perry, J. (1970). Emotions and object relations. *Journal of Analytical Psychology, 15*, 1–12.

10. Jung, C. (Ed.). (1964). *Man and his symbols*. Garden City, NY: Doubleday.

11. The fact that Jung apparently had affairs with at least two women analysts who trained with him is held by some to prove his masculine bias. In defending him, others point out that the issues of countertransference and appropriate therapeutic boundaries had not been worked out at that time.

12. Jung, C. (1966). Psychology of the transference. In *Collected works of C. G. Jung* (Vol. 16). Princeton NJ: Princeton University Press.

13. Jung, C. (1958). Foreword to the *I Ching*, commentary on *The Tibetan book of great liberation* and *The Tibetan book of the dead*, and Foreword to *Introduction to Zen Buddhism*. In *Collected works* (Vol. 11). Princeton, NJ: Princeton University Press. Commentary on *The secret of the golden flower*. In *Collected works* (Vol. 13). Princeton, NJ: Princeton University Press.

14. Jung, *Memories*, p. 246.

15. Jung, C. (1958). The holy men of India. In *Collected Works* (Vol. 11, p. 576).

16. Jung, *Memories*, p. 248.

CHAPTER 6

Abraham Maslow and Roberto Assagioli: Pioneers of Transpersonal Psychology

JOHN R. BATTISTA

ABRAHAM MASLOW AND ROBERTO ASSAGIOLI were both pioneers of transpersonal psychology. Maslow espoused a philosophy of science that set the stage for the development of humanistic and transpersonal psychology. He studied persons he considered self-actualized and described the spiritual values, beliefs, and actions of such individuals. He concluded that there is an inherently spiritual dimension to human nature and explicated a hierarchy of motivations that completes itself in spiritual self-realization. Maslow proposed the term *transpersonal* and addressed many of the basic concepts of the field.

Whereas Maslow explored fundamental issues in transpersonal psychology, Roberto Assagioli pioneered the practical application of these concepts in psychotherapy. Assagioli proposed a transpersonal view of personality and discussed psychotherapy in terms of the synthesis of personality at both the personal and spiritual levels. He dealt with the issue of spiritual crises and introduced many active therapeutic techniques for the development of a transcendent center of personality. This chapter reviews the theoretical and clinical foundations of transpersonal psychology and psychiatry as pioneered by Maslow and Assagioli, respectively.

MASLOW'S PHILOSOPHY OF SCIENCE

Maslow[1] was frustrated with the reductionistic methods he learned as a graduate student in psychology. As a result he emphasized the need for science to address significant human problems through the development of new methods. He emphasized that science and the scientific method should be applied to the study of subjective experience and not limited to objective phenomena. He suggested the development of a Taoist science[2] in which scientists observe and understand rather than influence and analyze. He was particularly critical of psychological theories that sought to reduce consciousness to unconscious phenomena or to reduce particular forms of conscious experience, such as spiritual states, to unresolved childhood issues. Overall, Maslow emphasized the phenomenological, holistic (nonanalytic), and empirical (non–a priori) nature of science. His basic concepts have now been widely accepted and slowly applied to psychology and psychotherapy.

Self-Actualization and Spirituality

Maslow[3,4] completed a long-term naturalistic study of persons he considered self-actualized and found striking similarities to traditional descriptions of enlightened persons. Self-actualized persons are reality-oriented, accept themselves and others, enjoy solitude, operate autonomously, and appreciate life, he reported. These individuals have peak experiences characterized by a state of oneness and kinship with other people. Self-actualized persons are humble, detached (not egocentric), humorous, and creative. They resist cultural beliefs, accept imperfections, and transcend dichotomies (e.g., reason–emotion, self–society, mystical–realistic; masculine–feminine). They have a desire to help, are efficient, and spontaneously engage in attempts to resolve social problems.

As a result of his study, Maslow[3] concluded that human beings have a positive, biologically based, instinctive nature that is fulfilled in spiritual self-actualization. He concluded that spirituality has a naturalistic meaning that does not necessarily make any religious or metaphysical assumptions. It was this conclusion that led him, with Stanislav Grof, to coin the term *transpersonal*[2] and to participate in the foundation of a new field, transpersonal psychology (see Chapter 2), distinct from humanistic psychology with which his work had always been associated.

In short, Maslow's work and life demonstrate how transpersonal psychology is a natural outgrowth of humanistic psychology. Maslow began by studying what it means to be fully human and ended by exploring transpersonal issues.

Self-Actualization Versus Narcissism

Maslow was a scientist and quite concerned that his work not be misunderstood and misused to support loose thinking, self-absorption, and self-inflation. He repeatedly went out of his way, therefore, to differentiate self-actualized individuals from those whom we generally call narcissists today. Maslow asserted[3,4] that people who are self-realized are oriented toward serving the world and are not self-absorbed. He emphasized that self-actualized persons are not preoccupied with their own feelings and motivations, overly sensitive to the criticism of others, or excessively concerned with what other people think of them. They are humble and loving toward others. They do not consider themselves prophets or enlightened beings who would revolutionize the world if only people would adopt their perspective.

Maslow emphasized the futility of seeking or searching for peak experiences. He stressed that a self-actualized, spiritual life is not an intense, orgasmic life characterized by a never-ending series of peak experiences. Although self-actualized life may involve intermittent peak experiences, it is better characterized by the experience of the sacred in the ordinary. He highlighted the feelings of peace and serenity that come from experiencing everyday life as sacred and called these moments *plateau experiences*[2] to distinguish them from peak experiences and to emphasize their importance in self-actualization.

Maslow also pointed out that spiritual growth commonly emerges from painful and difficult self-confrontations, not from affirmations of the positive, beautiful, and lovely. He coined the term *nadir experience*[2] to emphasize the importance to self-actualization of confrontations with death and near-death experiences. He tried to compensate for the cultural overemphasis and overinterest in peak experiences and the techniques designed to produce such spiritual breakthroughs.

A Hierarchical, Transpersonal Theory of Personality

Maslow was quite interested in how his self-actualized subjects differed from normal and neurotic individuals. On the basis of his research, Maslow proposed his famous hierarchy of needs, which is commonly taught in college psychology courses.[5] Maslow argued that the most basic human needs are physiological: the needs for oxygen, water, and food. These form the base of his hierarchical pyramid of human needs. When these needs are satisfied, needs for safety and security become prominent. If safety and security needs are satisfied, needs for love, affection, and belonging predominate. When these requirements are met, self-esteem needs emerge. Maslow considered these basic needs to represent *deficiency needs.* He meant that they all arise from an actual or perceived deficiency in the environment or self. The individual strives to complete these deficiencies through extracting what he or she needs from the physical, interpersonal, or social environment.

Maslow contrasted such deficiency needs with what he called *being–needs,* which include the need for creativity, beauty, simplicity, connection, meaning, service, advancement of knowledge, and society's improvement. Individuals pursue being–needs[3] after sufficiently satisfying their physiological, security, interpersonal, and self-esteem needs.

Maslow's hierarchy of needs and motivations provides a transpersonal model of development and theory of personality. As a developmental model, Maslow's work suggests that during the course of life each individual develops through a series of needs starting with basic physiological ones, followed by security–dependency needs and issues concerning belonging and self-esteem, and culminating in transpersonal or spiritual motivations.

The individual is also a hierarchically organized set of motivational structures. The physiological level is primary and dominates the other levels when it is not satisfied. The second order of motivations seeks to provide for security needs, and comes into play when the basic physiological needs are met. When security needs are satisfied, interpersonal motives for love and belonging emerge. When these interpersonal needs are sufficiently met, motives for self-esteem and self-assertion operate. Finally, when these personal needs are satisfied, motives for self-actualization and self-transcendence come into play. Maslow's theory implies that over the course of their lives, individuals experience themselves going up and down and in and out of this hierarchy as they respond to the stresses and rewards of life.

A Transpersonal Model of Social Organization

Maslow was particularly concerned with the application of his basic theory of motivation to the understanding of social organizations and structures. In the last few years of his life,[2] he further refined his hierarchy of motivations into a threefold model that included deficiency-motivated (theory x), humanistically motivated (theory y), and transcendentally motivated (theory z) individuals. Maslow's threefold model of levels of motivation is quite similar to Ken Wilber's[6] well-known model of prepersonal, personal, and transpersonal levels of development.

In his final conceptual paper, entitled "Theory Z," Maslow[7] tried to show how his three levels of human motivation could be applied to a wide variety of topics including business,[8] religion, psychotherapy, philosophy, and politics. He attempted to demonstrate how his three levels of motivation were organized into the operations of social structures including those of government, business, religion, interpersonal relations, and psychotherapy. For example, psychotherapy conducted at the deficiency level would operate by way of the traditional medical model in which the therapist is the knowledgeable authority who tells the person what to do and supplies him with what he needs. Psychopathology is conceptualized at this level in terms of inadequate parenting, learning, or gratification.

Psychotherapy conducted at the humanistic level is concerned with the person realizing his or her identity. The therapist offers an authentic encounter and relationship. Psychopathology is conceptualized as resistance to that potentiality. At the transpersonal level, psychotherapy is concerned with self-transcendence. The therapist serves as a compassionate teacher for the individual. Psychopathology takes the form of lacking zest in life or preoccupation with transcendent philosophical issues, such as meaning and justice. Maslow suggested the need to train and develop meta-counselors to deal with the soul-sickness of unmet metaphysical needs, which he called *meta-needs*.

Similarly, religions conducted on the deficiency level are concerned with a God of wrath. Religions at the humanistic level are concerned with a God of loving-kindness and with affirming the goodness of being human. Religions at the transpersonal level are concerned with spiritual realization; they use no concept of a personal God or utilize a God concept that is all-inclusive, paradoxical, and inexpressible.

Finally, business organizations[8] operating at the deficiency level use a managerial style of power–authority in which the employee is paid to do the job she is told to do. Businesses functioning at the humanistic level operate collectively through mutual respect. The employee is empowered to participate in the organization as fully as possible. Authority is assumed to be within each individual. Businesses at the transcendent level assume that all workers are devoted to service. The purpose of the business is to serve the client or consumer as fully as possible. Authority is assumed to be transcendent and ethically apparent to each individual. Maslow's work on the different hierarchical structures of personality organization and their relationship to different levels of psychopathology and psychotherapy anticipated the structural approach to transpersonal psychology taken by Wilber and other contemporary transpersonal theorists.

ASSAGIOLI'S TRANSPERSONAL VIEW OF ADULT PSYCHOLOGICAL DEVELOPMENT

Assagioli[9] conceptualized healthy adult development in two distinct stages. The first stage, or *personal psychosynthesis,* involves the integration, control, and balancing of the subpersonalities of the psyche through the development of a conscious center for the personality, which Assagioli called the *I*. The second stage, or *spiritual psychosynthesis,* involves the development of a spiritual center for the personality, which Assagioli called the *self*. This spiritual phase occurs as a natural outcome of contact between the personal center, or the I, and the creative and transforming spiritual energies of what Assagioli called the *superconscious*. The *superconscious* is a transpersonal and transcendent fountain of spiritual energy that can be contacted through a wide variety of techniques and practices such as meditation, active imagination, and music.

Personal Psychosynthesis

The first step in a personal psychosynthesis according to Assagioli[9,10] is exploring the structure of one's own psyche and becoming familiar with the contents of one's personal unconscious. He called this process *mapping*. Assagioli described subpersonalities that are formed through the conflicts and opposing forces of normal human experience. He also recognized the formation of personal unconscious *complexes* through trauma. In this preliminary stage of psychosynthesis, the client is taught about the personal unconscious, the superconscious, the subpersonalities, the self (the transcendent center), and the I (the personal center).

Assagioli[9] emphasized the importance of becoming familiar with one's subpersonalities, which may be unconscious, through the study of dreams and the use of psychological testing. Additionally, the client is encouraged to confront his subpersonalities by means of active imagination or daydreams,[11] in which the therapist helps the client visualize a variety of archetypal situations such as a voyage to the bottom of the sea or a visit with a witch, a wizard, a mythical beast, or a character such as Sleeping Beauty.

Assagioli also emphasized the coordination, integration, and control over the subpersonalities.[9,10] These tasks are accomplished by witnessing and observing the subpersonalities without being identified with them. This process of disidentification is similar to the insight meditation practice of Buddhism. Assagioli believed that through the disidentification process, the I, or personal center, is formed. He conceptualized this personal center as a projection into consciousness of the transpersonal self. In personal psychosynthesis, there is a reformation of the psyche around this personal center. This development[12] is an active and willed process facilitated by the therapist as teacher. An ideal form for this I, such as hero, teacher, or artist, is chosen and developed through the use of visualization, imagery, and guided fantasy. In this way the personal center develops and becomes more powerful and able to contain, integrate, and control the subpersonalities.

Spiritual Psychosynthesis

Once the I, or personal center, is developed to the point that it can effectively control and integrate the subpersonalities, the second stage of psychosynthesis is engaged: spiritual psychosynthesis.[9] First, symbols are used to evoke the experience of a spiritual or transcendent self.[13] This self, or spiritual center, is characterized by a sense of connection to all humanity and nature: a sense of unity with all things. The personal center is totally transcended in the experience of the self. Abstract symbols such as a rose, lotus, or sun, as well as personified symbols such as an angel, a sage, a master, or Christ, are used in this process.

Second, a variety of well-developed techniques such as meditation are used to facilitate spiritual development.[9,10] An inner dialogue technique[9] is used in which one asks questions of an inner
teacher or sage, who answers the questions. Clients are visually led
through spiritual quests such as the grail legend or *The Divine Comedy*.[9] Additionally, clients are visually guided through spiritual
cycles such as the blooming of a rose or the life cycle of wheat.[9]

Spiritual Crisis

Assagioli was well aware that the spiritual psychosynthesis
stage is commonly initiated by an existential crisis in which a person begins to question actively the meaning of existence, her self-
worth, or her values. Assagioli saw such a crisis as a natural and
common prelude to spiritual development. It is something to be
encouraged and understood as healthy rather than avoided or considered pathological.

Similarly, Assagioli recognized the difficulties that can occur as
the result of a spiritual awakening in an ill-prepared or undeveloped personality. In particular he spoke of the inflation of the personal I that can occur when a person is unable to integrate and
assimilate the flow of light and spirit into the personality. For this
reason he stressed the importance of a personal psychosynthesis
before a spiritual psychosynthesis is undertaken.

Relationship Between Psychosynthesis, Existential–Humanistic Psychology, Jungian Psychology, and Eastern Psychologies

Psychosynthesis has many connections with the existential–
humanistic movement. First, psychosynthesis emphasizes the
development of consciousness and the phenomenological basis of
psychotherapy. Second, Assagioli saw the psyche as inherently
growth-oriented and seeking to actualize itself, as does humanistic
psychology. Third, both psychosynthesis and the existential–
humanistic psychologies are concerned with values, meaning,
identity, and choice. Unlike some existentialists, however, Assagioli emphasized joy rather than loneliness, possibility over despair,
and meaningfulness more than meaninglessness.

Psychosynthesis is most closely related to Jungian psychology.[14]
Assagioli's overall view of the psyche was quite similar to Jung's;
his ideas concerning subpersonalities, the I, and the self are similar
to Jung's concepts of complexes, ego, and Self. Assagioli empha-

sized the formation of the psyche through its contact with opposites and the need to balance and synthesize opposites, much as Jung did. He also paralleled Jung's prospective, teleological view of symptoms, as well as Jung's view that there is a need to develop an ego before a spiritual transformation can be meaningfully undertaken. Psychosynthesis differs from Jungian psychology in that the therapist plays a much more active, educational, and directive role. Similarly, much more emphasis is placed on the use of the will in personal development. Finally, Assagioli had a more transpersonal view of the psyche and human development than Jung did. Assagioli perceived that a total reconstruction of the personality around a spiritual center is possible and spoke of the existence of a spiritual plane as a transpersonal as well as a personal reality.

Psychosynthesis is also kindred to both yoga and Buddhism. First, these disciplines all emphasize the control of the body, emotions, and intellect through disidentification and witnessing. Second, all of them stress the importance of meditation to personal development. Third, the active and instructive role of the therapist in psychosynthesis has more similarity to the teacher in the Eastern spiritual disciplines than to the traditional psychotherapist of psychodynamic psychotherapy.

CONCLUSION

Maslow and Assagioli were true pioneers of transpersonal psychology. Maslow's research on self-actualized persons furthered the empirical study of states of consciousness in psychology. His hierarchical model of motivation anticipated the structuralist models of contemporary transpersonal developmental theory. Maslow's application of his levels of motivation to business, religion, philosophy, psychology, and politics warrants further study. Similarly, Maslow's work on self-actualized persons can be expanded with the more sophisticated testing and research designs available today. For example, his idea that deficiency motivations need to be satisfied before being motivations emerge is readily testable. Overall, the field of transpersonal psychology is indebted to Maslow for his scientific approach.

Assagioli's work shows a mature synthesis of humanistic and Jungian psychology with Eastern spiritual traditions. His active, instructive view of the role of the therapist and his techniques for transpersonal development in spiritually oriented psychotherapy remain important elements that all transpersonal clinicians can benefit from.

NOTES

1. Maslow, A. (1969). *The psychology of science: A reconnaissance.* New York: Harper.
2. Maslow, A. (1972). *The farther reaches of human nature.* New York: Viking Press.
3. Maslow, A. (1962). *Toward a psychology of being.* Princeton, NJ: Van Nostrand.
4. Maslow, A. (1964). *Religions, values and peak-experiences.* Columbus: Ohio State University Press.
5. Maslow, A. (1954). *Motivation and personality.* New York: Harper.
6. Wilber, K. (1986). The spectrum of development. In K. Wilber, J. Engler, & D. Brown, *Transformations of consciousness.* Boston: Shambhala.
7. Maslow, A. (1969). Theory Z. *Journal of Transpersonal Psychology, 1,* 31–47.
8. Maslow, A. (1965). *Eupsychian management.* Homewood, IL: Irwin-Dorsey.
9. Assagioli, R. (1965). *Psychosynthesis: A manual of principles and techniques.* New York: Viking Press.
10. Whitmore, D. (1991). *Psychosynthesis counseling in action.* London: Sage.
11. Desoille, R. (1966). *The directed daydream.* New York: Psychosynthesis Research Foundation.
12. Assagioli, R. (1973). *The act of will.* London: Penguin Books.
13. Assagioli, R. (1976). *Transpersonal inspiration and psychological mountain climbing.* New York: Psychosynthesis Research Foundation.
14. Assagioli, R. (1967). *Jung and psychosynthesis.* New York: Psychosynthesis Research Foundation.

CHAPTER 7

The Worldview of Ken Wilber

ROGER WALSH AND
FRANCES VAUGHAN

KEN WILBER IS WIDELY REGARDED as one of today's foremost
transpersonal thinkers and theoretical psychologists. He has won
this reputation by creating syntheses of unprecedented scope
among diverse schools and disciplines including psychology, philosophy, sociology, anthropology, and religion. In a world of
increasing specialization, the range and richness of Wilber's vision,
together with his ability to integrate apparently conflicting viewpoints—East and West, psychology and philosophy, science and
religion—are all too rare. This chapter is intended to offer a synop-
tic introduction to Wilber's worldview.

THE SPECTRUM OF CONSCIOUSNESS

In his initial books *The Spectrum of Consciousness*[1] and a simplified
version of the same work, *No Boundary*,[2] Wilber uses the metaphor
of the spectrum, whose rich bands of color constitute a single

This chapter is adapted from R. Walsh and F. Vaughan (1994), "The World
View of Ken Wilber," *Journal of Humanistic Psychology*, 34 (2), 6–21. Copyright © 1994 Sage Publications, Inc. Reprinted by permission of Sage Publications, Inc.

underlying invisible entity: light. He suggests that consciousness displays a spectrum of levels and states with corresponding unconscious structures. He contends that different schools of psychology address different levels of this spectrum. The different schools are not contradictory and antagonistic, therefore, but complementary perspectives, each partially true. This spectrum view of consciousness forms the infrastructure for Wilber's ontological, epistemological, developmental, and evolutionary theories.

DEVELOPMENTAL THEORIES

In his book *The Atman Project,* Wilber[3] turns his attention to developmental psychology. Here he traces development from infancy to adulthood, comparing and integrating major conventional Western thinkers such as Sigmund Freud, Carl Jung, Jean Piaget, and Lawrence Kohlberg. He then traces development through further (transconventional, transpersonal) levels following tenets of the major non-Western schools. Wilber thus provides a developmental model that spans the full spectrum of human growth from infancy to enlightenment.

Because the personal level has been viewed as the acme of human development by most Western schools of psychology, a recurrent trap has been to dismiss or pathologize transpersonal levels. Indeed, because some transpersonal experiences such as the dissolution of ego boundaries bear a superficial resemblance to some pathological conditions, there has been a tendency to equate the two. For example, mystical experiences have been interpreted as regressions to union with the breast, ecstatic states viewed as narcissistic neurosis, enlightenment dismissed as regression to intrauterine stages, and meditation seen as self-induced catatonia. This is the trap that Wilber calls the pre-trans fallacy.

In *Transformations of Consciousness,*[4] Wilber refines his developmental stages and links them to specific pathologies and therapies, thereby producing spectra of development, pathology, and therapy. Developmental stages are linked to the appearance of corresponding basic structures: constituents of the psyche that, once they emerge, tend to endure. For example, basic structures include the sensoriphysical (Piaget's sensorimotor level) with its sensory data, the representational mind with its symbols and concepts, and the subtle level with its visions and archetypes.

The key idea of Wilber's spectrum of pathology is that each stage of development is predisposed to specific types of pathology and requires corresponding treatments. He divides these pathologies into the broad categories of *prepersonal, personal,* and *transpersonal.* He associates what he called the *prepersonal pathologies,* such as infantile psychosis and narcissistic and borderline personality disorders, with failures in early development. At the personal level, he includes neuroses and existential distress. Beyond these disorders are transpersonal pathologies associated with spiritual experiences and practices, such as kundalini crises, the dark night of the soul, or the spiritual emergencies described by Stanislav and Christina Grof.[5] For each of these stage-specific disorders, Wilber suggests a corresponding stage-specific treatment. For the earliest developmental failures manifesting as psychoses, he recommends pharmacological approaches; for narcissistic and borderline personality disorders, he suggests structure-building therapies; for neuroses, he recommends uncovering techniques; and for existential crises, he suggests existential therapy. For transpersonal disorders, he recommends a judicious mix of treatments developed over the centuries by contemplative traditions combined with psychotherapeutic approaches by a transpersonally sensitive therapist.

Challenges to Wilber's Developmental Scheme

Some clinicians have expressed concern that Wilber's developmental model is more theoretical than practical and does not necessarily match clinical observations.[6] Two challenges to Wilber's theory come from Jungian and existential perspectives. Michael Washburn[7,8] attempted to expand on Jung's theory of transpersonal development and, in doing so, to challenge Wilber's model. Washburn claimed that transpersonal development necessarily requires a U-turn, "a return to origins. . . . a going back before a higher going forth." Washburn's general idea is that some sort of return to the source or ground out of which the ego initially arose is an essential component of transpersonal development.

Wilber's disagreement with this idea in particular and the Washburn–Jung model in general was supported by a study of spiritual practitioners who had reached transpersonal developmental stages.[9,10] Contrary to Washburn's hypothesis, only some of them had experienced regressive crises.

The second challenge was presented by Kirk Schneider,[11,12] who criticized Wilber's claims for the existence, significance, and beneficence of higher transpersonal states of consciousness and developmental stages. He argued from an existentialist perspective that such states, especially the highest, are unprovable, logically contradictory, and humanly impossible. Unfortunately, Schneider's extensive knowledge of existentialism was not matched by his understanding of transpersonal experiences, and several complex assumptions and issues were insufficiently appreciated. Wilber noted some of these issues in his responses to Schneider.[13,14] The ensuing debate can be read in part as an example of a paradigm clash between existential and transpersonal worldviews. A similar paradigm clash occurs, as we will see, concerning Wilber's evolutionary theory.

EVOLUTION

Wilber next turned his attention to anthropology and applied the developmental schema from *The Atman Project* to human evolution. In *Up From Eden*, Wilber[15] traces the evolution of human consciousness, identity, culture, and religion and their dynamic interplay from the period of the first hominids up to the current time. Different stages of evolution, he suggests, have been marked by different predominant states of consciousness and identity, and these have been reflected in culture and religion. The general trend is a progressive development and freeing of consciousness, freeing first from exclusive identification with the body and then from various components of mind. Evolution is not a random concatenation of genetic and selective forces, he suggests, but an expression of a vast cosmological game of hide-and-seek in which consciousness creates matter (involution) and then evolves through successive physical, biological, mental, and spiritual (consciousness) levels to self-recognition. This general pattern of consciousness manifesting as the physical universe and then evolving to self-awareness is similar to Sri Aurobindo's view. Wilber's additional contribution is the attempt to tie the evolution of consciousness to contemporary psychology and anthropology.

A unique feature of *Up From Eden* is that Wilber hypothesizes two distinct lines of evolution. One is that of the average or collective consciousness; the other is that of the pioneers who precede and inspire the collective. He identifies these pioneers as the shaman, yogi, saint, and sage, who as evolutionary leaders plumbed successively greater depths of self and heights of consciousness. In contrast to the beliefs of scholars such as Mircaea Eliade, Jung, and Joseph Campbell, Wilber suggests that the techniques religious adepts use and the realizations they attain have evolved over time.

Up From Eden is the most controversial of Wilber's books. Anthropological critiques of it are similar to clinicians' criticisms of Wilber's map of pathology, namely, that the theory is logical and articulate, but it does not always match the data. The most detailed critique is that of Winkleman.[17] He argues, as do others,[16] that the theory is ethnocentric; it is rooted in a Western viewpoint and fails to encompass data from a representative sample of cultures. He also points out, as Wilber himself acknowledges, that the theory is based on a synthesis of the views of other theoreticians, such as Arieti, Gebser, Cassirer, and Neumann. There is no direct review of anthropological or archaeological data, and several claims contradict the findings of widely accepted anthropological research. The problem is that the enormous scope of the theory makes it unclear how conflicting data could easily disprove it and hence whether the theory is readily testable.

Winkleman also cites cultural relativism in criticizing the value system underlying Wilber's assessment of states and stages as more or less evolved. Cultural relativism argues that all perspectives and values are culture-laden and that "because there are no culture-free frames of reference, there are no absolutely objective criteria for comparing cultures and their traditions with respect to levels of development."[18]

There seem to be three possible responses to the cultural relativism criticism. Cultural relativism has itself been subject to two major criticisms. Theoretically, cultural relativism stands accused of what is called the *performative paradox:* of itself doing what it claims cannot be done. Claiming that no universal culture-free value judgments can be valid, it establishes its own principle as just such a valid universal rule; that is, it exempts itself from its own universal rule. In addition to this theoretical criticism, there now exists significant evidence that it is possible to make valid cross-cultural developmental assessments.[19] The third possible response to Winkleman's cultural relativism criticism is that Winkleman does not seem to consider Wilber's own criteria for assessing developmental stages. Wilber[20] advances the metaphor of the Chinese box that encloses box within box within box. He concludes that a stage can be said to be more developed when it (1) emerges later, (2) has access to the lower stage and its capacities, and (3) possesses additional capacities not available to previous stages.

It is important to note that a developmental or evolutionary sequence is not necessarily the same as a value hierarchy; that is, a later stage is not necessarily better than an earlier stage in the same way that a 10-year-old is not necessarily better than a 6-year-old. Many people seem to react negatively to developmental and evolutionary schemas in general and Wilber's model in particular because they do not appreciate this distinction.

Environmental philosopher Warwick Fox[21] criticized Wilber's theory for being anthropocentric: regarding humans as the most important and central factor in the universe. Wilber's view might be more accurately regarded as cosmocentric or theocentric, however, because it is ultimately centered in the Whole or Spirit, as source, context, and goal of evolution. In addition, Fox argues that Wilber's view is too linear and hierarchical and that species cannot be placed along a single linear scale of evolution, let alone a single scale of increasing perfection. Each species must be regarded as a perfect exemplar of its own kind.

Here again we have a paradigm clash. From a traditional, scientific (earth-centered) evolutionary view, Fox's concern may be correct. Yet from a cosmocentric evolutionary view, it may also be true that individual species, including humans, represent points on a vast purposeful developmental progression toward the whole and that this whole can be realized by humans.

Wilber's developmental and evolutionary themes are extended further in a massive new three-volume work *Sex, Ecology and Spirituality*.[22] In this work, Wilber links the evolution of consciousness to data in fields as diverse as physical, biological, and cultural evolution; psychology; anthropology; sociology; ecology; feminism; philosophy; and mysticism. The result is a synthesis of almost unprecedented scope.[43]

EPISTEMOLOGY

Conflicts such as those described in the preceding section raise the crucial question of how we can, or even *if* we can, assess the relative merits of competing worldviews that differ primarily in their metaphysics. Science alone seems inadequate to the task, and contemporary philosophy avoids metaphysics almost entirely, holding that such questions are unanswerable. Wilber[23,24] argues that there are three distinct "eyes of knowledge," or epistemological modes: the sensory, the intellectual or symbolic, and the contemplative.

Each of these modes has its own unique data and facts, and each realm of knowledge only partially overlaps others. To confuse these realms, such as by believing that contemplative knowledge can be reduced to intellectual understanding, is to commit a category error and to lose the unique information of each domain. Each domain does possess appropriate means of assessing the validity of knowledge in its own realm, however. Traditional scientific approaches are best suited for physical phenomena. Hermeneutics (interpretive approaches) best serve the symbolic realm; for example, the meaning of Shakespeare's *Hamlet* is determined better by hermeneutics than by scientific analysis of the ink with which it was written. Similarly, contemplative understanding is best evaluated with intersubjective testing by masters of this realm. Each method is valid in its own realm, but only in its own realm. Failure to realize this principle has produced enormous confusion and conflict among scientists, philosophers, and theologians.

SOCIOLOGY

Wilber's next excursion was into sociology; in *A Sociable God*,[25] he provides what he calls "a brief introduction to a transcendental sociology." Here his goal is a sociological framework capable of encompassing transpersonal experiences and practices. He uses the model of psychological maturation postulated in *The Atman Project* as a developmental framework for assessing levels of social interaction. This provides a corrective addition to current methods of sociological analysis, such as phenomenological hermeneutics, which have lacked criteria for differentiating among levels of social interaction. Wilber carefully linked these arguments with those of the German philosopher Jurgen Habermas.

Wilber's approach provides a means for avoiding the trap of making one level of social interaction and pathology paradigmatic for all, such as Marx and Freud did by interpreting all behavior in terms of economics and sexuality, respectively. Art, philosophy, religion, and all "higher" activities were then attributed to economic oppression or sexual repression, respectively.

The current trend toward increasing rationalization has been widely interpreted as evidence of an anti- or postreligious evolution. Wilber reframes this whole movement, however, as an appropriate phase-specific shift in which prerational worldviews yield to the rational on the way to the transrational–transpersonal. From this evolutionary perspective, the current phase is seen as antireligious only if religion is mistakenly regarded, as it often is, as consisting solely of prerational beliefs and behaviors rather than as diverse behaviors that may express any of the prerational–rational– transrational developmental levels. This perspective also allows a method of determining what Wilber calls the "authenticity" of a religion: the degree to which it fosters development to transrational levels. He differentiates *authenticity* from *legitimacy*, or the degree to which a religion fills the psychological and social needs, either healthy or unhealthy, of people at their current developmental level.

These different dimensions of religion have often been conflated. Differentiating them allowed Wilber in *Spiritual Choices* to outline a model for distinguishing religious groups that are likely to prove beneficial, problematic, or even dangerous.[26] In these times of religious confusion, such a model can be very useful.

PHYSICS

A topic of considerable contemporary confusion and conflict has been the relationship between physics and mysticism. The view that modern physics is discovering remarkable parallels to, and perhaps even proof of, ancient mystical claims has been championed by writers such as Fritjof Capra[27] and Gary Zukav.[28] This view has become remarkably popular, except among physicists.

In *Quantum Questions*[29] Wilber collected the writings of the great physicists—Albert Einstein, Werner Heisenberg, Erwin Schroedinger, and others—to see what they said about this question. Their conclusion? Physics and mysticism treat different domains. Physics can neither affirm nor deny mysticism. Indeed, Einstein claimed that "the present fashion of applying the axioms of physical science to human life is not only a mistake but has also something reprehensible in it."[30] Another physicist warned that "if I were an Eastern mystic the last thing in the world I would want would be a reconciliation with modern science . . . [because] to hitch a religious philosophy to a contemporary science is a sure route to its obsolescence."[31]

Wilber concludes, contrary to the beliefs of theorists such as Capra and Globus,[32] that there may be some identifiable parallels between descriptions from physics and certain mystical investigations but that these parallels are likely to be few, abstract, and certainly not proof of mystical claims. For Wilber, "genuine mysticism, precisely to the extent that it is genuine, is perfectly capable of offering its own defense, its own evidence, its own claims, and its own proof. . . . the findings of modern physics and mysticism have very little in common."[33]

ONTOLOGY

One of Wilber's central ideas is that reality is multilayered and that the levels of existence form an ontological hierarchy, or *holoarchy* as he prefers to call it, which includes matter, body, mind, and spirit. This is the *Great Chain of Being*, which has, "in one form or another, been the dominant official philosophy of the larger part of civilized humankind throughout most of its history."[34] For Wilber,[35] different levels of development involve identification with corresponding levels of the Great Chain. Humans identify first with the body, then with the ego–mind, and perhaps thereafter, as a result of contemplative practices, with more subtle mental realms and eventually pure consciousness itself. Development and evolution consist of movement up this hierarchy, and consciousness becomes increasingly refined, expansive, and free as this movement proceeds. Different levels tend to be associated with different worldviews; different schools of psychology, philosophy, and religion; and different psychopathologies and corresponding appropriate therapies.

Although they were historically dominant, the Great Chain of Being and all hierarchies, especially ontological hierarchies, now face severe criticism. Philosophically, ontological hierarchies are widely regarded as unprovable, although they are widely accepted in developmental psychology. Historically they have also been associated with patriarchal dominance and with a devaluing of the lower end of the spectrum, for example, the body, emotions, sexuality, and the earth. As Donald Rothberg[36] pointed out in an excellent review of the topic, these criticisms are not necessarily fatal, but they do point to distortions of the perennial philosophy that any hierarchical ontology, including Wilber's transpersonal theory, must take into account. Wilber attempts to incorporate these concerns by differentiating between natural and pathological hierarchies.

PERSONAL REFLECTIONS

The majority of Wilber's writings have been theoretical; however, he has written four intensely personal pieces. The first, a paper titled "Odyssey,"[37] provides an excellent autobiographical over-view of the development of his thought. The second, "On Being a Support Person,"[38] was catalyzed by his experience of providing support for his wife Treya, who discovered a breast cancer 10 days after they were married. Although many people become a support person at some time, almost nothing has been written about the role. Wilber shares openly his own pain, fears, conflicts, insights, and discoveries. He describes the difficulties involved (exhaustion, suppression of feelings, guilt, anger, resentment, and lack of out-side support), various ways of being skillfully supportive (offering empathy, being an emotional sponge, limiting advice giving, not suppressing the loved one's fears), and ways of getting support for oneself (support groups, psychotherapy, and spiritual practice). This paper has proved very valuable to others in similar roles.

Treya's last 24 hours are described in a remarkably poignant arti-cle "Love Story."[39] The whole saga of the Wilbers' battle with can-cer and their practice of the ars moriendi (the art of dying) is chron-icled in *Grace and Grit*.[40] The ars moriendi has long been a focus of individual practice in the world's spiritual traditions, but rarely has it been so powerfully portrayed by a couple committed to using life, death, and relationship for spiritual practice.

CONCLUSION

Wilber's theoretical system has its limits, but it also has enormous strengths. He has forged a systematic, broad-ranging, multidisci-plinary, integrative, visionary yet scholarly worldview based in psychology, grounded in philosophy, spanning sociology and anthropology, and reaching to religion and mysticism. His integra-tions of apparently conflicting schools and disciplines reduce con-flict and sectarianism; his incorporation of Asian traditions reduces Western ethnocentricity; and his contemporary interpretation of the perennial philosophy makes its wisdom comprehensible and helps us recognize that at their contemplative core, the world's great religions contain road maps and techniques for inducing transcendent states of consciousness. The scope of his synthesis is perhaps unparalleled.

Another of Wilber's contributions is the generous and uplifting view of human nature intrinsic to his system. Gordon Allport[41] remarked that "by their own theories of human nature, psycholo-gists have the power of elevating or degrading that same nature.

Debasing assumptions debase human beings; generous assumptions exalt them." Wilber's view of humanity journeying toward or awakening to Universal Consciousness is elevating indeed. Lewis Mumford[42] pointed out that the great human and social transformations throughout history stemmed in part from far-reaching transformations of humankind's self-images and involved three things: a broad-ranging synthesis of knowledge, recognition of a hierarchy of existence (the Great Chain of Being), and a purposive view of humankind as evolving toward "the good." According to Mumford, humankind's primary task is to align ourselves with this hierarchy and evolution. Wilber's system seems consistent with these criteria and this task.

NOTES

1. Wilber, K. (1977). *The spectrum of consciousness.* Wheaton, IL: Quest.

2. Wilber, K. (1981). *No boundary.* Boston: Shambhala Publications.

3. Wilber, K. (1980). *The Atman project.* Wheaton, IL: Quest.

4. Wilbur, K., Engler, J., & Brown, D. (Eds.).(1986). *Transformations of consciousness.* Boston: Shambhala Publications.

5. Grof, C., & Grof, S. (1993). Spiritual emergency. In R. Walsh & F. Vaughan (Eds.), *Paths beyond ego: The transpersonal vision* (pp. 137–143). Los Angeles: Tarcher.

6. Grof, C., & Grof, S. (1986). Spiritual emergence. *ReVision, 8,* 7–20.

7. Washburn, M. (1990). Two patterns of transcendence. *Journal of Humanistic Psychology, 30(3),* 84–112.

8. Washburn, M. (1988). *The ego and the dynamic ground: A transpersonal theory of human development.* Albany, NY: SUNY Press.

9. Wilber, K. (1990). Two patterns of transcendence: A reply to Washburn. *Journal of Humanistic Psychology, 30(3),* 113–136.

10. Thomas, L. E., Brewer, S., Kraus, P., & Rosen, B. (1993). Two patterns of transcendence: An empirical examination of Wilber's and Washburn's theories. *Journal of Humanistic Psychology, 33(3),* 66–81.

11. Schneider K. (1987). The deified self: A "centaur" response to Wilber and the transpersonal movement. *Journal of Humanistic Psychology, 27,* 196–216.

12. Schneider, K. (1989). Infallibility is so damn appealing: A reply to Ken Wilber. *Journal of Humanistic Psychology, 29,* 470–481.

13. Wilber, K. (1989). God is so damn boring: A response to Kirk Schneider. *Journal of Humanistic Psychology, 29,* 457–469.

14. Wilber, K. (1989). Reply to Schneider. *Journal of Humanistic Psychology, 29,* 493–500.

15. Wilber, K. (1981). *Up From Eden.* New York: Doubleday.

16. Staniford, P. (1982). Ken Wilber's transpersonal view of human evolution: A review of *Up From Eden. Journal of Transpersonal Anthropology, 67,* 163–166.

17. Winkleman, M. (1993). The evolution of consciousness: Transpersonal theories in light of cultural relativism. *Anthropology of Consciousness, 4(3),* 3–9.

18. Ibid., p. 5.

19. Habermas, J. (1979). *Communication and the evolution of society* (T. McCarthy, Trans.). Boston: Beacon Press.

20. Wilber, K. (Ed.). (1982). *The holographic paradigm and other paradoxes.* Boston: Shambhala Publications.

21. Fox, W. (1990). *Toward a transpersonal ecology: Developing new foundations for environmentalism.* Boston: Shambhala Publications.

22. Wilber, K. (1995). *Sex, ecology and spirituality: Vol. I. The spirit of evolution.* Boston: Shambhala Publications.

23. Wilber, K. (1996). *Eye to eye: The quest for the new paradigm* (Expanded ed.). Wheaton, IL: Quest.

24. Wilber, K. (1993). Eye to eye: Science and transpersonal psychology. In R. Walsh and F. Vaughan (Eds.), *Paths beyond ego: The transpersonal vision* (pp. 184–188). Los Angeles: Tarcher.

25. Wilber, K. (1983). *A sociable God: A brief introduction to a transcendental sociology.* New York: McGraw-Hill.

26. Anthony, D., Ecker, B., & Wilber, K. (Eds.). (1987). *Spiritual choices: The problem of recognizing authentic paths to inner transformation.* New York: Paragon House.

27. Capra, F. (1991). *The Tao of physics* (3rd ed.). Boston: Shambhala Publications.

28. Zukav, G. (1979). *The dancing wu li masters.* New York: William Morrow.

29. Wilber, K. (Ed.). (1984). *Quantum questions: Mystical writings of the world's great physicists.* Boston: Shambhala Publications.

30. Ibid., pp. ix–x.

31. Jeans, J. (1948). *Physics and philosophy.* Cambridge, England: Cambridge University Press.

32. Globus, G. (1986). Physics and mysticism: Current controversies. *ReVision, 8,* 49–54.

33. Wilber, *Quantum questions,* p. 26.

34. Lovejoy, A. (1936). *The great chain of being* (p. 26). Cambridge: Harvard University Press.

35. Wilber, K. (1993a). The great chain of being. In R. Walsh and F. Vaughan (Eds.), *Paths beyond ego: The transpersonal vision* (pp. 214–222). Los Angeles: Tarcher.

36. Rothberg, D. (1986). Philosophical foundations of transpersonal psychology: An introduction to some basic issues. *Journal of Transpersonal Psychology, 18,* 1–34.

37. Wilber, K. (1982). Odyssey: A personal inquiry into humanistic and transpersonal psychology. *Journal of Humanistic Psychology* 22, 57–90.

38. Wilber, K. (1988). On being a support person. *Journal of Transpersonal Psychology, 20,* 141–160.

39. Wilber, K. (1989, July/August). Love story. *New Age,* 32–112.

40. Wilber, K. (1991). *Grace and grit.* Boston: Shambhala Publications.

41. Allport, G. (1964). The fruits of eclecticism: Bitter or sweet. *Acta Psychologica, 23,* 27–44.

42. Mumford, L. (1956). *The transformations of man.* New York: Harper Brothers.

43. Walsh, R. (1995). The spirit of evolution: An overview of Ken Wilber's book *Sex, ecology, spirituality. Noetic Sciences Review,* summer, pp. 16–33. An expanded version of this overview is scheduled to appear in *ReVision* in 1996.

CHAPTER 8

The Consciousness Research
of Stanislav Grof

RICHARD YENSEN AND
DONNA DRYER

STANISLAV GROF WAS BORN in 1931 in Prague, Czechoslovakia, where he spent his youth and young adulthood. Trained in psychiatry and psychoanalysis, he came to the United States in 1967 on a Foundation's Fund for Research in Psychiatry Fellowship to join the faculty of Johns Hopkins University and soon became Chief of Psychiatric Research at the Maryland Psychiatric Research Center. In 1973 he left his research and academic posts to become scholar-in-residence at the Esalen Institute in Big Sur, California.

The outcome of Grof's research is a theoretical framework for understanding human consciousness that boldly challenges accepted Western beliefs about the psyche. He was one of the principal figures in the creation of the field of transpersonal psychology (see Chapter 2). Grof's theoretical contributions are well grounded in the careful observation and scholarly description of clinical experiences with thousands of patients undergoing psychotherapy while experiencing the effects of psychedelic drugs. He holds that the effects of psychedelics on consciousness resemble those of an amplifier or catalyst for the unconscious.[1]

75

OBSERVATION OF LSD SESSION: CONTENT AND PHENOMENOLOGY

In Czechoslovakia Grof conducted extensive research on the effects of LSD. He classified his observations of the subjective phenomenology of LSD experiences into four major experiential domains, described in the following sections.

Abstract Aesthetic Experiences

The most superficial level of reaction to LSD consisted of abstract aesthetic experiences that included all the sensory realms. These included geometric distortions and architectural patterns, optical illusions, hypersensitivity to sound, and synesthesias. These perceptual changes were enhanced by an amplification of fantasy. Grof suggested that these effects had little or no psychodynamic significance and may have resulted from simple physiological effects of LSD.

Psychodynamic Experiences and Systems of Condensed Experience (COEX)

This category of experience ranged from simple reliving of recent or remote events to complex reexperiencing of childhood traumas. There were more involved experiences such as enigmatic combinations of fantasy, symbolism resembling that of dreams, and defensive distortions or displacements. In people with relatively uncomplicated early lives, this layer of experience was resolved or integrated quickly. In people with difficult childhood circumstances, this type of experience extended for many sessions and required a great deal of skilled psychotherapeutic intervention for adequate resolution to occur.

Grof developed a concept for understanding the coincident structure of affect and memory in these experiences. He called the structures *systems of condensed experience*, or *COEX systems*, and he found they could explain and even predict clinical changes under the effects of LSD. Apparently simultaneously, on the other side of the Iron Curtain in Germany, Hanscarl Leuner conceived an almost identical concept to explain his observations concerning therapy with LSD, which he called *transphenomenal dynamic governing systems* or *TYDYSTS*.[2]

Both Grof and Leuner observed in LSD therapy sessions that

associative memory is organized and linked into systems that are made up of individual memories with similar feeling tone, affect, and thematic content. Once a COEX system was activated in an LSD session, it exerted a governing influence on the experience and could color the entire consciousness between LSD sessions. This passionate emotional charge was a summation of the affect from all similar life experiences from the past. Each COEX system had its own specific defenses. At their core, COEX systems contain vivid and colorful forgotten or repressed memories from infancy and early childhood. The core memories emerged as a series of complete relivings in successful therapy. Once a core memory was fully abreacted and integrated into the patient's conscious awareness, the entire COEX would lose its governing power and another COEX would emerge and dominate the session content. By continuing this process in repeated LSD sessions, psychological conflicts were systematically resolved. This approach to LSD therapy is called *psycholytic* (literally, mind dissolving) *therapy* and was practiced primarily in Europe.[3]

Grof mapped types of COEX systems to specific defense mechanisms and symptoms.[14] Some Jungians contend that COEXs and TYDYSTS are simply a restatement of Jung's concept of complexes. Grof mentions the similarity and says that COEXs are not identical to complexes, but he does not explain the differences beyond noting that the death–rebirth process has no unique status in Jung's theories.[9] In Grof's work the perinatal is the critical interface between the personal and transpersonal realms of consciousness.*

Perinatal: Portal Beyond the Separate Self

Grof noticed that as individuals resolved COEX issues, their LSD experiences came to be dominated by increasingly intense encounters with more universal concerns such as death and dying, agony, aging, and physical pain. Grof's subjects sometimes described themselves as feeling the suffering of all humanity. Their experiences alternated between this broader scope and intense personal agony concerning physical pain and the certainty that they were truly dying. Another universal concern that emerged was birth. After resolving their death agony, many patients told Grof that they

*Descriptions of COEXs and TYDYSTS so closely parallel Jung's earlier descriptions of complexes that the work of the three men must be viewed as independent confirmations of the same phenomena.—Ed.

were convinced they had relived the trauma of their own biological birth. Although he first called this the *Rankian phase*, Grof later realized that Otto Rank's concept of what constituted trauma did not entirely match the observations from the LSD research. Grof suggested that the fundamental trauma experienced in psychedelic sessions was the agony and vital emergency during the process of birth, not just separation from the mother as Rank emphasized.

The impressive clinical improvement patients experienced in work with the COEX systems often disappeared during the tumultuous Rankian passage. The previously distinct clinical syndromes now converged into a more uniform picture of collective dimensions. Grof formulated his central thesis around this observation. He proposed that the multidimensional death–rebirth domain is a universal basic matrix for all psychopathology.[4,5,6]

Grof was able to differentiate four stages within the death–rebirth process, which he termed the *basic perinatal matrices (BPMs)*. He used a temporal numbering sequence in which BPM I concerns intrauterine experiences and BPMs II through IV occur during the actual birth process; however, the sequence revealed itself in the serial LSD sessions in a slightly different order, and the following description is based on that order.

Basic Perinatal Matrix II

Patients entering the perinatal domain often described feeling caught in a cosmic vortex, or spiral; entering a long dark tunnel; or being swallowed by a monster. Common complaints included "hatband" headaches, ringing in the ears, difficulty in breathing, nausea, muscular tension, jerks and twitches, palpitations, excessive sweating, hot flashes alternating with chills, and pains in different parts of the body. On an emotional level, there were reports of overwhelming feelings of guilt and inadequacy, enormous anxiety, and a total loss of hope in an experience of complete despair. Patients wished for a passive suicide. There is a trapped character to the suffering at this level of consciousness, with a profound agony but with little release of emotion.

Basic Perinatal Matrix III

The difficult struggle increased to titanic and catastrophic proportions. As patients worked through the suffering, there eventually came a shift, usually accompanied by a final surrender. There was a new feeling of involvement in a meaningful passage: running the gauntlet or heading toward the light at the end of the tunnel. Patients reported an enormous sexual excitation and were confused by simultaneous experiences of intimate and revolting contact with blood, urine, and feces. Sadomasochistic visions abounded. Grof's patients reported paradoxical identifications with both the torturer and the victim. Pain intensified until it commingled with, and eventually became, pleasure.

This stage always seemed to culminate in a profound experiential encounter with death. When patients became cyanotic and exhibited a thready pulse, Grof became concerned that they might actually be dying because of cumulative toxicity from repeated administrations of LSD.[7]

Basic Perinatal Matrix IV

The passage from BPM III to BPM IV involved total surrender and a sense of annihilation on all imaginable levels. The process was indistinguishable from death for the subject. Following this complete surrender and death, there were visions of blinding white light, feelings of enormous expansion, feelings of narrowly escaping death, and associations to life experiences that involved fortuitous escape from mortal danger. Grof reported that patients felt cleansed and forgiven for their sins. There were overwhelming feelings of love, humility, and solidarity with all of humanity. There was an enhanced appreciation of the beauty of nature, and the senses were heightened. The experiential world of the patient was reborn. Renewed appreciation for basic human values of justice, service, love, self-respect, and respect for others was reported.

This transition marked the passage from negatively charged complexes to positively charged ones, and the entire character of the session content and intersession ideation changed from a self-reinforcing negative spiral toward a self-reinforcing positive spiral. Experience at this level influenced the process of perception and interpretation of reality in the intersession intervals. The transition from BPM IV to BPM I was a merging of transcendental elements into the expansive release and redemptive feelings that characterize BPM IV.

Basic Perinatal Matrix I

At this stage in the process, biological birth and spiritual rebirth led to feelings of cosmic unity and release from needs on every level. The oceanic and symbiotic quality of these experiences led Grof to the supposition of a parallel with an undisturbed intrauterine existence. Some of Grof's subjects gave anecdotal accounts of blissful, oceanic, intrauterine memories. The characteristics and consequences of this level encompassed the nine qualities of mystical experience delineated by Walter Pahnke.[8]

BPM I also rarely included negative intrauterine experiences such as attempted abortions, drug use, physical diseases, or emotional upheavals, which were reported by more seriously disturbed patients.

Perinatal Dynamics

Grof noted both biological and spiritual aspects to the perinatal phenomena. The biological aspects seemed to relate to the four stages of the birth process, and for each of the stages, there was a philosophical or spiritual counterpart.

BPM I related to undisturbed intrauterine existence in the biological dimension and to experiences of cosmic unity in the spiritual–philosophical dimension. BPM II related to the first clinical stage of delivery: uterine contractions before the cervix is dilated on the biological dimension and experiences of no exit or hell on the spiritual–philosophical dimension. BPM III related to passage through the birth canal on the biological dimension and to experiences of the death–rebirth struggle on the spiritual–philosophical dimension. BPM IV related to the moments of separation from the mother's body on the biological level and to experiences of ego death and rebirth on the spiritual–philosophical level.

The basic perinatal matrices make up a more global and affectively powerful level of organization than the systems of condensed experiences, but the two align with each other along similarities in feeling tone. For example, an inescapable life situation such as being trapped in an elevator may be part of a COEX that has as its core family fights in which the person as a child felt trapped and helpless. This core memory would have its deepest anchor in BPM II with the experience of hopeless despair, existential questioning, and no exit. Grof claims that all COEX systems have a specific root in one of the BPMs: Most positive COEX systems resolve into BPM I or IV, and most negative COEX systems into BPM II or III. Grof draws further parallels between the BPMs and Freudian erotogenic zones.

Transpersonal Experiences

Grof observed that after experiences of final perinatal resolution through ego death and rebirth, the subjective quality changed again. The experiential domain of consciousness continued to expand beyond the usual space–time boundaries of the skin-encapsulated ego. He labeled these experiences *transpersonal*. Grof divided transpersonal experiences into two categories: (1) expansions of ego boundaries into objective or "consensus" reality and (2) extensions of ego boundaries beyond the existing framework of consensus reality. The first category included experiences of identification with plants, the earth, all of life, or the universe as a totality; identification with ancestors; sequences with a past incarnation quality; and phylogenetic or evolutionary memories or experiences.

The second broad category of transpersonal experiences involved phenomena that are not part of objective reality in the Western philosophical tradition. Experiences that fell within Grof's second category included precognition, spirit communication, out-of-the-body experiences, telepathic or other paranormal phenomena, archetypal and complex mythological sequences, encounters with various deities, intuitive understanding of universal symbols, activation of chakra and kundalini energy, consciousness of the universal mind, and the supracosmic and metacosmic void.

APPLICATION OF THEORY TO PRACTICE

Transpersonal experiences, especially in psychedelic sessions, most often did not occur in a pure form. They were mixed with perinatal and biographical material. For example, an experience of a specific event from a person's life would blend into an intrauterine experience accompanied by visions of demons or deities from some other time and place. The experiences were multilevel, and the person might experience all these levels at once. Grof emphasized that for both theoretical and practical purposes it is extremely important to understand the ways in which different levels of the unconscious (i.e., COEXs, BPMs, and the transpersonal) seen in a session are related to the personality of the subject, his present life situation, his relationship to the therapist, his psychological problems, and many as yet unknown variables in the context within which the session is taking place. These factors have come to be known as the "set and setting," and Grof saw them as having more to do with the nature of the subject's experience than with the psychedelic used, the dosage, or other pharmacological factors.

The elements within a person's unconscious that were brought into conscious representation during a session were those that had the most intense positive or negative charge. The phenomenology of an LSD session reflected the key problems of the subject on the psychodynamic, perinatal, and transpersonal levels. Most often, these associations were not obvious but were more like dream material in their symbolism.

Even the most severely disturbed patients were able to traverse this terrain in the psycholytic therapy. Grof worked with some psychotic patients who were able to leave the hospital and go on with normal life after their work. The determining factor was their ability eventually to go through the death–rebirth experience. Other psychotic patients never were able to reach this point and did not improve.

Understanding Grof's map of the territory greatly aided the subjects in surrendering to their experiences, allowing a much greater toleration of intense discharges of emotion and patience in the face of extremely painful material. It was the peak, transcendent, or mystical experiences, however, that ultimately reorganized the individual psyche into a more coherent and conflict-free way of being.

DEVELOPMENT OF HOLOTROPIC THERAPY

During his 13 years at Esalen Institute, Grof developed a new technique he called *Holotropic* (from the Greek *holos*, meaning "whole," and *trepain*, meaning "moving toward") *Breathwork*. This form of therapy is a direct outgrowth of Grof's work with psychedelics and is designed to tap, without drugs, the powerful and healing energies available in the psyche. Grof realized that his theories could be applied to any method that created an altered state of consciousness, including meditation, Sufi dancing, chanting, or even intensive breathing. In addition, the official outlawing of psychedelic research created a need to find other ways to create the amplification or energizing of the unconscious that Grof found in the use of psychedelics (see Chapter 35).

CREATION OF NETWORKS FOR SPIRITUAL
EMERGENCY AND HOLOTROPIC WORK

During this period, Stan and Christina Grof coined the term *spiritual emergency* and created a network of helpers who could be called in case of such a crisis. Spiritual emergency is based on the idea that many nonordinary states of consciousness that involve changes of perception, emotional changes, or psychosomatic symptoms, are seen by traditional psychiatry as psychotic. These experiences may reflect spiritual or transpersonal crises rather than, or in addition to, other categories of psychiatric problems. The Grofs saw such crises as opportunities for healing and possibly conducive to growth if appropriately understood and supported. When a spiritual emergency is not differentiated from other psychiatric illnesses and treated, for example, with antipsychotic medication, harm could result. The Grofs believed that mental health professionals could be taught to differentiate mental illness from mystical states and difficulties in spiritual opening, honoring a distinction that had not been recognized by traditional psychiatry. In DSM-IV, for the first time, spiritual emergency is officially recognized and included (see Chapter 23).

The Grofs have also created a training organization to enable thousands of people worldwide to become certified Grof Breathwork practitioners (see Chapter 35).

CONCLUSION

Grof followed an empirical research path based on the work of Freud, Rank, and Jung but expanded to explore the great mysteries of human existence. Along the way he joined with the American human potential movement to form the new field of transpersonal psychology. Those who criticized Grof's work asserted that no one could prove that the experiences he observed and reported reflected the true nature of the human psyche. Within the prevailing scientific epistemological limits, there appears to be no way to arrive at a conclusive proof of Grof's theories. His theories are on the leading edge of a developing philosophy of science that includes both objective and subjective data. Perhaps a new scientific epistemology is needed before Grof's work can be validated and accepted more widely in scientific circles.

NOTES

1. Grof, S. (1976). *Realms of the human unconscious: Observations from LSD research* (p. 6). New York: Dutton.

2. Leuner, H. (1962). *Die experimentelle psychose.* Berlin: Springer-Verlag.

3. Yensen, R. (1985). LSD and psychotherapy. *Journal of Psychoactive Drugs, 17,* 267–277.

4. Grof, S. (1970). *Beyond psychoanalysis: I. Implications of LSD research for understanding of human personality.* Paper presented at the Second Interdisciplinary Conference on Voluntary Control of Internal States, Council Grove, Kansas.

5. Grof, S. (1970). *Beyond psychoanalysis: II. A conceptual model of human personality encompassing the psychedelic phenomena.* Paper presented at the Second Interdisciplinary Conference on Voluntary Control of Internal States, Council Grove, Kansas.

6. Grof, S. (1970). *Beyond psychoanalysis: III. Birth trauma and its relation to mental illness, suicide, and ecstasy.* Paper presented at the Second Interdisciplinary Conference on Voluntary Control of Internal States, Council Grove, Kansas.

7. Grof, S. (1972). Personal communication with R. Yensen.

8. Pahnke, W. N. (1963). *Drugs and mysticism: An analysis of the relationship between psychedelic drugs and mystical consciousness.* Doctoral dissertation, Harvard University, Cambridge, MA.

9. Grof, S. (1985). *Beyond the brain: Birth, death, and transcendence in psychotherapy* (pp. 187–193). Albany: SUNY Press.

CHAPTER 9

Consciousness, Information Theory, and Transpersonal Psychiatry

JOHN R. BATTISTA

TRANSPERSONAL PSYCHIATRY faces two challenges: first, the integration of knowledge about transpersonal states of consciousness into a general theory of consciousness that can address biological, psychological, and phenomenological data; second, the development of a general theory of consciousness into a psychological theory that can integrate transpersonal concepts of development, psychopathology, and psychotherapy. This chapter discusses an information theory approach to these goals.

AN INFORMATION THEORY OF CONSCIOUSNESS

Information theory allows holistic models such as Ken Wilber's to be developed into testable scientific theories.[1] Similar information theories of consciousness were independently developed by E. Roy John[2] and me[3] in the 1970s. These theories hypothesize that consciousness is information and that different forms of consciousness refer to different, more encompassing, levels of information. Events of a particular level are conscious when they surpass a threshold amount of information for that level. If they do not surpass that level, the events are unconscious, or out of awareness.

The concept of information is widely misunderstood. Information is often thought of as an entity that is carried by a signal and exists independent of some information-processing structure. Instead, information theory defines information as knowledge, which can be measured in terms of the amount of uncertainty reduction that a particular signal or stimulus provides to a receiver.[4] It is a change in the level of organization (negentropy) of one system as the result of interaction with another system.

For example, although the maximum amount of information that this book could convey can be mathematically determined, the actual amount of information it does convey can only be understood in relation to a particular reader. For an individual who cannot read English, the book conveys no information. For the individual who is full of questions about transpersonal issues, it can convey more information than for someone not interested in the field or already familiar with the material.

STATES OF CONSCIOUSNESS AND INFORMATION THEORY

Physical interactions define a basic level of information by differentiating a particular physical state from all potential states. From this perspective, the physical world is neither objective nor subjective but active: It stands out from, or exists, as the result of an interaction among previously existing forms. David Bohm (see Chapter 20) suggested that this physical level of information has a root or basic consciousness that is sensory; that is, the physical world is literally "in-the-form-of" (informed by) a "sensation" (measurement, impact) of the world with which it is connected. Similarly, many biologists and psychologists have written about a basic, cellular, sensory–physical level of consciousness that operates independently of the nervous system.

In human beings, representations of the physical world by the sensory nervous system (physical or sensory consciousness, which may be called "information one") are transduced into a pattern of nervous impulses that are transmitted to the brain. The central nervous system processes the sequence and pattern of input, generating a new level of information: information two. This new level of information—the meaning of sensory input to the central nervous system—is called *perception*. The process is interactive rather than passive. The brain monitors sensory input to see if it is within "expected" levels. Physical input leads to consciousness only when input fails to occur within programmed levels: when it is novel. This is the reason that infants are particularly attentive and responsive to alterations in stimulus intensity, movements of stimuli, or edges of stimuli. Most sensory information processing occurs outside of awareness because sensory input conforms to expectations. Perception thus results from processing uncertainty associated with sensory input; it is the meaning of sensory uncertainty to the organism. Perception is information about sensation.

Affects refer to a third order of information: information about perceptual uncertainty. Affects, which function as conscious drives, activate the system behaviorally much as increases in sensory uncertainty activate perception. Affects require the coordination of perception with an action to resolve the perceptual uncertainty associated with them. The source of that resolution might be an external object such as food, another person (such as a mother), or a part of one's body, as in sucking one's thumb. The actions that resolve the uncertainty associated with perceptions represent a third level of information, which we experience as *emotion*. The resolution of perceptual uncertainty is experienced as a positive affect: satisfaction, gratification, pleasure, or release of tension. Affects therefore signal increases and decreases in perceptual uncertainty, whereas emotions are formed by actions used to resolve these uncertainties.

This theory of emotions, which can be traced back to William James and is kindred to the work of Stanley Keleman,[5] is consistent with Stanley Schacter and Jerome Singer's[6] finding that a particular state of physiological arousal is compatible with a number of different emotions depending on the context within which it occurs. The theory is also consistent with phenomenological, observational, and empirical data[7] showing that positive affects result from decreased uncertainty, whereas negative affects result from increased uncertainty.

Emotional consciousness (information three) involves complex relational actions with objects of perception and creates a new type of uncertainty. The resolution of this uncertainty results in a new order of consciousness in which emotions become the objects, rather than the subjects, of conscious awareness. This new order of consciousness, subjective awareness, constitutes a fourth level of information. In this level of awareness, one's emotional life is experienced as a stable object, as embodied, and exists in relation to other stable entities: other embodied, emotional beings. This is what Daniel Stern[8] called the *intersubjective self*. This is the first order of consciousness in which an *I* can be experienced, and it is indicated developmentally by the capacity to recognize one's self in a mirror, something that normally occurs in the second year of life. It is important to realize, however, that what is being referred to here is an awareness of having emotional consciousness, not an awareness of being aware. It is subjective or direct awareness, not reflective, self-aware awareness.

Extensive data showing that awareness tends to occur only under conditions of moderate uncertainty are consistent with this basic hypothesis.[3] This noncognitive, subjective form of information processing is also consistent with our common perceptions of human life. For example, children naturally use play as a means of working through emotional uncertainty without conceptualizing emotions. Dreams and the elaboration of emotions in visual–motor representations, such as painting or dance, also help work through the uncertainty of emotions independently of cognition.

Reflective awareness, or *cognition*, a fifth level of information, results from information about subjectivity. Generally, this process involves conceptualizing one's being as an object, a "self" or person in a system of other persons and selves, and evaluating that self in terms of particular qualities, categories, or capacities such as social roles. This self-concept is referred to as *ego* in common parlance. This level could be termed the *level of ego consciousness*. Cognition is a learning process that involves verbal conceptualization. Such cognition is concrete in the sense that it is rooted in actual experience. At this level concepts themselves cannot be operated on independently of the concrete situations in which they are embedded.

At the next, sixth level of awareness, *self-awareness*, the categories of cognition can be operated on in the imagination; that is, they can be removed from concrete situations. This task can be done objectively through a process we describe as abstract thinking. Alternatively, it can be done subjectively in a holistic, nondiscriminating manner, which we refer to as intuition. Abstract thinking and intuition are thus hypothesized to consist of complementary forms of a sixth level of information that involves analytic and holographic modes of information processing in the brain (see my article and chapter on the holographic model[9,10] for a discussion).

Abstract thinking and intuition are integrated into a sense of self-awareness that is independent of the immediate physical or social situation. Self-awareness constitutes a sixth level of information that results from processing uncertainty, in which one gains information about the process of reflective awareness, or ego awareness, and notices the way one structures and organizes this information. Self-awareness normally results in the capacity to sense and develop knowledge about one's self. This awareness is commonly conceptualized in contemporary psychiatry as knowledge about one's self or personality. This knowledge is inner awareness, or inner sight (insight), into the nature of one's actual self. As such, it should be distinguished from outer awareness, or outsight, into how one appears, one's attributes, and how one would like to appear or thinks one should be, which characterize the previous level, ego structure of consciousness.

The seventh level of information refers to information or consciousness about self-awareness. Awareness of the ongoing process of being aware results in the capacity to suspend labeling, constructing, and interpreting of ego consciousness with reference to a self that experiences these things. This process allows self-awareness to be replaced by pure awareness, or awareness without object–unitive consciousness. EEG data on unitive states of consciousness reveal a synchronization of the brain during such states consistent with the brain acting as a coherent whole.[3] Claude Domash[11] suggested that the brain in such a synchronized state could be likened to a superfluid and respond as a totality to any incoming stimulus; therefore, the brain in this order of consciousness could function as a sense receptor of quantum-mechanical input. The quantum-mechanical interconnectedness of the universe central to the ontological interpretation of quantum mechanics (see Chapter 20) could explain the ability of individuals in a unitive state to obtain knowledge through extrasensory perception.

This theory of consciousness can be expanded to include an eighth level of information that involves the universe as a whole. Such an eighth order of consciousness, *transcendent* or *transcendental consciousness*, would involve the capacity to experience pure consciousness as an object of awareness, rather than as consciousness itself. Some might call the eighth order of consciousness God or Brahman: a dynamic, transcendent reality. Because the transcendence of pure awareness cannot be objectively apprehended by embodied consciousness, it cannot be proved that this realm exists by objective means, although many individuals have come to believe in the reality of the transcendent plane as a result of miraculous or unexplainable phenomena. If such a transcendent form of consciousness does exist, the capacity of transcendent consciousness to influence all other forms of consciousness is a reasonable supposition, considering the general capacity of higher information-processing structures to regulate lower information-processing structures.[1]

With the inclusion of spiritual or transcendent levels of consciousness, this theory recapitulates the Great Chain of Being articulated in the perennial philosophy and discussed by Wilber.[12] The postulate is that there is one undivided, conscious universe grounded in physical, sensory, informational interaction and organized into perceptual, emotional, subjective, self-aware, transpersonal, and transcendent structures of consciousness. In this way, the universe is revealed as one undivided whole, separated into immanent and transcendent informational planes of awareness.

From this perspective, human beings are no longer the sole proprietors of consciousness. The entire physical world is conscious at the sensory level. Computers would have a basic perceptual consciousness. All animals with a central nervous system would be expected to share at least in perceptual and emotional consciousness. Other mammals appear to share subjective consciousness, and some primates appear to have at least rudimentary cognitive awareness.

PSYCHOPATHOLOGY AND PSYCHOTHERAPY

Each level of information processing gives rise to distinct kinds of psychopathology that require specific types of treatment. The first level of consciousness involves the construction of sensations from ongoing contact with the environment, and it begins in utero. Pathology here arises through failure of proper development of one or more sensory modalities, such as congenital deafness or color blindness. Treatment may consist of training the person to assume the functions of the missing inputs or physical interventions such as surgery or hearing aids. The therapist may function as auxiliary sensor, decision maker, and trainer and may at times assume the role of caretaking organizer and prescriber.

The second level of consciousness involves integration of sensations into conscious perceptions. Autism may constitute the purest form of the failure to register sensation. More subtle impairments may include dyslexia. Treatment at this level consists of helping the individual compensate for the impaired sensory processing, usually involving biological or neurological approaches such as pharmacology or, in alternative traditions, Neurolinguistic Programming.

The third level of consciousness involves the integration of percepts into coherent emotional patterns. Pathology here involves the inability to separate emotions from perception and, therefore, the emotional fusion of fantasy and reality: inner and outer. Symptoms include hallucinations, delusions, projection, and ideas of reference. Treatment for this severe or psychotic level of psychopathology is usually biological, including medications. The therapist also must provide supportive psychotherapy and socialization analogous to the role of a good parent to a young child.

The fourth level of consciousness involves regulating emotion to permit the emergence of a coherent sense of self. Symptoms at this level include dissociation, splitting, and rage attacks, which reflect a fragmented self; grandiosity, devaluation, schizoid withdrawal, and projective identification, reflecting a self unable to separate itself from others; and substance abuse, sexual perversions, sexual or physical abuse, rocking, head banging, and self-mutilation, revealing a basic problem in emotional self-regulation. All of these behaviors and ego functions are indicative of a severe or borderline level of psychopathology. Treatment involves providing an empathic, understanding, and even gratifying relationship, but the key is probably working through the emotional self–other confusion in which the person is embedded. This process involves empathic confrontation and understanding in the context of clear, consistent boundaries. The result is outsight: the capacity to see oneself from the outside in interaction with others in order to be a functional, separate person.

The fifth level of information processing involves the separation of identity from one's subjective experience through the internalization of one's own experience and of the reactions and descriptions of others. These internalizations ideally result in the establishment of a positive, accurate, socially adaptive identity and the capacity to control emotions and impulses intrapsychically. Failure here results in a negative self-image or socially maladaptive means of relating to society. Symptoms include impulsivity, acting out, denial, lying, cheating, lack of concern for others, and displacement of responsibility. These behaviors and ego functions are indicative of a moderate or characterological level of psychopathology. Such characterologically disturbed individuals are commonly brought to the therapist's office by their parents, spouse, or representatives of society rather than through their own motivation. The therapist must intervene to help the person accept a social reality bigger than she is, transcending the ego to enter a larger social system. This task often requires educating the client concerning how the world works, persuading her to change her behaviors, and establishing social reinforcers for modifying her behavior, as well as working with family members to help them develop clear and consistent expectations for the individual that acknowledge her own wishes, wants, needs, and capacities.

The sixth level of consciousness involves the differentiation of identity from self and the reconciliation of ideal and real self-images and internalized beliefs into an authentic, existential self. Failure here is indicated by an impersonal, nonintimate self, an inauthentic self structure characterized by an inaccurate self-image, or confusion about how to be in the world. Symptoms include intellectualization, emotional distance, ambivalence, passive–aggressive behavior, reaction formation, and doing–undoing. These behaviors and ego functions refer to a mild or neurotic level of psychopathology. Successful resolution of this developmental stage manifests in acceptance, humor, sublimation, and integration: ego functions characteristic of healthy, adult functioning. The initial step in therapy here is to help the client distinguish a real, embodied self from false or ideal self-images. In neurotic persons, embodied experience is often disavowed as needy, immature, or frightening and is replaced by strivings for perfection or demands for higher levels of functioning. One role of the therapist is to encourage the person to claim, honor, and integrate these split-off dimensions of self as the foundations for authentic life. The neurotic person needs "inner sight": to be aware of his true, embodied self and to have empathy for it. The therapist models authentic relationship in this process and offers an emotional engagement within the limits and boundaries of the therapeutic role.

This humanistic process of life-transforming psychotherapy is particularly well facilitated by a therapist who has some familiarity with spiritual, transpersonal life. This experience allows the therapist to approach the individual seeking to claim his own life with compassion and empathy, not only because she has been there, but also because she can see the entire process in context. Although existential–humanistic therapy may not be directly transpersonal, the transpersonal development of the therapist facilitates the authentic development of the client. (Similarly, in dealing with more severely disturbed persons, the nonjudgmental and compassionate nature of the transpersonally informed thera-pist helps patients to perceive and accept themselves.)

The seventh level of the self involves stopping the tendency of self-awareness to construct a restricted, isolated self and allow-ing the emergence of a realized self. Such a realized self is char-acterized by transpersonal states of consciousness, resolution of polarity, compassion, and altruism. Difficulties may involve the defensive misuse of spirituality (see Chapter 24) and inflation of the ego.

Such inflation can appear psychotic and needs to be distin-guished from psychotic states (see Chapter 23). Although this process is interior, it may benefit from a spiritual teacher, guide, or instructor. A therapist could serve as this guide if he or she were properly trained and developed. Such a "therapy" would be truly transpersonal and has been attempted in Jungian analysis and in psychosynthesis as well as in the transpersonal psychotherapies that employ contemplative techniques.

This developmental model of psychopathology defines a contin-uum of health and illness beginning with psychosis and progress-ing through borderline and characterological levels into neurotic, healthy, and transpersonal psychological structures.[13] This contin-uum defines a hierarchy of ego functions that is consistent with empirical findings.[14,15]

CONCLUSION

An information theory of consciousness was used to present a transpersonal theory of development that identified seven self structures (sensory, perceptual, emotional, subjective, identified, existential, and realized) that result from the resolution of seven developmental tasks: organization of ongoing contact with the environment into discrete sensory events, organization of sensory events into perceptions, separation of inner and outer, separation of self and other, internalization of an identity, differentiation of an authentic self from one's identity, and transcendence of the con-structive nature of self-awareness. This developmental theory was used to define an empirically supported continuum of health and illness (psychotic versus nonpsychotic, borderline versus normal, characterological versus socialized, authentic versus neurotic, and realized versus pseudospiritual) and to describe the different roles therapists take on the basis of their therapeutic interventions: caretaking organizer, empathic analyst, social agent, authentic other, and guide.

A process of transpersonal theory development has been presented. A theory of consciousness that includes transpersonal states is used as the basis for understanding development. This theory of development is used to order and understand psychopathological structures. The understanding is used to organize the kinds of interventions that a psychiatrist, psychologist, or psychotherapist must make to facilitate the development of an individual. In this way a transpersonal perspective on development, psychopathology, and psychotherapy has been constructed.

NOTES

1. Battista, J. (1977). The holistic paradigm and general system theory. *General Systems, 22,* 65–71. Reprinted in W. Gray, J. Fidler, & J. Battista (Eds.). (1982). *General systems theory and the psychological sciences.* Oceanside, CA: Intersystems Press.

2. John, E. R. (1976). A model of consciousness. In G. Schwartz & D. Shapiro (Eds.), *Consciousness and self-regulation.* New York: Plenum Press.

3. Battista, J. (1978). The science of consciousness. In K. Pope & J. Singer (Eds.), *The stream of consciousness* (pp. 55–87). New York: Plenum Press.

4. MacKay, D. (1969). *Information, mechanism and meaning.* Cambridge, MA: MIT Press.

5. Keleman, S. (1987). *Embodying experience.* San Francisco: Center Press.

6. Schacter, S., & Singer, J. (1962). Cognitive, social and physiological determinants of emotional state. *Psychological Review, 69,* 379–399.

7. Battista, J., & Almond, R. (1973). The development of meaning in life. *Psychiatry, 36,* 409–427.

8. Stern, D. (1985). *The interpersonal world of the infant.* New York: Basic Books.

9. Battista, J. (1978). The holographic model, holistic paradigm, information theory and consciousness. *ReVision, 2,* 99–102.

10. Battista, J. (1982). Informational holism: Toward an integration of the holographic and analytic models of consciousness. In W. Gray, J. Fidler, & J. Battista (Eds.), *General systems theory and the*

psychological sciences. Oceanside, CA: Intersystems Press. Reprinted in J. Van Gigch (Ed.). (1987). *Decision making about decision making.* Cambridge, MA: Abacus Press.

11. Domash, C. (1976). The transcendental meditation technique and quantum physics. In D. Orme-Johnson (Ed.), *Scientific research on transcendental meditation* (Vol. 1). Weggis, Switzerland: Maharishi European Research University Press.

12. Wilber, K. (1993). The great chain of being. *Journal of Humanistic Psychology, 33,* 52–55.

13. Battista, J. (1981). The structure of health and illness: An ego functions approach. In W. Reckmeyer (Ed.), *General systems research and design: Precursors and futures.* Louisville, KY: Society for General Systems Research. Revision reprinted in W. Gray, J. Fidler, & J. Battista (Eds.). (1982). *General systems theory and the psychological sciences.* Oceanside, CA: Intersystems Press.

14. Battista, J. (1982). Empirical test of Vaillant's hierarchy of ego functions. *American Journal of Psychiatry, 139,* 356–357.

15. Battista, J. (1983). *The continuum model of health and illness: An empirical investigation.* Unpublished manuscript.

CHAPTER 10

Shamanism and Healing

ROGER WALSH

SHAMANISM CAN BE DEFINED as a family of traditions whose practitioners focus on voluntarily entering altered states of consciousness in which they experience themselves or their spirits traveling to other realms at will and interacting with other entities to heal others or help their community.[1] Shamanism is found in cultures all over the world, from Siberia and the Americas to Africa and Australia. Shamanism also has ancient roots: Paleolithic art from Europe dated to over 17,000 ago and from South Africa dated to 25,000 years ago appear to show shamanic practices.

The focus on what is called spirit travel, while in altered states of consciousness, which is also known as soul flights or soul journeys, distinguishes shamans from other magicoreligious healers. For example, priests may lead rituals and medicine men may heal, but they rarely enter altered states. Mediums may enter altered states, but they do not journey. Yogis and meditators may sometimes journey, but this is not a central focus of their practice. Finally, those suffering mental illness may enter altered states, but they are helpless victims rather than intentional creators of these states.

SHAMANIC TECHNIQUES

Shamanic techniques for inducing altered states include psychological, social, and physiological approaches. These techniques constitute one form of what has been called the "technology of the sacred" or the art of transcendence. The psychological techniques involve exercises undertaken both before and during the ritual. Common preparatory techniques include periods of solitude, contemplation, and prayer as well as creation of the appropriate mind-set and environmental setting. The latter two techniques may include donning the shamanic mask and clothing and gathering the family or tribe. The group provides support and encouragement and, by its presence and dependency, reinforces belief in the shaman's power and importance. The powerful effect of set and setting are well recognized by contemporary psychologists from research into psychedelics.[2,3]

Timing of shamanic rituals is also regarded as important. Journeying is usually done at night so that the "spirits" and geography of the shamanic otherworlds can be better seen. In psychological terms, this process might be understood as an example of perceptual release, the process by which subtle objects become recognized when stronger stimuli are withdrawn.

Physiological techniques for shamanic journeys are often ascetic and commonly used beforehand. Shamans may go for a day or more without food, sleep, sex, or even water. They may also expose themselves to temperature extremes such as the icy cold of winter streams or the searing heat of the sweat lodge. During a seance, shamans may subject themselves to intense rhythmic stimulation such as dancing and drumming and may also ingest one or more drugs. Any or all of these techniques may disrupt normal physiological functioning sufficiently to destabilize the ordinary state of consciousness. The use of psychedelics and rhythmic stimulation is particularly interesting (see Chapters 21 and 32).

Psychedelics

Archaeological records suggest that shamanic drug use may extend back for more than 3,000 years. Currently, Siberian and Latin American shamans often employ psychedelics as booster rockets to launch their cosmic travels. In Siberia a preferred substance has been the mushroom known as *Amanita muscaria,* or agaric. Among the many drugs used in Latin America, two of the most powerful and popular psychedelics are peyote and yage, or ayahuasca. The latter is made from an Amazonian "visionary vine" called *Banisteriopsis*[4] along with potentiating additives. Yage is chemically complex, but the most important psychoactive ingredient may be harmaline.[5] However, shamans do not attribute the effects to chemicals but to the spirit that dwells within the plant.

Yage appears to elicit strong visual experiences. Users describe long sequences of dreamlike visions that appear in a spiritually significant progression. Yage is famous for provoking specific images, particularly jungle scenes and visions of tigers, snakes, and naked women.[5] Several Westerners including Michael Harner have described their amazement on ingesting the substance at the power of the imagery and its consistency with native reports.[6,7] On the other hand, I interviewed three Western psychologists who took yage in an urban setting well away from a jungle and reported no jungle imagery whatsoever.

Yage is particularly interesting with regard to shamanism because of claims for its healing and telepathic effects. In South America it is known as "the great medicine," which, through its intercession with the spirits, can either reveal remedies or produce healing. In contrast to Western notions of medicine, yage is believed to be curative whether the patient or the healer swallows it.[5]

Native reports abound in stories of yage-empowered journeys, flying, and extrasensory perception. One anthropologist reported that "on the day following one Ayahuasca party, six of nine men informed me of seeing the death of my chai, my mother's father. This occurred a few days before I was informed by radio of his death."[8] Reports of such paranormal phenomena are common in many shamanic cultures. Needless to say, the interpretation and significance of such reports is hotly debated by anthropologists.

Rhythm

Rhythmic stimulation, whether by music, singing, or dancing, has long been known to induce altered states, and shamans have used all of these techniques. Drums and rattles are the most widely used shamanic instruments. When a drum is played at a tempo of about 200 to 220 beats per minute, most Western novices report that they can journey successfully, even on their first attempt. Indeed the remarkable ease of induction of these states and their experiences are one clear reason for shamanism's recent popularity. This ease contrasts dramatically with the months of practice usually required by most meditative and yogic disciplines before significant altered states appear. The drum is sometimes used even in these more recent traditions, however, such as in Korean Zen.

Drumming probably facilitates shamanic states and journeying through several mechanisms. First, it may act as a concentration device that continuously reminds the shaman of her purpose and reduces the mind's incessant tendency to wander. It also probably drowns out distracting stimuli and enables the shaman to focus attention inward. Heightened concentration seems to be a key element in effective spiritual disciplines,[9,10] and shamans appear to have found one of the quickest and easiest ways to develop it.

In addition to assisting concentration, drumming is commonly assumed to harmonize neural activity with the vibrational frequency of the sound. Two studies that appear to support this idea have been widely quoted.[11,12] In both reports, brain waves measured by electroencephalography of subjects listening to drumming seemed to show auditory driving responses. Auditory driving occurs when a repetitive sound provokes corresponding firing frequencies in the brain. These studies are certainly suggestive and have been widely quoted as proof of the neural effects of drumming. Unfortunately, the studies are flawed, and it is impossible to draw firm conclusions from them.[13] Whatever the neural mechanisms may be, however, anyone who has been entranced by music or dancing is well aware of the powerful potential of rhythm for affecting states of mind.

The ability to access altered states appears to be a learnable skill. Entering a specific state for the first time may be hard, but with subsequent practice it can become easier and easier. For example the person who smokes marijuana may experience little or no effect initially; however, further attempts may meet with increasingly dramatic success. The result is a phenomenon, most curious and surprising to pharmacologists, known as reverse tolerance, in which the drug's effects become not less but more powerful with repeated use. The phenomenon probably also applies to other means of inducing altered states such as drumming. This learning effect helps explain why experienced shamans enter altered states with a minimum of ritual and preparation, in contrast to novice shamans, who use elaborate ceremonies.[14]

THE MAKING OF A SHAMAN

The process by which individuals become shamans shows similarities across cultures. Often an individual receives a call to become a shaman in adolescence. The call may occur through visions, dreams, or an illness. The visions or dreams may be of spirits or ancestors demanding that the individual become a shaman. The illness may seem physical, such as an epileptiform disorder, or psychological, such as wild, erratic, perhaps even psychotic behavior. In contemporary terms, such disorders would be regarded as culture-specific examples of what have been called spiritual emergencies, spiritual emergences, and transpersonal crises.[1,10,17,18]

The individual may be reluctant or ambivalent about the calling to become a shaman because of the rigors of the initiation and the responsibilities of a shaman. Indeed, the shaman-to-be often suffers greatly from the initiatory call or illness. This ordeal may culminate in an experience of death and being reduced to bones, followed by rebirth as a shaman.[1,3,10]

After the initial call, most individuals require some training with or apprenticeship to a practicing shaman. Crucial to the shaman's development is healing the initiatory illness. Although shamans have been described as wounded healers, practicing shamans have been found to be robust, psychologically healthy individuals; that is, they have healed themselves or been healed of their initiatory illness.[1,14] Although early reports of shamanism portrayed practitioners as individuals suffering from serious psychopathology, including psychosis, or as charlatans, cumulative evidence argues against this view.[1] Most shamanic cultures, in fact, clearly distinguish between true shamans and "crazy people" who only claim to be shamans.

SHAMANIC HEALING RITES

Although there are broad cultural variations, there is a common core to most shamanic healing rites (see Chapter 21 for a detailed report of one such shamanic ritual). The afflicted individual usually gathers his or her family and frequently the whole tribe, involving them in the rite. After appropriate preparations, such as fasting, the shaman begins the ritual. He or she enters an altered state using drumming, hallucinogens, or other means. The shaman then goes on a spirit journey either to the underworld or to the celestial realms. The shaman seeks the cause of the individual's ill-ness, which is usually considered to be the work of spirits. The shaman must then bargain or battle with the spirits. If successful, the shaman returns to ordinary consciousness and completes the ritual with instructions to the patient.

Communal involvement recruits powerful group processes that can be profoundly healing to the individual and the community. Such social forces have been relatively neglected in transpersonal writings. Some shamanic rituals deal with the community rather than an individual's affliction. For example, when hunting tem-porarily becomes difficult, the shaman may conduct a ritual to dis-cover the cause. He goes on a spirit journey and may declare the cause of the communal misfortune to be the violation of a tribal taboo by several individuals. Those people must confess in a cathartic process that reveals and resolves community tensions.

IMPLICATIONS OF SHAMANISM FOR TRANSPERSONAL PSYCHIATRY

Shamanism is so widespread among cultures and of such antiquity that some people have suggested it arose from a common cultural core early in human history. In some ways modern Western culture may be considered aberrant in rejecting elements of shamanism such as the use of altered states of consciousness and hallucinogens to obtain transcendent visions. Indeed, fully 90% of the world's cultures make use of one or more institutionalized altered states of consciousness, and in traditional societies these are, almost with-out exception, sacred states. According to Bourguignon, this is "a striking finding and suggests that we are, indeed, dealing with a matter of major importance."[15] Clearly, humankind has devoted enormous energy and ingenuity to the task of altering conscious-ness. Indeed it may be that the "desire to alter consciousness peri-odically is an innate normal drive analogous to hunger or the sex-ual drive."[16] Shamans can be considered humankind's earliest systematic explorers of altered states of consciousness.

Shamanism offers an important model of healing and healers. This model emphasizes that healing may involve the experience of descent into the underworld and a death–rebirth episode. From these chaotic states, an individual may emerge with greater strength and vigor and a sense of deepened spiritual meaning or purpose in life. Psychological distress may be in the service of spiritual and psychological development. This shamanic model has been elaborated by Carl Jung and Michael Washburn (see Chapter 5) and by Grof as the notion of a spiritual emergency (see Chapter 8). Because shamanic cultures distinguish between true shamans and madmen, they recognize and emphasize the difference between psychopathology and spirituality, between the prepersonal and the transpersonal.

CONCLUSION

Whatever the precise neural and chemical mechanisms involved, it is clear that shamans have discovered a wide variety of psychological, physiological, and chemical aids to modify consciousness. Shamans developed a range of techniques that constituted perhaps the world's first technology: a technology of the sacred for modifying consciousness. The techniques were simple and probably first discovered accidentally such as when the tribe faced hunger, fatigue, and dehydration in their struggle for existence or accidentally ate psychedelic plants. Because of their pleasurable and valuable effects, these techniques were likely remembered and repeated. When they were collected and set within a tradition and cosmology, shamanism was born. In this way humankind's first road map to transcendent states likely was discovered and rediscovered in different times and places; through these states poured the visions of transcendence that sustained and inspired humankind for thousands of years.

NOTES

1. Walsh, R. (1990). *The spirit of shamanism*. Los Angeles: Tarcher.
2. Grof, S. (1980). *LSD psychotherapy*. Pomona, CA: Hunter House.
3. Grof, S. (1988). *The adventure of self discovery*. Albany: SUNY Press.
4. Dobkin de Rios, M. (1972). *Visionary vine*. San Francisco: Chandler.
5. Stafford, P. (1983). *Psychedelics encyclopedia*. Los Angeles: Tarcher.
6. Harner, M. (Ed.). (1973). *Hallucinogens and shamanism*. New York: Oxford University Press.

7. Naranjo, C. (1975). *The healing journey.* New York: Ballantine Books.

8. Stafford, *Psychedelics encyclopedia,* p. 353.

9. Goleman, D. (1988). *The meditative mind.* Los Angeles: Tarcher.

10. Walsh, R., & Vaughan, F. (Eds.). (1993). *Paths beyond ego: The transpersonal vision.* Los Angeles: Tarcher.

11. Neher, A. (1961). Auditory driving observed with scalp electrodes in normal subjects. *Electroencephalography and Clinical Neurophysiology, 3,* 449–451.

12. Neher, A. (1962). A physiological explanation of unusual behavior in ceremonies involving drums. *Human Biology, 34,* 151–160.

13. Achterberg, J. (1985). *Imagery and healing: Shamanism and modern medicine.* Boston: New Science Library.

14. Eliade, M. (1964). *Shamanism: Archaic techniques of ecstasy* (p. 80). Princeton, NJ: Princeton University Press.

15. Bourguignon, E. (Ed.). (1973). *Religion, altered states of consciousness, and social change.* Columbus: Ohio State University Press.

16. Weil, A. (1972). *The natural mind.* Boston: Houghton Mifflin.

17. Grof, C., & Grof, S. (1992). *The stormy search for self.* Los Angeles: Tarcher.

18. Grof, S., & Grof, C. (Eds.). (1989). *Spiritual emergency.* Los Angeles: Tarcher.

CHAPTER 11

The Contribution of Hinduism and Yoga to Transpersonal Psychiatry

BRUCE W. SCOTTON AND J. FRED HIATT

> The Christian [read Westerner] is too absorbed in the outer
> world and then we just lose God altogether. And the Hindu
> is so absorbed in the inner life that he tends to lose the outer
> life and India can go to pieces like that. So the future of the
> world depends on the meeting of these two opposite tradi-
> tions. And always truth is in the meeting of the opposites.
> *Father Bede Griffith*

THE RANGE AND DEPTH of Indian philosophical and metaphysical thought are among the greatest in the world. Any attempt to cover the subject in detail is beyond the space limitations of the present book. This chapter provides a conceptual overview of the mind-set of a culture that leads to a dramatically different life from that of the West.[1]

BASIC ASSUMPTIONS

Inherent in the Hindu worldview is an evolutionary view of consciousness, a development that can be completed in one lifetime.

104

Indian theory, including Hindu, Buddhist, and Jain religions, begins from what Carl Jung termed the *introverted perspective*. Human experience is primary, and is all that is possible to know. Any knowledge about the outside world, including the corroboration or negation of other observers, is subject to the distortions of our own mind. Mental experience is not only primary but is the only given; all else is speculation. This view is the exact complement to contemporary Western rational positivism, which asserts that all we can know is external and objective.

Within this perspective, Hindu theories teach one to sharpen the perceptions of the mind; the metaphor most frequently used is to *polish the mirror of the mind*. Hindu theory building differs from that of the West in that it is experiential. The goal is not to construct a theory that is neat and rational but to construct one which leads to a different experience of life. This difference has tended to make Westerners suspicious of Hindu thought as "mystical." For Hindus, however, the experiential purpose of theory building provides a built-in quality control; if the theory does not alter one's experience of life for the better, it must be changed or exchanged for another. Against such a criterion, almost all Western theories fail miserably.

Hindu theories begin with the painful condition of the subject as he begins self-exploration, trapped in an aging body that is subject to anxieties, disease, and death and to wants that are only intermittently satisfied. The theories seek a better life, almost invariably through disidentifying from the individual's physical existence and progressively identifying with greater and greater parts of the whole of existence. This change in identity is not speculative but experienced. Although often arduous and painful, this development in consciousness ends in great joy and peace.

A second major quality of Hindu thought is the acceptance of the validity of many different paths of development. Many different personal deities may point the way to evolution, and many different methods of self-development may facilitate it. If the hallmark of Western religion is the truth of monotheism, that the divine is ultimately one, the hallmark of Hinduism is that the human experience of spirituality is manifold. The plethora of Hindu gods has led to the general misconception that Hinduism is polytheistic. In fact, because reality is based on inner rather than outer experience, the gods, like everything else, are seen as inner, and they are as variable as the human mind. The ultimate oneness of being is granted but is perceived as the ground of being from which all experience, including gods, arises. Each of the different paths and guides may be useful and appropriate for some people.

Another major difference between Hindu and Western thought relates to the view of time and space. Unlike the Western idea of progressive development through time, Hinduism views time cyclically. The world does not develop linearly but evolves in immense cycles in which the world is created and then slowly winds down as its inhabitants become more and more distant from its spiritual underpinning. Finally, the world is destroyed, and creation begins all over. Whatever happens now has happened thousands of times before. Furthermore, the world is only one of many planes of existence even within our own cycle of creation. The resulting picture makes humans much more a tiny grain of sand on the cosmic beach and much less the conqueror of the planets and atoms that Westerners envision.

A final essential concept is that of karma. Through her actions, each person creates her particular life. Actions of a particular type, whatever their nature, produce experiences that match that type. These experiences persist until the person learns the lesson and stops performing actions that harm herself or others. Hinduism takes the concept of the accumulation of such actions a step further and holds that such accumulated karma is carried over from one lifetime to the next and that a particular soul or jivatman will be forced to continue to be reborn until the lessons are learned and no more karma is generated.

THE PATH TO EVOLUTION OF THE SELF

As might be expected in such an introverted culture, evolution of the self is sought not from the outside but from within. Teachings and practices exist to help one discover the potential that lies within.

Two concepts convey this perspective: (1) *Atman* is the highest aspect of the self. Eternal and omniscient, it dwells in perpetual peace as the play of the material world, *maya*, goes on about it. All spiritual paths are meant to put the person in touch with her essence, atman. First, she becomes conscious of the existence of atman, then she gradually gives up attachment to the ego and lives from atman, participating in the material world but not attached to it. (2) *Brahman* is the ground of being, that which underlies all existence and transcends the dichotomy of being and nonbeing. It is the essential oneness that defies all attempts to describe or qualify it. Words can only point the way but cannot identify it.

Ultimately, atman is brahman. The Vedas (Hindu sacred writings) say *tat tvam asi*, which means "thou art that" or your essence is the ground of being. The Hindu path of development leads first to disidentification from the ego, then to higher states of consciousness involving intuition and peace, and finally to unitary consciousness, which stands beyond subject and object differentiation.

AYURVEDA

Ayurveda is the classical Indian system of health maintenance and medical treatment. Derived from the Sanskrit terms *ayu* meaning "life" or "daily living" and *veda* meaning "knowing," it means "the science of life." This truly holistic medical system encompasses science, religion, and philosophy and includes physical, mental, and spiritual aspects of the person in its healing approach. For this reason, it has been described as "a science of truth as expressed in life."[2] In addition to its spiritual context, ayurveda differs from Western medicine in defining normality in terms of the individual rather than statistically and in emphasizing acceptance, observation, and experience rather than questioning, analysis, and logical deduction.

According to tradition, the basic principles of ayurveda originated 5,000 years ago with the *rishis* (revered wisemen of antiquity) and are outlined in the Vedas.[3] Underlying all Hindu philosophy is the goal of achieving enlightenment. Because the first step toward enlightenment is purification of the gross body, ayurveda is the foundation and prerequisite to understanding and fully benefiting from *yoga* (mental and physical exercises) and *tantra* (rituals and practices).

Ayurveda is based on the Samkhya philosophy of creation, which holds that cosmic consciousness is the source of all existence and manifests in all things.[4] The most basic principle and source of the universe is *Prakriti*, the female creative energy that is the One that desires to become the Many. This primordial physical energy has three attributes, or *gunas*. *Rajas* (movement) is the active kinetic force. *Satva* (stability, essence, awakening, and light) and *tamas* (inertia, matter, ignorance, and darkness) are inactive potential energies that need rajas to manifest the organic and inorganic universes, respectively. When the balance between these gunas is disturbed, the evolution of the universe occurs. The first manifestation from Prakriti is *mahad* (cosmic intellect). From this, ego is formed. Ego then manifests in the five senses, five motor organs, and mind, from satva, and in the five elements and corresponding physical phenomena that affect the five senses, from tamas. The five basic elements are ether, air, fire, water, and earth, formed in that order, with each arising from the preceding element. From earth, all organic life and the mineral kingdom arise, that is, all matter; therefore, all elements are in all matter, and matter and energy are one.

The five elements manifest in the body as three principles, or *doshas*, that govern all biological and psychological functions in the body, mind, and consciousness.[5] They act as basic constituents; govern the creation, maintenance, and destruction of tissue; and are responsible for psychological phenomena such as emotions. From ether and air, the air principle, *vata dosha*, is manifested. It is movement; in the body it is the subtle energy that governs biological movement such as breathing or cytoplasmic movement. Psychologically, it is responsible for nervousness, fear, pain, spasms, and feeling energetic. The fire principle, *pitta dosha*, comes from the fire and water elements and is heat and energy. It manifests as metabolism, digestion, assimilation, temperature, and intelligence. Psychologically, pitta arouses anger and jealousy. Earth and water manifest as the water principle *kapha dosha*. This provides the physical structure of the body and maintains body resistance. It manifests as lubricants, immunity, biological energy for the heart and lungs, and memory. Psychologically, it is responsible for attachment, greed, envy, calmness, forgiveness, and love.

At the mental and energic levels of being, the three gunas correspond to the dosha. People are born with a particular constitution that is composed of one, two, or all three of these types. Those with a satvic temperament are healthy and pure in body and mind. They find it easier to attain self-realization than other types. People with a rajasic temperament tend to be aggressive and extroverted and are often interested in power and prestige, whereas those of tamasic temperament, which manifests in ignorance and inertia, tend to be lazy and selfish and capable of hurting others.

Health and disease are a result of the inherent relationships between energy and matter and between individual and cosmic spirit and consciousness. The constitution interacts with the macrocosm to produce the balance of energies and final functioning of the body and mind. In some cases, the same life energies that are involved in the process of becoming enlightened become imbalanced, leading to disturbance in the dosha and hence to disease. By properly attending to the balance of energies, the body is capable of healing itself and slowing or reversing the processes of disease and deterioration.

In ayurveda, disease is classified in several ways: whether it is physical, psychological, or spiritual in origin; the parts of the body in which it manifests (e.g., intestines) and starts, which may be different from each other; the bodily dosha; and other causative factors. The types of diseases to which one is prone are related to the constitution and imbalances of either the body or the mind. Psychological ailments can lead to disturbances of dosha and thence to physical disorder, and the reverse can occur. Emphasis is placed on not repressing emotions because this is certain to eventuate in disease. Rather, one should allow oneself to experience the emotion, observe it with detachment, and allow it to dissipate.

Ultimately, all of one's manifestation springs from one's spiritual state before conception. This state gets concretized in one's constitution at the moment of conception and sets the stage for both personality and the way the body is prone to function. Actual manifestation is influenced by a dynamic interplay of these givens with energy from outside one's body, for example, from food or social interactions. Dysfunction can arise from any level of one's being and can manifest in other levels. Conversely, correction of the imbalances can be directed at any level. Ayurveda incorporates interventions aimed at all levels to maximize not only the return to health, but also progress along the road to self-realization and spiritual attainment.

YOGA

The term *yoga* comes from the same Indo-European root word as the English word *yoke* and refers to linking the lesser self to its highest aspect. It is a system, or family of systems, for development of the self and consciousness.

Traditionally there were originally three types of yoga. *Bhakti yoga* is a system focusing on devotion and love as a path to development of the self. Usually the practitioner chooses one of the Hindu deities and an aspect of that deity representing qualities that speak to the practitioner. Through the use of chanting, singing of traditional songs of worship, repetition of the names of the god (a form of mantra), and meditation on the image and qualities of the god, the practitioner is drawn beyond his ego. A frequent task is to visualize the god so frequently and in such detail that the image of the god becomes a constant part of the yogin's mental landscape. Westerners are probably most familiar with the Hare Krishna movement as an example of this sort of yoga; however, it must be noted that our version is an Americanized one adapted from a long and respected tradition in India.

Karma yoga focuses on works and actions in the world. The Hindu philosophical tradition makes it clear that actions can generate good karma as well as bad and that action freed of ego attachment generates no karma. Karma yoga first teaches actions that generate better states of mind and then actions that come from lack of ego involvement. In the Bhagavad Gita, a devotional work that is acknowledged by many as the epitome of Hindu expression, Lord Krishna admonishes Arjuna not to shrink from the battle he must fight with his cousins but to fight it without ego attachment. The karma yogin is to identify the bidding of the Highest that dwells within and to do its bidding whether that results in his revilement or his celebration. Mother Teresa of Calcutta is frequently mentioned as a modern-day example of someone who practices karma yoga.

Jnana yoga is the yoga of understanding and discrimination. Jnana yogins study the ancient and traditional texts, which are broadly divided into two groups. *Sruti* applies to the most ancient texts, the Vedas, and carries the connotation that the text is divinely inspired. *Smrti* applies to other texts such as the *Puranas*, the great epics the *Ramayana* and the *Mahabharata*, and the laws of *Manu* (the Hindu Adam), which are of great age and venerability and therefore carry much weight of tradition. Finally, there are specific texts that convey the viewpoint of a specific philosophical school or religious group. Among these are many commentaries on the older texts and such groupings as the tantras and the agamas.

The jnana yogin usually settles on one particular tradition and mines it for years, reading the texts with an eye toward altering his consciousness in the direction described therein. In fact, the texts usually give directions for developing the states they describe. In addition, the yogin practices meditations designed to develop his discrimination between states of consciousness and his ability to enter various states at will.

References are often made to forms of yoga other than the three discussed. These are usually combinations of the three types. Mixing of the three types is common practice and has been recommended as far back as in the Gita. Several of these schools deserve mention.

Patanjali's *Yoga Sutras,* the universally acknowledged yogic text, presents an *ashtanga,* or eight-limbed yoga. His system includes certain abstentions, observances, postures *(asanas),* methods of breath control *(pranayama),* and withdrawal of the attention from the outer world to be fixed on objects of meditation.

Hatha (meaning force or determined effort) *yoga* emphasizes realization through work on the body with asanas and pranayama. These physical practices can result in powerful alterations of consciousness. Many Westerners know yoga only through hatha yoga and have little understanding of the developmental goal that lies beyond the bending, stretching, and puffing. Unfortunately, many Westerners purport to teach yoga but have appropriated the bodily movements without much understanding of the spiritual basis for them, which only furthers the confusion. Contact with traditional hatha yoga can be found in the West by looking for teachers who can detail descent from a lineage of Hindu teachers and by listening for the teacher's attention to the spiritual aspects of the discipline.

Kundalini yoga closely relates to hatha yoga (see Chapter 25). *Kundalini* is defined as a powerful energy that lies dormant at the base of the spine until it is awakened to course up to the head like a serpent uncoiling. As the serpent energy rises in the body, it activates various energy centers called *chakras* (wheels), which are felt to contain abilities and potentialities of the human being. The most important chakras are along the spinal column, behind the eyes, and at the crown of the head. Kundalini yoga consists of asanas, pranayama, and visualizations designed to guide the kundalini energy to the crown chakra, with the resultant highest self-development. As Gopi Krishna noted concerning his experience with kundalini, the unfolding of the energy can be spontaneous and the course rocky and painful[6] (see Chapter 25).

Tantric (meaning loom, religious pattern, or ritual) *yoga* is derived from the tantras, a specific group of texts for enlightenment in the current, most decadent, era, the *Kali Yuga.* On the basis of the idea that many people in this era are so tied to physical existence that they cannot easily renounce attachment to it, tantric yoga seeks to take the energy of physical–sensory experience and use it for the higher development of the self. In addition to mantra, meditation, asana, ritual, and visualization, tantric yoga involves *yantra,* the use of mystical diagrams to access certain states and qualities of experience. Two prominent themes of tantra are two of the major preoccupations of physical life: sex and death. Tantric practice seeks to use our strong attachment–revulsion responses to these themes to fuel more sophisticated perceptions of our selves.

A major division within tantra is between those who pursue the "right-hand" path and work with imagery and those who pursue the "left-hand" path, or *vama marga,* and use sexual partners, cremation grounds, and intoxicants in their work. It is the left-hand path that has captured the imagination of many Westerners and contributed to the dismissal of all of yoga by some observers. Contrary to these prejudices, however, the vama marga appears to be a genuine spiritual path rather than an excuse for behavior against the norm. For instance, many warnings are issued that one must be an unusual, heroic practitioner to even enter the dangerous left-hand path. Those who do practice *maithuna,* or sacred sexual intercourse, must spend hours in ritual preparation, envisioning their partners as the incarnation of Shiva or Shakti. They are enjoined not to experience orgasm but to send the energy upward for higher uses. Such practice certainly does not constitute easy access to sexual release.

RELEVANCE TO TRANSPERSONAL PSYCHIATRY

The traditions of Hinduism are of primary importance to a newly enlarged study of the mind because they contain thousands of years of knowledge accumulated on the basis of the highest levels of mental experience. The specific systems for generating such experience, although tried and true in the East, are only beginning to be known and used in the West. Knowledge of this tradition is an essential part of the education of anyone seeking a comprehensive view of the mind. It is important, however, to note that knowledge and experience of the spiritual realms that concern Hinduism in no way replaces the need for therapeutic work at lower levels of development. In many ways, Western and Eastern systems of the mind are complementary, the former specializing in the study and treatment of lower levels of mental functioning with a relative lack of knowledge about higher levels of consciousness and the latter with the opposite specialization and blind spot.

At the very least, knowledge of the clinical presentation of spiritually based phenomena seems essential to avoid misdiagnosing and inappropriately treating a subgroup of patients. Many Westerners, including clinicians, wish to continue to work on their self-development throughout their life and may wish to draw on the accumulated knowledge of the Hindu tradition in this process. Exposure to the life and mind-set of Hindu culture may serve to spur the growth of the reader by allowing her to get some distance from our own culture's pervasive materialism. To free one's consciousness from the restricted field available in any culture's consensually validated reality is a major step in the development of higher consciousness.[7]

NOTES

1. Boss, M. (1965). *A psychiatrist discovers India* (H. Frey, Trans.). London: Oswald Wolff.

2. Lad, V. (1984). *Ayurveda: The science of self-healing* (p. 47). Santa Fe, NM: Lotus Press.

3. Basham, A. L. (1967). *The wonder that was India*. New Delhi, India: Rupa.

4. Zimmer, H. (1969). *Philosophies of India*. Bollingen Series XXVI. Princeton, NJ: Princeton University Press.

5. Thakkur, C. G. (1974). *Introduction to ayurveda*. New York: ASI Publishers.

6. Krishna, G. (1971). *Kundalini: The evolutionary energy in man*. Boulder, CO: Shambhala.

7. Berger, P., & Luckman, T. (1966). *The social construction of reality*. Garden City, NY: Doubleday.

CHAPTER 12

The Contribution of Buddhism to Transpersonal Psychiatry

BRUCE W. SCOTTON

BUDDHISM MAY BE UNIQUE among the world's religions in that it arose not as a system of worship of some higher power but as the record of one man's attempt to free himself from the suffering of human existence. Centuries of development have resulted in the elucidation of many subsystems of Buddhist thought and practice. Today Buddhism is generally considered to consist of two major arms: the *Theravada*, or way of the ancient ones, prevalent in Sri Lanka, Burma, and much of Southeast Asia, and the *Mahayana*, or great vehicle, prevalent in Tibet, Nepal, China, Korea, and Japan. The relationship among the various teachings is beyond the scope of this chapter, which focuses on Buddhist principles that are potentially informative to the discipline of transpersonal psychiatry.

Although the study of consciousness in Western psychiatry dates back about 150 years, the study of consciousness in Buddhism dates back 2,500 years. Like Western psychology, Buddhism places a value on empirical verification and practical effectiveness. One is not to trust the teachings implicitly but to test

114

them oneself and evaluate their effects. Because of this empirical and practical approach, Buddhism may be particularly accessible to the West. Unlike the Western tradition, however, Buddhism does not attempt to separate religious or spiritual concerns from psychology. This chapter examines (1) the basic beliefs about the nature of reality essential to Buddhism; (2) the psychology, or map of the mind, that Buddhism constructs from these basic beliefs; (3) the teachings and practices given to followers: the therapy of Buddhism; and (4) the result and outcomes of these practices.

PHILOSOPHICAL PRINCIPLES

There are four "noble truths" about human existence that arise from observations of consciousness. First is the truth of *dukkha:* that suffering is universal. There are three types of suffering, including (1) physical: birth, aging, and death; (2) mental: frustrated desires; and (3) essential: arising from the five *skandhas,* or aggregates, which are discussed later in the chapter. Second is the truth of *samudaya:* that suffering is caused by our attraction to and repulsion from things, ideas, and events. This leads to a cycle of "dependent origination," or rebirth. *Rebirth* in this context means rebirth of the ego in each moment as well as from lifetime to lifetime.[1] Third is the truth of *nirodha:* that suffering can be stopped by liberation from the chain of dependent origination. Finally, there is the truth of *marga,* or the "noble eightfold path": the way of the cessation of suffering. The noble eightfold path consists of correct views, correct intention, correct speech, correct action, correct livelihood, correct effort, correct mindfulness, and correct concentration.[2]

There are two other beliefs, or seals, that are essential to Buddhism. The first is *anatta,* or the belief that there is no core, essential, enduring self or ego. This belief emerges from breaking down the process of awareness and finding that the ego is neither a part of awareness nor the sum of the parts of awareness. The other essential belief of Buddhism is *annicca,* the impermanence of everything. Buddhists believe that change and movement are characteristic of existence. Everything is in change or flux. The idea of a fixed or permanent ego or self is perceived as an illusion that is created in an attempt to cope with the ever-flowing flux of reality.

THE PSYCHOLOGY OF CONSCIOUSNESS

The *abhidharma* (the psychology and philosophy of Buddhism) is pragmatic. It describes that which serves to lead to a personal experience of Buddhahood as reported by those who, collectively, have spent centuries watching internal events and ordering them, just as those in the West have watched and ordered external events. Buddhist psychology tends to be descriptive of states of consciousness rather than concerned with their development.[3] This focus reflects the view that consciousness arises anew with each circumstance.

Consciousness is defined as the relationship between subject and object. The subject can have one of three qualities: the quality of craving, the quality of aversion, or the absence of either one of them; the third quality allows free will. Consciousness that is not bound by craving for or aversion to worldly things is termed *directed* (toward deliverance). Consciousness still bound to worldly reactions is termed *undirected*.

One important school of abhidharma describes eight different types of consciousness (*vinjnanas*). The first five are the sense consciousnesses of seeing, hearing, tasting, smelling, and touching. The sixth, *manovinjnana*, is intellectual consciousness, which sorts out and judges the first five. It produces attraction and repulsion and the illusion of an objective world. The seventh, *manas*, or mind, observes the stream of becoming: the totality of being, as well as the individual. The eighth, *alayavijnana*, is universal or "store" consciousness. Alayavijnana is a pervasive mindlike medium that is capable of storing traces of experience and their structures, which may become actual experience under suitable conditions.

Humans are is made up of five skandhas, or aggregates, that result from and produce karma. The first is the *rupa skandha*, or corporeality. This is the group of sense organs with their objects, relationships, and psychological consequences. Second is *vedana skandha*, or feelings: all the reactions arising from sensations and from inner causes. The third, *samjna skandha*, consists of perceptions that help one to discriminate among experiences; it includes reflective and intuitive perception. The fourth, *samskara skandha*, is the group of mental formations, or the character of the individual arising as the consequence of volition. Finally, there is the *vijnana skandha*, or the consciousness that coordinates the previous four and represents the potentiality of pure consciousness.[4]

One can differentiate between personality, which is composed of the different aspects people present at different moments, and individuality, which is the false idea of a fixed uniqueness or separate-ness. The idea of individuality contradicts the basic tenet of anatta, or the lack of separate existence. One may demonstrate markedly different personalities, therefore, from circumstance to circumstance.

Emotions are defined as ego-centered attitudes that make the mind restless when something occurs. Emotions are considered to be different from feeling, which may be positive, negative, or neu-tral, and from positive mental events such as tranquillity. Six basic emotions are considered. *Attachment* consists of a yearning after things. *Anger* is a vindictive attitude toward other beings. *Arrogance* is an inflation of mind about things that are in fact transient. *Lack of intrinsic awareness* is not being aware of one's fullest capac-ity, that is, the capacity for nirvana. *Indecision* is to be of two minds about the truth. *Opinionatedness* is to be attached to a particular dogma.[5]

SPIRITUAL TEACHINGS

The path of Buddhism leads from *samsara*, or conditioned exis-tence, to *nirvana*. It is called the middle path because it avoids extremes (for example, of existence and nonexistence). It affirms human experience of both the being in conditioned existence and the emptiness or cessation of being in nirvana. *Unitive conscious-ness*, or the union of self and all that exists, is considered to be the highest form of Buddhist practice. Ego and separateness are seen as early stages of development that must first be reached and then transcended. This view differs from that of traditional Western psychology, which has tended to look on experiences of oneness as regression.

According to Buddhism, there is a higher consciousness, *bodhi*, which transcends rational consciousness. Why then do we not operate in that higher consciousness? There are three root causes of unenlightened existence: *lobha*, or greed and desire; *dosa*, or hatred and ill will; and *moha*, or ignorance and delusion.[6]

Instruction given by teachers is quite variable. Buddhism emphasizes a method rather than a stable truth so that different teachings are given to different followers.[7] However, three princi-pal aspects of the path to enlightenment can be identified. The first is the renunciation of cyclic existence. The second is the aspiration for enlightenment for all beings. Basic to all Buddhism of the Mahayana tradition is the *bodhisattva vow*, which is the affirmation that the follower will not permanently enter the state of nirvana until he can help all other beings attain that state. Essential to this affirmation is the idea of compassion: to help and assist others in a nonjudgmental way along the spiritual path. Intrinsic to this idea is the assumption that each of us has been born basically "rich" in a spiritual way.[8] This view differs from Western individualism with its emphasis on personal advancement in competition with others.

The third aspect of the path is a correct view of emptiness, or *sunyata.*[9] Much emphasis is placed in Buddhist practice on emptiness: Through being nothing, one is everything; by desiring nothing, one transcends suffering; by not grasping, naming, or seeking existence, one sees into the true nature of reality and experiences creative life. Emptiness and emptying are an essential focus of Buddhist fullness.

Meditation is essential to Buddhist practice and involves mastery of two important dimensions of consciousness. *Samatha,* or one-pointedness, emphasizes freedom from distraction and focus on a chosen object or concept. *Vipassana,* or insight, emphasizes the focused awareness of outer and inner events in one's consciousness.[10]

Specific forms of meditation are often prescribed for people of specific temperaments. Those with desire prominent in their makeup may be advised to meditate on the decay of a corpse, for example. Those strong in antipathy may be advised to meditate on and manifest the four divine behaviors: *maitri* (benevolent love), *karuna* (compassion), *mudita* (joy), and *upekkha* (impartiality). These prescriptions for meditation aim directly at changing the structure of consciousness, in contrast to Western psychotherapy, which tends to be indirect and focused on removing blockages to awareness. Because the mind is seen as creating the world, a prescription is likely to be an instruction to work directly with perceived energy and to shift it where it is needed or to visualize and create in reality something that is needed. This is the *tantric* or *mantrayana* approach, which expresses the transcendent in the sensory world.

In the initial state of meditation, there are five factors, each of which counteracts an obstacle. *Vitarka,* the mental taking hold, overcomes indolence. *Vicara,* the detailed mental investigation, overcomes skepticism. *Priti,* joy with physical sensations, overcomes ill will. *Sukha,* or bliss, overcomes regret, frivolity, and restlessness. *Samadhi,* absorption and concentration, overcomes sensuality. As meditation deepens, the energy of the first four factors is progressively absorbed into the fifth. Vitarka and vicara subside, therefore, and one arrives at individual clarity with penetration to the underlying emotional tone. Later priti subsides, and one is left with equanimity. At this point the special features of meditation can operate, that is, inspection, *smriti*, and full awareness, *samprajanaya*. Bliss subsides, and one is left with thorough lucidity and perspicuity of inspection.

For one who is seriously pursuing the path of enlightenment in Tibetan Buddhism, there is a series of progressive initiations. The first one takes refuge in the Buddha, the *dharma* (the eternal law), and the *sangha* (the community of those following the Buddha).

A way to gauge one's progress toward enlightenment is provided by the existence of 10 fetters, which are ranked in order of difficulty to overcome: (1) the belief in permanent personality, (2) doubt, (3) clinging to rules and rituals, (4) sensual desire, (5) aversion, (6) craving for existence in a world of pure form, (7) craving for existence in a world of nonform, (8) pride, (9) restlessness, and (10) ignorance. In the Theravadan tradition, one is declared to have seen the goal of nirvana and is called a "stream winner" when he has overcome the first three fetters. He becomes a "once returner" when he has partially overcome numbers 4 and 5, and a "never returner," one who need never come back to physical incarnation, when he has overcome 1 through 5. An *arahat*, or enlightened one, has overcome all 10 of the fetters.[11]

THERAPY AND HEALING ISSUES

Insight into the real nature of things results in the destruction of one's previous understanding of the world. This shift may produce disturbing mental images like those of the wrathful deities seen on meditation paintings, or *thangkas*. Unless it is combined with compassion and love from the heart, this can be a highly toxic experience. Buddhism suggests, therefore, that psychosis can be seen as the breakdown of one's worldview without sufficient emotional support from within.[12] Severe mental illness, however, is most often understood in the framework of Buddhism as caused by the pursuit of a lifestyle contrary to the inherent disposition of the person and contrary to his spiritual destiny. In serious cases, the highest spiritual aspect (manas) is believed to withdraw from the five aggregates, or skandhas.[13] Hypnosis, drugs, and alcohol are seen as loosening those aggregates. Such loosening may allow the occupation of the parts from the outside by discarnate beings.[14] Patients who are possessed may undergo exorcism by recitation of Pali texts; strengthening the patient with diet and medications follows. When the patient is lucid, psychological work begins.[15]

Less severe mental illness is generally understood in terms of a discordance of the five aggregates. Depending on the presence or retreat of certain aggregates, the person experiences a change in consciousness. Sometimes emotional shocks such as the false report of his mother's death or even pouring boiling water on a patient may be used to call back the displaced part.

Forceful or quick cures are seen as displacing the problem, however, and are only used in the least serious cases. Generally, mental illness is understood to be brought on by the patient's mind and to require a basic restructuring of consciousness. This approach is consonant with the basic approach of transpersonal and depth psychotherapies.

RESULTS OF THIS SYSTEM OF THOUGHT

Universal compassion and tranquillity constitute the principal goals of Buddhism. In attempting to write of the results of a system for transcendence, one inevitably encounters the problem alluded to by all the wisdom traditions: That which can be named is, by definition, not truly transcendent. Although many practitioners affirm that the system produces the claimed alterations in experience of the world, the experiences are ineffable, and one must cite phenomena and case examples that lie outside the current range of knowledge and suggest the working of powerful forces. The description of three cases personally known to the author will serve as examples.

The phenomenon of the *tulku* represents one aspect of Tibetan Buddhism inexplicable to Western science. A *tulku* is an important teacher or leader of a monastery who chooses to reincarnate in body after body to continue his mission. Tulkus traditionally are chosen from amongst the children in an area in which the previous incarnation had decreed he would reappear. To be selected as the tulku, however, the child is required to pick without mistake all of the previous teacher's possessions out of a set of 10 to 20 closely matched pairs of objects. In each pair, only one object belonged to the previous teacher. Although the chances are 1 in 2 for one right choice, the chance of getting all of them right becomes infinitesimal. The knowledge of recently discovered tulkus for their previous incarnations has been commented on by several Western writers.[16,17] One of my teachers, Thartang Tulku Rinpoche, was chosen in such a manner.[18]

An Asian Buddhist woman had meditated for years under the guidance of a renowned Theravadan master. One day she called together her grown children, a group that included a Western-educated physician, an army officer, and academicians. At least one of them had to travel many miles. She prepared food for them and asked them to sit with her in meditation. She addressed each one and then, in meditation, voluntarily took leave of her body. The local townspeople heard from servants about the event and asked to be allowed to build a shrine to house her body; however, wishing as little publicity as possible, the children arranged a private burial. I interviewed three of the six children individually, obtaining the same story from each, along with the same request that their name and residence not be made public.

For a period of 3 days near the end of a meditation retreat, a young woman saw the world only as patterns of vibrating golden energy and could not assemble these vibrations to form people or objects. This occurrence corresponded with the retreat teacher's understanding of the first stage of enlightenment, in which the world is seen to be a mental construct based on patterns of energy. With this interpretation, the young woman functioned calmly (after an initial period of fear at the perceptual change) and after 3 days reconstituted a normal physical world but with a new understanding of it. She showed no ill effects, although she proceeded to change her work and living situation radically and appropriately over the next few years. When last seen, approximately 10 years after the experience, she was a well-adjusted mother.

CONCLUSION

Buddhism contains a comprehensive system for understanding the functioning of the mind and producing higher states of consciousness, a system that has been carefully elucidated over the course of two and one half millennia. Because of its empirical nature and pragmatic approach, the Buddhist system may be particularly accessible to Westerners. The brief survey provided by this chapter may serve to introduce the clinician to ways of conceptualizing and experiencing the world that, although deviant from those of our culture, may constitute spiritual emergence or normal variants rather than pathology. Readers may wish to explore the Buddhist tradition further to widen their view of the ways that reality may be constructed or to further their own development.

NOTES

1. Buott, E. (Ed.). (1955). *Teachings of the compassionate Buddha* (p. 42). New York: Penguin Books.
2. Govinda, A. (1974). *The psychological attitude of early Buddhist philosophy* (pp. 47–75). New York: Samuel Weiser.
3. Govinda, *Psychological attitude*, p. 115.
4. Gyatso T. (1971). *Opening of the wisdom eye* (pp. 37–38). Madras, India: Theosophical Publishing.
5. Guenther, H., & Kawamura, L. (1975). *Mind in Buddhist psychology* (pp. 64–81). Emeryville, CA: Dharma Publishing.
6. Govinda, A. (1969). *Foundations of Tibetan mysticism* (p. 238). New York: Samuel Weiser.
7. Govinda, *Psychological attitude*, p. 4.
8. Trungpa, C. (1973). *Cutting through spiritual materialism* (p. 99). Berkeley, CA: Shambhala Publications.
9. Sopa, L., & Hopkins, J. (1976). *Practice and theory of Tibetan Buddhism* (p. xv). New York: Grove Press.
10. Willis, J. (1973). *Diamond light* (p. 50). New York: Simon & Schuster.
11. Govinda, *Psychological attitude*, pp. 107–108
12. Govinda, *Foundations*, p. 176.
13. Burang, T. (1974). *Tibetan art of healing* (S. McIntosh, Trans.) (p. 89). London: Robinson & Watkins.
14. Ibid., p. 90.
15. Ibid., p. 93.
16. David-Neel, A. (1965). *Magic and mystery in Tibet* (pp. 112–126). London: Corgi.
17. Govinda, A. (1972). *The way of the white clouds* (pp. 163–167). London: Rider.
18. Thartang, T. (1976, November 9). Personal communication.

CHAPTER 13

Kabbalah and Transpersonal Psychiatry

ZALMAN M. SCHACHTER-SHALOMI

TRANSPERSONAL THERAPISTS need maps of spiritual development to help individuals toward greater integration. In the West one of these spiritual maps is in the Kabbalah, the literary and oral body of Jewish mysticism. This library of works includes early material from between the time of the Old and New Testaments and later developments, like the Zohar schools of Spain and Provence in the thirteenth to fourteenth centuries and the Cordoverian and Lurianic schools in Safed in the sixteenth century. More recent material comes from classical Hasidism in the late eighteenth century.

FOUR LEVELS OF REALITY

The Kabbalah describes a four-world cosmology. It locates the body and its energies in the world of *Assiyyah*. Assiyyah is the realm of sensation, action, and behavior. The Jewish code of religious practice known as *Halakhah* operates largely in the realm of Assiyyah. On this level, religion trains people in behaviors intended to please God by obedience to his laws. Piety expresses itself here mostly as *G'millut Hhassadim*, the doing of kind and helpful works and observance of the Commandments. Habits, addictions, and body issues belong in the realm of Assiyyah. In working with these problems, the Kabbalist uses appropriate methods such as behaviorism. Indeed, behaviorism is the psychology of the Assiyyah level; a person is considered an object in the world of objects, according to what Martin Buber called the *I–It relationship*.

The second level of reality is that of the *Ru'aHh* (literally, "the breath" or "spirit"). This is the world of *Yetzirah*, or formation, and involves feeling, images, values, and myths. On this level people are treated as persons, as subjects like ourselves, in what Buber called the *I–Thou relationship*. Here piety is measured in terms of devoutness: the sincere feeling one invests in prayer and worship. The purification of emotions is a central task on this level and a prerequisite for full entry into the world of the Kabbalah.

The third realm of reality is the world of *B'riyyah*, or Creation: the world of thinking and philosophy. B'riyyah includes the faculties of concepts, ideas, hypotheses, and theories. Piety expresses itself on this level in how one invests time and awareness in the study of Torah and the esoteric teachings.

The fourth level of reality is *Atzilut*, which translates as "emanation." This is the world of being, intuition, inner teaching, *Sod* (literally, "secret" or "mystery"), and the anagogical level of interpretation. Atzilut is the source of inspiration, the place where we speak of God as a person, clothing the divine in a "root metaphor": an archetypal image like father, mother, king, healer, beloved, and friend. These images put us on the soul level of *Hhayah*, creating a covenantal relationship with the divine. Dealing with an individual's resistance to Atzilut is often the concern of the Kabbalist in working with a student or disciple.

THE S'FIROT AND THE TREE OF LIFE

In addition to the four levels of reality, the Kabbalah organizes the world with the 10 S'firot, attributes and dimensions of reality that apply to God, souls, spirits, and all creation. God is in everything and one can see aspects of God in everything; the Kabbalists found that the system of using these 10 attributes helped them see aspects of God in all sorts of worldly entities. The 10 S'firot of Kabbalah and their literal translations are: *KETER* (crown); *HhOkHMAH* (wisdom); *BINAH* (understanding); *HhESED* (grace); *G'VURAH* (strength); *TIF'ERET* (beauty); *NETZAHh* (victory); *HOD* (glory); *Y'sOD* (foundation); and *MALKhUT* (kingship).

The diagram in Figure 13.1 is sometimes called the *Tree of Life* and reveals significant relationships among the S'firot. Those grouped on the right side are the "soft, gentle" ones, and those on the left side are "hard," or "severe." The contrast also involves intuition and knowledge, or masculine and feminine. The arrangement of

FIGURE 13.1

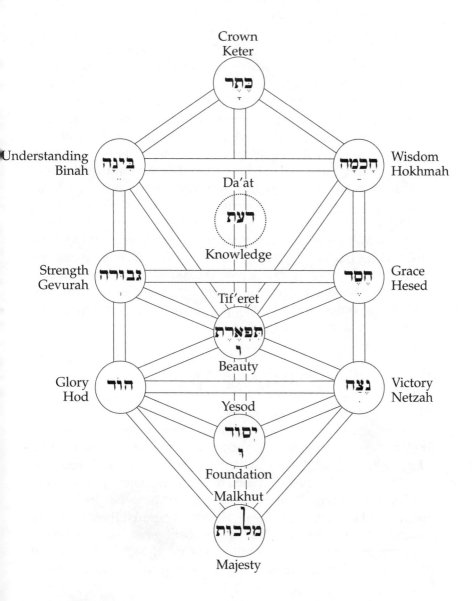

the S'firot resembles the human body, with the head at the top of the diagram and the genitals at the base. Because a major process of mysticism is to see connections between the "real world" and the divine, conceptual tools such as these are helpful.

COSMOLOGY AND ARCHETYPES

In the Kabbalah, the Godhead is called *Resha d'la yad 'a ud'la ityad'a,* "the head that is beyond knowing and becoming known." Yet the Godhead wanted to become known. So the *EYN SOF* emanated *Partzufim* (from the Greek for "mask"), which includes *Adam Qadmon* ("primal human"), *Atiq Yomin* ("ancient of days"), *Abba* ("father"), *Imma,* ("mother"), *Ben* ("son"), and *Bat* ("daughter").

Much that deals with Jewish liturgy, ritual, and celebration is really a "sacred technology" for interacting with the Partzufim. For example, the Sabbath is divided into several phases in which one comes home on Friday night to *Imma* (mother), as *Binah* (understanding) and *Malkhut* (kingship). On Sabbath morning, the individual rises to *Keter* (crown), *Hhokhmah* (wisdom), and *Binah* (understanding), spending the afternoon with the "minor visages" like *Hhessed* (grace) on the Tree of Life, which corresponds to Abraham and Miriam. Finally, Saturday night is involved with *Malkhut* (Bat) on the Tree of Life, that is, David and Rachel. In each case the individual attunes to the archetype and its connection to God, thus recharging the soul's energy for functioning in the world. The daily liturgy is also designed to take a person up and down through the four worlds, thus attuning the individual to cosmic reality.

ON DEATH

Hasidic eschatology taught the Hasid the importance of dying in full possession of his consciousness. Often a *nigun*—a Hasidic melody—and a deathbed scene are interwoven. A story is told of a Hasidic *rebbe* (rabbi) who invited 10 men to his deathbed and taught them a new melody. When the men had learned the melody well enough to carry it by themselves, the rebbe leaned back, offering his soul to God, and expired. Hasidim prepared themselves for death by asking the rebbe for advice about what "unification" to meditate on in the moments of their passing. R. SimHhah Bunim of Pshysskha compared death to sleep: He who prepared himself properly for sleep, offering his soul up to God, would be able to pass on to the other life with ease.

Viewed in eschatological terms, the moment of death becomes the event of initiation. Death can be extremely painful. The pangs of birth, the pangs of death, and the pangs of the Messiah are often described as constituting one and the same kind of separation. Yet if the Hasid has been truly prepared, death can be like removing a hair from the milk, or like walking out one door and into another. The freed self, the self that is capable of choosing freely and making decisions, has no problem with the death experience; but to free a Hasid from the pangs and the pain and the attachments, a master may have to use severe techniques such as mortification.

If death is the goal orientation of life, it is only when death means union with the Eyn Sof (the Infinite One). To ensure such a union, the individual must be clear and pure when he or she comes before the Lord in the Heavenly Court. This task requires disciplined action during life. For example, anyone who indulges the seeking of sense pleasure for its own sake becomes earthbound. Sensual indulgence leads to identification with the body. This identification of the person with his body, the implicit faith that the body is a true self, must be broken. The Hasid needs to discover that beyond the flesh there is another self. For this purpose, the Hasid practices *itkafia*, or self-denial. Each time the Hasid says "no" to his physical wants, he separates himself from his bodily identity. This attitude is close to that of Francis of Assisi, who spoke of his body as "Brother Ass." A more positive means is prayer offered in great *kavanah* ("sincerity" or "intent"). In such prayer, one becomes oblivious to the body and the environment.

At death, the earthbound soul may be unable to separate itself from the body. This puts the soul in danger of experiencing a decay of consciousness and turning into nothingness. For this reason, an angel, *Dumah,* is charged with preventing this decay. To do this, he asks each person for his Hebrew name: his spiritual identity. To avoid forgetting this identity after death, owing to the shock of dying, Hasidim are taught mnemonic devices.

Unatoned sins stain the soul. The soul then has to descend into *Gehenna.* Gehenna was often described in lurid physical detail as fire and extreme cold, yet the rabbis translate it as meaning the pains of anxiety caused by the absence of "background noise" from worldly concerns and to the depth of realization of the wrong done. Every evil passion fulfilled must be seared out of the soul, and the soul, as if cauterized by this shock, is healed of the spiritual hemorrhage flowing from the self-inflicted psychic wound of the evil act.

When a soul is ready to enter *Gan Eden* ("paradise"), it must first be immersed in the River of Light that flows from the fervent perspiration of the Heavenly Hosts as they sing glory to the Highest. This immersion rids the soul of the remaining earth images (even those that were good in themselves) so that the soul may, without further illusions, see heaven as it really is. In life, Hasidim enact this immersion with the *miqveh* (ritual bath). Almost every Hasidic master imparted to his disciples the secrets of the miqveh, which symbolically contains the River of Light. The four walls of the miqveh represent the four letters of the Divine Name. In dipping into the miqveh four times, one intends by this total submersion to be included in God. The miqveh is often discussed and interpreted as the feminine element of the Divine: Dipping in the miqveh therefore constitutes a return to the Divine Womb. This return, being "absorbed into the very Body of the King"[1] is the final spiritual aim: The soul merges finally in God, as a drop in the ocean.

SPIRITUAL WORK AND COUNSELING

Habad Hasidism turns dogmatic statements into methodological ones; that is, religious doctrines are translated into psychological terms. The eschatological teachings of Hasidism are reflected, therefore, in the work of the rebbe and the Hasid and in their relationship. For example, the phases of the soul's journey after physical death correspond to the tasks the Hasid must master, working with the rebbe: purgation, preparation, and finally, enlightenment. The eschatological teachings therefore provide a model for the work that the aspirant must do: The Hasid's work is a spiritual laboratory.

KABBALAH TODAY

In classical Kabbalah the root metaphor, S'firot, Partzufim, worlds, souls, and angels were seen as fixed and revealed by God through prophets, seers, and sages. The transpersonal therapist can help clients with this root metaphor work. Here one's connection with the right, healing, and salvific Partzufim needs to be repaired. Such repair is called *Tiqqun* in the Kabbalah. Other forms of Tiqqun include helping clients to gain free access to all the four worlds from Assiyyah to Atzilut and balancing an individual's Tree of Life so that he or she does not tilt toward being overly generous and open, the side of Hhessed (grace), nor to being severe, tight, and closed, the side of G'vurah (strength).

In the later stages of life, when individuation and self-actualization become concerns, the person has to deal with mortality and depression. The task is to access the Partzuf of Atiq Yomin, the Ancient of Days. Gaining access to this archetype helps the individual transcend transitory existence. The Partzuf of Adam Qadmon, the primal person, is also important in the individual's philosophical and contemplative homework. Although it is relatively easy to talk and think about the three lower worlds of the ladder—Assiyyah, Yetzirah, and B'riyyah, dealing with sensation, feelings, and intellect—it is more difficult to understand and gain access to Atzilut. These lower three realms have biological and evolutionary parallels in the reptilian, limbic, and cortical parts of the brain, which correspond to Assiyyah, Yetzirah, and B'riyyah, respectively. More tools are needed to enable one to activate and "domesticate" the Atzilic functions.

There are other techniques in the Kabbalah for opening the everyday, contracted, mind of *MoHhin d'qatnut* to the more awakened mind of *MoHhin d'gadlut* (literally, "the brain of enlargement"). The mere reading about these techniques is not likely to help one who seeks to practice them, however. Individuals learn from emulating real people who have mastered these sacred arts. Newer methods are also emerging today that might help one achieve these states of consciousness with less ascetic expense to the body. There are also effective imaginal exercises growing out of the Kabbalah. Elsewhere, I have written about interactive and "socialized" meditation; the use of *niggunim,* or chants, and movement; and the practice of prayer with special intentions or *kavvanot,* as well as teaching stories and blessings.

CONCLUSION

The transpersonal therapist gains from the encounter with Kabbalah by meeting a system that has a powerful terminology for inner states and transpersonal regions. The terrors one may encounter by entering into unusual and frightening regions of reality yield to a naming and thus can be tamed. Balance is achievable once one knows which S'firoth are out of balance. The confusion of levels of awareness can be reduced by knowing in which "world" an experience was encountered.

It is of great therapeutic–strategic value to help Jewish clients by referring to the Kabbalah. Otherwise, they might regress to childish icons of God and obsessive–compulsive piety in their intense need to make peace with their spiritual urgings. In opening to them avenues for integrating awe-filled experiences, the therapist reassures the client and ensures the blessed impact of these unsettling moments. Kabbalah is not limited to Jews, however. In fact knowing of the S'firot and the worlds can make it easier to connect with other mystical systems.

It is crucial that the therapist use the language and terminology in conjunction with his or her own experience with the teachings. Without some personal encounter, the language of Kabbalah is mere jargon and adds to the already confusing psychobabble abounding in the helping professions.

NOTES

1. Sperling, H., & Simon, M. (Trans.). (1933, 1956). *The Zohar* (vol. 1). London: Soncino Press, p. 217b.

REFERENCES

Ariel, D. S. (1992). *The mystic quest: An introduction to Jewish mysticism.* New York: Shocken Books.

Bakan, D. (1965). *Sigmund Freud and the Jewish mystical tradition.* New York: Schocken Books.

Ben-Amos, D., & Mintz, J. P. (Trans. and Eds.). (1993). *In praise of the Baal Shem Tov.* Northvale, NJ: Jason Aronson.

Buber, M. (1975). *Tales of the Hasidim: Vol. I. The early masters.* New York: Schocken Books.

———. (1975). *Tales of the Hasidim: Vol. II. The later masters.* New York: Schocken Books.

Dan, J. (1987). *Gershom Scholem and the mystical dimension of Jewish history.* New York: New York University Press.

Dresner, S. H. (1987). *The zaddik.* New York: Abelard Schuman.

Green, A. (1981). *Tormented master: A life of Rabbi Nahman of Bratslav.* New York: Schocken Books.

———. (Ed.). (1987). *Jewish spirituality* (2 vols.). New York: Crossroad Publishing.

———. (1993). *Seek my face, speak my name: A contemporary Jewish theology.* Northvale, NJ: Jason Aronson.

Halevi, Z. ben S. (1972). *Tree of life: An introduction to the cabala.* London: Rider.

———. (1974). *Adam and the Kabbalistic tree.* New York: Samuel Weiser.

———. (1976). *The way of Kabbalah.* London: Rider.

———. (1977). *A Kabbalistic universe.* London: Rider.

———. (1986). *Kabbalah and psychology.* Bath, England: Gateway.

———. (1987). *The anointed: A Kabbalistic novel.* London: Arkana.

Harris-Wiener, S., & Omer-Man, J. (1993). *Worlds of Jewish prayer: A Festschrift in honor of Rabbi Zalman M. Schachter-Shalomi.* Northvale, NJ: Jason Aronson.

Heifetz, H. (Ed.). (1978). *Zen and Hasidism.* Wheaton, IL: Quest Books.

Heschel, A. J. (1973). *A passion for truth.* New York: Farrar, Straus & Giroux.

Hoffman, E. (1981). *The way of splendor: Jewish mysticism and modern psychology.* Boulder: Shambhala Publications.

Idel, M. (1988). *Kabbalah: New perspectives.* New Haven, CT: Yale University Press.

———. (1988). *The mystical experience in Abraham Abulafia* (J. Chipman, Trans.). Albany: SUNY Press.

Jacobs, L. (1972). *Hasidic prayer.* New York: Schocken Books.

Kamenetz, R. (1994). *The Jew in the lotus.* San Francisco: Harper San Francisco.

Kaplan, A. (1978). *Meditation and the Bible.* York Beach, ME: Samuel Weiser.

———. (1985). *Jewish meditation: A practical guide.* New York: Schocken Books.

———. (1988). *Meditation and Kabbalah.* York Beach, ME: Samuel Weiser.

———. (1990). Innerspace: Introduction to Kabbalah, meditation and prophecy. In A. Sutton (Ed.), *Inner spaces.* Brooklyn: Moznaim.

———. (1995). *Sefer Yetzirah: The Book of Creation.* Northvale, NJ: Jason Aronson.

Kushner, L. (1981). *The river of light: Spirituality, Judaism and the evolution of consciousness.* San Francisco: Harper & Row.

Liebes, Y. (1993). *Studies in the Zohar* (A. Schwartz, Trans.). Albany: SUNY Press.

Matt, D. C. (Ed.). (1983). *Zohar: The book of enlightenment*. New York: Paulist Press Classics of Western Spirituality.

Meltzer, D. (Ed.). (1976). *The secret garden*. New York: Seabury Press.

Musaph-Andriesse, R. C. (1982). *From Torah to Kabbalah: A basic introduction to the writings of Judaism*. New York: Oxford University Press.

Nigal, G. (1994). *Magic, mysticism and Hasidism: The supernatural in Jewish thought* (E. Levin, Trans.). Northvale, NJ: Jason Aronson.

Newman, L. (Ed. and Trans.). (1975). *The Hasidic anthology: Tales and teachings of the Hasidim*. New York: Schocken Books.

Raphael, S. P. (1974). *Jewish views of the afterlife*. Northvale, NJ: Jason Aronson.

Schachter-Shalomi, Z. (1975). *Fragments of a future scroll*. Philadelphia: Leaves of Grass Press.

———. (1991). *Spiritual intimacy*. Northvale, NJ: Jason Aronson.

———. (1993). Paradigm Shift. In E. Singer (Ed.), *Paradigm shift*. Northvale, NJ: Jason Aronson.

———. (1994). *Gate to the heart*. Philadelphia: Aleph Publications.

———, & Miller, R. S. (1995). *From age-ing to sage-ing: A profound new vision of growing older*. New York: Warner Books.

Scholem, G. (1954). *Major trends in Jewish mysticism*. New York: Schocken Books.

———. (1969). *On the Kabbalah and its symbolism* (R. Manheim, Trans.). New York: Schocken Books.

———. (1976). *On the mystical shape of the Godhead* (J. Neugrosschel, Trans.). New York: Schocken Books.

———. (1978). *Kabbalah*. New York: New American Library.

———. (1987). *Origins of the Kabbalah* (A. Arkush, Trans.). Philadelphia: Jewish Publication Society.

Shapiro, D. (1989). Judaism as a journey of transformation: Consciousness, behavior and society. *Journal of Transpersonal Psychology, 21*, 12–59.

Steinsaltz, A. (1988). *The long shorter way*. Northvale, NJ: Jason Aronson.

———. (1988). *The strife of the spirit*. Northvale, NJ: Jason Aronson.

———. (1989). *The sustaining utterance: Discourses on Chasidic thought*. Northvale, NJ: Jason Aronson.

———. (1992). *The thirteen petalled rose* (Y. Hanegbi, Trans.). Northvale, NJ: Jason Aronson.

Tishby, I., & Lachover, F. (Eds.). (1989). *The wisdom of the Zohar* (3 vols.; D. Goldstein, Trans.). London: Oxford University Press.

Trachtenberg, J. (1974). *Jewish magic and superstition: A study in folk religion.* New York: Atheneum.

Winkler, G. (1981). *Dybbuk.* New York: Judaica Press.

———. (1982). *The soul of the matter.* New York: Judaica Press.

The Zohar (5 vols.; H. Sperling & M. Simon, Trans.). (1933, 1956). London: Soncino Press.

CHAPTER 14

Transpersonal Psychology: Roots in Christian Mysticism

DWIGHT H. JUDY

ONE MAJOR ROOT of transpersonal psychology in the West is Christian mysticism, which is a strain of Christian theology and practice that includes the following characteristics:

1. God is understood as inherently present within the human being, and individuals are challenged to a lifelong task of self-development in loving and serving all humanity and creation.
2. Jesus Christ is the model and inner guide for this personal development.
3. Personal growth is undertaken in the historic context of Christian sacramental worship, theological reflection, and community support. This path ordinarily involves a focus on meditative prayer.

This strain of thought and practice is rooted in the teachings of Jesus and the practice of the early Desert Fathers and Mothers. This "perennial wisdom" of Christianity was particularly well expressed by a number of Christian mystics during the High Middle Ages in Europe.

NEW TESTAMENT TEACHINGS AND
DESERT FATHERS AND MOTHERS

Jesus said: "Love God with all your heart and mind and soul and strength, and love your neighbor as yourself" (Luke 10:27). Jesus defined *neighbor* to mean "all humanity." The common ethic in Jesus' time was that love of neighbor meant love within one's own group only and active hostility beyond one's group, clan, or nation.[1] To this Jesus gave the great teaching:

> You have learned that they were told, "Love your neighbor, hate your enemy." But what I tell you is this: Love your enemies and pray for your persecutors; only so can you be children of your heavenly Father, who makes his sun rise on good and bad alike, and sends the rain on the honest and the dishonest. If you love only those who love you, what reward can you expect? . . . There must be no limit to your goodness, as your heavenly Father's goodness knows no bounds. (Matt. 5:43–48)[2]

Christian mysticism has held forth the challenge of growing into the fullness of love that Jesus proclaimed as a process of personal transformation from ego-bound consciousness to a state of cosmic consciousness. In some cases this process has been described as an inner marriage between the individual and God. In other cases it has been described as surrender to God. In the church's attempt to describe this process in the language of doctrine, it has been called *sanctification*. By *sanctification*, or its more recent term, *divinisation*, the Christian church has declared the possibility that an individual might grow toward incorporating the completeness of God within his or her own mind and heart. A scriptural basis for this process is contained in many places, but none is more eloquent than the injunction to "let this mind be in you which was also in Christ Jesus" (Philippians 2:5).

Christian mysticism points to the example of Jesus for much of its form. In the opening of the Gospels, Jesus is sent into the wilderness to sort out his relationship to God and worldly power. Jesus' retreat for self-examination has played a prominent role in Christian mysticism. The earliest Christians, who were called the *Desert Fathers and Mothers*, modeled their lives on a self-examining retreat into the desert regions in Syria, Palestine, and Egypt. They were well established by the third century and flourished for at least another 300 years. The record of the interior life of these individuals is well described in *The Early Fathers from the Philokalia*.[3] They rigorously examined their own inner demons in utter emotional nakedness before God. Hallmarks of their life were simplicity of spiritual practice and divinisation of self through complete self-honesty. Desert Mothers and Fathers cultivated the human spirit with a rigor that matched the discipline of advanced practitioners of other major spiritual traditions. Their experience provides a direct lineage for contemporary transpersonal experience, practice, and insight.

Thomas Merton[4] described the Mothers and Fathers as establishing the prototype for individual self-consciousness. Their isolated life in the desert was an assertion of the worth of the individual that was unusual for the time.[5] In this respect, all of the West owes much to them for their capacity to experience their autonomy.

In addition to the cultivation of the inner Christ and a loving devotion to God in all people, Christianity's emphasis on the crucifixion–resurrection of Jesus has brought the archetype of death–rebirth into a central place in the Western mind. This archetype remains central to transpersonal practice in our time. The great cycles of the Christian year focus on birth, death, and rebirth. Annually, through the seasons of Christmas and Easter, this pageant of the seasons is rehearsed. Of course, the festivals of the seasons are based on the more ancient practices of the land-based spiritual traditions of Europe, marking the season of darkness with a hope for the birth of light and marking the renewal of springtime with the festival of rebirth.

Christianity treats these seasons as occasions for renewal of individual and communal life. The crucifixion points metaphorically to the necessity for ego surrender in the transformation process leading to divinisation or sanctification. In the perpetual remembrance of this death in the Eucharist, or Holy Communion, Christian practice continually rehearses the possibility of divinisation.

As a metaphysical construct, the resurrection points to the indomitable creativity of the universe and is taken by Christians as the signpost of the capacity of God to renew all life forms. It gives a dynamic quality to Christian life, reminding one not to be satisfied with the status quo, particularly when structures of society perpetuate human suffering. The resurrection also symbolizes the potentiality of the living quality of Christ as an archetypal presence within the heart and mind of persons in any age.

MEDITATIVE PRAYER PRACTICE

The Desert Fathers and Mothers practiced meditative prayer as a method for self-knowledge and interior growth. A brief quotation from the *Philokalia* indicates something of the sophistication of self-awareness and spiritual experience that these renunciants discovered through their simple practices.

> The highest state of prayer has two forms. . . . The sign of the first order is when a man collects his mind, freeing it of all worldly thoughts, and prays without distraction and disturbance, as if God Himself were present before him, as indeed He is. The sign of the second is when, in the very act of rising in prayer, the mind is ravished by the Divine boundless light and loses all sensation of itself or of any other creature, and is aware of Him alone, Who, through love, has produced in him this illumination. In this state, moved to understand words about God, he receives pure and luminous knowledge of Him.[3]

In the sixth century, Benedict codified the life of monastics in what has become known as *The Rule of St. Benedict*. One of the key principles of the Rule is a particular way of meditating, called *lectio divina*, which involves meditating on a brief phrase of scripture. The intent of the practice is to bring holy wisdom to the practitioner. Meditation on Jesus, or the *Jesus Prayer*, became the mainstay of Eastern Orthodox practice and is exceptionally well described in *The Way of a Pilgrim*.[6] Meditative devotion to Mary was also well established in Europe. The fourteenth-century text *The Cloud of Unknowing*[7] describes contemplative prayer focused on the word *God* or *love*.

It is intriguing that meditative prayer has had such a strong presence in Christian practice throughout the ages but was almost lost in the first half of the twentieth century.[8] At the present time, there is a major renewal of these prayer forms among both Protestants and Roman Catholics in the Western world. Many authors have been important to this endeavor, including Thomas Merton,[4] Morton Kelsey,[9,10] M. Basil Pennington,[11] and Thomas Keating.[12,13] In one of the most popular of these contemporary practices, centering prayer,[11] the practitioner meditates on a single word of scripture of his or her choice, such as God or love. The word is joined with a practice of the presence of "contemplative love." It is a profound method of both self-awareness and inner healing. Whatever the mind brings forth is allowed to be present. There is no internal repression. Whatever thought, image, memory, or vision arises is then answered with the spirit of contemplative love and with the meditation word.

Matthew Fox[14,15] has been noteworthy in restating the essential Christian theology underlying Christian mysticism. My own *Christian Meditation and Inner Healing*[16] describes the major practices of Christian meditation, and *Healing the Male Soul*[17] gives special attention to the effects of the Desert spirituality on Christian practice.

SPIRITUALITY OF THE HIGH MIDDLE AGES

For the purposes of this chapter, the period in Europe from the eleventh through the sixteenth centuries will be called the *High Middle Ages*. These years can be viewed as a single period because the quality of mind among Christian mystics exhibited throughout this period was strikingly uniform. Figures such as Meister Eckhart, Hildegard of Bingen, Teresa of Avila, John of the Cross, Dante, Ignatius of Loyola, Bonaventure, and Thomas Aquinas worked with concepts strikingly similar to those found today in transpersonal conferences, with discussions of inner imagery, inner healing process, processes of spiritual growth, and the relationship of inner work to social life.

Space limitations prevent a thorough review of the history of Christian mysticism in this period. For the reader who would like to pursue this subject further, a significant place to begin is with Evelyn Underhill's *Mysticism*,[18] written in 1911. This chapter focuses on a few key concepts from Bonaventure (thirteenth century), Dante (fourteenth century), Teresa of Avila (sixteenth century), John of the Cross (sixteenth century), and the anonymous writing *The Cloud of Unknowing* (fourteenth century). From these sources emerges a discussion of the general transpersonal themes, a transpersonal cartography of the human soul, and models of psychological–spiritual development.

TRANSPERSONAL THEMES IN CHRISTIAN MYSTICISM

One of the great gifts of Christian mysticism of the High Middle Ages is its portrayal of a sense of human dignity and interconnectedness with the universe. The Christian mystics' appreciation of the inherent dignity of the human being is eloquently stated in *The Cloud of Unknowing:*

> Beneath you and external to you lies the entire created universe. Yes, even the sun, the moon, and the stars. They are fixed above you, splendid in the firmament, yet they cannot compare to your exalted dignity as a human being.
>
> The angels and the souls of the just are superior to you inasmuch as they are confirmed in grace and glorious with every virtue, but they are your equals in nature as intelligent creatures. By nature you are gifted with three marvelous spiritual faculties, Mind, Reason, and Will, and two secondary faculties, Imagination and Feeling. There is nothing above you in nature except God himself.[7]

Teresa of Avila, in her distinctive way, makes the same point regarding human dignity. It is necessary to "truly understand that within us lies something incomparably more precious than what we see outside ourselves. Let's not imagine that we are hollow inside."[20] Indeed, what was "inside" for Teresa was the fullness of God. She asks the reader to imagine that God is a "mighty King who has been gracious enough to become your Father; and that He is seated upon an extremely valuable throne, which is your heart."[20]

This emphasis on human dignity in Christian mysticism brings with it a profound understanding of the capacities of the human being to connect and interact with all aspects of the universe. I believe that humanity has lost something of the exalted understanding of human nature contained in these texts. Transpersonal theory seeks to establish, in a new way, the dignity of the human being and the inherent capacities of the psyche for connections: internal connections between mind and body and external connections between the individual human psyche, the collective field of thought and emotion surrounding the individual, and the archetypal powers that draw us beyond our own time.

TRANSPERSONAL CARTOGRAPHY OF THE HUMAN SOUL

Bonaventure lived from 1217 to 1274 and was a professor at the University of Paris and minister general of the Franciscans. His work *The Soul's Journey into God*[21] contains a model of spiritual development that holds within it a map of human consciousness. The chapters describe seven stages of meditation. The relationship of human consciousness to God begins with one's relationship to the physical universe, to one's body, and to the senses. This first level of consciousness, perhaps for Bonaventure, is the most accessible. He delights in the sensory world and the mysteries revealed in the universe through the senses. In addition to experiencing this sensory data, Bonaventure asks another question: What does it tell one about the nature of God that one is a creature of sensory awareness? This question contains a method of philosophical reflection that was prominent in Bonaventure's time: going from the microcosm of one individual's experience to intuit a meaning for the macrocosm of the universe.

Bonaventure guides the reader to look into the natural powers of the human mind. Here he discusses memory, imagination, mathematics, reason, and other properties of the mind. He describes the human capacities for reason and provides a sophisticated discussion of the many qualities of mind that were important in his time. Again, he asks the question of the meaning for one's understanding of God that these capacities of the mind are available. What does it say about God that humans possess such natural powers within themselves?

After laying this foundation concerning the natural capacities of humans, Bonaventure turns to the potential for human transformation of motivations and intentions in his discussion of the redeeming work of Christ. This realm is a more fundamental level of the human being, less visible even than that of reason. It is the arena of the human heart, the interior realm of life choices: decisions of both action and emotional states. Bonaventure offers within the heart the potentiality of transformation of the individual into a more loving being.

Moral purification was deeply addressed by another cartographer of the soul, Dante, in the fourteenth century. In Dante's description of Purgatory, the seven deadly sins of pride, envy, sloth, jealousy, hatred, greed, and lust[22] were purified through meditative practice. Dante adds an additional perspective to that of Bonaventure. His Hades[23] is a realm where every evil is encountered. As he descends the rungs of Hades, he encounters all types of atrocities that human beings have inflicted on each other. One of the challenges that Dante brings to contemporary transpersonal thought is the need to address the question of evil directly: what has historically been called *sin* in Christian thought. An area of compatibility between Dante's cartography of the soul and contemporary transpersonal psychiatry is that the depth of the shadow dimension of the human being must be addressed. It cannot be ignored. For Dante, in fact, this realm of depth—the shadow, death, and destruction—is the gateway to interior growth. Hades must be encountered before any additional interior growth is possible.

One enters a still deeper level of the soul in Bonaventure's contemplation of God. Two modes are described: contemplating God as being, and contemplating God as goodness. Now there is a direct relationship with the Absolute. As we contemplate these essentials of the universe, there is still a separation between our perceiving capacities and that which we contemplate. In Bonaventure's final stage, however, there is a complete merging of individual consciousness with the Ultimate in an experience of ecstatic oneness. Dante's final stage of contemplation concerns "Primal Love."[24] He discovered, as did Bonaventure, that God is essential goodness.

The nature of consciousness we have been describing could be diagrammed as seen in Figure 14.1:

FIGURE 14.1

sensory world

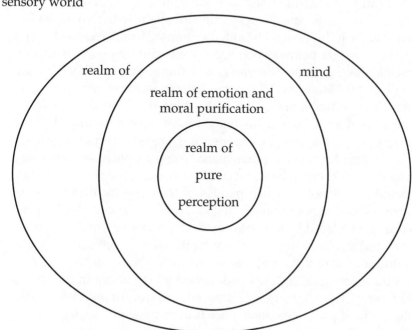

realm of   mind

realm of emotion and
moral purification

realm of

pure

perception

MODELS OF PSYCHOLOGICAL–SPIRITUAL DEVELOPMENT

With this model of the soul before us, let us turn to the primary model for psychological–spiritual development that emerged from the tradition of Christian mysticism. This model has its roots in the writings of the third-century Greek philosopher Plotinus, who conceptualized spiritual development as a three-stage process involving purification, illumination, and unification. *Purification* involves the same kind of emotional and motivational self-examination described by Dante in *Purgatory*. *Illumination* appears from the direct perception of reality as in Bonaventure's contemplation of God as being and as goodness. Plotinus' stage of *unification* involves absorption of the individual into the Divine and lies in the realm of pure perception, illustrated by Dante's merging with Primal Love and with Bonaventure's giving over of reason into ecstasy.

Underhill,[18] drawing on the experience of many Christian mystics, expands this model into five stages: awakening of the self, purification of the self, illumination of the self, dark night of the soul, and the unitive life. This model fits remarkably well with the course of spiritual development described by Teresa of Avila in the sixteenth-century text *Interior Castle*.[20] *Interior Castle* presents a thoughtful and mature statement on the lifelong progress of the individual from a life consumed by outward affairs to the mystical marriage of the individual with God, the Spouse, in the innermost region of the soul. Her pathway is especially relevant for people with high imagination, psychic awareness, and strong emotionality.[25] In fact, her chapter "Mansions VI" is one of the most important writings in Western spiritual literature on unusual interior experiences, such as flights of the soul out of the body. I have often recommended this chapter to people who are experiencing a rapid spiritual emergence accompanied by intense phenomena. These people have universally found this writing to be very beneficial, because they discover a historical companion and rich parallel of their psychic experience. In Teresa's final state of union with God, such intense spiritual experiences are replaced by a simple day-to-day awareness of Divine presence and guidance in a life of love for the world.[25] Teresa, like Dante, found the heart of the universe, deep within her own heart, to be a loving source guiding the mind toward loving action in the world. Referring to the diagram in Figure 14.1, therefore, it may be said that the realm of pure perception, once fully integrated into one's being, illumines our senses, emotions, mind, and actions with love.

For John of the Cross, a contemporary of Teresa's, the way toward final alignment with the Divine in the realm of pure perception is not through the interior prayer of imagination (kataphatic style), but rather through a process of letting go (apophatic style). For John of the Cross, it is only in the absence of image that God is perceived. "To come to the knowledge you have not you must go by a way in which you know not."[19] I believe that the final results of the purification–illumination process are the same, although the pathways are very different for persons of the apophatic versus kataphatic personalities.

CONCLUSION

The practice of Christian mysticism has elaborated models of consciousness and of spiritual development. It has established methods for the exploration of the interior realms and for the discernment of life purpose. Christian mysticism is one of the primary unbroken traditions of conscious reflection on the interior qualities of the human mind in the West. It constitutes a root of psychology itself, as well as of transpersonal psychology. Many of the riches of this tradition remain to be brought forth in our current era. As these historical sources become more readily available, a fruitful dialogue with proponents of transpersonal psychology can take place.

NOTES

1. Furnish, P. V. (1972). *The love commandment in the New Testament* (pp. 65–66). Nashville: Abingdon.
2. *The new English bible.* (1971). New York: Cambridge University Press.
3. Kadloubovsky, E., & Palmer, G. E. H. (Eds. and Trans.). (1954). *Early fathers from the Philokalia.* London: Faber. Quotation on pp. 299–300.
4. Merton, T. (1960). *The wisdom of the desert.* New York: New Directions.
5. Workman, H. B. (1962). *The evolution of the monastic ideal.* Boston: Beacon Press.
6. French, R. M. (Trans.). (1952). *The way of a pilgrim and the pilgrim continues his way* (2nd ed.). Minneapolis: Seabury Press.

7. Johnston, W. (Ed.). (1973). *The cloud of unknowing and the book of privy counseling.* Garden City, NY: Doubleday. Quotation on p. 129.

8. Morello, Fr. A. (1980). Personal communication.

9. Kelsey, M. T. (1983). *Companions on the inner way: The art of spiritual guidance.* New York: Crossroad.

10. Kelsey, M. T. (1976). *The other side of silence: A guide to Christian meditation.* New York: Paulist.

11. Pennington, M. B. (1980). *Centering prayer: Renewing an ancient Christian prayer form.* Garden City, NY: Doubleday.

12. Keating, T. (1992). *Invitation to love: The way of Christian contemplation.* Rockport, MA: Element.

13. Keating, T. (1991). *Reawakenings.* New York: Crossroad.

14. Fox, M. (1983). *Original blessing: A primer in creation spirituality.* Santa Fe, NM: Bear & Co.

15. Fox, M. (1991). *The coming of the cosmic Christ.* San Francisco: Harper San Francisco.

16. Judy, D. (1991). *Christian meditation and inner healing.* New York: Crossroad.

17. Judy, D. (1992). *Healing the male soul: Christianity and the mythic journey.* New York: Crossroad.

18. Underhill, E. (1990). *Mysticism: A study in the nature and development of man's spiritual consciousness.* New York: Doubleday.

19. Kavanaugh, K., & Rodriguez, O. (Trans.). (1973). *Ascent to Mt. Carmel: The collected works of St. John of the Cross* (p. 67). Washington, DC: ICS Publications.

20. Kavanaugh, K., & Rodriguez, O. (Trans.). (1980). *The collected works of St. Teresa of Avila* (Vol. 2). Washington, DC: ICS Publications. Quotations on pp. 143–144.

21. Cousins, E. (Trans.). (1978). *Bonaventure: The soul's journey into God, the tree of life, the life of St. Francis.* New York: Paulist Press.

22. Dante Alighieri (1955). *The comedy of Dante Alighieri, the Florentine, Cantica II, Purgatory (Il Purgatorio)* (D. L. Sayers, Trans.). New York: Penguin Books.

23. Dante Alighieri (1949). *The comedy of Dante Alighieri, the Florentine, Cantica I, Hell (Il Inferno)* (D. L. Sayers, Trans.). New York: Penguin Books.

24. Dante Alighieri (1962). *The comedy of Dante Alighieri, the Florentine, Cantica III, Paradise (Il Paradiso)* (D. L. Sayers, Trans.). New York: Penguin Books.

25. Judy, D. (1996). *Embracing God: Meditating with Teresa.* Nashville: Abingdon.

CHAPTER 15

Native North American Healers

DONALD F. SANDNER

HEALTH CARE PRACTITIONERS in traditional tribal societies throughout the world tend to be of two kinds. The first kind is specific, grounded, and factual. They are skilled men and women with a wide knowledge of native plants and their uses who can prepare and employ many natural remedies. They may also be wound healers and bonesetters, familiar with many aspects of physical therapy and body manipulation (massage). Close observers of the body and its reactions, they are the early pharmacologists and physiologists, and many of their remedies remain in the National Formulary.[1]

The second type of health care practitioner, especially prominent among native North Americans, employs another kind of healing, which is transpersonal, highly involved with myth and rituals, and holistic in the sense that its procedures are meant to treat the body, mind, and soul at the same time. This healing treats disharmony of the whole and tries to restore a natural state of health. It involves contact with a supernatural reality: a realm of spiritual beings.

The shaman is the person in the tribe most adept in these transpersonal methods. He has acquired the power to communicate with the spirits, to go on out-of-body journeys in search of a

145

lost soul, to usher the dead into the other world, or to gain a boon such as good hunting conditions for his tribe. He does these tasks with the help of his spirit animals or spirit guardians. They are his allies and effect the transition between this world and the other.

Medicine men and women are also part of this transpersonal healing tradition. They do not enter the spirit world in deep trance as shamans do, but they operate with supernatural sanction and they are conduits for supernatural power.

ETIOLOGY AND TREATMENT OF ILLNESS

Native American peoples recognized four main causes of illness: offending the spirit world by breaking a taboo, intrusion of an object or spirit into the body, soul loss, and witchcraft. Each called for a specific type of treatment.

Many problems and illnesses in tribal life are considered to be the result of offending divine powers by breaking strict taboos or neglecting the observance of proper rituals. Such disrespect is thought to bring about divine retribution of the most painful kind. For example, the withdrawal of game is considered to be a divine retribution for offending divine powers among the Inuit. Similarly, among the tribes of the Southwest, the lack of rain and the withering of vital food crops is commonly understood in terms of an offense against divine forces. For an individual, decline and illness are commonly considered to be punishment for breaking taboos. To correct this condition, the medicine man tries to reconnect the person with the offended transcendent power. The patient is purified by being placed in a prepared space that has been emptied of noxious influences. With songs, prayers, and rituals, sacred power is induced to enter this space and act on the patient. During the ceremony, the patient is often identified with the power. This identification with sacredness, which is at the heart of tribal healing, has been ignored and forgotten in our own scientific medicine.

North American tribal societies also believe that illness results from the intrusion of objects or spirits into the body. Doctors attempt to cure these pathological intrusions by sucking them out. Using a sucking tube or his mouth, with the aid of prayers, songs, and his guardian spirits, the doctor sucks out the offending object or spirit and banishes it. The object may be in the form of a noxious worm or insect, a bit of fluff, or a small stone. Sometimes it can be seen only by the doctor. This form of healing is widespread; in

North America it was especially prominent among the Ojibway.

Soul loss is another major cause of illness. In this syndrome the illness is caused by the soul, or one of several souls, becoming separated from the body or possessed by malevolent powers. It may even be abducted to the land of the dead. The patient feels heavy with loss of interest and vitality in life. Doctors seek to cure soul loss by enticing the soul back into the body with prayers and rituals. If this does not suffice, the shaman enters into deep trance and, with the help of his allies, goes forth into the other world to recapture the lost soul and bring it back. This kind of soul retrieval was found in North America as part of Shoshoni and Northwest Coast culture until recent times. It may have been more widespread in the past.

Finally, witchcraft is considered to be a common cause of illness in North America and throughout the traditional tribal world. Witches, who are commonly associated with incest and believed to be able to travel at night as were-animals, are said to cause illness by projecting toxic substances into the victim's body, a practice sometimes called bean-shooting. Medicine men and shamans seek to combat witchcraft illness by seeing inwardly the identity of the witch and turning the evil power back on him or her, freeing the victim. It is believed that medicine men sometimes become witches when their healing powers have waned because of malice or need for goods and power. For this reason medicine men are often feared as well as respected and admired.[2]

There is a suggestion that the causes of illness in tribal life—object and spirit intrusion, soul loss, taboo violation, and witchcraft—can be equated with our own psychiatric categories of dissociative reaction, depression, compulsive disorder, and paranoia, respectively.

VARIATIONS IN HEALING PRACTICES AMONG NATIVE AMERICAN HEALERS

The Far North

The complex of traditional shamanism was always strongest in areas nearest the Siberian homeland. The Eskimo peoples of the Far North recognized a great goddess, Sedna, who controlled the sea creatures on which their lives depended. Whenever hunting was bad and famine threatened, it was believed that some taboo from

Sedna had been broken. The shaman was called on to send his soul out-of-the-body across the sea to the great whirlpool that was the entrance to Sedna's home. The shaman would then soothe Sedna by gently cleaning and combing her long black hair. She would relent and tell him why the sea creatures had not been released and what the Eskimo people must do to regain her favor.[3] This communal healing ritual was revered as one of the greatest feats of healing known to the tribal world.

The Northwest Coast

In North America the greatest degree of shamanic differentiation occurred on the Northwest Coast among the Tlingit. The Tlingit shaman was wild in appearance with uncut, unkempt hair, reaching to the ground, and necklaces of animal bones or claws around his neck. Decked out with animal hides, drum, rattle, and animal masks, he became the very personification of otherworldly power. His position was hereditary, but receiving his inheritance depended on his ability to attract guardian spirits who would help him perform amazing feats. He needed several guardian spirits to fulfill all his functions. An aspiring candidate had to spend long periods in isolation, fasting and purging himself, never washing or combing his hair, to acquire the necessary spirits. The spirits then taught him songs to summon them to do his bidding in the future.

If the cause of the disease was a lost or abducted soul, the Tlingit shaman, unlike his Eskimo and Siberian counterparts, did not make intense journeys into another world. He hunted for the soul in the surrounding woods with the help of assistants. They carried soul catchers, small bone instruments with open mouths at both ends, with which they caught the fugitive soul, brought it back, and blew it into the patient's body.[4]

The Plains

The greatest transpersonal ritual in North America, the vision quest, is most closely associated with the Plains Indians. It was found in many variations, however, in the eastern woodlands, the Great Plains, the Arctic and subarctic, and all the way to the Northwest Coast and California. Sometimes it was a boy's puberty ritual practiced only in adolescence (Winnebago and Central Algonquin); sometimes it was continued from puberty all through life (Plateau, Salish). In the central Great Plains area, it was mature men only who sought the vision (Arapaho, Gros Ventre).[4] Only in the South and the Southwest, where influences from Mexican civilization had been strong, did the vision quest lose its primacy.

The vision quest still is the predominant Native American method of establishing a direct link to the spirit world. It is also the basis for most healing rituals, especially among the peoples of the Plains. One Teton Sioux man expressed his understanding this way: "It is a general belief of the Indians that after a man dies his spirit is somewhere on the earth or in the skies, we do not know exactly where, but we believe that the spirit still lives. So it is with Wakan Tanka. We believe that his spirit is everywhere, yet he is to us as the spirits of our friends whose voices we cannot hear."[5] (*Wakan Tanka* means Great Spirit.)

The vision quest varies from group to group, but most often it involves isolation on a sacred mountain without food or water for 4 days and nights. Even then there is no certainty that a vision will come, but if it does, it becomes a guide for life. The vision might be of a small insignificant creature such as a mouse or an insect, or it might consist of a powerful medicine animal such as a wolf or a bear. Ordinarily people are content with small visions, but a medicine man needs powerful helpers.

The Lakota medicine man had to be able to see what caused the patient's illness and remove it. He would prepare by fasting and praying. Then he would appear in his full regalia, sometimes with an animal mask with the animal's hide thrown over his shoulders; a bear's head and hide are especially powerful. He would sing his special medicine songs and stroke the patient with feathers or magical objects until he saw the pathogenic object. Then he would quickly put his lips to that spot and suck it out. He would put the object in a bowl or wrap it up and hurry it away. The patient then confidently expected to improve. One medicine man said he could cure just by singing and concentrating but that the patient needs to see an object. It appears, therefore, that a healing ritual must include both the concrete and the transpersonal to be complete.[7]

The Plains Indians, such as the Lakota Sioux, also have a powerful communal ritual in the sun dance. Here, as in the vision quest, the greatest importance is attached to the individual experience of the dancers. In addition to the rigorous fasting and dancing, there is the intense pain of wooden pegs piercing the flesh of the dancer's chest and attached by strong cord to the central pole. As the dancer goes through the hot day without food or comfort of any kind and as the pegs tear through his flesh, the dancer is in ecstatic union with his sun father who represents Wakan, the spirit power that inheres in the world.[6]

The Northeast Woodlands

In the Northeast Woodlands among the Algonkian-speaking people, there was a wide range of healing modalities. Among the Ojibway, who inhabited the Great Lakes region, many doctors specialized in herbal cures, using plant remedies that were handed down through the generations. There was a special healing society called the Midewiwin, which had as one of its main functions the safeguarding of this extensive plant lore.[8] When the herbal cures failed, however, there were medicine men who sucked out the offending object or spirit, such as previously described for the Plains tribes.[5]

At the top of the healing hierarchy were the true shamans. Their diagnostic and curative powers were manifested by the shaking tent, a trance ritual that called on the shaman's spirit helpers to produce amazing effects. The shaman, bound and naked, was closed inside a strong, well-grounded tent. Loud sounds such as wind and running water would come from the tent, and it would begin to sway rhythmically back and forth. Various animals would be seen and heard. The shaman, with the aid of his spirit helpers, then answered questions about healing, witchcraft, and matters of tribal welfare. Finally, he crawled from the tent, unbound but exhausted.[9]

The Southeast

In the southern part of North America, as the distance from the Bering Straits grew greater, the shamanic influence became weaker, and a healing system based on knowledge rather than trance ceremonies was more prevalent. Curing societies and herbal medications increased in importance. The Cherokee, whose historic country was North Carolina, Georgia, and Tennessee, were a prime example. They were experts in plant healing. One of their early leaders, Sequoyah, had developed a written form for their language so that they were able to record in notebooks all the herbal lore handed down from generation to generation. The notebooks also contained exact formulas and other rituals to be performed when the herbal medicines were given.

About 400 specific plant remedies were recorded. For instance, the bark of the wild hydrangea was used for stomachache. It could also be used to make an antiemetic for children or be made into a poultice for sore muscles. A tea brewed from the black-eyed Susan was curative for dropsy or could be used as a poultice for sores or snakebite. The Cherokee doctors also had other physical cures such as vapor baths, massages, sucking, scarification, and induced emesis, but there was always a proper herbal formula to connect the physical herbal cure to its supernatural origin.[10]

The Southwest

The Pueblo Indians, including the Hopi, the Zuni, and the Rio Grande Pueblos, live in small adobe villages (pueblos) in northern Arizona and New Mexico and cope with the arid conditions through intensive farming. Many of their rituals, besides being for healing, are devoted to producing enough rain to nourish the corn. They are known for their beautiful pottery and their great plaza dances put on by secret societies based in the *kivas*, which are underground chambers for ritual use. Much of this culture is influenced by the great Mexican civilization to the south; here again, shamanic influence is weak. The secret rites are presided over by the elders, who have absolute authority; although trance dancing is not predominant, the kiva rites are so secret that they have seldom been seen or described by outsiders. The Zuni are representative of this group.

The symbolism at the heart of the Zuni curing societies, connecting them in one vast system, centers on the six beast gods who guard the six directions, bring in the healing power, and protect the secret rites, including the *katchina* (or *koko*) dances. These six gods are generally described as the mountain lion of the north, the bear of the west, the badger of the south, the white wolf of the east, the eagle of the empyrean, and the mole of the underworld. All the curing societies derive their power from these six gods, and all their members have at one time been severely ill, close to death, from natural or supernatural causes. All have been protected and restored to health by these beast gods.

In the Zuni system, disease is most often caused by a pathogenic object manipulated by a witch. The patient must go to a sucking doctor. After he has been cured, the patient must present himself at the next meeting of his doctor's curing society. He is then initiated into that society as a life member. The initiation consists of singing sacred songs, invoking the beast gods, using various rituals to further extract the disease, and painting the initiate as an animal, most often the bear. Sometime during the ceremony, the initiate dies and is brought back to life as a full-fledged member.[11]

CONCLUSION

The spiritual practices of Native North America have carried the burden of tribal and individual healing for centuries. It is the spiritual attitude of devotion and submission to a higher power in the face of illness and death that may be the most effective medicine for healing.

In modern psychology, Carl Jung recognized the value of such an attitude and realized its importance for Europeans and Euro-Americans as well as Native Americans and other tribal people (see Chapter 5). As part of his analytical psychology, Jung developed a technique of active imagination, which is close to a modern version of the vision quest. Instead of the forceful methods of isolation, deprivation, and self-inflicted pain used by the Plains Indians to induce vision states, Jung recommended a quieter and more meditative way of immobilizing all outer-directed ego activity: First the mind is stilled; then a spontaneous image is allowed to enter the field of inner awareness. This image is regarded with serious open-minded attention and allowed to play itself out spontaneously. Afterward, some record must be made of this occurrence: a drawing, a narrative, or some dramatic action. Finally, this experience must be incorporated into everyday life.

In our scientific medical system, there is an enormous emphasis on technology and a demand for the quick and complete cure it sometimes brings. But there is a darker side to this technology. If one has listened, as I have, to patients telling their stories of bleak inhuman encounters with medical supermachines and their technicians, one must realize that this process, effective as it often is, may produce an alienating fearfulness that defeats the larger purpose of mind–body healing. A balance between technical, secular knowledge and spiritual power seems to be the desired goal. Western medicine has pioneered one-half of that balance, and Native Americans, as well as other tribal people, have developed the other half. Should some harmony and cooperation come about between the two sides, a measure of true holistic healing will have been achieved.

Native American healing, as it has been presented here, does much to forward the goal of holism. The shamanism of the North with its deep trance states and its strenuous journeys for soul retrieval, depends on a highly developed experience of another world. This experience is something most people have long forgotten and can perceive now only as a remote phenomenon. In a softer version, however, such as a vision quest, it is more familiar and accessible. Here we may find a meeting place for the two concepts of curing and healing.

I offer in closing an example of a spontaneous vision I had while on the Navajo reservation near Monument Valley, Colorado. It incorporates the sense of harmony that balances body, mind, and soul. I was on the top of a small rise looking toward the west, where the sun was setting in a big red ball. But between where I stood and the horizon, there was a great thunderstorm, and dark clouds were just above the setting sun. As I watched, a great branching streak of lightning flashed from the clouds across the red face of the sun. It was a breathtaking sight, and in the next moment an inner vision overlaid that outer sight. Two great snakes leaped across the red face of the sun crossing each other. They came together in one brief instant and then faded into that greater glory. It was the vision of a sacred union between the earth, the snakes, and the Father Sun. It carried the feeling and meaning of a full life lived against the background of the great spirit, once and forever, and it filled me with joy.

NOTES

1. Vogel, V. J. (1973). *American Indian medicine.* Norman, OK: University of Oklahoma Press.

2. Sandner, D. (1979). *Navaho symbols of healing* (pp. 247–248). New York: Harcourt Brace Jovanovich.

3. Woodhead, H. (Ed.). (1992). *The spirit world* (pp. 68–70). Alexandria, VA: Time-Life.

4. Benedict, R. (1922). The vision quest in Plains culture. *American Anthropologist, 24,* 1–23.

5. Woodhead, *Spirit world,* p. 125.

6. Lewis, T. H. (1990). *The medicine men: Oglala Sioux ceremony and healing.* Lincoln: University of Nebraska Press.

7. Woodhead, *Spirit world,* pp. 136–141.

8. Hultkrantz, A. (1992). *Shamanic healing and ritual drama* (pp. 46–47). New York: Crossroad.

9. Ibid., pp. 38–39.

10. Woodhead, *Spirit world*, pp. 104–105.

11. Bunzel, R. (1932). *Zuni ceremonialism* (p. 20). Albuquerque: University of New Mexico Press.

CHAPTER 16

Aging and Adult Spiritual Development: A Transpersonal View of the Life Cycle Through Fairy Tales

ALLAN B. CHINEN

BECAUSE OF THE CONTRIBUTIONS of Sigmund Freud, Jean Piaget, John Bowlby, and Lawrence Kohlberg, psychiatry recognizes the importance of emotional and cognitive development in childhood. Carl Jung, Erik Erikson, George Vaillant, and Daniel Levinson emphasized that development continues throughout adulthood. Jung argued that adult development is spiritual in nature, and the transpersonal theme has become increasingly prominent with the work of David Gutmann, James Fowler, Rick Moody, John Kotre, L. Eugene Thomas, Harold Koenig, and Zalman Schachter-Shalomi, among others.

Most religions stress the importance of spiritual development in the adult years. Because different traditions describe divergent spiritual tasks, it is difficult to formulate a cross-culturally valid model of adult transpersonal development. For this task, aid comes from an unexpected source: folk fairy tales from around the world. Although most familiar stories like "Cinderella" are about children or adolescents, a large number feature protagonists in middle and

155

later life. These "middle and elder tales" are similar across the world and present a cross-cultural, ecumenical perspective on the spiritual tasks of adult development.[1,2]

SETTLING DOWN AND THE LOSS OF MAGIC

A tale from Wales, "The Man Who Married a Fairy," highlights the transpersonal dimension of moving from youth to adult life:

> Once upon a time, a young man came upon a group of fairies dancing in a circle. One fairy was so beautiful, he fell in love with her, seized her, and ran off. He asked her to marry him, and she agreed on two conditions: he had to discover her name, and never strike her with iron. After much trial, he learned her name, married her, and they began a family. One day, the husband struggled to bridle an unruly horse. In anger, he threw the iron bit at the animal but the bridle accidentally hit his wife. She vanished, leaving her husband and children heartbroken.

Stories similar to this Welsh tale can be found around the world. Examples include "The Stork Wife" from Japan and "Never Ask Me About My Family" from the Kikuyu of Africa, among others. When all these tales are compared, two cross-cultural motifs become evident. First, a young man or woman marries a magical or supernatural being. Second, because of a small human fault, the man or woman loses the magical spouse. These recurrent motifs reflect major developmental tasks of adolescence. The fact that the protagonist is young and marries indicates that the story is about adolescence and early adulthood. The magical or supernatural spouse, in turn, symbolizes youth's encounter with numinous, transpersonal, or divine experiences.[3] Most indigenous cultures recognize the importance of these adolescent experiences by having initiation ceremonies, such as Native American vision quests. In modern Western society, aside from a few remaining traditional rites like the Bar Mitzvah, there are no formal ways of recognizing or fostering adolescent spiritual experiences. For most youth, therefore, transpersonal inspiration takes secular forms like romantic love, ideological idealism, use of "mind-expanding" drugs, or social activism.[4] Adolescent inspirations arise from two psychological developments: sexual maturation, which intensifies emotional experience, and the advent of "formal operations," or the ability to think abstractly in universal, idealistic terms.

The second theme in these stories is the loss of the magical spouse, some time after marriage. This loss reflects the normal diminishment of transpersonal concerns as adolescents move into adult life and assume secular responsibilities like earning a living or raising children. In these fairy tales, the loss of magic usually comes from some small human fault, like becoming angry in the Welsh tale. This motif emphasizes that the loss of numinous inspiration is not due to a moral failure but simply to the course of normal human life; that is, the loss is a normal development. Idealistic young social reformers adopt more conventional corporate roles to support their families; young devotees of a guru turn away from mystical practices in maturity; and the numinous romances of youth fade into ordinary marriages—or divorces.

MIDLIFE AND THE DEMONIC

A story from Japan, "The Bonesetter," highlights the spiritual tasks of midlife:

Once upon a time, there lived a famous warrior who was also a physician. His wife was equally well-known for her intelligence and accomplishments. One evening, she went to the outhouse and when she lifted her robe, a hairy hand touched her buttocks. She was indignant and cried out, "Try that again, and you'll regret it!" The next evening, when the wife went to the outhouse, she took a sword with her. As she lifted her robe, a hairy hand touched her on the buttocks. She raised her sword and chopped off the hand. The molester screamed and fled into the moonlight. The wife picked up the hand and found that it was green, with webbing between the fingers. She showed the hand to her husband, who guessed that it was the hand of a water demon. That night, the demon knocked at the window and asked for its hand back. The husband reached over to his weapons and pulled on the string of his bow as a warning. The demon fled. The next night, the demon returned and pleaded for its hand. The husband plucked his bowstring again and the demon fled. The third night, the demon begged once more for its hand and the husband asked why the demon wanted it, since it was shriveled up. The creature explained that water demons knew all the secrets of healing, so that he could rejoin the dead hand to his arm. So the husband and wife offered to give the demon his hand if he told them his secrets of healing. The demon agreed and taught the husband and wife. The next morning, the husband and wife found two beautiful fish lying on their porch, a gift from the water demon. From that day on, the couple practiced their healing arts, bringing comfort and health to the sick. And so they lived in prosperity, honor, and happiness the rest of their days.

The protagonists of this tale are married already, in contrast to the young man in the first Welsh tale. The story thus deals with the middle period of life, adulthood, rather than with youth. A large number of stories about adulthood portray similar dramas, like "Solomon's Advice" from Italy, "The Godfather" from Germany, and "The Angry Wife" from Russia. These tales highlight three cross-cultural themes. First is the encounter with something demonic or evil: the dark side of life, or the underworld. Second, the encounter does not involve a heroic battle in which the dark side is defeated, as occurs in youth tales. The focus is on negotiating or reconciling with the demonic. The third theme is that healing or some other great boon is the result of the demonic experience.

In real life, the encounter with the underworld often takes the form of illness, depression, death, or tragedy: when "bad things happen to good people." At midlife, old traumas that have been long repressed or ignored often resurface.[5,6] At this time the optimistic, heroic ambitions of youth collapse and the proverbial midlife crisis often results, compelling individuals to question the very meaning of life. The result of the dark encounter is healing, however, as the Japanese fairy tale makes clear. The healing result of a demonic experience reflects ancient shamanic tradition (see Chapter 10). In shamanic experience, the individual descends to the underworld, struggles with demonic forces, and returns with the power to heal.

Significantly, many shamans are initiated at midlife. An example dramatizes this process: Emanuel Swedenborg was an eminent seventeenth-century Swedish scientist and engineer. He devoted his youth to rational, secular pursuits, ignoring matters of soul and spirit as is normal in early adult life. At 55 years of age, Swedenborg began having troubling dreams and visions, filled with horrifying images of demons, war, murder, and cannibalism, followed by visions of paradise, ecstatic love, and compassion. He had encountered the dark and the light aspects of the divine. Moved by his dreams and visions, Swedenborg abandoned his scientific and administrative posts and began a highly productive new period in his life, elaborating a mystical philosophy. Jung experienced a similar midlife encounter with the underworld (see Chapter 5).

ELDER TALES

An Italian tale called "The Shining Fish" highlights the spiritual tasks of old age:

Once upon a time, an old man and his wife lived in a house over-looking the sea. In youth, the man was a fisherman, but in old age he could only gather fallen wood in the forest, selling it for kin-dling. He and his wife had three sons who became fishermen, but each son drowned at sea in storms. One day in the forest, the old man met a stranger with a long white beard. The stranger said he knew of the old man's hard life, gave the old man a small leather bag, and vanished. The purse was filled with gold! The old man threw away his wood and hurried home. Along the way, he wor-ried that his wife would squander the fortune and decided not to tell her about it, so he hid the money under a pile of manure. The next day, the old man awoke to find that his wife had unknow-ingly sold the manure to obtain money for food. There was no manure left—and no gold.

The old man went to work in the forest and met the stranger again. The stranger gave him another purse filled with gold, and the old man rushed homeward. Along the way he feared his wife would waste the money and decided to say nothing to her. He hid the gold under ashes in the fireplace. The next day he awoke to find that his wife had sold the ashes as fertilizer to gain money for food. The heartbroken old man went back to work in the for-est and met the stranger a third time. The stranger gave the old man a large bag filled with live frogs and told him to sell the frogs and buy one large fish. Then the stranger vanished. The old man sold his frogs in the village and was tempted to buy many things at the market. But he decided to follow the stranger's instructions and bought the largest fish he could find. He returned home late in the evening, so he hung it outside his house from the roof. That night it stormed, and the old man and woman prayed for any fishermen caught at sea. In the middle of the night, a group of young fishermen pounded on the door and thanked the old man for saving their lives. They explained that they were caught at sea by the storm and did not know which way to row until the old man put out a light for them. The old man then saw that the fish he hung from his roof was shining with such a great light it could be seen for miles around. From then on, each evening, the old man hung out the shining fish to guide the young fishermen home, and they shared their catch with him. So he and his wife lived in honor and prosperity the rest of their days.

This Italian tale is typical of "elder stories" that feature protagonists specifically called "old." Tales similar to "The Shining Fish" include "The Six Statues" from Japan, "The Fishermen and the Genie" from Arabia, and "The Straw Ox" from Russia, among others. The present tale illustrates several cross-cultural themes found in elder stories. The tale opens with an old man and his wife living in poverty. This theme is present in elder tales around the world and dramatizes the multiple losses of old age. To make the theme even more poignant, the story says that the couple's children all died, perhaps the deepest loss an adult can suffer. Yet in this dismal situation, the old man meets a stranger who gives him a bag of gold. Magic returns unexpectedly, and the story goes on to reveal the nature of this "magic." The old man keeps the treasure for himself and does not tell his wife. He acts out of suspicion and greed and loses the treasure, not once but twice, to emphasize the point: Numinous inspirations in later life are not for personal, material gain. The stranger reappears with a third gift and advises the old man to buy the largest fish available at the market. The injunction is odd. A single large fish is hardly practical; dried fish or sausages would be less perishable. The old man nevertheless obeys the stranger, presumably because he knows how poor his own judgment can be. Here the story introduces a major theme in elder tales: self-transcendence, or going beyond the rational ego, to heed a "higher," transpersonal authority. The theme is clear in "An Aged Mother's Sorrow" from Germany, "The Magic Forest" from Yugoslavia, and "The Magic Towel" from Japan, among other elder tales.

Most religions emphasize that such self-transcendence is a major task of old age.[7,8,9,10] Christianity, for example, stresses that later life is a time to prepare for death by turning away from secular concerns and cultivating spiritual virtues. Jewish tradition considers old age a sign of God's blessing and a time for studying the Torah and grasping its deeper wisdom. In ancient China, Confucius described 50 years of age as a turning point, when the individual shifts from material concerns to learning the "mandate of heaven." In India the life cycle was traditionally divided into four distinct phases. The first two involved secular concerns, like earning a living and raising a family. The third phase began at midlife, when an individual saw his "son's sons." The task was to leave the family, become a hermit, and pursue spiritual development through meditation and yoga. Enlightenment,

or self-transcendence, represented the fourth and final stage.
In the story, the old man hangs the fish outside from the rafters.
Symbolically, the old man transcends his greed and offers the fish
to the world. The fish then becomes a beacon that saves the lives
of several young fishermen. So the old man brings magic into the
world, which helps the next generation. He dramatizes what
Erikson called "generativity," or the nurturing of the younger
generation: one's own children, students, or employees. The
story, however, adds a crucial point: Generativity is a spiritual
development.[11] The story is Italian and uses a traditional symbol
of Christ—the fish—to emphasize the spiritual theme. In effect,
the old man mediates between the material world and the divine
realm.

Such mediation is the traditional role of elders in indigenous cultures, from the !Kung in Africa to the Micronesians of the Pacific
and the Kirghiz of Afghanistan.[12,13,14] Even in secular modern Western culture, the turn toward spiritual development in old age
occurs. Alfred North Whitehead provides a good example. In adolescence, Whitehead was intensely interested in religious questions, but he put them aside in early adulthood, when he embarked
on a career in mathematics, writing the *Principia Mathematica* with
Bertrand Russell. Whitehead had a long, illustrious, secular career
as a mathematician and university administrator, but when he
retired from his academic post in Britain, he began writing essays
on metaphysics and theology, at a time when both were in ill-
repute. Like the old man buying a large fish and hanging it from
his roof, Whitehead did something that appeared crazy or irrational. Yet the result was a boon to a new generation of theologians
and philosophers.

Many prominent scientists, from Sir Isaac Newton to Nobel laureates Jacob Monod and Jonas Salk, have shown a similar shift
from rigorous science to spiritual concerns in later life. Numerous
writers, artists, and musicians have exhibited a similar course of
development, like Tolstoy, Beethoven, Rembrandt, Michelangelo,
Donatello, Titian, El Greco, and Turner.[15,16] Systematic studies have
confirmed that men and women move toward humanitarian,
moral, and religious issues with age.[17,18,19] These transpersonal concerns usually take a more personal form, as private reflections at
home, for instance, rather than public attendance at church or synagogue. The transpersonal shift also correlates with better morale
and healthier psychological adjustment.[20,21]

CLINICAL APPLICATIONS

The cross-cultural scheme of adult spiritual development portrayed by fairy tales has important clinical implications, because transpersonal issues change with age. In adolescence and early adulthood, the challenge is to accept, validate, experience, and then leave behind transpersonal inspirations. As many have commented, when adolescents do not have a spiritual context for their numinous experiences, they often go astray, using drugs, for example. On the other hand, it is often difficult to exchange spiritual experiences for practical, worldly realities. The case of Arthur illustrates the latter.

A graduate student in philosophy, Arthur came to therapy for depression. He had meditated for several years and had several numinous, ecstatic experiences. He preferred to discuss these inspiring episodes and their meaning to him rather than exploring the reasons for his depression or challenging a major factor behind it, namely, his social anxiety and withdrawal. Therapy focused on practical issues, therefore, like how to meet people and manage his anxiety. As Arthur's focus shifted away from his ecstatic experiences and toward relationships and work, his depression steadily improved. Although Arthur experienced something of a loss of magic, just as fairy tales depict, he entered more fully into the human world.

At midlife, the developmental issues shift. The task here is to focus on the dark side of life: the complement to the adolescent focus on idealism and inspiration. The case of Paul, an Episcopal priest, highlights the issue. Paul came to therapy in his late 30s for depression, feeling "burnt-out" in his ministry. He had wanted to be a priest since he was a child and had found the work deeply rewarding in the first years after his ordination. Over the years, however, he found himself increasingly dissatisfied with his vocation. Two major issues emerged in therapy: his problems with anger and his reactions to his deceased alcoholic father. Paul rarely expressed anger and was somewhat frightened as he found himself more and more irritable with people. At the same time he came to terms with his anger, pain, and shame about his father from years before. In struggling with many intense and distressing feelings Paul experienced an encounter with the underworld as depicted in fairy tales of midlife. Through the process, however, Paul deepened and renewed his spiritual vocation. He found himself more patient and compassionate in his ministry and experienced new meaning in this work.

In the last third of life, the tasks of transpersonal development again shift. The focus now is explicitly spiritual, not so much resolving past issues and meeting personal needs but transcending the ego. The case of Robert illustrates the process. Robert came to therapy in his 60s, distressed by his wife's emotional withdrawal from him. They had been happily married for some 20 years previously, but she became increasingly involved in leading women's groups and complained that Robert was too demanding. Robert had been in therapy many years earlier and so recognized to some extent that his frustrations with his wife echoed a distressed childhood, disrupted by his family's escape from Nazi Germany. His parents were demoralized by the experience, having lost most of their relatives in the Holocaust.

As an adolescent, Robert had to assume the enormous responsibility of helping his family settle in America. Consequently, he had not had much experience of being taken care of. In therapy, Robert did not focus on the traumas of his past but rather on the new experiences he began to have while meditating and practicing yoga. He had extraordinary ecstatic episodes and out-of-body experiences. Robert began to see these events in shamanic terms, as a crossing between worlds, between the natural and spiritual realms. He then realized that this "crossing" had been his role throughout his life, first helping his family settle in America and learning a new culture, and later as a scientific researcher, developing interdisciplinary projects.

Robert began writing essays concerning science and spirituality, which he published in various scientific journals. Significantly, as he found profound inner fulfillment in his work, Robert's wife became more emotionally open and expressive toward him. Robert thus embarked on a fruitful new phase of this life. What is striking about Robert's experience is how he transcended past traumas, reframing them in a spiritual context. He did not deny or avoid these traumas as is normal in youth, nor did he plunge into them as is typical of midlife. Instead he integrated these painful events in a wider, deeper way.

Age itself does not determine the tasks of transpersonal development, because young people facing death grapple with issues that usually arise in the last third of life. Individuals with AIDS, for example, often struggle with explicitly spiritual issues. The case of Tim highlights the point. Tim was a gay man, deeply tormented by his sexual orientation. When he was diagnosed with AIDS, Tim was profoundly distressed by self-blame and self-loathing. In therapy he was able to link his distress to being raised in a fundamental Protestant sect and being told as a child that he had to take care of other people, not himself. These insights did not alleviate his sense of guilt and sin, however. Then in one session, he fell silent for a long period; he later described his experience as being filled with the Holy Spirit.

After this transformative episode, Tim no longer felt guilt or self-blame but could accept himself and his condition. Psychologically Tim experienced an accelerated developmental process, encountering the underworld, as is the task of midlife, and then transcending the ego to enter an explicitly spiritual domain, as is typical of later life.

CONCLUSION

Traditional fairy tales about adults, gathered from around the world, provide rich, cross-culturally valid insights about transpersonal development in the adult years. The stories contain four important lessons for transpersonal psychiatry. First, spiritual experiences and concerns are normal in human life. They often occur at predictable stages, and they are not rare. Second, transpersonal experiences correlate with greater maturity in adulthood, contradicting the traditional psychiatric belief that religious concerns reflect immature or neurotic wish-fulfillment. Third, in the course of normal adult development, individuals shift from a secular, materialistic, practical, rational perspective, to a spiritual, transcendent, and even mystical viewpoint. Finally, the life cycle approach has important clinical implications, because transpersonal experiences play different roles at different stages of adult life.

NOTES

1. Chinen, A. (1989). *In the ever after: Fairy tales and the second half of life*. Wilmette, IL: Chiron.

2. Chinen, A. (1992). *Once upon a midlife: Classic stories and mythic tales to illuminate the middle years*. Los Angeles: Tarcher.

3. Magen, Z., & Aharoni, R. (1991). Adolescents' contributing toward others: Relationship to positive experiences and transpersonal commitment. *Journal of Humanistic Psychology, 31*, 126–143.

4. Bernstein, J. (1987). The decline of rites of passage in our culture: The impact on masculine individuation. In L. Mahdi, L. Carus, S. Foster, & M. Little (Eds.), *Betwixt and between: Patterns of masculine and feminine initiation.* LaSalle, IL: Open Court.

5. Vaillant, G. (1977). *Adaptation to life: How the best and brightest came of age.* Boston: Little, Brown.

6. Levinson, D., Darrow, C., Klein, E., Levinson, M., & McKee, B. (1978). *The seasons of a man's life.* New York: Ballantine Books.

7. Isenberg, S. (1992). Aging in Judaism: "Crown of glory" and "days of sorrow." In T. Cole, D. Van Tassel, & R. Kastenbaum (Eds.), *Handbook of the humanities and aging.* New York: Springer.

8. Kakar, S. (1979). Setting the stage: The traditional Hindu view and the psychology of Erik H. Erikson. In S. Kakar (Ed.), *Identity and adulthood.* Delhi: Oxford University Press.

9. Wei-ming, T. (1978). The Confucian perception of adulthood. In E. Erickson (Ed.), *Adulthood* (pp. 113–120). New York: Norton.

10. Caligiuri, A. (1980). Maturing in the Lord: Reflections on aging and spiritual life. In *Studies in Formative Spirituality, 1,* 368–378.

11. Rubinstein, R. (1994). Generativity as pragmatic spirituality. In Thomas, L. E., & Eisenhandler, S. (Eds.), *Aging and the religious dimension.* Westport, CT: Auburn House.

12. Gutmann, D. (1987). *Reclaimed powers: Toward a new psychology of men and women in later life.* New York: Basic Books.

13. Shahrani, M. N. (1981). Growing in respect: Aging among the Kirghiz of Afghanistan. In P. Amoss & S. Harrell (Eds.), *Other ways of growing old.* Stanford, CA: Stanford University Press.

14. Biesele, M., & Howell, N. (1981). The old people give you life: Aging among !Kung hunter-gatherers. In P. Amoss & S. Harrell (Eds.), *Other ways of growing old.* Stanford, CA: Stanford University Press.

15. Funk, J. (1982). Beethoven: A transpersonal analysis. *ReVision, 5,* 29–41.

16. Munsterberg, H. (1983). *The crown of life: Artistic creativity in old age.* New York: Harcourt Brace Jovanovich.

17. Fowler, J. W. (1981). *The stages of faith: The psychology of human development and the quest for meaning.* San Francisco: Harper & Row.

18. Haan, N. (1981). Common dimensions of personality: Early adolescence to middle life. In D. Eichorn, J. Clausen, N. Haan, M. Honzik, & P. Mussen (Eds.), *Present and past in middle life.* New York: Academic Press.

19. Tornstam, L. (1994). Gero-transcendence: A theoretical and empirical exploration. In L. E. Thomas & S. Eisenhandler (Eds.), *Aging and the religious dimension.* Westport, CT: Auburn House.

20. Koenig, H. (1990). Research on religion and mental health in later life: A review and commentary. *Journal of Geriatric Psychiatry, 23,* 23–53.

21. Koenig, H. G., Cohen, H. J., Blazer, D. G., Pieper, C., Meador, K. G., Shelp, F., Goli, V., & DiPasquale, B. (1992). Religious coping and depression among elderly, hospitalized medically ill men. *American Journal of Psychiatry, 149,* 1693–1700.

CHAPTER 17

Meditation Research: The State of the Art

ROGER WALSH

There are enough research projects here to keep squadrons
of scientists busy for the next century.

Abraham Maslow

MEDITATION RESEARCH IS A YOUNG but vigorous field. More than 1,500
publications have demonstrated a variety of psychological, physiological, and chemical effects of meditation. Different types of meditation appear to elicit overlapping but distinct effects. The most frequently studied practice has been Transcendental Meditation (TM).
Transpersonal psychiatrists and psychologists have researched meditation hoping to forge a mutually beneficial link between the practices of the consciousness disciplines and the experimental techniques of science; however, the variables examined to date, such as
heart and respiration rate, have often been relatively objective and
gross compared to the subjective and subtle shifts in awareness, emotions, and values that constitute the traditional goals of meditation. It
is hoped that future research will address the relationship between
meditation and these traditional goals of meditative practice.

This chapter is adapted from R. Walsh and F. Vaughan (Eds.), *Paths beyond
ego: The transpersonal vision* (Los Angeles: Tarcher, 1993). Copyright © 1993
by Roger Walsh and Frances Vaughan. Reprinted by permission of The
Putnam Publishing Group/J. P. Tarcher Inc.

PSYCHOLOGICAL EFFECTS

The range of experiences that can emerge during meditation is enormous. Experiences may be pleasant or painful. Intense emotions such as love or anger can alternate with periods of calm and equanimity. Although meditation is not simply a relaxation response, continued meditative practice does lead toward greater calm, positive emotional experience, perceptual sensitivity, and introspective awareness. Advanced meditation experiences include feelings of peace, joy, love, and compassion; insight into the nature of mind; and a variety of transcendent states that can run the gamut of mystical experiences.[1,2]

Enhanced perceptual ability allows insight into psychological processes and habits. One of the initial insights is commonly the realization that one's usual state of mind is out of control, unaware, fantasy-filled, and dreamlike. Classical claims that the untrained mind is like a wild drunken monkey and that taming it is the art of arts and science of sciences soon make sense to the beginning meditator.

To date most knowledge of meditative experiences has come from personal accounts; however, there have been a large number of experimental studies of the effects of meditation on personality, performance, and perception. Intriguing findings include evidence for enhancement of creativity, perceptual sensitivity, empathy, lucid dreaming, self-actualization, self-control, and marital satisfaction.[2,3,4] Studies of TM suggest that it may foster maturation as measured by scales of ego, moral, and cognitive development; intelligence; academic achievement; and self-actualization.[1,5]

A fascinating study of perception examined the Rorschach test responses of Buddhist meditators ranging from beginners to enlightened masters.[2,6] Beginners showed normal response patterns, whereas subjects with greater concentration, rather than reporting the usual images such as animals and people, simply saw the patterns of light and dark on the Rorschach cards. Their minds showed little tendency to elaborate these patterns into organized images, a finding consistent with the claim that concentration focuses the mind and reduces the number of associations.

Further striking findings characterized subjects who had reached the first of the four stages of Buddhist enlightenment. Although their Rorschach responses were not obviously different from those of nonmeditators, these subjects viewed the images they saw as creations of their own mind and were aware of the moment-to-moment process by which their stream of consciousness became organized into images.

The subjects who had reached initial enlightenment displayed evidence of normal conflicts around issues such as dependency, sexuality, and aggression; however, they showed remarkably little defensiveness and reactivity to these conflicts. In other words, they accepted and were unperturbed by their neuroses.

Those few meditators who were at more advanced stages of enlightenment gave reports that were unique in three ways. First, they saw, not only the images, but the ink blot itself, as a projection of mind. Second, they showed no evidence of drive conflicts and appeared free of psychological conflicts. This finding is consistent with claims that psychological suffering can be dramatically reduced in advanced stages of meditation. Third, these masters systematically linked their responses to all 10 cards into an integrated, single theme. The result was a systematic teaching about the nature of human suffering and its alleviation. The meditation masters transformed the Rorschach testing into a teaching for the testers.

PHYSIOLOGICAL EFFECTS

Physiological research began with sporadic investigations of spectacular yogic feats such as altering body temperature and heart rate. When some of these claims proved valid, more systematic investigation was begun. The introduction of better controls led to the recognition that many physiological effects initially assumed to be unique to meditation could be induced by other self-control strategies such as relaxation, biofeedback, or self-hypnosis.[7] For example, initial studies of TM meditators showed a marked reduction in metabolic rate as measured by reduced oxygen consumption, carbon dioxide production, and blood lactate levels, suggesting that meditation leads to a unique hypometabolic state. Subsequent studies confirmed a reduced metabolic rate, but better controls suggested that the effects were not unique to meditation.[2]

The cardiovascular system is clearly affected.[24] During meditation, heart rate drops, and with regular practice, blood pressure also falls. Meditation can therefore be a useful treatment for mild high blood pressure. Some practitioners can increase blood flow to the body periphery, thereby raising the temperature of fingers and toes. Tibetan tumo masters who specialize in this feat are reported to demonstrate their mastery by meditating seminaked in the snows of the Tibetan winter, sometimes competing to see who can dry the greatest number of wet shawls with their body heat. Blood chemistry may also shift.[2,4] Hormone levels may be modified; lactate levels may fall, which is sometimes regarded as a measure of relaxation; and cholesterol may be reduced.

In summary, it is clear that meditation elicits significant physiological effects. Although a few studies of TM have reported distinct patterns of blood flow and hormone levels, overall it is not yet clear to what extent the physiological effects are unique to meditation or common to a variety of self-control methods.

EEG Studies

The most common measure of brain activity during meditation has been electroencephalography (EEG). This measure of cerebral electrical activity is valuable but gross; it is roughly comparable to measuring activity in Chicago by placing a dozen microphones around the city. Although it remains unclear whether there are brain-wave patterns unique to meditation, intriguing findings have emerged. With most meditative practices, the EEG slows and alpha waves (8–13 cycles per second) increase in amount and amplitude. In more advanced practitioners, even greater slowing may occur, and theta patterns (4–7 cycles per second) may appear. These findings are consistent with deep relaxation.

Not only do the brain waves slow, they also may show increasing synchronization or coherence between different cortical areas. Some TM researchers suggest that this effect provides a basis for enhanced creativity and psychological growth.[1] However, it is always difficult in EEG research to extrapolate from brain waves to specific states of mind. It is humbling to realize that greater coherence can also occur in epilepsy and schizophrenia.

Some skeptics have attempted to explain the effects of meditation as merely the result of drowsiness or sleep; however, this explanation fails for several reasons. Although meditators may become drowsy, especially novices, this occurrence is recognized by contemplative traditions as a specific trap: the "defilement of sloth and torpor" is the Buddhists' picturesque description. Second, the experience of nondrowsy meditation is very different from that of sleep. Finally, the EEG pattern of meditation is quite distinct from that of sleep.[4,8]

It is increasingly recognized that the left and right cerebral hemispheres have distinct, although overlapping, functions. Because meditation may reduce left-hemisphere functions such as verbal analysis, it is believed that meditation might involve a reduction of left-hemisphere activity or an activation of the right hemisphere, or both. There is preliminary evidence of some enhanced right-hemisphere skills in meditators such as the ability to remember and discriminate among musical tones. EEG studies suggest, however, that there may be relative left-hemisphere deactivation during the initial few minutes of a sitting but that thereafter both hemispheres seem to be affected equally.[8,9]

Yogis and Zen practitioners may respond differently to sensory stimulation, in manners consistent with their respective methods and goals of practice. Yogis, whose practice involves internal focus and withdrawal of attention from the senses, show little EEG response to repeated noises. Zen monks, whose practice involves open receptivity to all stimuli, show continued EEG responsiveness to a repeated sound rather than habituation to it, as is found in nonmeditators.[4] Although repeated studies have found less clear-cut differences,[8] these findings remain intriguing because the electrophysiological data are consistent with the different goals and experiences of yogic and Zen practitioners. Moreover, the lack of EEG habituation in the Zen monks is consistent with other reports. Continuous freshness of perception is characteristic of both Maslow's self-actualizers and contemplatives who practice Buddhist "mindfulness" or the Christian "sacrament of the present moment."[2,10]

THERAPEUTIC EFFECTS

Research suggests that meditation can be therapeutic for various psychological, psychosomatic, and social disorders. Responsive psychological disorders include anxiety, phobias, posttraumatic stress, muscle tension, insomnia, and mild depression. Regular, long-term meditation seems to reduce both legal and illegal drug use; it has been found to help prisoners by reducing anxiety, aggression, and recidivism. Psychosomatic benefits may include reduction in blood pressure and cholesterol levels and in the severity of asthma, migraine, and chronic pain.[2,3,11]

These therapeutic effects may reflect enhancement of general psychological and physical health. In fact, TM meditators use lower than average amounts of psychiatric and medical care. Meditators in their mid–50s measured 12 years younger than controls on scales of physical aging.[12] Of course, it is unclear how much of this superior general health is due to meditation and how much is due to associated factors such as self-selection, prior good health, and a healthy lifestyle.

One well-controlled study clearly demonstrated dramatic effects on the aged. Nursing-home residents of an average age of 81 who learned TM performed better on multiple measures of learning and mental health than did residents taught relaxation, given other mental training, or left untreated. Most striking, however, was the fact that after 3 years all the meditators were alive, whereas only 63% of the untreated residents survived.[1] For thousands of years, yogis have claimed that contemplative practices increase longevity, a claim that can no longer be ignored.

The most startling research claim is that meditators can exert "action-at-a-distance." TM researchers see reality as a field of consciousness; they argue, therefore, that minds are interconnected and that meditation groups of sufficient size can influence non-meditating individuals and society at large. Several studies have reported that TM groups have beneficially influenced social problems. These benefits included reduced rates of crime, violent death, traffic accidents, and terrorism. When a group meditated in the Middle East, the intensity of conflict in Lebanon decreased.[13]

These findings are certainly dramatic; however, most of this and other research on TM has been conducted by members of the TM organization. Because unconscious biases can easily affect research findings, studies by researchers independent of the TM organization are essential. If the findings of action-at-a-distance are independently and reliably confirmed, the implications—for everything from philosophy and physics to peace and politics—will be remarkable.

COMPLICATIONS

A general principle in psychiatry states that any therapy powerful enough to be helpful is also powerful enough to be harmful. Although the principle seems to hold true for meditation, serious casualties are rare. Meditators may experience psychological difficulties at any stage; however, problems are more frequent in beginners, those doing intense practice without adequate supervision, and people with preexisting psychopathology. Some difficult experiences may ultimately prove to be cathartic and beneficial, a process TM calls "unstressing."

The range of difficulties is wide, including emotional lability with episodes of anxiety, agitation, depression, and euphoria. Psychological conflicts may surface, and somatic symptoms such as muscle or gastrointestinal spasms may appear. Meditators may ruminate obsessively or be confronted by painful existential questions. On rare occasions, defenses may be overwhelmed and result in a psychotic break, especially in those with a history of previous psychosis.[14] Advanced practitioners may also experience difficulties, although these are more likely to be subtle and to involve existential or spiritual concerns.[14,15]

Finally, dramatic and temporarily disabling symptoms may arise as a normal part of the process of development through the stages of meditation, a phenomenon now appropriately understood as an experience best diagnosed by the new V code in DSM-IV for nonpathological spiritual experience.

Given that meditation can produce both benefits and difficulties, can we predict which people will be affected in which way? Studies of TM suggest that those who persist successfully share certain traits. They are more interested in internal experiences, are more open to unusual ones, and feel they have strong self-control. They may be less emotionally labile than others and possess high concentration and alpha-wave activity. They appear to be less psychologically disturbed and more open to recognizing and acknowledging unfavorable personal characteristics. The results of future research may allow the identification of people who will respond optimally, those at risk for negative effects, and means of enhancing favorable responses.

CONCLUSION

Research has demonstrated that meditation may produce a large number of effects and therapeutic benefits. Some experimental designs and control groups have been less than ideal, however. Most meditation subjects have been beginners by traditional standards. It is often unclear whether meditation is more effective for clinical disorders than other self-regulation strategies such as relaxation training, biofeedback, and self-hypnosis. On the other hand, meditators often report that their practice is more meaningful, more enjoyable, and easier to continue than other approaches and that it fosters an interest in self-exploration.[2,10]

Exactly how meditation produces its many effects remains unclear. Many mechanisms have been suggested. Possible physiological processes include lowered arousal and increased hemispheric synchronization. Possible psychological mechanisms include relaxation, desensitization, dehypnosis, and development of self-control skills, insight, and self-understanding.[2] Perhaps the most encompassing explanation is the classic one: that meditation fosters psychological development.[6]

Although much has been learned experimentally about meditation, research is still in its early stages. As yet relatively little can be said about the relationships between the traditional goals of meditation and experimental measures. More attention has been given to heart rate than to heart opening. Future research ought to pay attention to advanced practitioners and their transpersonal goals such as enhanced concentration, ethics, love, compassion, generosity, wisdom, and service.[16] The vision of a mutually enriching bridge between meditation and science remains only partly realized, but it also remains worth seeking.[16]

NOTES

1. Alexander, C. (1991). Growth of higher stages of consciousness. In C. Alexander & E. Langer (Eds.), *Higher stages of human development*. New York: Oxford University Press.

2. Shapiro, D., & Walsh, R. (1984). *Meditation: Classic and contemporary perspectives*. Hawthorne, New York: Aldine de Gruyter.

3. Kwee, M. (Ed.). (1990). *Psychotherapy, meditation and health*. London: East-West.

4. Murphy, M., & Donovan, S. (1988). *The physical and psychological effects of meditation*. San Rafael, CA: Esalen Institute.

5. Alexander, C., Rainforth, M., & Gelderloos, P. (1992). Transcendental meditation, self actualization and psychological health: A conceptual overview and statistical meta-analysis. *Journal of Social Behavior and Personality, 6,* 189–247.

6. Wilber, K., Engler, J., & Brown, D. (Eds.). (1986). *Transformations of consciousness: Conventional and contemplative perspectives on development*. Boston: New Science Library/Shambhala.

7. Shapiro, D. (1982). Comparison of meditation with other self-control strategies: Biofeedback, hypnosis, progressive relaxation. *American Journal of Psychiatry, 139,* 267–274.

8. West, M. (Ed.). (1987). *The psychology of meditation.* Oxford, England: Clarenden Press.

9. Earle, J. (1981). Cerebral laterality and meditation. *Journal of Transpersonal Psychology, 13,* 155–173.

10. Walsh, R., & Vaughan, F. (Eds.). (1993). *Paths beyond ego: The transpersonal vision.* Los Angeles: Tarcher.

11. Kabat-Zinn, J. (1990). *Full catastrophe living.* New York: Delacorte.

12. Orme-Johnson, D., & Alexander, C. (1988). *Critique of the National Research Council's report on meditation.* Fairfield, IA: Maharishi International University.

13. Orme-Johnson, D. (1988). International peace project in the Middle East: The effects of the Maharishi technology of the unified field. *Journal of Conflict Resolution, 32,* 776–812.

14. Epstein, M., & Lieff, J. (1981). Psychiatric complications of meditation practice. *Journal of Transpersonal Psychology, 13,* 57.

15. Wilber, K. (1993). The spectrum of pathologies. In R. Walsh & F. Vaughan (Eds.), *Paths beyond ego: The transpersonal vision.* Los Angeles: Tarcher.

16. Shapiro, D. (1990). Meditation, self control, and control by a benevolent other. In M. Kwee (Ed.), *Psychotherapy, meditation and health* (pp. 65–123). London: East-West.

CHAPTER 18

Psychedelics and Transpersonal Psychiatry

GARY BRAVO AND
CHARLES GROB

But I may add a new possibility for scientific investigation
of transcendence. In the last few years it has become quite
clear that certain drugs called "psychedelic," especially LSD
and psilocybin, give us some possibility of control in this
realm of peak-experiences. It looks as if these drugs often
produce peak-experiences in the right people under the
right circumstances, so that perhaps we needn't wait for
them to occur by good fortune.

Abraham Maslow

ABRAHAM MASLOW, A REVERED FOUNDER of transpersonal psychology, advised investigating any technology that might be helpful in
producing the "core-religious revelation" and the healing power
that went along with it. Psychedelic drugs were once touted to be
this technology. They were seen as breakthrough tools for understanding the mind, mental illness, and spirituality. Indeed, psychedelics were perceived to be as important to the science of consciousness as the telescope was to astronomy or the microscope to
biology.[2]

THE HISTORY OF PSYCHEDELICS

Psychedelic plants have been used by shamans in indigenous cultures for thousands of years as reliable tools for inducing altered states of consciousness.[3] The peyote cactus in Mexico, the ayahuasca brew in the Amazon basin, the iboga root in central west Africa, and the *Psilocybe* mushrooms in central America are just a few of the psychoactive plants that were used in healing, divinatory, celebratory, and initiation rites.[4] In Asia, the foundations of the Hindu religion were influenced by a psychoactive substance called *soma*, the exact identity of which remains a mystery, but it may have been a psychedelic mushroom. In addition, it has been argued that the Eleusinian mysteries of ancient Greece involved a fungus with a lysergic acid derivative for its central rites, thus influencing the founders of the Western philosophical tradition.[5] Modern European exploration of the effects of mind-altering chemicals began to surface in the reports of Samuel Coleridge, Thomas DeQuincey, and Charles-Pierre Baudelaire, although to general opprobrium.

The peyote cactus extract mescaline was the first compound to be identified by modern chemists as a psychedelic, and its power to induce visions and religious exaltation was appreciated early on, as well as its power to evoke a state similar to psychosis. William James reported his personal exploration of consciousness with both mescaline and nitrous oxide. After LSD was discovered in 1943, widespread interest in psychedelics as tools to understand the mind developed in psychiatry. LSD, the most potent psychoactive chemical then known, excited hope for the discovery of the biochemical underpinnings of mental illness. The ability of LSD to loosen ego defenses and magnify the contents of the unconscious led to its use in psychoanalysis.[6] Reports of early experimentation were confined to scholarly journals, but when Aldous Huxley published *The Doors of Perception* in 1954 about his experiences with mescaline, the intellectual world began to take notice.[7]

Freewheeling experimentation with psychedelic drugs began to emerge after Timothy Leary, Richard Alpert, and others began to work with psilocybin and LSD under the auspices of the Harvard psychology department. Although their work was groundbreaking, their style was seen as proselytizing and their methods were viewed as loose and unscientific by their colleagues. The high levels of publicity they generated resulted in their dismissal from Harvard.[8]

As psychedelics became more popular, the government began to place tighter controls on their clinical and experimental use. Despite this restraint, the use of LSD spread in the new youth culture under the banner "Turn on, tune in, and drop out" and became associated with "hippies" and the antiwar movement.[9] Psychedelics had gone out of the labs and clinics and into the street and were seen as major contributors to, if not directly responsible for, the nonconformity and rebellion of large groups of youths, which was threatening to the status quo. Media coverage of this phenomenon became highly sensationalized, and LSD was demonized in the popular culture. The new spirituality opened up by psychedelics threatened the powerful religious institutions. Finally, possession of psychedelics was outlawed in 1966, and research ceased, except for a few projects that survived into the 1970s.[8] For example, intelligence agencies continued to use psychedelics for their own purposes as agents of mind control and warfare, demonstrating that psychedelics were not inherently benevolent.[9] Eventually, psychiatry lost interest in psychedelics, and the whole area became seen as somewhat illegitimate and passé.

The use of psychedelics in the general populace seemed to peak in the late 1960s and early 1970s. In the mid–1980s, a previously obscure drug, 3,4-methylenedioxy-methamphetamine (MDMA), popularly called *ecstasy*, was made illegal by the Drug Enforcement Administration. There was protest by some psychiatrists and therapists who had been quietly using MDMA in their practices for several years. In a controversy that was highly reminiscent of the psychedelic debates 20 years earlier, the psychiatrists argued that MDMA, by facilitating trust and openness in the patient, was a valuable adjunct to psychotherapy. The government regulators countered that MDMA was highly abusable and potentially brain damaging. Despite the ban, MDMA went on to become popular with young people at special dance parties called *raves*.[10]

The 1990s have seen a resurgence of interest in the significance of psychedelics. For the first time in years, the Food and Drug Administration has allowed basic studies in humans with a number of different psychedelic substances.[11]

PSYCHEDELICS AND THE NEUROSCIENCES

Psychedelic drugs are chemical substances that have the common effect of producing very powerful and unique psychoactive effects without causing physical addiction. The classical psychedelics, which include LSD, psilocybin, dimethyltryptamine (DMT), and mescaline, resemble endogenous neurotransmitters. Some occur naturally in plants and animals and even in the human brain (DMT), whereas others are synthetic or semisynthetic (LSD).

Psychedelic drugs are the most potent psychoactive substances known to science, and they can cause significant alterations in affective state, emotional expression, body image, perception, cognition, and sense of reality. Neuroscientists in the past 3 decades, although limited to animal studies, have found psychedelics to be invaluable tools for mapping neurotransmitter systems in the brain. Studies have shown that psychedelics bind to specific types of serotonin neuroreceptors in the brain, deregulating the serotonergic system's control of multiple brain regions.

There is growing interest on the part of psychopharmacologists in correlating psychedelic drug interactions in the living human brain with subjective human experience. This research could shed light on uniquely human experiences such as perception, thinking, dreaming, hallucinations, delusions, creativity, and transcendent consciousness. Until then, one must rely on phenomenological theories to explain how psychedelics affect consciousness. The most plausible hypothesis is that the chemicals somehow inhibit the brain's normal pattern of processing information, allowing access to an ocean of stimuli that normally are filtered out of awareness.[12]

It has also been hypothesized that psychedelics improve the communication and coherence between the two halves of the brain.[13] The Czech LSD researcher Stanislav Grof[14] described psychedelics as nonspecific amplifiers of the unconsciousness and has used LSD as though it were a microscope to chart the regions of the unconscious as reported by his patients (see Chapter 8).

PSYCHEDELICS AND SPIRITUALITY

The "transcendent" experiences evoked by psychedelics in the 1960s were a whole generation's introduction to altered and spiritual states of consciousness and helped catalyze the development of transpersonal psychology (see Chapter 2). These "peak experiences," as Maslow called them, led many Westerners to look to esoteric and Eastern spiritual systems to learn more about the realms of consciousness unacknowledged by orthodox psychology but often addressed in the Eastern consciousness disciplines. Charles

Tart[15] surveyed Western practitioners of Tibetan Buddhism and found that 77% of them had had major psychedelic experiences. A little more than half of the respondents reported that these experiences were very or fairly important to their general spiritual life, although only 10% said that they still used psychedelics. This interesting finding has not been expanded on in further research in part because of the societal taboos surrounding the topic.[16]

It is a tenet of transpersonal psychiatry that mystical experiences can be healing and transformative. Psychedelics used wisely can certainly catalyze mystical experience in the prepared and predisposed, thus perhaps providing the best hope for a true science of "experimental mysticism." This type of approach is exemplified by the famous "Good Friday" experiment done by Walter Pahnke and associates[17] at Harvard in 1962, in which psilocybin was administered to 10 graduate students of divinity in a chapel during a Good Friday service. A placebo was administered to 10 control subjects in a double-blind fashion. A typology of mystical experience had been prepared to survey the subjects. It was found that the experiences of the psilocybin group were significantly more like the mystical typology than those of the controls. Interestingly, a 25-year follow-up of the subjects revealed that all those who had taken psilocybin "still considered their original experience to have had genuinely mystical elements and to have made a uniquely valuable contribution to their spiritual lives."[18]

One of the most important advances in psychedelic scholarship and theory has been an appreciation for the role of altered states of consciousness and ritual in healing.[19] Psychedelic plants are one tool among the many methods used by shamanic healers to produce an altered state of consciousness.[20] The power of ritual in setting the proper context for healing has also become more recognized and is a restatement of the role of "set and setting" as major determinants of the altered-state experience. As the effects of ritual, drumming, dance, meditation, breathwork, hypnosis, and many other techniques to induce altered awareness have become well known, is not yet clear if there is anything unique or special to the "psychedelic" state of consciousness at all.[21]

There are many unanswered questions about the relationship of spirituality and transpersonal psychiatry to psychedelic drugs. In the study of spirituality, there has been a long-standing debate about the relative merits of a drug-induced versus a natural mystical experience. One of the main differences is that in a drug experience the revelation comes to an unprepared mind; therefore, its effect is not as lasting as in someone who, through methods such as prayer and discipline, has a foundation on which to actualize that vision. As the religious scholar Houston Smith says, "Drugs appear able to induce religious experiences; it is less evident that they can produce religious lives."[22]

A potential trap seen with psychedelics is that the user feels he "needs" the drug to have a spiritual experience and never grasps that the psychedelic is just "unlocking" an experience latent in the user. This feeling leads to "craving," even if subtle, which is contrary to the goals of most spiritual paths. Certainly there are those for whom one psychedelic experience has been life transforming, and there are others who tend to repeat the experience again and again compulsively with little change demonstrated in their day-to-day consciousness. Although the place of psychedelics in spiritual practice remains controversial, many transpersonalists have argued that psychedelics can serve as an awakener to other states of being and realms of consciousness.[16] Once the message is heard, however, the individual needs to transform his or her life gradually through spiritual practice to manifest the transpersonal vision.

PSYCHEDELICS AND TRANSPERSONAL PSYCHIATRY

What contributions can experience with psychedelic drugs give to the theory and practice of transpersonal psychiatry? First, the transpersonal paradigm is the only psychiatric worldview that can begin to categorize and explain the range of phenomena elicited in the psychedelic experience. Second, we believe that psychedelics offer the best hope of linking transpersonal psychiatry and the predominant "biological" paradigm of modern psychiatry. Simply stated, this paradigm holds that human psychopathology fundamentally stems from physiological malfunctioning of the nervous system and that drugs provide the easiest and most elegant method of correcting this malfunction. Ironically, psychedelic drugs, by showing how minuscule amounts of chemicals can have profound effects on behavior and experience, helped usher in the psychopharmacological revolution in psychiatry. Paradoxically, as psychedelic research with humans was shut down, the biopsychiatric paradigm rose to power.

MOTIVATION FOR USING PSYCHEDELICS

There seems to be a universal urge for the mind to experience altered states of consciousness.[23] Many psychedelic users are looking for ways to enhance sensory experience and "get high." People looking for this level of experience usually get frightened if deeper levels of consciousness emerge, resulting in panic reactions and "bad trips." Many users blend the categories of recreational and spiritual use by taking psychedelics at concerts and raves to enter a "group mind."[24] Psychedelics have also been credited with inspiring creativity, providing another reason people continue to take them, although formal studies have not shown consistent results in this regard.[25]

Psychedelics used in groups can facilitate tremendous emotional bonding, especially if this result is emphasized in the set and setting.[26] Traditional societies use psychedelic rituals as methods to enhance social cohesion and share a worldview. The Native American Church, using formalized peyote rituals, functions in this way and has demonstrated therapeutic effects in its members, particularly in the area of alcoholism. In Brazil there are recently developed and legally sanctioned churches that use the potent psychedelic brew ayahuasca as the central sacrament in their liturgy. There have been myriad other utopian communities and religions that have sprung up from the psychedelic vision. Most of these have not lasted, but they testify to the ubiquitous human need to give structure to the psychedelic experience.

DANGERS OF PSYCHEDELICS

Specific problems associated with psychedelic psychotherapy are discussed in Chapter 32, but there are some general issues to be noted when discussing psychedelics and spiritual growth. There has been concern that psychedelics can cause damage in the user that can manifest on physical, psychological, or spiritual planes. Although most studies show that there are no long-term physical sequelae of most psychedelics and no permanent brain damage,[27] many spiritual adepts warn of damage to the astral or subtle bodies, such as "holes in the aura." These concerns deserve further investigation.

Psychedelics often produce a "conversion experience" and can lead to ego inflation. A frequent criticism of psychedelics is that they reduce drive and motivation in heavy users, but this has been difficult to assess because of value judgments by investigators about what are healthy and worthwhile goals. Also, psychedelics can precipitate existential depressions and crises in those who find their lives shallow or unfulfilling when viewed from a psychedelic-influenced state of mind and can precede "spiritual emergence." They can also induce psychoses in predisposed individuals, although this is rare when psychedelics are used therapeutically.

Maslow, who suggested the investigation of drugs as a possible method to bring the "core religious revelation" to those who haven't had it, was not blind to the dangers of drugs:

> Drugs, which can be helpful when wisely used, become dangerous when foolishly used. The sudden insight becomes "all," and the patient and disciplined "working through" is postponed or devalued. Instead of being "surprised by joy," "turning on" is scheduled, promised, advertised, sold, hustled into being, and can get to be regarded as a commodity.[1]

CONCLUSION

Psychedelic research continues to offer a most useful scientific procedure for investigating transpersonal states of consciousness. Psychedelic research may hold an important key to understanding brain mechanisms associated with spirituality and its pathological distortions. Such research may allow researchers to evaluate and understand the role of peak experiences in personality transformation and development. We hope that this valuable tool will once again become the source of meaningful transpersonal research.

NOTES

1. Maslow, A. H. (1964). *Religions, values, and peak-experiences.* New York: Viking Press. Quotations on pp. 27 and x.

2. Clark, W. H. (1969). *Chemical ecstasy.* New York: Sheed & Ward.

3. Dobkin de Rios, M. (1984). *Hallucinogens: Cross-cultural perspectives.* Albuquerque: University of New Mexico Press.

4. Ott, J. (1993). *Pharmacotheon: Entheogenic drugs, their plant sources and history.* Kennewick, WA: Natural Products.

5. Wasson, R. G., Kramrisch, S., Ott, J., & Ruck, C. A. P. (1986). *Persephone's quest: Entheogens and the origins of religion.* New Haven, CT: Yale University Press.

6. Neill, J. R. (1987). "More than medical significance": LSD and American psychiatry, 1953 to 1966. *Journal of Psychoactive Drugs, 19,* 39–45.

7. Huxley, A. (1954). *The doors of perception.* New York: Harper & Row.

8. Stevens, J. (1987). *Storming heaven: LSD and the American dream.* New York: Harper & Row.

9. Lee, M., & Shlain, B. (1985). *Acid dreams.* New York: Grove Weidenfeld.

10. Watson, L., & Beck, J. (1991). New Age seekers: MDMA use as an adjunct to spiritual pursuit. *Journal of Psychoactive Drugs, 23,* 261–270.

11. Strassman, R. J. (1995). Hallucinogenic drugs in psychiatric research and treatment: Perspectives and prospects. *Journal of Nervous and Mental Disease, 183,* 127–138.

12. Hofmann, A. (1986). *Insight outlook.* Atlanta, GA: Humanics New Age.

13. Mandell, A. (1985). Interhemispheric fusion. *Journal of Psychoactive Drugs, 17,* 257–266.

14. Grof, S. (1975). *Realms of the human unconscious: Observations from LSD research.* New York: Dutton.

15. Tart, C. (1991). Influences of previous psychedelic drug experiences on students of Tibetan Buddhism: A preliminary exploration. *Journal of Transpersonal Psychology, 23,* 139–173.

16. Walsh, R. (1982). Psychedelics and psychological well-being. *Journal of Humanistic Psychology, 22,* 22–32.

17. Pahnke, W. N., & Richards, W. A. (1966). Implications of LSD and experimental mysticism. *Journal of Religion and Health, 5,* 175–208.

18. Doblin, R. (1991). Pahnke's "Good Friday experiment": A long-term follow-up and methodological critique. *Journal of Transpersonal Psychology, 23,* 1–28. Quotation on p. 23.

19. Lukoff, D., Zanger, R., & Lu, F. (1990). Transpersonal psychology research review: Psychoactive substances and transpersonal states. *Journal of Transpersonal Psychology, 22,* 107–148.

20. Harner, M. (1982). *The way of the shaman.* New York: Bantam Books.

21. Walsh, R. N. (1990). *The spirit of shamanism.* Los Angeles: Tarcher.

22. Smith, H. (1993). Do drugs have religious import? In R. Walsh & F. Vaughan (Eds.), *Paths beyond ego: The transpersonal vision*. Los Angeles: Tarcher/Perigee. Quotation on p. 93.

23. Weil, A. (1986). *The natural mind: An investigation of drugs and the higher consciousness*. Boston: Houghton Mifflin. (Original work published 1972)

24. Millman, R. B. , & Beeder, A. B. (1994). The new psychedelic culture: LSD, ecstasy, "rave" parties and the Grateful Dead. *Psychiatric Annals, 24*, 148–150.

25. Krippner, S. (1985). Psychedelic drugs and creativity. *Journal of Psychoactive Drugs, 17*, 235–245.

26. Adamson, S., & Metzner, R. (1988). The nature of the MDMA experience and its role in healing, psychotherapy and spiritual practice. *ReVision, 10*(4), 59–72.

27. Strassman, R. (1983). Adverse reactions to psychedelic drugs: A review of the literature. *Journal of Nervous and Mental Disease, 172*, 577–595.

CHAPTER 19

Parapsychology and Transpersonal Psychology

CHARLES T. TART

IN THE LAST FEW DECADES A number of representative national surveys have found high percentages of apparently "normal" people reporting "psychic" experiences. Table 19.1 is a summary of the surveys reported by Haraldsson.[1]

TABLE 19.1
PERCENTAGE OF RESPONDENTS FROM FOUR COUNTRIES
REPORTING PSYCHIC EXPERIENCES

Type of experience	Country			
	Iceland	Britain	Sweden	USA
Psychic dreams	36	29	19–28	—
Waking ESP (telepathy)	27	29	14–29	58
Contact with the dead	31	12	9	27
Hauntings	—	18	14	—
Poltergeists	—	9	3	—
Out-of-the-body experience	8	—	6–12	—
Some psychic experience	64	64	—	—

Note. ESP = extrasensory perception.

Traditional scientists reject the reality of psychic phenomena, however, reflecting what sociologists call *scientism:* a hardening of

186

conventional theories into a rigid belief system. Psychic phenomena (psi) challenge scientism. Furthermore, an open-minded exploration of psi counteracts the widespread invalidation of otherwise healthy individuals who report transpersonal and psi experiences.

FUNDAMENTAL PSI: THE BIG FOUR

The vast majority of people, both professionals and laypersons, believe or disbelieve in psi effects for nonrational and emotional reasons rather than as a result of empirical evidence.[2,3,4,5,6] There are four fundamental types of psi that have been established by many laboratory experiments.

Telepathy, the first kind of extrasensory perception (ESP), literally means mind-to-mind communication. A specific thought or emotion is accurately cognized or "perceived" by another person, even though the people are not in sensory communication with each other and there is no reasonable way of inferring the content of the "sender's" mind. The typical telepathy laboratory experiment involves selecting some kind of target material for the sender or "agent" to concentrate on sending while the receiver is sensorially isolated from the agent, typically by being in another room or even hundreds of miles away. The targets may be randomized fixed symbols, such as those on playing cards, allowing statistical assessment of whether the achieved scores can be reasonably ascribed to chance variation or are unlikely enough to postulate telepathy. The targets may be more broadly ranging items like randomly selected pictures of various scenes. Analysis in the latter case involves using a judge, who is blind concerning what scene is intended to go with what response, to match scenes and responses.

Telepathy, like the other types of psi, is difficult to produce on demand in the laboratory. Only about one of every three psi experiments carried out by experienced parapsychologists has yielded statistically significant results.[7] There is considerable variation among individual experimenters, with some almost never getting significant results and others regularly getting them. This is not surprising, given the extensive research demonstrating that the experimenter is usually part of the experiment.[8] Research on how qualities of the experimenter affect psi performance is still meager, but an initial study showed that experimenters perceived as warm and friendly get more significant psi results than those perceived as cold and distant.[9] Similarly, the appearance of psi events in psychotherapeutic situations is affected by the therapist's openness to the phenomenon. Furthermore, "real-life" instances of psi usually are determined by strong emotional intensity, whereas laboratory conditions are seldom of much emotional intensity. Considering the strong affective intensity often seen in psychotherapeutic situations, it is not surprising that strong psi sometimes manifests there, the analysis of which can lead to important clinical insights.[10,11,12,13]

Clairvoyance, from the French for "clear seeing," is the perception of the state of physical matter when that state is not currently known to any human mind. In the laboratory, experimenters typically test clairvoyance by shuffling a deck of cards without looking at them and shielding them from the would-be percipient, such as by putting them in a desk drawer. The percipient is then asked to write down the order of the cards. A wide variety of target materials have been used in telepathy and clairvoyance experiments with successful results, ranging from pictures that have been photographically reduced in size to microdots,[14] to patterns of electrical impulses within a computer.[15,16,17]

Precognition, the third form of ESP, is the ability to predict future events, events that have not occurred at the time the percipient attempts to describe them and that cannot be rationally inferred from a knowledge of current conditions. The typical test procedure has consisted of asking a percipient to predict the sequence of cards in a deck before it is shuffled. Although there have been more than enough experiments to establish the reality of precognition, the scoring rate in these experiments—the information transfer rate—is significantly below that obtained in experiments with telepathy and clairvoyance.[18]

Psychokinesis (PK) is the ability of the mind to affect physical matter or physical energy directly. The classical test procedure has involved asking a participant, the PK agent, to wish for a certain face of a die or several dice to turn up on a particular throw, when the agent could not mechanically intervene in any known way. Modern studies have shown PK effects in such diverse target systems as radioactive decay,[19,20,21] temperature,[22] and electronic random-number generators.[23]

OTHER POSSIBLE PSI PHENOMENA

In addition to telepathy, clairvoyance, precognition, and PK, there are a variety of other ostensible psi phenomena that have been observed sufficiently to allow a reasonable, but not yet conclusive, case for their existence. Following are descriptions of a few that are of particular relevance to transpersonal psychology and psychiatry.

Psychic healing refers to PK-like effects in which an ostensible psychic healer, sometimes operating in sensory isolation from the patient, promotes physical healing through his or her efforts. Grad's[24,25] classic studies showing that sterile saline solution in hermetically sealed glass containers had a healing effect on injured barley seeds when the solution had been held between the hands of a known healer is an excellent demonstration of the feasibility of laboratory research in this area. The current widespread use of therapeutic touch[26,27] illustrates the clinical application of this sort of healing, as does LeShan's[28] work on two major types of psychic healing.[29]

In out-of-the-body experiences (OBEs), the person feels he is located outside of his physical body, yet the reality and clarity of consciousness during the OBE is so great that the person does not consider it a dream or hallucination.[30] Occasionally the OBE experiencer finds herself at some distant location and observes previously unknown or improbable events that are confirmed by investigation. In one experimental situation, a young woman awakening from an OBE marked by an unusual EEG pattern correctly reported a 5-digit random number that was hidden on a shelf well above her head.[31]

Psychologically, the OBE is a major source of the belief that humans have a soul and that such a soul survives death. People who have OBEs generally say something to the effect that they do not "believe" that they will survive death; they "know" it! A comprehensive review of the psychological aspects of OBEs can be found in the work of Harvey Irwin.[30]

Belief in reincarnation is widespread in modern culture: Gallup[32] found a 23% belief rate for Americans. The most impressive evidence of reincarnation comes from Ian Stevenson's studies of hundreds of children who spontaneously recalled past lives.[33,34,35,36,37] These children, most often of preschool age, frequently insisted on being taken to see their former families in some other town or village. In these evidential cases, the other families were unknown to the child's family, yet some unique and accurate descriptions of the family had been given by the child.

RELIGION AND PSI

Scientific proof of the existence of psi makes little difference to organized religions, which all implicitly accept some sort of psi as part of the mechanism of supernatural action. Every religion also reports psi-like events, or miracles, which are cited to prove that the belief system of that particular religion is right and others are wrong. Modern scientific research shows, however, that there is no exclusivity of psi. An anthropologist once told me an amusing anecdote that illustrates this fact. A Christian missionary visiting a secluded tribe in the Amazon preached to the members about the miracles Christ had performed, including raising a man from the dead. In conversation afterward, the Indians told the missionary they were extremely impressed with this Christ fellow. Their own shaman had raised a man from the dead just last week, and it was a tremendous amount of work!

TOWARD A MORE ADEQUATE VIEW OF THE NATURE OF THE MIND

It is now commonly accepted that we live in a neurologically based world-simulator, that is, that we do not directly experience the world outside our own nervous systems.[38] What we experience is an electrochemical pattern within our brain that is only a partially accurate simulation of the outside world. The existence of basic psi requires that we alter the world-simulation model in two ways. First, we may occasionally have psychic contact with events in the "external" world (including the contents of other people's minds), so that the simulation we experience as reality may have inputs affecting it other than ordinary sensory input. Second, we need to postulate that mind exists in a (poorly understood) way that is independent of the physical properties of matter and the nervous system as we currently know them. This different, "nonphysical" aspect of mind strongly interacts with the brain and nervous system, however, so that the properties of brains must be understood if we are to have a complete understanding of mind as it is normally experienced. I have theorized about this process in detail elsewhere.[39]

The fact that mind seems to have a nonphysical aspect to it does not mean that it automatically has some sort of direct access to the truth about things independent of the world-simulation process. The classical parapsychological example of this precept is the sheep–goat effect, discovered by Schmeidler[40] and repeatedly verified by many experimenters.[41,42,43] Before a multiple-choice-type ESP test is given, participants indicate on a questionnaire whether or not they believe in ESP. Those who do are classified as sheep. Those who do not are called goats. Repeated studies have found that the believers tend to score above chance expectation and the nonbelievers tend to score below chance. The only plausible mechanism for significant below-chance scoring is that the unconscious minds of the nonbelievers occasionally use ESP to detect the correct target and then influence their conscious mind to think of any target but the correct one.

CONCLUSION

Parapsychological studies have demonstrated strong evidence for the existence of several forms of psi and should play a unique role in the transition from a modern to a postmodern worldview. If one respects the methodology of science, parapsychological findings force one to broaden one's intellectual horizons to a view of mind as something capable of transcending the current limits.

NOTES

1. Haraldsson, E. (1985). Representative national surveys of psychic phenomena: Iceland, Great Britain, Sweden, USA and Gallup's multinational surveys. *Journal of the Society for Psychical Research, 53*, 145–158.

2. Tart, C. (1980). Are we interested in making ESP function strongly and reliably? A reply to J. E. Kennedy. *Journal of the American Society for Psychical Research, 74*, 210–222.

3. Tart, C. (1983). The controversy about psi: Two psychological theories. *Journal of Parapsychology, 46*, 313–320.

4. Tart, C. (1986). Attitudes toward strongly functioning psi: A preliminary study. *Journal of the American Society for Psychical Research, 80*, 163–173.

5. Tart, C. (1986). Psychics' fear of psychic powers. *Journal of the American Society for Psychical Research, 80*, 279–292.

6. Tart, C. (1984). Acknowledging and dealing with the fear of psi. *Journal of the American Society for Psychical Research, 78*, 133–143.

7. Tart, C. (1973). Parapsychology. *Science, 182*, 222.

8. Tart, C. (1978). Review of the book *The human subject in the psychological laboratory* by I. Silverman. *Journal of the American Society for Psychical Research, 72*, 285–288.

9. Schmeidler, G., & Maher, M. (1981). Judges' responses to the nonverbal behavior of psi-conducive and psi-inhibitory experimenters. *Journal of the American Society for Psychical Research, 75,* 241–257.

10. Ehrenwald, J. (1977). Parapsychology and the healing arts. In B. Wolman, B. Dale, G. Schmeidler, & M. Ullman (Eds.), *Handbook of parapsychology* (pp. 541–556). New York: Van Nostrand Reinhold.

11. Eisenbud, J. (1970). *Psi and psychoanalysis: Studies in psychoanalysis of psi-conditioned behavior.* New York: Grune & Stratton.

12. Eisenbud, J. (1982). *Paranormal foreknowledge: Problems and perplexities.* New York: Human Sciences Press.

13. Eisenbud, J. (1983). *Parapsychology and the unconscious.* Berkeley, CA: North Atlantic Books.

14. Puthoff, H., Targ, R., & Tart, C. (1980). Resolution in remote viewing studies: Mini-targets. In W. Roll (Ed.), *Research in Parapsychology 1979* (pp. 120–122). Metuchen, NJ: Scarecrow Press.

15. Schmidt, H. (1969). Precognition of a quantum process. *Journal of Parapsychology, 33,* 99–108.

16. Schmidt, H. (1969). Clairvoyance tests with a machine. *Journal of Parapsychology, 33,* 300–306.

17. Targ, R., & Tart, C. (1985). Pure clairvoyance and the necessity of feedback. *Journal of the American Society for Psychical Research, 79,* 485–492.

18. Tart, C. (1983). Information acquisition rates in forced-choice ESP experiments: Precognition does not work as well as present-time ESP. *Journal of the American Society for Psychical Research, 77,* 293–310.

19. Beloff, J., & Evans, L. (1961). A radioactivity test for psychokinesis. *Journal of the Society for Psychical Research, 41,* 41–54.

20. Onetto, B. (1968). PK with a radioactive compound, cesium 137. In W. Roll, R. Morris, & J. Morris (Eds.), *Proceedings of the Parapsychological Association, No. 5,* 18–19.

21. Wadhams, P., & Farrelley, B. (1968). The investigation of psychokinesis using beta particles. *Journal of the Society for Psychical Research, 44,* 736.

22. Schmeidler, G. (1973). PK effects upon continuously recorded temperature. *Journal of the American Society for Psychical Research, 67,* 325–340.

23. Radin, D., May, E., & Thomson, M. (1986). Psi experiments with random number generators: Meta-analysis, Part 1. In D. Weiner & D. Radin (Eds.), *Research in parapsychology 1985* (pp. 14–17). Metuchen, NJ: Scarecrow Press.

24. Grad, B. (1965). Some biological effects of the "laying on of hands": A review of experiments with animals and plants. *Journal of the American Society for Psychical Research, 59,* 95–127.

25. Grad, B. (1967). The "laying on of hands": Implications for psychotherapy, gentling, and the placebo effect. *Journal of the American Society for Psychical Research, 61,* 286–305.

26. Krieger, D. (1979). *The therapeutic touch: How to use your hands to help or to heal.* Englewood Cliffs, NJ: Prentice-Hall.

27. Krieger, D. (1981). *Foundations for holistic health nursing practices: The renaissance nurse.* Philadelphia: Lippincott.

28. LeShan, L. (1974). *The medium, the mystic, and the physicist: Toward a general theory of the paranormal.* New York: Viking Press.

29. Murphy, M. (1992). *The future of the body.* Los Angeles: Tarcher.

30. Irwin, H. (1985). *Flight of mind: A psychological study of the out-of-body experience.* Metuchen, NJ: Scarecrow Press.

31. Tart, C. (1968). A psychophysiological study of out-of-the-body experiences in a selected subject. *Journal of the American Society for Psychical Research, 62,* 3–27.

32. Gallup, G. (1982). *Adventures in immortality: A look beyond the threshold of death.* New York: McGraw-Hill.

33. Stevenson, I. (1975). *Cases of the reincarnation type (Vol. 1).* Charlottesville: University of Virginia Press.

34. Stevenson, I. (1977). *Cases of the reincarnation type: Vol. 2. Ten cases in Sri Lanka.* Charlottesville: University of Virginia Press.

35. Stevenson, I. (1980). *Cases of the reincarnation type: Vol. 3. Twelve cases in Lebanon and Turkey.* Charlottesville: University of Virginia Press.

36. Stevenson, I. (1983). *Cases of the reincarnation type: Vol. 4. Twelve cases in Thailand and Burma.* Charlottesville: University of Virginia Press.

37. Stevenson, I. (1987). *Children who remember previous lives: A question of reincarnation.* Charlottesville: University of Virginia Press.

38. Tart, C. (1987). The world simulation process in waking and dreaming: A systems analysis of structure. *Journal of Mental Imagery, 11,* 145–158.

39. Tart, C. T. (1990). Psi-mediated emergent interactionism and the nature of consciousness. In R. Kunzendorf & A. Sheikh (Eds.), *The psychophysiology of mental imagery: Theory, research and application* (pp. 37–63). Amityville, NY: Baywood.

40. Schmeidler, G., & McConnell, R. (1958). *ESP and personality patterns.* New Haven, CT: Yale University Press.

41. Edge, H. L., Morris, R. L., Palmer, J., & Rush, J. H. (1986). *Foundations of parapsychology: Exploring the boundaries of human capability.* Boston: Routledge & Kegan Paul.

42. Krippner, S. (Ed.). (1978). *Advances in Parapsychological Research* (Vol. 2). New York: Plenum Press.

43. Rao, K. R. (1966). *Experimental parapsychology: A review and interpretation.* Springfield, IL: Thomas.

CHAPTER 20

Contemporary Physics and Transpersonal Psychiatry

JOHN R. BATTISTA

PHYSICS AND REALITY

Beginning with the sixteenth century, when science began to challenge the Christian church, Western culture came to believe that science would be capable of explaining the "real," objective world in terms of universal, predictable, deterministic forces independent of the observer. This belief has been called into question, however, by the findings of twentieth-century physics.

Einstein's special theory of relativity showed that matter, energy, space, and time are not characteristics of an objective reality but relative to the observer's. For example, an imaginary traveler approaching the speed of light would notice that a scientist conducting experiments on a stationary platform is using a ruler shorter than her own, using a clock that is running slower than her own, and calculating mass against a standard that is heavier than her own. The scientist would notice exactly the same things about the traveler.[1]

The developments of quantum physics have led to equally profound reconceptualizations of ideas of reality and the relationship between the observer and the world, but they are more difficult to grasp. Quantum theory emerged from Max Planck's success in resolving a disparity between experimental findings and classical mechanics known as the *ultraviolet catastrophe*. Classical mechanics predicted that if you heat blackened metal in a furnace until it is white hot, exchanges inside the furnace would transfer all the energy to shorter wavelengths so that the furnace would emit all its energy in the ultraviolet range or beyond. This was not found to be true. Planck resolved this problem by suggesting that energy is packaged in quanta, or chunks, of different sizes that are a function of the frequency of the light wave that carries them. Each wavelength carries a different-sized energy packet. Radio waves, with a very long wavelength and low frequency, carry tiny energy packets, just enough to alter the spin of an electron. Light in the visible spectrum carries larger energy packets, from approximately 1.5 to 3 electron volts, which can excite an atom. Gamma rays, of very short wavelength and high frequency, come in gigantic quanta of millions of electron volts, capable of killing a cell or altering its DNA.

In the classical view, light was thought to be an energy wave with energy evenly distributed throughout the wave. In the quantum view, light energy is carried in action-packets: photons guided by light rays. Louis Victor de Broglie theorized not only that all light waves are associated with particles, but also that all particles are associated with waves. De Broglie argued that a wavelength could be assigned to all matter such that its wavelength was equal to Planck's constant[2] divided by its momentum. This radical and revolutionary concept was confirmed by Clinton Davisson's and Lester Germer's experiments. Erwin Schroedinger then extended de Broglie's idea mathematically into a general wave equation for electrons, which forms the heart of quantum physics. The quantum-mechanical wave theory has been applied to nuclear physics, chemical bonds, and a wide variety of related topics, and its predictions have been repeatedly verified.

It has been difficult to understand the implications of the Schroedinger wave equation for the nature of reality, however, and for the relationship between the observable world and consciousness. This difficulty stems from the fact that the "waves" of the Schroedinger wave equation are not physical, like light waves or water waves; only their mathematical form is wavelike. Three basic interpretations of the Schroedinger wave equation have been made: the epistemological approach of Niels Bohr, the classical approach of John von Neumann, and the ontological approach of David Bohm.

THE EPISTEMOLOGICAL INTERPRETATION

The epistemological interpretation of quantum physics followed from Werner Heisenberg's uncertainty principle. Heisenberg argued that the situation of a quantum physicist is analogous to that of a scientist who is trying to examine a particle in a microscope. To observe a particle, the scientist must bombard the particle with at least one photon; this alters the observed particle's position and motion.

Heisenberg was able to calculate that the uncertainty with which the particle's position can be determined multiplied by the uncertainty with which the momentum can be determined must be equal to or greater than Planck's constant. Planck's constant thus defines a basic unit of uncertainty about the universe.

Heisenberg's uncertainty principle led Bohr to declare that quantum physics can say nothing about the world that exists "outside of" measurements. The experimental situation and the measurements must be seen as an interconnected totality. As a result, quantum physics can only make predictions about "measurement-observations," not about the "real" world that we assume to exist independent of our observations. More generally, one can never have total knowledge of the world through physics because the physicists' way of obtaining knowledge about the world alters the world being observed. Moreover, space, time, energy, and matter are not fixed and immutable properties of the world but should be understood as phenomena of experience that depend on the state (velocity) of the observer relative to that which is being observed.

These implications of twentieth-century physics are in accord with the beliefs and findings of transpersonal psychiatry. Transpersonal theorists generally agree that the reality people experience is a construction of the individual. Similarly, transpersonal psychiatrists would generally agree that any attempt to know reality through observation is not objective but influenced by the observer's biases. Only an enlightened person sees things as they are; however, these beliefs are derived from psychological experiments and experiences. They are neither proved nor disproved by physics. The observer effect and the constructive nature of perception are revealed in our day-to-day observations of human behavior. For example, anyone who has listened to a couple fighting or attended a hotly contested sporting event must be impressed by the capacity of two individuals to interpret the same events in very different ways. Similarly, the famous field–ground pictures, which can be seen as two faces or a goblet, or as an old person or a young woman, must convince us that our perceptions of reality are a constructive and interactive process. It is interesting that the constructive and interactive nature of perceptual reality is revealed in the domains of twentieth-century physics and twentieth-century psychology, but it is not true that the validity of the constructive and interactive nature of perception observed in people is dependent on or proved by the findings of relativity theory or quantum mechanics. Phenomena of the quantum realm are not necessarily true of the psychological realm any more than forces that influence molecular interactions are necessarily the forces that influence international relations.

This conservative, epistemological approach is consonant with Ken Wilber's[3] criticism of the attempt to use physics to support a mystical worldview (see Chapter 7). However, many transpersonalists, physicists, and interpreters of science have not accepted this conservative position. They have gone on to interpret what quantum physics "really" implies about reality and the role of consciousness in it. This is not surprising considering the Western cultural tradition of using physics to understand and interpret the world. When this step is taken, however, it is important to be aware that one is walking into a kind of quicksand that has consumed many physicists and philosophers and confused many transpersonalists.

THE CLASSICAL INTERPRETATION

The classical interpretation of quantum physics emerged from von Neumann's extension of Paul Dirac's quantum field theory. It considers the Schroedinger wave equation to provide a complete description of reality. The reality this equation refers to, however, is not the reality of the observed world but a quantum reality that "exists" separate from the observable reality of measurements. Each observable state results from the "collapse" of the quantum state given by the Schroedinger wave equation in the measurement process. If this quantum theory is interpreted physically, it holds that it is possible to exist in several different places at the same time and to exist in several different states at once.

The most compelling reason to interpret the Schroedinger wave equation in this way stems from the difficulty physicists have in understanding the results of Thomas Young's famous two-slit experiments when they involve the passage of a single particle. Even though particles pass through the two-slit apparatus one at a time, the spectrum of their measured positions was the same as if two particles had gone through the apparatus at once and inter-fered with one another. The classical interpretation of quantum physics explains these findings by arguing that the particle went through both slits at the quantum level of reality but was "reduced" to having appeared to have gone through one slit by the measurement process.[4,5]

Transpersonal or spiritually oriented theoreticians have con-tended that the reality implied by the classical interpretation of quantum physics is related to the structure of reality expressed by Eastern mystics, shamans, and enlightened teachers.[6,7] Similar thinking has led a number of scientifically oriented theoreticians to hypothesize that there must be a quantum-mechanical process operating in the brain that involves consciousness.[4,7,8,9,10,11,12] A vari-ety of brain mechanisms have been proposed to operate quantum mechanically to explain the uncertainty, free will, and wholeness of consciousness as well as psychic phenomena, time travel, and many other "nonstandard" states of consciousness.

Criticisms of the classical ontological interpretation of quantum physics, what Robert Anton Williams[13] called the fundamentalist interpretation of quantum mechanics (to liken it to the fundamen-talist Christian interpretation of the Bible), have focused on the measurement or observation problem, generally discussed in terms of "Schroedinger's cat." The argument goes something like this: Suppose you have an electron whose spin can be measured to be either up or down. According to the classical interpretation of quantum physics, before the spin state of the electron is measured to be up or down, it exists in a quantum state that is neither up nor down but a superposition of these alternatives. Now suppose you hook up the measuring apparatus used to determine the spin to a second device that releases poison gas into a box containing Schroedinger's cat if the spin is up and releases food and water into the box containing the cat if the spin is down. When in this process can we say that Schroedinger's cat is dead or alive? Is it dead when spin was measured by the instrument, when the scien-tist heard the apparatus click up or down, or when the scientist opened the box and looked inside? How do we explain how the world of quantum reality "collapsed" into the world of observable reality?

Quantum reality is used to "explain" findings in the observable world, yet it does not explain how those findings got there. The situation is similar to using a theory of the unconscious to explain conscious phenomena. Consciousness can no more be reduced to the unconscious than the observed world can be explained as a reduction of a quantum world.

CONSCIOUSNESS EXPLANATIONS

Some physicists have been uncomfortable with the inability of the classical interpretation to explain the findings of the observable world and have introduced an "explanatory" concept into the classical interpretation of quantum theory: consciousness. Eugene Wigner[14] is generally credited with being the first physicist to propose that the consciousness of the observer "causes" the collapse of the wave equation to a particular state. It has been pointed out in criticism of this solution to the observation problem[13] that if human consciousness causes the collapse of the wave function, one cannot explain the existence of the universe before human beings existed.

Questions like these have prompted some physicists to provide answers that make Wigner's idea that consciousness causes the collapse of the wave function look conservative. For example, David Mermin[13] has argued that the moon does disappear when no one looks. Similarly, John Wheeler[13] argued that consciousness travels back in time to the big bang to attune the universe to the very conditions that support the emergence of human beings. Some psychologists such as Stephen Wolinsky[15] have taken up these ideas, saying that quantum physics proves consciousness creates reality.

ONTOLOGICAL INTERPRETATIONS

To escape from the impasse of the classical interpretation of quantum mechanics' inability to explain the collapse of the wave function, other physicists have built on the idea that the wave function never collapses into observed reality. Instead they interpret the wave equation as observed reality (many worlds, many minds) or assume that there is a physical reality that quanta inform (one mindful world). Each of these approaches is a true ontological interpretation of quantum physics.

The "many worlds" approach of Hugh Everett[16] and the "many minds" approach of Henry Stapp[16] both assert that the wave function is a complete description of reality. Unlike the classical interpretation, however, these approaches contend that the reality of the wave function is not a quantum reality but the observed reality of people. In the many worlds approaches of Everett, the conscious observer is given a purely physical interpretation, and the consciousness of the observer has no effect on the evolution of the universe, much as in classical physics. Everett avoids the observer problem posed by the collapse of the wave function by positing that all options evolve in a world that is constantly branching. In terms of Schroedinger's cat, in one universe Schroedinger's cat is alive, and in another, the cat is dead. These universes continue to evolve through time. The "many minds" approach of Stapp is like the many worlds approach of Everett except that the mind is considered to be entirely different from matter and able to become conscious of matter without influencing it in any way. Although these approaches offer a more consistent approach than the classical interpretation of quantum physics, they offer no inherent advantage because they simply hypothesize the existence of multiple realities to account for the limitations of the classical interpretation. Their hypotheses about reality are not only unproved, they appear to be unprovable.

Bohm and Basil J. Hiley's[16] ontological approach to quantum theory (one mindful world) stems from the work of de Broglie, who argued that matter should be thought of as "wave-groups" carrying energy and momentum compactly. The "wave-packet" is what is normally observed as the "particle." The guiding ripples inside it, however, are made up of many neighboring wavelengths, which gang together to make the resultant pattern. These sets of ripples are in phase near the center of the group, but elsewhere they get out of step and cancel. Yet each individual component–wave may be regarded as a guide that extends far ahead and behind. It is the wave that guides the group–particle to a bright fringe in an interference pattern. The guide–ripples of a moving particle travel faster than the group, the reverse of the case for water ripples. In fact, these ripples travel at a speed that is greater than the speed of light itself. This breaks the no relativity rule, because the guide–ripples are only phase–waves, an all-pervading pattern that carries no energy with that speed. "You might fancy the ripples being there ahead of the particle to mark out the interference pattern and tell the particle where to go."[1] This guide-wave theory was severely criticized by Wolfgang Pauli at the 1927 Solvay Congress and was abandoned until 1952, when Bohm refuted many of the criticisms raised against it. However, the nonlocality implied by de Broglie's approach was thought of as an even worse violation of reality than the "nonexclusive physicality" implied by the classical interpretation of quantum physics.

De Broglie's theory might have been permanently discarded without the indirect influence of Einstein. Einstein had been an ongoing critic of the classical interpretation of quantum theory as a complete theory. Einstein, Boris Podolsky, and Nathan Rosen[4,8,13,16,17,18] proposed a famous thought experiment, commonly called the EPR experiment after its authors. They argued that quantum theory could not be a complete theory because of its implications: For example, if an experiment is conducted in one part of the universe that determines the spin of an electron, quantum mechanics insists that the spin of another electron in another part of the universe would be constrained even if no measurement were made. EPR argued that either quantum theory was incomplete because the spin was determined all along by some "hidden," or invisible, variables or there must be an instantaneous nonlocal connection between the two particles, a possibility they dismissed as too "spooky" to be taken seriously. EPR's position seemed to be disproved when von Neumann was able to show that no local, hidden variables were possible. It appeared, therefore, that von Neumann's classical approach had to be accepted and the whole ontological approach dropped, or a nonlocal, hidden variable theory to quantum physics had to be accepted. After Bohm[16] showed that nonlocal, hidden-variable theories of quantum mechanics were possible and consistent with the empirical findings of quantum theory, Bell[4,13,16] was able to delineate testable predictions of such a nonlocal, hidden-variable theory. Amazingly, the phenomenon of nonlocality was confirmed, initially by John Clauser[4,16] and more recently and definitively by Alain Aspect.[4,16] If quantum theory refers to some ontological reality, therefore, that reality must involve a nonlocal, quantum-mechanical, interconnectivity like that originally proposed by de Broglie.

Bohm and Hiley[16] developed de Broglie's idea of nonlocal, guide waves into a new ontological interpretation of quantum physics. In this approach Bohm argues that particles exist with well-defined positions at all times, although we are inhibited from knowing them exactly. Particles are nonlocally interconnected with one another. Rather than interpreting the Schroedinger wave equation as a complete description of reality, as in the classical interpretation, Bohm and Hiley interpret the Schroedinger wave equation as a "quantum potential" that "informs" and guides matter. They make the analogy to radio waves that "inform" a radio receiver. The radio receiver is informed by radio waves, and yet the energy used by the radio is not that of the radio waves but that of the receiver. Furthermore, Bohm and Hiley point out that radio waves are in many ways nonlocal in that they do not fall off with distance and depend only on the frequency and not the amplitude of the wave, as per quantum physics in general.

In line with this approach, Bohm and Hiley interpret the findings of the two-slit experiments as a result of the interaction between the particle and the slits. The particle and slits are "informed" by the quantum potential that contains information about whether there are two slits open or one. A kind of basic sensory awareness is available to matter at all times; in fact, it cannot be separated from it. According to Bohm and Hiley, it literally "in-forms" it; that is, it is the form of it. In this way the concept of information is used to break down the distinction between matter and consciousness. Relativity theory implied that matter, energy, space, and time are not immutable properties of the universe that can be separated from the observer. Bohm and Hiley's perspective clarifies that the observer effect should not be limited to or conceived of as human consciousness. Observation is an integral part of the universe. There is an interconnection among all parts of the universe that involves an elementary information-awareness.

Furthermore, the work of Bohm and Hiley suggests the existence of what they call "more subtle" levels of information that interact with the quantum potential. A set of hierarchically organized levels of information structures arises naturally from Bohm and Hiley's work. Bohm and Hiley's ideas about a basic quantum level of information that interacts with the information of higher ordered structures provide the possibility of integrating their work with information theories of consciousness and transpersonal theories of development that use hierarchically ordered information-processing structures (see Chapter 9).

Interpreted through Bohm and Hiley, twentieth-century physics reveals a "holistic paradigm"[18] showing that knowledge is conscious, consciousness cannot be separated from matter, consciousness is hierarchically organized, the observer cannot be removed from what is observed, and the world of knowledge is based on quantum-actions, or information events that involve the interaction of parts of one interconnected, conscious universe.

This holistic paradigm bears many similarities to the paradigmatic beliefs of transpersonal psychiatry. Transpersonal psychiatry holds that reality is both transcendent and immanent: It cannot be separated from matter but cannot be fully understood as material. Reality is conscious: it cannot be captured as an object independent of the subject. Transpersonal psychiatry holds that there is one interconnected reality of which we are all a part that transcends our normal physical and deterministic conceptualizations of reality. Many transpersonal psychiatrists believe reality to be hierarchically organized. All transpersonal psychiatrists perceive consciousness as the key to understanding reality.

CONCLUSION

There is a basic parallel between the reality paradigms of contemporary physics and those of transpersonal psychiatry. The reality paradigms of physics and transpersonal psychiatry have been expressed in several different, parallel ways. In the epistemological approach to quantum mechanics, the idea of a transcendent reality is dropped, and observation is accepted as the domain of physics. This view is paralleled within transpersonal psychiatry by the Soto school of Zen Buddhism, which emphasizes sitting and "suchness" and eschews concerns with what is real or true beyond or apart from awareness.

The classical interpretation of quantum physics emphasizes a separate and transcendent reality that is "beyond" ordinary, observed reality and is used to "explain" it. This theme is paralleled in transpersonal psychiatry by the general cultural concepts of spirituality, which have emphasized a separate, transcendent reality that is "really real" and provides the true meaning and cause of everyday, ordinary observed events. I believe that the classical approach to physics and the transcendental approach to psychology both make a basic category error that results in obscuring, rather than revealing, conscious reality. Finally, the ontological interpretation of quantum physics seeks to reveal reality through its theory. It uses concepts of information and hierarchical organization to reveal an interconnection among all parts of one undivided, conscious universe. This approach is paralleled in transpersonal psychology by theoreticians such as Wilber and myself who have used hierarchy and information concepts in an attempt to reveal the nature and structure of conscious reality (see Chapter 9).

Although the parallels among physics and transpersonal psychiatry are interesting, one field does not prove the other. Physics, like psychiatry and psychology, has been driven to these beliefs by its methods of knowing. These beliefs are valuable because they help to inform about reality. It must not be forgotten, however, that reality is active, related, participatory, and conscious. It is not something that can be captured in or by a theory that stands independent of our knowledge of it. Although the integration of ontological approaches to physics and psychology might lead to a more integrated general theory of reality, the result could never be reality or capture the experience of enlightenment. That goal requires the development of awareness.

NOTES

1. Rogers, E. (1963). *Physics for the inquiring mind* (p. 740). Princeton, NJ: Princeton University Press.

2. Brillouin, L. (1964). *Scientific uncertainty and information.* New York: Academic Press.

3. Wilber, K. (1985). Of shadows and symbols. In K. Wilber (Ed.), *Quantum questions.* Boston: Shambhala Publications.

4. Penrose, R. (1994). *Shadows of the mind.* Oxford, England: Oxford University Press.

5. Capra, F. (1976). *The Tao of physics.* Boston: Shambhala Publications.

6. Zukav, G. (1979). *The dancing Wu Li masters.* London: Rider/Hutchinson.

7. Sarfatti, J. (1979). Scientific commentary. In B. Toben (Ed.), *Space, time and beyond.* New York: Dutton.

8. Herbert, N. (1994). *Elemental mind.* New York: Penguin Books.

9. Walker, E. H. (1970). The nature of consciousness. *Mathematical Biosciences, 7*, 46–63.

10. Marshall, I. N. (1989). Consciousness and Bose–Einstein condensates. *New Ideas in Psychology, 7*, 73–83.

11. Eccles, J. (1994). *How the self controls its brain.* New York: Springer-Verlag.

12. Zohar, D. (1990). *The quantum self.* New York: Quill/William Morrow.

13. Williams, R. A. (1993). *Quantum psychology.* Phoenix: New Falcon Publications.

14. Wigner, E. (1967). *Symmetries and reflections.* Cambridge: MIT Press.

15. Wolinsky, S. (1993). *Quantum consciousness.* Norfolk, CT: Bramble Books.

16. Bohm, D., & Hiley, B. J. (1993). *The undivided universe.* London: Routledge.

17. Polkinghorne, J. C. (1984). *The quantum world.* Princeton, NJ: Princeton University Press.

18. Battista, J. (1977). The holistic paradigm and general system theory. *General Systems, 22,* 65–71.

CHAPTER 21

The Contribution of Anthropology to Transpersonal Psychiatry

LARRY G. PETERS

THIS CHAPTER ILLUSTRATES several cross-cultural, transpersonal principles of healing through a presentation of Tamang shamanism. These principles first are related to rites of passage and then are applied to a case of borderline personality disorder.

HEALING RITUALS: THE TAMANG OF NEPAL

The healing rituals of the Tamang of Nepal have many features in common with indigenous healing practices the world over and employ several important transpersonal principles of healing. In Tamang villages, shamans (bombo) have a social role analogous to that of a psychotherapist; they diagnose and treat spiritual, psychological, and interpersonal problems. For example, a woman experienced symptoms of headache, blurred vision, and backache; after a frightening episode in which she nearly spilled boiling water on her son, she became extremely agitated, complained of being almost blind, and took to her bed. A shamanic ritual was scheduled for the following evening. These rites normally last from dusk until dawn and involve the patient's entire extended family.

During the diagnostic part of the ritual, the shaman drummed rapidly and entered an altered state of consciousness (ASC). In this state, he "channeled" a tutelary deity who announced that the Yama Dhut, the army of the Lord of Death, had stolen the patient's soul. With the woman's soul absent, another spirit had come to possess the woman.

As the drumming continued, the patient also entered an ASC, with tremors that soon became convulsive. She yelled in anger at the shaman and her family and attempted to destroy the ritual altar. The shaman and his disciple restrained her, waving a mala (rosary) over her to control the possessing spirit. The patient and the shaman, who sat next to her, began to shake in unison, thereby exorcising the spirit by "transferring" it into his body before dispatching it. After a short recess, the shaman began to dance, calling on his spirit helpers to accompany him on his "journey" to retrieve the woman's soul. Suddenly the shaman collapsed, fell onto the floor, and lay there trembling. He narrated what he saw during his journey, "as if in a dream," into the spirit world. The shaman bargained with the Army of Death, promising a sacrifice to lure them away from the woman's soul, which he "saw" wandering near the Castle of Death. He restored the soul to the patient by placing a "soul flower," symbol of the god of creation and life, on her forehead (which is where the Tamang believe the soul resides). Before closing the ceremony, the shaman asked the family to huddle together, arms wrapped around each other and the patient. A blanket was placed over them, and the shaman threw burning millet over it, symbolically restoring the family's unity. After the final ritual act, everyone in the patient's network sat together touching and embracing.

Cross-Cultural Principles

The Tamang healing rite reveals transpersonal elements that are present in the healing systems of many cultures and that may be useful in psychiatry. First, the rite brings the patient's condition to a painful spiritual crisis that is cathartic and healing.[1] The release from social etiquette allows the free expression of emotion that may resolve interpersonal conflicts.[2]

Second, the healing rites involve altered states of consciousness, in which there is partial or full dissociation. The therapeutic effects of dissociation in ceremonial contexts have been described in relation to numerous indigenous cultures.[3] Such altered states, combined with suspension of social conventions, enable individuals to experience extremely powerful emotions. These experiences are similar to therapeutic "regressions in the service of the ego," described in the transcultural psychiatric literature as "dissociations in the service of the self."[4]

Third, these intense experiences are given structure and meaning through the use of potent spiritual symbols, rituals, and myths. During the Tamang ritual, the patient's soul was said to have been stolen by the Army of Death. The shaman dramatically rescued the soul and put a sacred soul flower on the patient's forehead, a symbol of the return of soul, vital passion for life, and renewed connection to the creator god, who is also the god of wisdom, love, and healing. The anthropologist Claude Lévi-Strauss[5] argued that such symbolic ritual gestures reach the patient's unconscious conflicts in ways that the spoken word cannot.

Fourth, there is an alteration in the patient's relationship to community and cosmos. The Tamang ritual not only creates social support,[6,7] but also generates what Stanislav and Christina Grof[8] call a "spiritual emergency." This is an intense emotional crisis that often includes themes of death and renewal but presents opportunities for healing through a deeper connection to nature, divinity, and other people. A structured ritual crisis, therefore, gives the patient access to the transpersonal healing forces of community and spirit.

RITES OF PASSAGE

Cross-cultural rites of passage, like healing rituals, assist people through life crises and have a similar transformational structure.[9] Rites of passage, such as puberty rites or initiations into sacred vocations, have three phases: separation, transition, and worldly return. Separation involves leaving one's familiar surroundings, lifestyle, and identity. This occurs in healing rites with the patient's assumption of the sick role, the suspension of normal everyday obligations, and the creation of a sacred space for the ritual.

The second phase, *liminality*, falls between social categories and states of being. The initiates are "travelers in a transitional area."[10] This state corresponds to the suspension of everyday social conventions in healing rituals. Altered states of consciousness are often induced here, for example through fasting, psychedelic ingestion, continual dancing, or sensory deprivation. These states parallel the ASCs induced in Tamang healing rites by drumming. During the liminal period of initiation, everything is done to cause a "disintegration of the personality."[11] The neophytes are typically referred to as "dead" or "being in the womb." Fear, pain, and death themes all serve to make the experience a dramatic crisis. These emotions are interpreted in mythic terms and thus given structure and meaning within a transcendent context. This process is also clear in the spiritual catharsis of healing rites.

In the final phase, the novice is reintegrated into the community, reborn and transformed. As the chrysalis becomes the butterfly, the child becomes the adult and the novice becomes a shaman. This reintegration parallels the restoration of community solidarity in healing rituals. As with all rites of passage, the result is a new, more complex role, not simply restoration of previous functioning. Passage is developmental and involves growth and adaptive change in work, sentiments, and interpersonal relations.

Transitional Crisis

In some cultures, behavior that is considered psychopathological by Western culture is understood as a transitional crisis. For example, the "wild man" behavior among the Bena Bena of New Guinea involves adults who have delayed assuming full, mature, culturally defined responsibilities. Wild-man behavior is characterized by violent antisocial activity. The episode is explained as being due to a spirit possession and accepted as a part of transition to adult life. The individual is reintegrated into the community, and the episode is quickly forgotten and leaves no social stigma.[12]

The transition involves crisis, ASCs, exceptions to social convention, spiritual meaning, and community support. When these factors are absent, problems result. In another New Guinea group observed by Phillip Newman,[13] for example, wild man behavior leads to a permanent loss of status, and the person is not allowed or expected to fulfill normal adult obligations. The wild-man episode is not valued as a transitional period. Perhaps as a consequence, chronic recurring episodes are common, in contrast to the experience of the Bena Bena. This information suggests that lack of social support and a sacred initiatory context can convert a transitional crisis into chronic psychopathology.

Evidence for this suggestion comes from various studies. Rin and Lin[14] compared prevalence rates of schizophrenia in four aboriginal tribes and ethnic Chinese in Taiwan. They found that among the aboriginals, schizophrenia was characterized by acute onset and a relatively favorable course and prognosis, in contrast to the urban, more Westernized Chinese, who have significantly higher prevalence rates. Pow Meng Yap[15] found similar prognostic data to the aboriginals favoring the illiterate, spiritually oriented, and least Westernized Chinese in Hong Kong. T. Adeoye Lambo[16] also ascertained that tribal patients with schizophrenia had a "lower prevalence of chronicity" and "shorter duration of psychotic episodes" than patients from more acculturated African groups, who developed chronic and deteriorating types of psychosis. E. Fuller Torrey[17] found that tribal highland groups in New Guinea had a schizophrenia rate one-tenth that of districts exposed to Western civilization. A World Health Organization international pilot study on schizophrenia showed that patients in developing countries had a more favorable course than those in developed countries. Traditional spiritual beliefs and stable social support systems appear to exert a protective effect.[18]

Borderline Personality Disorder as a Rite of Passage

Rollo May[19] argues that in Western society, suicide and major personality disorders such as borderline personality disorder (BPD) stem from a lack of meaningful sacred myths to guide the formation of identity. As Clifford Geertz[20] writes, myths and rituals are models of what a culture maps as real or valuable as well as models for personal behavior and identity. Lacking rituals to bring those myths and values alive, individuals are liable to remain confused.

Many features of transitional crises appear in BPD. Fasting, altered states of consciousness, body mutilation, and the use of psychoactive drugs are typical of rites of passage and of BPD. Moreover, other transitional crisis experiences, such as body fragmentation, dismemberment, and mutilation, occur frequently in BPD. These "symptoms" parallel the emphasis on death, dying, dismemberment, and disintegration in both puberty and shamanic rites of passage. The self-destructive acting-out of BPD patients often occurs in trancelike states involving temporary regressive experiences of merging, fusion, and loss of boundaries. Although they are considered pathological in traditional psychiatry, these altered states are typical of the liminal transitional stage in tribal rites of passage.

Significantly, Wen-Shing Tseng and John McDermott[21] consider the possibility that BPD is a Western "culture-related specific psychiatric condition." Moreover, Joel Paris[22] suggested that BPD is rapidly increasing in Western and developing societies, whereas more traditional societies, which provide clear mores and structures for the young, might protect against BPD. In other words, the borderline syndrome, like many other chronic psychiatric disorders, is less prevalent in cultural contexts with meaningful rites of passage.[23]

From a transpersonal, anthropological view, the self-destructive symptoms of BPD can be interpreted as attempts at self-transformation, or "rites of passage"; the attempts have "gone wrong," according to M. Sandra Reeves and Alina Tugend,[24] because of a lack of social support, guidance with ASCs, and sacred rituals that can provide structure for profound emotions. Individuals with BPD are dependent on their own resources. Worse, the altered states and unconventional behavior that characterize BPD are labeled deviant, "crazy," or psychotic and are not placed within a meaningful context. I suggest that the individual with BPD becomes fixated in an ill-structured, liminal state and so repeats concrete "ritualistic" acts of self-destruction that are unacceptable in contemporary culture but would be given a sacred meaning within tribal societies.

A case illustrates this thesis. Betsy was a highly intelligent, well-educated, and attractive 30-year-old. She had been hospitalized in a psychiatric facility on numerous occasions in between periods working as a licensed mental health counselor. Her psychiatric admissions were usually for suicidal gestures involving multiple lacerations to her arms and breasts. She often drank heavily and ingested numerous prescribed psychotropic medications, which induced an ASC. During these ASCs, she always solicited help. One hospitalization followed frightening hallucinations of spiders and other creatures dismembering her and tearing at her flesh. Psychological testing during this hospitalization led to her diagnosis of BPD.

Betsy called her mother a "witch" who wanted to "consume" her and control her life. When hospitalized, Betsy dreaded her mother's visits, and after seeing her mother, she often became self-destructive and made attempts at self-mutilation. During her suicidal and self-mutilation episodes, Betsy described a pressure building up inside her, brought on by a witch who took control and "polluted" her, filling her with "pus, worms, and maggots." After cutting herself and seeing the blood drip down her hands, however, Betsy felt calmed.

Betsy was emphatically advised not to continue her career as a therapist. This advice is counter to what often occurs in other societies, however: Shamans are often initiated because of an episode of bizarre behavior and apparently psychotic experience. These events are interpreted as deviant or crazy behavior by the indigenous culture but are also culturally reframed as a spiritual "calling" from which recovery is expected. When Betsy made a similar interpretation of her experience, she began a remarkable process of transformation.

After nearly a decade of parasuicidal behaviors and intermittent hospitalizations, Betsy decided to leave her native state and resume her profession in another. She explained that she realized that her encounter with mental illness made her able to understand others who were suffering similar experiences and to be more deeply empathic with them. Contrary to what her doctors said, Betsy concluded she was better qualified to be a therapist because of her own inner journey. She came to believe in the inherent value of her "illness," a belief that set her on a renewed path of service.

Today Betsy is a therapist working with adolescents and youths; she has gone without episodes of self-mutilation or suicidal attempts for 4 years. Her healing seems contrary to conventional psychiatric expectations but is consistent with the cross-cultural, transpersonal principles of healing and transformation discussed earlier.

Paralleling a rite of passage, Betsy's transformation involved painful crises, altered states of consciousness, self-mutilation, and suspension of social convention. Healing did not begin, however, until Betsy renewed the transpersonal values that motivated her to become a therapist in the first place, seeing a spiritual meaning in all her suffering. Furthermore, she experienced a dramatic change in role and responsibility, changing from dependent daughter to responsible therapist, when she moved to a new status in another state. Her new community role provided the container for healing, that is, the return of soul and passion for life.

Individuals with BPD do not have the cultural "container" that indigenous cultures provide in rites of passage. These rituals, myths, and symbols channel powerful, chaotic, and "primitive" emotions into a new, stable identity by providing transcendent meaning and cultural context to critical life periods. This "education for transcendence"[25] helps build a self structure that can use and integrate experiences of intense affect and nonordinary consciousness. I suggest that chronic borderline states are attempts to achieve healing (spiritual, psychological, and interpersonal) that typically fail in our culture because of lack of social education, support, sacred myths, and rituals that mark and channel life's difficult passages.

CONCLUSION

Although psychological and spiritual crises offer opportunities for transformation and growth, it is important not to romanticize psychopathology. In some cases, such as in schizophrenia or manic-depressive illness, biological elements may severely interfere with development. A cross-cultural, anthropological perspective, however, suggests that in many individual situations, remarkable transformation is possible provided social support and sacred rituals are available. Crisis, suspension of convention, altered states of consciousness, transcendent symbols, and community can transmute apparent psychopathology into psychological and spiritual growth.

Clinically, therefore, other cultures offer much wisdom for modern Western psychiatry. From this perspective, the role of a psychotherapist is closer to that of initiation master—a creator of community—than to a medical doctor. Reclaiming this role represents an initiation—an initio, or return to origins—for psychology and psychiatry: embracing the ancient shamanic roots of medicine, reintegrating spirit and community in transpersonal psychiatry.

NOTES

1. Kiev, A. (1964). The study of folk psychiatry. In A. Kiev (Ed.), *Magic, faith, and healing*. New York: The Free Press.

2. Lewis, M. (1989). *Ecstatic religion* (2nd ed.). Harmonsworth, England: Penguin Books.

3. Prince, R. (1974). The problem of spirit possession for the treatment of psychiatric disorders. *Ethos: Journal of the Society for Psychological Anthropology, 1*, 315–333.

4. Bourguignon, E. (1965). The self, the behavioral environment and the theory of spirit possession. In M. Spiro (Ed.), *Context and meaning in cultural anthropology*. New York: The Free Press. Quotation on p. 50.

5. Lévi-Strauss, C. (1963). The effectiveness of symbols. In C. Lévi-Strauss (Ed.), *Structural anthropology*. New York: Basic Books.

6. Peters, L. G. (1978). Psychotherapy in Tamang shamanism. *Ethos: Journal of the Society for Psychological Anthropology 6(2)*, 63–91.

7. Kennedy, J. (1973). Cultural psychiatry. In J. J. Honigmann (Ed.), *Handbook of social and cultural anthropology*. Chicago: Rand McNally.

8. Grof, S., & Grof, C. (1989). *Spiritual emergency: When personal transformation becomes a crisis*. Los Angeles: Tarcher.

9. Achterberg, J., Dossey, B., & Kolkmeier, L. (1994). *Rituals of healing: Using imagery for health and wellness*. New York: Bantam Books.

10. Turner, V. (1962). Three symbols of passage in Ndembo circumcision ritual. In N. Gluckman (Ed.), *Essays on the ritual of social relations*. Manchester, UK: Manchester University Press. Quotation on p. 146.

11. Eliade, M. (1958). *Rites and symbols of initiation* (R. Trask, Trans.). New York: Harper & Row. Quotation on p. 72.

12. Langness, L. L. (1967). Hysterical psychosis: The cross-cultural evidence. *American Journal of Psychiatry, 124,* 143–152.

13. Newman, P. (1964). Wild man behavior in a New Guinea highland community. *American Anthropologist, 66,* 1019–1028.

14. Rin, H., & Lin, T. (1962). Mental illness among Formosan aborigines as compared with the Chinese in Taiwan. *Journal of Mental Science, 108,* 134–146.

15. Yap, P. M. (1960). The possession syndrome: A comparison of Hong Kong and French findings. *Journal of Mental Science, 106,* 114–137.

16. Lambo, T. A. (1965). Schizophrenic and borderline states. In A. V. S. DeReuck & R. Porter (Eds.), *Transcultural psychiatry*. Boston: Little, Brown. Quotation on p. 72.

17. Torrey, E. F. (1980). Schizophrenia and civilization. New York: Aronson Press.

18. Sartorius, N., Jablensky, A., & Shapiro, R. (1978). Cross-cultural differences in the short-term prognosis of schizophrenic psychosis. *Schizophrenia Bulletin, 4,* 102–113.

19. May, R. (1991). *The cry for myth*. New York: Bantam Books.

20. Geertz, C. (1973). Religion as a cultural system. In C. Geertz (Ed.), *The interpretation of culture*. New York: Basic Books.

21. Tseng, W.-S., & McDermott, J. F. (1981). *Culture, mind and therapy*. New York: Brunner/Mazel. Quotation on p. 42.

22. Paris, J. (1992). Social factors in borderline personality disorder. *Canadian Journal of Psychiatry, 37,* 510–515.

23. Peters, L. G. (1994). Rites of passage and the borderline syndrome: Perspectives in Transpersonal Anthropology. *Anthropology of Consciousness, 5,* 1–15.

24. Reeves, M. S., & Tugend, A. (1988). Suicide's unanswerable logic. In L. C. Mahdi, S. Foster, & M. Little (Eds.), *Betwixt and between: Patterns of masculine and feminine initiation.* LaSalle, IL: Open Court.

25. Katz, R. (1973). Education for transcendence: Lessons from the !Kung Zhu/twasi. *Journal of Transpersonal Psychology, 5(2),* 136–155. Quotation on p. 136.

CHAPTER 22

Western Analytical Philosophy and Transpersonal Epistemology

ALLAN B. CHINEN

FOLLOWING WESTERN SCIENCE, most psychiatrists reject belief in God, gods, or spirits. Yet transpersonal psychiatry draws on spiritual traditions that postulate the existence of such beings. The result is a philosophical conflict for transpersonal clinicians. The issue is not idle speculation. If "spiritual entities" do not exist, experiences of God or gods must be imaginary, and belief in them would be immature or pathological. If such beings do exist, psychiatry must consider questions such as whether "possession" by spirits actually occurs and how possession might differ from states such as multiple personality disorder.[1,2,3]

The clash between transpersonal tradition and modern science can be traced to at least three epistemological principles that determine how science judges the truth of a claim or theory. The first principle is *skepticism*, which questions and challenges traditional received doctrines, such as faith in God's reality or the existence of souls. The second principle is *empiricism*, which demands that beliefs be based on direct experience that is available to any qualified observer. The third principle is *materialism*, which holds that the same processes that govern inanimate objects govern all other phenomena in the world, including spiritual entities such as gods or souls.

In this chapter, I locate these three epistemological principles within the history of Western philosophy, noting alternatives from that tradition. Subsequently, I propose a possible resolution for the conflict between transpersonal tradition and scientific psychiatry from an unexpected source: analytical philosophy, which is the branch of Western thought that gave rise to logical positivism.

A HISTORICAL TOUR

Skepticism has a long history in Western thought; its most dramatic example is found in the work of the ancient Greek philosopher Socrates (469–399 B.C.E.). Through his question-and-answer method, now well-known as the *Socratic dialogue*, Socrates challenged the accepted religious and philosophical conventions of his time. As happens to many social gadflies, Socrates was condemned to death. This suppression of skepticism became even more pronounced when Christianity became a state religion in medieval Europe, emphasizing revealed doctrine and centralized ideological authority. The skeptical spirit flowered again during the Renaissance, with the British philosopher David Hume (1711–1776) as a leading exponent. More recently, the skepticism resurfaced as *deconstructionism*. Proponents of this school, like Jacques Derrida, argue that texts—and all other symbolic expressions—have no fixed, public meaning. Everything is subject to question and reinterpretation.

In Western philosophy, the skeptical spirit has been opposed by the "absolutist" tradition, which argued that absolute, or indubitable, knowledge is possible. One form of absolutism is *rationalism*, exemplified by Plato (428–348 B.C.E.), who argued that pure reason gives us absolute knowledge. A second form of absolutism is *fideism*, the reliance on faith as a foundation of absolute knowledge, exemplified by Christian theologians like Augustine (354–430) and Aquinas (1224–1274). After the medieval "age of faith," pure rationalism flourished again in the Renaissance with René Descartes (1596–1650), widely considered one of the first modern Western philosophers.

The second epistemological principle governing science is empiricism. Like skepticism, empiricism has a long, honored history in philosophy, with Aristotle (384–322 B.C.E.) as a prominent proponent. Although he was a student of Plato, Aristotle insisted on the importance of careful observation. Aristotle dissected animals and insects, and his observations led him to formulate a notion of evolution, as well as basic concepts of embryology. Empiricism retreated when Christianity became dominant in medieval Europe, but it resumed its evolution after the Renaissance, with such figures as John Locke (1630–1704). Francis Bacon (1561–1626) soon included experimental manipulation as part of empiricism, moving beyond simple, passive observation.

In the late nineteenth century, empiricism evolved into *logical positivism*, which holds that to have any meaning a statement must refer to sensory observation. Partly in reaction to this narrow scientific definition of *observation*, proponents of the Romantic movement insisted that empiricism embrace emotions and intuition. Writers like William Blake (1757–1827), Samuel Coleridge (1772–1834), and Ralph Waldo Emerson (1803–1882) extolled the importance of passion and mystery in human knowledge. Johann Goethe (1749–1839) exemplified the Romantic view, arguing for an inclusive model of science in which poetry, art, and traditional science constituted a single knowledge-seeking enterprise. Soren Kierkegaard (1813–1855) and recent existentialists like Albert Camus, Jean-Paul Sartre, and Karl Jaspers elaborated on the Romantic tradition, insisting that human experience is fundamentally irrational. Phenomenologists like Edmund Husserl, Martin Heidegger, and Maurice Merleau-Ponty went on to argue that introspection qualifies as evidence as much as detached sensory observation. The "New Age" movement builds on this broadened empirical tradition by arguing that nonordinary experiences, produced by psychedelics, meditation, yoga, vision quests, and so on, are included in the framework of observation and evidence. Many transpersonal psychiatrists implicitly accept this broadened version of empiricism.

The third epistemological principle of science is materialism. Like skepticism and empiricism, materialism can be traced back to early Greek philosophers. Democritus (460–370 B.C.E.), for instance, argued that everything is composed of tiny indestructible units he named *atoms*. Materialism went underground during the Christian era but reappeared during the Renaissance. Thomas Hobbes (1588–1679), for instance, argued that mental experiences are the result of purely mechanical processes involving atoms, a position prevalent in modern psychiatry. Charles Darwin (1809–1882) placed mental processes within an evolutionary perspective, and contemporary sociobiologists, like E. O. Wilson, continue the Darwinian tradition by arguing that religion is a biological adaptation just like language use or the opposable thumb; that is, the same processes that determine biology govern spiritual matters. Even earlier, the German philosopher Ludwig Feuerbach (1804–1882) held that God did not create humanity; humanity created God by inventing religion. Karl Marx (1818–1883) introduced yet another materialist view, arguing in part that religion is a tool used by the ruling classes to keep the lower classes pacified.

Opposed to materialism is *idealism,* or *spiritualism,* the doctrine that reality is ultimately composed of pure ideas or some sort of spiritual "substance." Plato exemplified this view, postulating the existence of eternal Forms that stand behind the fleeting sensory experiences of transient material objects. Plotinus (204–270) elaborated on Plato's philosophy and proposed that there is one ultimate Form, the Form of Forms, which he identified with God. This neo-Platonic tradition provided a rich philosophical framework for subsequent Jewish, Christian, and Islamic mysticism. Idealism experienced a revival beginning in the seventeenth century, with George Berkeley, Gottfried Leibniz, Baruch Spinoza, and Johann Fichte. Georg Hegel (1770–1831) offered a particularly important version of idealism. Hegel argued that reality is ultimately "pure Reason," a "World Mind" that evolves toward a state of increasing integration, following a dialectic process in which thesis generates antithesis and then moves to synthesis. Hegel's dialectic is important to transpersonal psychiatry because it underlies Ken Wilber's theory of consciousness.[4]

Skepticism, empiricism, and materialism usually conflict with absolutism, rationalism, fideism, and idealism. Descartes attempted to reconcile the two conflicting camps by dividing the world into two domains, one material and the other mental or spiritual. Skepticism, empiricism, and materialism apply to the material realm. Absolutism, rationalism, fideism, and idealism apply to the mental or spiritual domain. Immanuel Kant (1724–1804) later offered another integration, redividing the world not between mind and matter but between human experience and reality itself. Kant argued that human experience is structured in specific, universal ways, exemplified by logic.

Kant profoundly influenced Western thought. Structuralists like Ferdinand de Saussure, Claude Lévi-Strauss, Roland Barthes, Michel Foucault, and Noam Chomsky extended Kant's search for universal structures into linguistics, anthropology, literature, and sociology. Sigmund Freud did the same in psychology: His theory involving the ego, id, superego, and oedipal complex involves Kantian-type structures. Carl Jung's notion of archetypes also exemplifies the kind of innate structures Kant postulated.

Twentieth-century analytical philosophy, which includes G. E. Moore, Bertrand Russell, Ludwig Wittgenstein, and Gilbert Ryle as leading proponents, continued Kant's tradition in a slightly different vein. They analyzed everyday concepts and language use as examples of basic structures that shape human experience. Analytical philosophers usually reject metaphysical claims about spiritual entities; however, when it is considered in a broader, more explicitly Kantian fashion, analytical philosophy helps reconcile the conflict between scientific and spiritual claims in transpersonal psychiatry. I shall explain this statement by analyzing an example: a transpersonal trance vision.

CONCEPTS OF TRUTH

A person in an altered state of consciousness, like a shamanic or meditative trance, may have a vision of an animal-spirit helper. The vision may be repeated in other trance episodes in such a vivid manner that the individual may conclude the visions are true. But what criteria are used to determine whether the visions are true or hallucinations? Here analytical philosophy takes a step back and asks a more fundamental question: What do we mean by *true?* That is, what is involved in the concept of truth?

The most common notion is that an experience is true if it represents a real situation. The trance vision would be true if the animal spirit actually existed. Implicit here is the concept of *objective* rather than *subjective* existence. The former requires that other people be able to see the same animal helper, under the right conditions, for example, if they enter the proper kind of trance. If the animal spirit were idiosyncratic to one individual, the vision would not be true in an objective sense.

This concept of truth has been called various names in philosophy, including "the correspondence concept of truth," because it holds that an experience must correspond with reality to be true. Science relies on this representational concept of truth, as does jurisprudence. The goal for both is the elucidation of facts independent of an observer's personal reactions.

Implicit in the objective concept of truth is a second notion: that of subjective truth. In this view, an individual's vision of a spirit animal is treated as an inner experience. The question is not whether the spirit animal actually exists but what the individual's vision means. Psychoanalysts, for instance, might interpret the visions as they would a dream, symbolizing the individual's unconscious concerns. The vision can also be interpreted in terms of a particular cultural or religious system, and if the individual's experience fits into the system, the vision is meaningful and "subjectively true." (Most traditions, from Huichol shamanism to Tibetan Buddhism, have criteria for separating authentic or "true" visions from false ones.) Two elements define subjective truth: (1) suspension of the question of objective truth and (2) consistency or coherence within a larger meaning system. (Hence the name of this concept in philosophy, the *coherence concept of truth*.)

Hermeneutic philosophers like Wilhelm Dilthey, Hans-Georg Gadamer, and Jurgen Habermas emphasize the coherence concept of truth, as do phenomenologists like Husserl, Heidegger, and Merleau-Ponty. Hermeneutics and phenomenology both suspend questions of external reality to introspect on inner experience and delineate its structures. Hence one might call this notion the hermeneutic or phenomenological concept of truth. "Awareness meditations" like vipassana and the systems built on these experiences, such as Buddhist Abhidharma psychology, also use the hermeneutic concept of truth. Similarly, contemporary transpersonal theorists like Ken Wilber, Stanislav Grof, and Michael Washburn use the hermeneutic mode, outlining various structures in consciousness.

There is a third notion of truth, often called *pragmatic truth*, first explicated by the American philosophers William James (see Chapter 3), Charles Pierce, and John Dewey. According to this school, an experience is "true" if it helps an individual master a situation or solve a problem. Experiences or beliefs are considered to be actions like any other actions, and true experiences and beliefs are those with positive consequences. In the example of the animal spirit, the vision may inspire the individual to change his or her life, for example, switching careers to become a shamanic healer. If the overall result is salutary, the vision would be considered true in a pragmatic sense. Engineering, applied technology, medicine, and other therapies rely on the pragmatic concept of truth. Pragmatic truth provides transpersonal clinicians with powerful support: The therapeutic effects of using altered states of consciousness help establish the "validity" or "truth" of transpersonal psychiatry (see Chapters 8, 10, 11, 12, 25, 29, 32, 33, 35).

A fourth type of truth involves metaphors. Here an experience is taken to be an imperfect characterization of a far more complex, and perhaps ineffable, reality. In the example of the spirit animal, the trance experience would not be interpreted as a representation of an inner or outer reality but as a metaphor for a complex, mysterious phenomenon. Two elements are important in this concept of truth: (1) reference to something undefined or ineffable and (2) a specific experience that "points to" this mysterious reality. Mystics commonly use the metaphoric concept of truth, emphasizing that their descriptions are only analogies for an ultimate reality that transcends words or images. "New Age" literature uses the metaphoric concept of truth, for instance, in talking about spiritual energy, vibrations, or auras. Taken literally, as objective claims, the assertions are problematic because spiritual energies or vibrations are not reliably or universally perceived, nor do instruments detect these phenomena, in contrast to light, sound, and heat, which are paradigmatic examples of energy and vibration. As metaphors for more complex phenomena, the terms *spiritual energy* and *spiritual vibration* have greater and more plausible meaning.

The metaphoric mode has various standards by which to judge the "truth" of an expression. Particularly "good" metaphors, for instance, produce an "Aha!" feeling, the sense that the symbol "fits" the mysterious reality in question and reveals something new about the situation. At the same time, a good metaphor also evokes a sense of mystery, wonder, and openness. Metaphoric truth can therefore be judged by how fitting, full, rich, and evocative it is. Because it is difficult to make these judgments precisely, these standards have been most clearly elucidated in the humanities. It is no accident that transpersonal psychology arose out of humanistic psychology: The metaphoric concept of truth is even more prominent with spiritual experiences, and transpersonal literature relies heavily on metaphors and arguments-by-analogy.

A final notion of truth might be called the *presentational concept.* Here an experience is accepted just as it is, without reference to anything beyond it. The immediate experience is not taken to be a symbol or representation of anything else but as something complete in itself. In the case of the spirit animal, the trance vision would be accepted simply as it is experienced, without judgment or analysis. An everyday example of this type of truth comes from modern art: An abstract painting is enjoyed as a visual experience of color and shape. The image is not interpreted as a portrait of anything real, nor even as an expression of a subjective state. Significantly, descriptions of enlightenment experiences from various traditions emphasize the presentational concept of truth: In enlightenment, an individual is said to see things just as they are, without analysis, explication, or distortion.

MODES OF TRUTH

The five concepts of truth described are directly related to basic logical modalities, as analyzed by modal logic.[5,6] The different modes of truth represent basic modes of human understanding. An analogy—a metaphor—is useful here. The different modes of truth are like distinct sensory modalities, each with characteristic features. Representational truth is analogous to sight, which provides a clear view of objects, separate from the observer. The hermeneutic notion is like smell, a sense that usually triggers immediate and highly personal reactions, such as pleasure, repulsion, or vivid memories. The emphasis on such personal, inner experience is central to the hermeneutic mode of truth. The pragmatic mode is equivalent to touch, which determines texture and weight by rubbing or moving an object. Action is central to touch, as it is to the pragmatic concept of truth. The metaphoric mode is analogous to hearing, which in general is less localized and specific than sight and constantly open to all directions, that is, less definite. Sound, particularly in music, is also capable of expressing many complex, ill-defined emotions that escape literal or verbal description. Finally, the presentational concept of truth is like taste: an immediate experience that is rarely questioned or analyzed but is often enjoyed for its own sake, for instance in wine-tasting.

The analogy with sensory modalities is useful in emphasizing that all the modes of truth are necessary for a full understanding of the world. Relying only on sight or hearing leads to impoverished information. Similarly, relying only on representational or phenomenological modes of truth gives inadequate knowledge. Transpersonal phenomena in particular require a multimodal approach, or a pluralistic epistemology.

Modes of truth are conceptually distinct from the structures of consciousness described by transpersonal theorists such as Wilber, Grof, and Washburn, which describe the organization of various elements in consciousness: the structure of an experience. In contrast, modes of truth involve how the experience, whatever its structure, is interpreted and related to "reality," that is, as objective fact, subjective illusion, and so on. Another analogy is useful: Most transpersonal theorists describe the syntax of experience, or how various elements of consciousness like the ego or body image are linked with each other according to definite principles. This idea parallels the way that words are organized by definite grammatical rules into sentences. Modes of truth, on the other hand, involve semantics: how an experience, with all its organized elements, is interpreted or related to "the world," paralleling the different ways a word relates to its referent. The difference here might be summed up by two distinct questions: (1) How do the elements of an experience relate to each other? (2) How does the experience relate to reality, truth, being, or existence? The first question is phenomenological and structuralist; the second, epistemological and ontological. The example of mystical experience may clarify the distinction.

Mystical experiences are often described in terms of union with the cosmos, direct experience of the unity of all things, or transcendence of the subject–object duality. These various formulations explicate the syntax, or structure, of mystical experience. Modes of truth, on the other hand, involve ontological interpretation: Is the mystical experience taken to be objective fact or subjective reality? Or is it used pragmatically, for instance, to inspire creativity or counteract depression?

Attending to the different modes of truth helps clarify various conceptual confusions. For example, many transpersonal theorists point out the similarities in mystical experiences described by exponents of widely different traditions. These parallels are taken as evidence for the universality of mystical experience, which is presented, in turn, as evidence for the validity or truth of mystical consciousness. This reasoning confuses the phenomenological and representational modes of truth. The similarities in descriptions do indeed suggest that mystical states follow certain rules that hold for all people in the same way that human languages have similar "deep structures." This universality, however, does not mean that mystical experiences reveal anything about the objective world. All the mystical episodes might be hallucinations. The claim for the universality of mystical experience involves the phenomenological mode, which can be tested by the direct subjective experience of many different individuals. Whether those mystical states portray objective reality involves a representational claim, which requires a different kind of testing, usually that involved in science.

In fact, the findings of modern physics are frequently cited as evidence for the truth of mystical experiences, for example, that all aspects of the cosmos interact and are part of a unitary whole. This argument also confuses different modes of truth. In mystical experience, part of the sense of unity, or transcendence of the subject–object duality, comes from the usual mode in which mystical states are experienced, the presentational mode. Here the mystical episode is experienced just as it is, without reference to anything beyond itself. No duality is experienced, because no analysis or reflection is involved. But this means that no representational or phenomenological claims can be made, because those modes require analysis and reflection. No correlation can be made, therefore, between mystical episodes experienced in the presentational mode and modern physics theory, which uses the representational mode. To be sure, mystical experiences can be approached in the representational mode and subjected to various tests. For instance, if an individual having a mystical experience is truly one with the cosmos, he or she should have knowledge of all the cosmos. Scores on tests of telepathy and clairvoyance should be highly and reliably correlated with mystical experiences, as is often claimed in spiritual traditions. This is a matter for scientific investigation (see Chapter 20).

In most of the recent discussions of the relation between physics and mystical experience, the meaning appears to be metaphoric; that is, the parallels between quantum physics and mystical consciousness are analogical, not literal. The metaphoric meanings are important, however, because many scientific insights and paradigms come from metaphors. To be scientifically useful, however, metaphors must be translated into specific, concrete, testable claims, that is, shifted into the representational mode from the metaphoric one.

The status of science remains controversial in transpersonal psychiatry. Modes of truth help clarify the issues. Different modes of truth may apply to the same object of attention, as the example of mystical experience showed. But the complement holds: The same mode can apply to different objects of consciousness. This means that the representational mode, so closely allied with science, can be used in principle for any object of study, including all transpersonal phenomena. The scientific study of phenomena such as shamanic trances and mystical experiences is possible, therefore, in principle: a basic tenet of transpersonal psychiatry. The empirical work of Charles Tart, Roger Walsh, Grof, and much earlier, James (See Chapters 3, 8, 17, 19) illustrates this application of the representational mode to transpersonal phenomena.

CONCLUSION

Common sense often assumes that truth is either subjective or objective. In that case, transpersonal psychiatry would have to be like either physics and chemistry, dealing with material processes such as electrons and plants, or the humanities, involved with inner worlds, often imaginary. Western analytic philosophy reveals that there are other modes of truth, which reflect deep structures of the human psyche, as explicated by modal logic. All the modes of truth are needed for an adequate understanding of the human condition: from the mundane to the sublime, childhood to elderhood, and prepersonal to transpersonal. To paraphrase the mathematician-philosopher Alfred North Whitehead, the question is not simply whether transpersonal experiences are true or not. The real question is, true in what sense? Only a rich, multimodal approach will allow transpersonal psychiatry to come of age and achieve its full potential as a truly scientific, humanistic, practical, and spiritual discipline.[7]

NOTES

1. McDermott, R. A. (1993). Transpersonal worldviews: Historical and philosophical reflections. In R. Walsh & F. Vaughan (Eds.), *Paths beyond ego: The transpersonal vision.* Los Angeles: Tarcher.

2. Rothberg, D. (1986). Philosophical foundations of transpersonal psychology: An introduction to some basic issues. *Journal of Transpersonal Psychology, 18,* 1–34.

3. Walsh, R., & Vaughan, F. (1993). On transpersonal definitions. *Journal of Transpersonal Psychology, 25,* 199–208.

4. Wilber, K. (1993). The great chain of being. *Journal of Humanistic Psychology, 33(3),* 66–81.

5. Chinen, A. (1988). Modes of understanding and mindfulness in clinical medicine. *Theoretical Medicine, 9,* 45–71.

6. Chinen, A. (1987). Semiotic modes and the development of perspective in clinical object relations. *Psychoanalysis and Contemporary Thought, 10,* 373–406.

7. Harman, W. (1994). The scientific exploration of consciousness: Towards an adequate epistemology. *Journal of Consciousness Studies, 1,* 140–148.

PART III

Clinical Practice

DIAGNOSIS

TRANSPERSONAL PSYCHOTHERAPY

PSYCHOPHARMACOLOGY

SPECIAL TECHNIQUES

ETHICS AND PROFESSIONAL DEVELOPMENT

CHAPTER 23

Diagnosis: A Transpersonal Clinical Approach to Religious and Spiritual Problems

DAVID LUKOFF,
FRANCIS G. LU, AND
ROBERT TURNER

TRADITIONAL PSYCHIATRY has tended to ignore or pathologize religious and spiritual issues. Yet these issues are among the most important cultural factors structuring human experience. In addition, studies have shown that mental health professionals are frequently called on to assess and treat religious–spiritual issues. The Group for the Advancement of Psychiatry reported that "manifest references to religion occur in about one-third of all psychoanalytic sessions."[1] In other studies, psychologists reported that at least 1 in 6 of their clients presented issues that involve religion or spirituality;[2] 29% of psychotherapists agreed that religious issues are important in the treatment of all or many of their clients;[3] and 4.5% of therapy patients brought mystical experiences into treatment.[4]

RELIGION, SPIRITUALITY, AND PSYCHOPATHOLOGY

The view that religion and spirituality are associated with psychopathology has a long history in the theory, research, and practice of psychiatry.[5] Yet studies indicate that religion is linked to psychological well-being and provides a source of meaning and purpose in life.[6] A meta-analysis of religious commitment and mental health found them to be positively related. Church-affiliated individuals showed greater happiness and satisfaction with marriage, work, and life.[7] Studies also found a significant positive correlation between the self-reported quality of relationships with divine others (e.g., Christ, God, Mary) and several measures of well-being.[8] Similarly, people reporting mystical experiences have scored lower on psychopathology scales and higher on measures of psychological well-being than controls.[9,10,11] Numerous studies have also documented the non-pathological nature of near-death experiences (NDEs) (see Chapter 29).

RELIGIOSITY GAP

Perhaps one reason that religion and spirituality have been associated with psychopathology is the "religiosity gap" between mental health professionals and the general public. Surveys conducted in the United States consistently show that both the general public and psychiatric patients attend church more frequently than mental health professionals, believe in God at a significantly higher rate, and consider religion to be more important in their lives.[3,12]

The spiritual beliefs and practices of mental health professionals have not been researched to the same extent, but the limited data available do not suggest the existence of a "spirituality gap." In one survey, 51% of psychologists characterized their spiritual beliefs and practices as involving an alternative spiritual path rather than an organized religion.[2] Another survey of psychiatrists, psychologists, social workers, and marriage and family counselors found that 68% indicated that they seek a spiritual understanding of the universe and one's place in it.[3] The authors concluded that "there may be a reservoir of spiritual interests among therapists that is often unexpressed due to the secular framework of professional education and practice."[3]

CULTURAL SENSITIVITY ISSUES IN CLINICAL PRACTICE

In traditional psychiatry, the narrow focus on biological factors, combined with the historical biases against religious and spiritual experiences, impedes culturally sensitive understanding and treatment of religious and spiritual problems. This problem is particularly apparent when ethnic minorities and non-Western societies are considered. Traditional healers often conceptualize and treat patients' complaints as having spiritual causes.[13] When the cultural context of the individual is considered, some individuals who present with unusual religious or spiritual content are found to be free of psychopathology and suffering from a culturally appropriate reaction to stress[14] (see Chapter 21). For example, Maurice Eisenbruch[14] described "cultural bereavement" syndrome among Cambodian refugees characterized by visits from supernatural forces and yearning to complete obligations to the dead. Through the use of culturally validated ritual, a Buddhist monk or traditional healer may successfully restore the patient's link with the past and help with reintegration into the community.

Non-Western traditional cultures also distinguish between serious mental illness and the spiritual problems experienced by some shamans-to-be[15,16] (see Chapter 10). Anthropological accounts show that babbling confused words, displaying curious eating habits, singing continuously, dancing wildly, and being "tormented by spirits" are common elements in shamanic initiatory crises. In shamanic cultures, spiritual crises are interpreted as an indication of an individual's destiny to become a shaman rather than a sign of mental illness. Individuals in Western cultures occasionally experience similar problems,[17,18] which sometimes lead them into the allied health professions.[19]

In Asian cultures, spiritual problems are distinguished from psychopathology. For example, a well-known pitfall of spiritual practice recognized in many Asian traditions is "false enlightenment," associated with delightful or terrifying visions, especially of light.[20] When these spiritual traditions are transplanted into Western contexts, such problems still occur.[21]

RELIGIOUS OR SPIRITUAL PROBLEM

To redress the lack of sensitivity to the religious and spiritual problems that become the focus of psychiatric treatment, we proposed a new diagnostic category for DSM-IV: "religious or spiritual problem." The definition in DSM-IV reads as follows:

> This category can be used when the focus of clinical attention is a religious or spiritual problem. Examples include distressing experiences that involve loss or questioning of faith, problems associated with conversion to a new faith, or questioning of other spiritual values that may not necessarily be related to an organized church or religious institution.[67]

Although the terms *religion* and *spirituality* are sometimes used interchangeably, in this chapter we use the term *religion* to stand for adherence to the beliefs and practices of an organized religious institution and the term *spirituality* to refer to the relationship between a person and a transcendent reality, not involving a specific religious affiliation.

In the following sections, a typology of religious and spiritual problems is presented, and instances in which such problems coexist with Axis I mental disorders are discussed.

Types of Religious Problems

Religious problems have received much more attention than spiritual problems in the clinical and research literature. There are about a dozen journals devoted to pastoral counseling and several more to "Christian psychiatry." Additionally, there are professional organizations and conferences that address religious problems.

The most common examples of religious problems described in the clinical literature are loss or questioning of faith, change in denominational membership or conversion to a new religion, intensification of religious beliefs and practices, and joining or involvement with a new religious movement or cult.

Loss or Questioning of Faith

Dorothy Barra, Erica Carlson, Mark Maize, and colleagues[22] conducted a survey and reviewed the anthropological, historical, and contemporary perspectives on religious loss as a grief-engendering phenomenon. They concluded that "a break in one's religious connectedness, whether in relation to traditional religious affiliation or to a more personal search for spiritual identity, frequently resulted in individuals experiencing many of the feelings associated with more 'normal' loss situations."[22] They cited one case of a graduate student who described giving up belief in her organized religion of origin. She reported feeling alienated, fear, anxiety, anger, hopelessness, and even suicidal ideation, the common sequelae of a grief reaction. Edward Shafranske[23] described a man of professional accomplishment whose life was founded on the bedrock of conservative Roman Catholic Christianity. He came to doubt the tenets of his religion and, in so doing, declared he had lost the vitality to live. Jack Kornfield[24] has also described grief reactions related to loss of spiritual connection.

Change in Denominational Membership or Conversion to a New Religion

A serious loss may be experienced when persons from differing religious backgrounds marry or a person moves to a community that does not have a branch of his or her original religious group.

Intensification of Adherence to Beliefs and Practices

Newly religious patients often experience conflicts between their former and current lifestyles, beliefs, and attitudes. Spero[25] described the case of a 16-year-old adolescent from a reform Jewish family who underwent a sudden transformation to religious orthodoxy. The dramatic changes in her life, including long hours studying Jewish texts, avoidance of friends, and sullenness at meals, led to her referral to a psychoanalyst. A mental status examination uncovered no Axis I or II disorders. The analysis dealt with the impact of religious transformation on her identity and object relations.

Voluntary intensification of religious practice may be the result of a powerful religious experience. This event can lead to problems when the person either does not feel free or does not know how to talk about it. Intensification of religious practice is also a common coping mechanism used to deal with trauma and is associated with the need to find meaning in the distressing event to avoid a breakdown of identity.

Involvement in New Religious Movements and Cults

The issue of cults has been controversial (see Chapter 30). The American Psychiatric Association's Committee on Psychiatry and

Religion[26] called upon psychiatrists to "help temper the anticult fanaticism that often afflicts a distressed family" and to resist labeling nonconformists as mentally ill. In particular, psychiatrists were under pressure in the early 1980s, after the Jonestown massacre, to sanction the forcible deprogramming and involuntary hospitalization of religious seekers who were "turning East."[27]

More than 90% of persons who join new religious groups leave within 2 years.[28] Post[27] points out that "if brainwashing goes on, it is extremely ineffective." For the vast majority, such "radical religious departures" are part of their adolescent or young-adult identity exploration. Vaughan[29] reported that many individuals who leave destructive groups say that the experience contributed to their wisdom and maturity by forcing them to meet the challenge of restoring their integrity. Nevertheless, some genuinely dangerous and destructive groups do arise under the banner of religion, and the experience can lead to serious psychological difficulties in those unfortunate enough to belong to the groups. Finally, Bogart[30] reviewed the various disturbances and problems that can occur in the relationship between a student and his or her spiritual teacher. Often students transitioning from the "culture of embeddedness" with their teachers into more independent functioning seek psychotherapeutic help.

Types of Spiritual Problems

The definition of *spiritual problems* in the DSM-IV includes the "questioning of other spiritual values which may not necessarily be related to an organized church or religious institution."[67] For some individuals, it may involve questioning their whole way of life, purpose for living, and source of meaning.

Mystical Experience

The definition of a mystical experience used by researchers and clinicians varies considerably,[31] ranging from Neumann's[32] "upheaval of the total personality," to Greeley's[33] "spiritual force that seems to lift you out of yourself," to Scharfstein's[34] "everyday mysticism." A definition of mystical experience that is both congruent with the major theoretical literature and clinically applicable would characterize it as a transient, extraordinary experience marked by feelings of unity and harmonious relationship to the divine and everything in existence, as well as euphoric feelings, sense of gnosis, loss of ego functioning, alterations in time and space perception, and the sense of lacking control over the event. Numerous studies assessing the incidence of mystical experience support the conclusion reached by Bernard Spilka, Ralph Hood, and Richard Gorsuch[35] that 30–40% of the population have had mystical experiences, suggesting that these are normal rather than pathological phenomena.

A case example of a spiritual problem from a report of the Group for the Advancement of Psychiatry (GAP)[36] illustrates how a mystical experience can become the focus of treatment. The patient was a woman in her early 30s who sought out therapy to deal with unresolved parental struggles and guilt over a younger brother's psychosis. Approximately 2 years into her therapy, she underwent a typical mystical experience, including a state of ecstasy, a sense of union with the universe, a heightened awareness transcending space and time, and a greater sense of meaning and purpose to her life. This experience increasingly became the focus of her continued treatment as she worked to integrate the insights and attitudinal changes that followed. The report stated:

> Her mood was ecstatic (if you prefer a theological term) or euphoric (if you prefer psychiatric vocabulary); it persisted for about ten days. She felt that everything in her life had led up to this momentous experience and that all her knowledge had become reorganized during its course. For her, the most important gain from it was a conviction that she was a worthwhile person with worthwhile ideas, not the intrinsically evil person, "rotten to the core," that her mother had convinced her she was.[36]

Because of the rapid alteration in her mood and her unusual ideation, the authors considered diagnoses of mania, schizophrenia, and hysteria. But they rejected these because many aspects of her functioning were either unchanged or improved, and overall her experience seemed to be "more integrating than disintegrating." They concluded that "while a psychiatric diagnosis cannot be dismissed, her experience was certainly akin to those described by great religious mystics who have found a new life through them."[36] Her subsequent treatment focused on expanding the insights she had gained and helping her to assimilate the mystical experience. Nobel[37] noted that although mystical experience may result in greater psychological health, the process is sometimes disruptive and may prompt individuals to seek treatment.

Near-Death Experience

For a discussion of the near-death experience, see Chapter 29.

Spiritual Emergence or Emergency

Asian spiritual practices that entered the West starting in the 1960s have been found to be associated with a variety of psychological difficulties for some persons. Stanislav and Christina Grof[21] have collected case reports illustrating the more common presentations, including mystical experiences, kundalini awakening (a complex physiopsychospiritual transformative process described in the yogic tradition), shamanistic initiatory crisis (a rite of passage for shamans-to-be in indigenous cultures, commonly involving physical illness or psychological crisis, or both), and psychic opening (the sudden occurrence of paranormal experiences).

These problems present with intensities ranging from a mild form of "spiritual emergence" (a gradual unfoldment of spiritual potential with no disruption in psychological–social–occupational functioning) to a severe form of "spiritual emergency" (an uncontrolled emergence of spiritual phenomena with significant disruption in psychological–social–occupational functioning). In general, the milder forms of spiritual emergence should not be diagnosed or treated as mental disorders but rather as religious or spiritual problems that can result in long-term improvement in overall well-being and functioning. The more severe forms of spiritual emergency, which some view as developmental crises, may be associated with mental disorders or exacerbate preexisting Axis I or II disorders.

Assagioli[38] (see Chapter 6), in his classic paper "Self-Realization and Psychological Disturbances," also noted the association between religious–spiritual practices and psychological problems. For example, persons may become inflated and grandiose as a result of their religious–spiritual experiences: "Instances of such confusion are not uncommon among people who become dazzled by contact with truths too great or energies too powerful for their mental capacities to grasp and their personality to assimilate."[38] In Jungian analysis, "the crisis experience, far from something to be overcome or avoided, is essential to psychological and religious growth; in fact, it is so important that it is sometimes purposely induced during the analytical process."[39] Jung's viewpoint was that this induced crisis experience has religious–spiritual as well as therapeutic dimensions.

Meditation

Walsh and Roche[40] noted that altered perceptions may occur during initial phases of intensive meditation but that these are not necessarily pathological (see Chapter 17). Such experiences, if distressing, should be categorized as religious or spiritual problems. The clinical literature also documents, however, that meditation can occasionally precipitate psychological difficulties. Meditation, especially Buddhist forms, may have a special attraction for persons with borderline and narcissistic personality disorders because the doctrine legitimates and rationalizes their lack of self-structure and integration.[41] When meditative practice exacerbates a latent or preexisting disorder, the diagnosis of *religious or spiritual problem* should be used in conjunction with the appropriate Axis I or II disorder.

Medical or Terminal Illness

Religious and spiritual beliefs and practices often influence the ways that patients react to medical illness. The religious or spiritual aspects of patients' lives are often ignored, however, or only superficially explored by consultation–liaison psychiatrists.[42]

This is particularly true in the case of terminal illnesses that raise fears of physical pain, the unknown risks of dying, the threat to integrity, and the uncertainty of life after death. It is important that consultation–liaison psychiatrists, doctors, and nurses work together with clergy in caring for dying patients,[42] because profound religious and spiritual changes often occur during terminal illness.

It is interesting that the psychiatric nursing profession has demonstrated greater awareness than the medical profession of the spiritual problems of hospitalized patients and has established a diagnostic category of spiritual distress to cover two treatment situations: (1) when religious or spiritual beliefs conflict with a prescribed health regimen and (2) when there is distress associated with a patient's mental or physical inability to practice religious or spiritual rituals.[43]

RELIGIOUS OR SPIRITUAL PROBLEM CONCURRENT
WITH MENTAL DISORDER

DSM-IV includes a section for "other conditions that may be a focus of clinical attention."[67] This definition introduces a third possible relationship with a mental disorder that was not included in DSM-III-R. In addition to recognizing that a religious or spiritual problem can occur without a mental disorder and can exist with an unrelated concomitant mental disorder, the new definition specifically notes the possibility that an individual can have a mental disorder that is related to the problem, as long as the problem is sufficiently severe to warrant independent clinical attention. For example, the diagnosis *religious or spiritual problem* could be assigned along with bipolar disorder if the religious–spiritual content is addressed in the treatment of a manic episode. Or *religious or spiritual problem* can be coded along with obsessive–compulsive disorder if treatment addresses religious scrupulosity. This definition greatly expands the potential use of this category, because the symptoms and treatment of many mental disorders include religious and spiritual aspects.

Jerome Kroll and William Sheehan[44] found that hospitalized psychiatric patients are as religious as the general population, and they suggest that patients may turn to religion additionally during crises. At St. Elizabeth's Hospital in Washington, D.C., the Chaplain Program, headed by Clark Aist, conducts a "spiritual needs assessment" on each inpatient, concluding with a treatment plan that identifies religious–spiritual needs and problems, the role of pastoral intervention, and recommended religious–spiritual activities. Following are some examples of common co-occurrences.

Alcohol and Drug Dependence and Abuse

The strong relationship between religious–spiritual commitment (e.g., church attendance) and the avoidance of alcohol and illicit drugs is well established. Unfortunately, not much is known about the religious–spiritual dimensions of addiction treatment because religious–spiritual variables have been neglected in research.[45] It is known, however, that patients in alcohol treatment who become involved with a religious community after treatment have lower recidivism rates than those who do not.[46]

Twelve-Step programs dominate addiction treatment in mental health settings, and religion–spirituality plays a central role. One of the 12 steps mentions "a Power greater than ourselves"; the final step mentions a "spiritual awakening"; 5 of the 12 steps make a specific reference to God; and the phrase "as we understand Him" appears twice. The founders of Alcoholics Anonymous (AA) did not ponder whether religious and spiritual factors are important in recovery, but rather whether it is possible for alcoholics to recover without the help of a higher power.[45] Jung told Bill W., the cofounder of Alcoholics Anonymous, that "craving for alcohol was the equivalent, on a low level, of the spiritual thirst of our being for wholeness."[46] Jung maintained that recovery from addiction required a religious experience in order to be released from the curse of pathology.[47] Similarly, some theorists and clinicians within the field of transpersonal psychology have approached addictions as essentially spiritual crises rather than mental disorders.[48]

Obsessive–Compulsive Disorder

Superficially, religious rituals and obsessive–compulsive behaviors share some common features: the prominent role of cleanliness and purity, the need for rituals to be carried out in specific ways and numbers of times, and the fear of performing the ritual incorrectly. David Greenberg and Eliezer Witztum[49] described an individual whose concern with saying his prayers correctly led him to spend 9 hours a day in prayer instead of the usual 40–90 minutes of other ultraorthodox Jews. In such cases, Greenberg and Witztum recommend meeting with the patient's religious leader present and that "during assessment, the terms and symbols of the religion of strictly religious patients should be used . . . [to] enable the patient to feel as comfortable as possible."[49] When these religious factors warrant independent clinical attention and are explicitly addressed in treatment, the diagnosis of *religious or spiritual problem* should be coded along with obsessive–compulsive disorder.

Greenberg and Witztum proposed the following criteria for differentiating obsessive–compulsive behaviors from religious practices: (1) The compulsive behavior goes beyond the letter of the religious law; (2) the compulsive behavior is focused on one specific area and does not reflect an overall concern for religious practice; (3) the choice of focus of obsessive–compulsive behavior is typical of the disorder (e.g., cleanliness and checking, obsessive thoughts of blasphemy toward God, or fear of illness); and (4) many important dimensions of religious life are neglected. These criteria should be viewed as guidelines and applied in a culturally and contextually sensitive manner. Some genuine, intense religious experiences can be awesome and frightening, preoccupy the individual for a period of time, and lead to the performance of private rituals. Greenberg and Witztum remind clinicians that "differentiating religious beliefs and rituals from delusions and compulsions is difficult for therapists ignorant of the basic tenets of that religion."[49]

Psychotic Disorders

Co-occurrence of a mental disorder and a religious or spiritual problem is frequent among the psychotic disorders, especially manic psychosis. One study of hospitalized bipolar patients found religious–spiritual delusions present in 25% and that the hallucinations were usually religious.[50] Edward Podvoll[51] discussed the similarities between manic psychotic episodes and mystical experiences. From the medical-model perspective, these similarities suggest that "there may have been many mystics who may well have suffered from manic-depressive illness—for example, St. Theresa, St. Francis, St. John."[50] David Lukoff[55] proposed a new diagnostic category of Psychotic Episode with Mystical Features to accommodate this coexistence of genuine mystical features with a psychotic disorder. For such patients, the diagnosis of *religious or spiritual problem* could be coded along with the concomitant Axis I disorder.

Some individuals with schizophrenia present with delusions of being Christ or receiving direct communication from God. Even in these cases, the treatment literature documents that there is often therapeutic value in addressing a person's religious ideation.[53] When a person develops the grandiose delusion that he is God or the messiah, the valid religious–spiritual dimensions of the experience can be salvaged through psychotherapy: "What remains . . . is an ideal model and a sense of direction which one can use to complete the transformation through his own purposeful methods."[38] Transpersonal psychotherapy can be especially valuable in the postpsychotic period because it promotes the integration of the healthy parts of religious–spiritual experiences in psychosis.[54] One woman wrote that following her hospitalization, she could look back and say, "Listen, I had this incredible experience. It integrated and made sense of everything that had ever happened to me or that I had ever done. It showed me the meaning and purpose of life. It was a birth into a state of consciousness I did not even know existed, but which is now a permanent part of my life."[55]

DIFFERENTIAL DIAGNOSIS BETWEEN PSYCHOPATHOLOGY AND RELIGIOUS–SPIRITUAL PROBLEMS

The clinician's initial assessment of powerful spiritual experiences can significantly influence the eventual outcome. With mystical experience, negative reactions by professionals can intensify an individual's sense of isolation and block her efforts to seek assistance in understanding and assimilating the experience. Lukoff[55] noted that individuals undergoing powerful religious or spiritual experiences are sometimes at risk for being hospitalized as mentally ill.

Barnhouse[56] pointed out that the pathological significance of religious language can seldom be determined by the immediate content alone, especially if differential diagnosis with psychotic disorders is being considered. She suggested that a religious history be part of the standard evaluation. Robert Spitzer, Miriam Gibbon, and Andrew Skodol,[57] Robert Lovinger,[52] and Greenberg and Witztum[49] have also discussed assessment methods for distinguishing religious–spiritual problems from psychopathology that presents with religious content. Greenberg and Witztum proposed the following criteria to distinguish between normative, strictly religious beliefs and experiences resulting from psychotic symptoms. Psychotic episodes usually (1) are more intense than normative religious experiences in the person's religious community, (2) are terrifying, (3) are preoccupying, (4) are associated with deterioration of social skills and personal hygiene, and (5) involve special messages from religious figures.

The DSM-IV specifically notes that clinicians assessing for schizophrenia in patients from socioeconomic or cultural situations different from their own must take cultural differences into account:

> Ideas that may appear to be delusional in one culture (e.g., sorcery and witchcraft) may be commonly held in another. In some cultures, visual or auditory hallucinations with a religious content may be a normal part of religious experience (e.g., seeing the Virgin Mary or hearing God's voice).

Ken Wilber argues that confusion between intense spiritual experiences and psychosis has been created by theorists who fail to make the critical distinction between prerational states and authentic transpersonal states (see Chapter 7). He reports that although some writers have reduced the transpersonal to the prepersonal (e.g.,

Freud), transpersonal therapists have an opposing tendency to elevate prepersonal experiences to the transpersonal level (e.g., Jung).

Criteria for making the differential diagnosis between psychopathology and authentic spiritual experiences have been proposed by Tomas Agosin,[58] Grof and Grof,[21] and Lukoff.[55] There is considerable overlap among the proposed criteria. Lukoff suggested using good prognostic indicators to help distinguish between psychopathology and authentic spiritual experiences. The criteria he designed to aid in the identification of individuals who are in the midst of a spiritual emergency that has psychotic features include (1) good preepisode functioning, (2) acute onset of symptoms during a period of 3 months or less, (3) stressful precipitants to the psychotic episode, and (4) a positive exploratory attitude toward the experience. Individuals who meet these criteria for a spiritual emergency should be treated with transpersonal psychotherapy, hospitalization should be avoided, and medication should be minimized.

Efforts to differentiate mystical experiences from psychopathological phenomena have focused on schizophrenia,[59] psychosis,[60,61] psychoactive substance-induced mental disorders,[17] and epilepsy.[62] Near-death experiences have also been differentiated from similar-appearing psychoactive substance-induced hallucinations, meditative states, and organic brain disorders (see Chapter 29).

It is often difficult to distinguish spiritual emergencies from episodes of mental disorder. Agosin[58] pointed out that "both are an attempt at renewal, transformation, and healing." John Perry[63] described the acute psychotic episode as an attempt to access the energy and images of the archetypal unconscious to heal a broken sense of self. He argued that in many cases it is the prepsychotic personality that is the problem, and the psychosis is a compensatory movement aimed at constructing a more impassioned life. In addition, the outcomes from both spiritual emergencies and psychotic episodes are greatly influenced by the set and setting. The tragic outcomes that can occur when an individual in the midst of a spiritual emergency is inappropriately hospitalized and medicated have been noted in the literature.[21] Agosin described such an individual who had an important spiritual breakthrough: "Unfortunately, my patient was unable to find a way to nourish that infusion . . . and she soon thereafter returned to a depressed, suicidal state."[58] Yet some individuals who have been mistreated in this manner still manage to recover and carry on with their spiritual quest.[18]

CONCLUSION

In general, mental health professionals have not accorded religious and spiritual issues in clinical practice the attention warranted by their prominence in human experience. Scott Peck, a psychiatrist who has written several books on the spiritual dimensions of life, including the best-selling *The Road Less Traveled*, gave an invited address that drew a standing-room-only crowd at the 1992 Annual Meeting of the American Psychiatric Association. He pronounced psychiatrists "ill-equipped" to deal with either religious–spiritual pathology or health. Continuing to neglect religious–spiritual issues, he claimed, would perpetuate problems like "occasional, devastating misdiagnosis; not infrequent mistreatment; an increasingly poor reputation; inadequate research and theory; and a limitation of psychiatrists' own personal development."[64]

Reviews of the research on religious and spiritual dimensions of healing indicate that recognition of these factors has been increasing in all of the allied mental health professions including rehabilitation, addiction counseling, nursing, and social work.[65,66] The transpersonal movement, in particular, has made a number of contributions to the literature on assessment and treatment of religious and spiritual problems. It is hoped that these developments will increase the accuracy of diagnostic assessments, reduce iatrogenic harm from misdiagnosis, and increase the mental health professional's respect for individual beliefs and values.

NOTES

1. Group for the Advancement of Psychiatry. (1968). *The psychic function of religion in mental illness and health*. New York: Author.

2. Shafranske, E., & Maloney, H. (1990). Clinical psychologists' religious and spiritual orientations and their practice of psychotherapy. *Psychotherapy, 27*, 72–78.

3. Bergin, A., & Jensen, J. (1990). Religiosity of psychotherapists: A national survey. *Psychotherapy, 27*, 3–7. Quotation on p. 3.

4. Allman, L. S., De La Roche, O., Elkins, D. N., & Weathers, R. S. (1992). Psychotherapists' attitudes towards clients reporting mystical experiences. *Psychotherapy, 29*, 564–569.

5. Larson, D. B., Pattison, M., Blazer, D. G., Omran, A., & Kaplan, B. (1986). Systematic analysis of research on religious variables in four major psychiatric journals, 1978–1982. *American Journal of Psychiatry, 143,* 329–334.

6. Larson, D. B., & Larson, S. S. (1991). Religious commitment and health. *Second Opinion, 17,* 27–40.

7. Bergin, A. (1983). Religiosity and mental health: A critical re-evaluation and meta-analysis. *Professional Psychology, 14(14),* 170–184.

8. Pollner, M. (1989). Divine relations, social relations, and well-being. *Journal of Health and Social Behavior, 30,* 92–104.

9. Caird, D. (1987). Religion and personality: Are mystics introverted, neurotic, or psychotic? *British Journal of Social Psychology, 26,* 345–346.

10. Hood, R. W. (1974). Psychological strength and the report of intense religious experience. *Journal for the Scientific Study of Religion, 13,* 65–71.

11. Spanos, N. P., & Moretti, P. (1988). Correlates of mystical and diabolical experiences in a sample of female university students. *Journal for the Scientific Study of Religion, 27,* 105–116.

12. American Psychiatric Association. (1975). *Psychiatrists' viewpoint on religion and their services to religious institutions and the ministry.* Washington, DC: Author.

13. Westermeyer, J., & Wintrob, R. (1979). "Folk" explanations of mental illness in rural Laos. *American Journal of Psychiatry, 136,* 901–905.

14. Eisenbruch, M. (1991). From post-traumatic stress disorder to cultural bereavement: Diagnosis of Southeast Asian refugees. *Journal of Nervous and Mental Disease, 180,* 8–10.

15. Murphy, J. (1978). The recognition of psychosis in non-Western societies. In R. L. Spitzer & D. F. Klein (Eds.), *Critical issues in psychiatric diagnosis.* New York: Raven Press.

16. Noll, R. (1983). Shamanism and schizophrenia: A state specific approach to the "schizophrenia metaphor" of shamanic states. *American Ethnologist, 10,* 443–459.

17. Lukoff, D. (1991). Divine madness: Shamanistic initiatory crisis and psychosis. *Shaman's Drum, 22,* 24–29.

18. Lukoff, D., & Everest, H. C. (1985). The myths in mental illness. *Journal of Transpersonal Psychology, 17(2),* 123–153.

19. Achterberg, J. (1988). The wounded healer: Transformational journeys in modern medicine. In G. Doore (Ed.), *Shaman's path.* Boston: Shambhala Publications.

20. Kornfield, J. (1989). Obstacles and vicissitudes in spiritual

practice. In S. Grof & C. Grof (Eds.), *Spiritual emergency: When personal transformation becomes a crisis.* Los Angeles: Tarcher.

21. Grof, S., & Grof, C. (Eds.). (1989). *Spiritual emergency: When personal transformation becomes a crisis.* Los Angeles: Tarcher.

22. Barra, D., Carlson, E., Maize, M., Murphy, W., O'Neal, B., Sarver, R., & Zinner, E. (1993). The dark night of the spirit: Grief following a loss in religious identity. In K. Doka & J. Morgan (Eds.), *Death and spirituality.* Amityville, NY: Baywood. Quotation on p. 292.

23. Shafranske, E. (1991, August). *Beyond countertransference: On being struck by faith, doubt and emptiness.* Paper presented at the meeting of the American Psychological Association, New Orleans, LA.

24. Kornfield, J. (1993). *A path with heart: A guide through the perils and promises of spiritual life.* New York: Bantam Books.

25. Spero, M. H. (1987). Identity and individuality in the nouveau-religious patient: Theoretical and clinical aspects. *Psychiatry, 50,* 55–71.

26. APA Committee on Psychiatry and Religion. (1989). *Cults and new religious movements.* Washington, DC: American Psychiatric Association. Quotation on p. 7.

27. Post, S. G. (1993). Psychiatry and ethics: The problematics of respect for religious meanings. *Culture, Medicine, and Psychiatry, 17,* 363–383. Quotation on p. 374.

28. Levine, S. (1986). *Radical departures: Desperate detours to growing up.* San Diego, CA: Harcourt Brace Jovanovich.

29. Vaughan, F. (1987). A question of balance: Health and pathology in new religious movements. In D. Anthony, B. Ecker, & K. Wilber (Eds.), *Spiritual choices: The problem of recognizing authentic paths to inner transformation* (pp. 265–282). New York: Paragon House.

30. Bogart, G. C. (1992). Separating from a spiritual teacher. *Journal of Transpersonal Psychology, 24(1),* 1–22.

31. Lukoff, D., & Lu, F. (1988). Transpersonal psychology research review: Mystical experience. *Journal of Transpersonal Psychology, 21(1),* 161–184.

32. Neumann, E. (1964). Mystical man. In J. Campbell (Ed.), *The mystic vision.* Princeton, NJ: Princeton University Press.

33. Greeley, G. (1974). *Ecstasy: A way of knowing.* Englewood Cliffs, NJ: Prentice-Hall.

34. Scharfstein, B. (1973). *Mystical experience.* New York: Bobbs-Merrill.

35. Spilka, B., Hood, R., & Gorsuch, R. (1985). *The psychology of religion: An empirical approach.* Englewood Cliffs, NJ: Prentice-Hall.

36. Group for the Advancement of Psychiatry. (1976). *Mysticism: Spiritual quest or mental disorder.* New York: Author. Quotations on pp. 804, 806.

37. Nobel, K. D. (1987). Psychological health and the experience of transcendence. *The Counseling Psychologist, 15,* 601–614.

38. Assagioli, R. (1989). Self-realization and psychological disturbances. In S. Grof & C. Grof (Eds.), *Spiritual emergency: When personal transformation becomes a crisis.* Los Angeles: Tarcher. Quotations on pp. 36, 38.

39. Smith, C. D. (1990). Religion and crisis in Jungian analysis. *Counseling and Values, 34,* 177–186. Quotation on p. 178.

40. Walsh, R., & Roche, L. (1979). Precipitation of acute psychotic episodes by intensive meditation in individuals with a history of schizophrenia. *American Journal of Psychiatry, 136,* 1085–1086.

41. Engler, J. (1986). Therapeutic aims in psychotherapy and meditation. In K. Wilber, J. Engler, & D. Brown (Eds.), *Transformations of consciousness.* Boston: Shambhala Publications.

42. Waldfogel, S., & Wolpe, P. (1993). Using awareness of religious factors to enhance interventions in consultation–liaison psychiatry. *Hospital and Community Psychiatry, 44,* 473–477.

43. Carpenito, L. (1983). *Nursing diagnosis: Application to clinical practice.* Philadelphia: Lippincott.

44. Kroll, J., & Sheehan, W. (1989). Religious beliefs and practices among 52 psychiatric inpatients in Minnesota. *American Journal of Psychiatry, 143,* 329–334.

45. Miller, W. (1990). Spirituality: The silent dimension in addiction research. *Drug and Alcohol Review, 9,* 259–266.

46. Jung, C. G. (1987). The Bill W.–Carl Jung letters. *ReVision, 10(2),* 19–21. Quotation on p. 20.

47. Jung, C. G. (1973). *Letters* (G. Adler, Ed.). Princeton, NJ: Princeton University Press.

48. Grof, C. (1993). *The thirst for wholeness: Addiction, attachment, and the spiritual path.* New York: HarperCollins.

49. Greenberg, D., & Witztum, E. (1991). Problems in the treatment of religious patients. *American Journal of Psychotherapy, 45,* 554–565. Quotations on pp. 557, 563.

50. Goodwin, F., & Jamison, K. (1990). *Manic-depressive illness.* New York: Oxford University. Quotation on p. 362.

51. Podvoll, E. (1987). Mania and the risk of power. *Journal of Contemplative Psychotherapy, 4,* 95–122.

52. Lovinger, R. (1984). *Working with religious issues in therapy.* New York: Jason Aronson.

53. Bradford, D. (1985). A therapy of religious imagery for paranoid schizophrenic psychosis. In M. Spero (Ed.), *Psychotherapy of the religious patient*. Springfield, IL: Thomas.

54. Lukoff, D. (1988). Transpersonal therapy with a manic-depressive artist. *Journal of Transpersonal Psychology, 20(1)*, 10–20.

55. Lukoff, D. (1985). The diagnosis of mystical experiences with psychotic features. *Journal of Transpersonal Psychology, 17(2)*, 155–181. Quotation on p. 177.

56. Barnhouse, R. T. (1986). How to evaluate patients' religious ideation. In L. Robinson (Ed.), *Psychology and religion: Overlapping concerns*. Washington, DC: American Psychiatric Press.

57. Spitzer, R. L., Gibbon, M., & Skodol, A. (1980). The heavenly vision of a poor woman: A down to earth discussion of DSM-III differential diagnosis. *Journal of Operational Psychiatry, 11*, 169–172.

58. Agosin, T. (1992). Psychosis, dreams and mysticism in the clinical domain. In F. Halligan & J. Shea (Eds.), *The fires of desire*. New York: Crossroad. Quotations on pp. 52, 62.

59. Wapnick, K. (1969). Mysticism and schizophrenia. *Journal of Transpersonal Psychology, 1*, 49–67.

60. Buckley, P. (1981). Mystical experience and schizophrenia. *Schizophrenia Bulletin, 7*, 516–521.

61. Oxman, T., Rosenberg, S., Schnurr, P., Tucker, G., & Gala, G. (1988). The language of altered states. *Journal of Nervous and Mental Disease, 176*, 401–408.

62. Sensky, T. (1983). Religiosity, mystical experience, and epilepsy. In F. C. Rose (Ed.), *Research progress in epilepsy*. New York: Pitman.

63. Perry, J. (1974). *The far side of madness*. Englewood Cliffs, NJ: Prentice-Hall.

64. Peck, S. (1993). *Further along the road less traveled*. New York: Simon & Schuster. Quotation on p. 243.

65. Lukoff, D., Turner, R., & Lu, F. (1992). Transpersonal psychology research review: Psychoreligious dimensions of healing. *Journal of Transpersonal Psychology, 24(1)*, 41–60.

66. Lukoff, D., Turner, R., & Lu, F. G. (1993). Transpersonal psychology research review: Psychospiritual dimensions of healing. *Journal of Transpersonal Psychology, 25(1)*, 11–28.

67. American Psychiatric Association. (1994). *Diagnostic and statistical manual of mental disorders* (4th ed.). Washington, DC: Author. Quotations on pp. 685, 675, 281.

CHAPTER 24

Offensive Spirituality and Spiritual Defenses

JOHN R. BATTISTA

IN THE LATE 1970s Christopher Lasch[1] dismissed spirituality, New Age beliefs, and humanistic–transpersonal psychology as narcissistic self-absorption. Alternatively, Marilyn Ferguson[2] perceived spirituality and transpersonal psychology as the dawning of a new age of higher consciousness in which the self-centered perspective of Western culture would be transcended in love for humanity and earth. The tension between these two points of view evolved slowly in the ensuing years into a useful and realistic question: When are spiritual beliefs, practices, and experiences healthy or unhealthy?

Initial attempts to distinguish healthy and unhealthy spirituality focused on distinguishing spiritual awakenings and spiritual crises from psychotic states. Psychiatry has long recognized that psychotic states may include religious delusions or self-aggrandizing attributions of spiritual insight. Transpersonally oriented therapists since Roberto Assagioli[3] have recognized that individuals undergoing a spiritual awakening may enter altered states of consciousness that may appear to be psychotic. Such an individual may have sensory experiences that are like hallucinations, develop beliefs that are like delusions, or experience ego inflation that is like a manic state. The concern of transpersonally oriented therapists has been that individuals undergoing a spiritual crisis or spiritual opening will be mis-perceived, misdiagnosed, and mistreated as psychotic.[4] The transpersonal literature has emphasized that such experiences may be better understood in terms of the transpersonal context within which they arose than the psychiatric context of psychotic disorders.[4] The extension of the psychotic–nonpsychotic distinction to include a new category, "spiritual emergence or spiritual emergency," has been a valuable outgrowth of the transpersonal movement.

Similarly, the work of Francis Lu and David Lukoff and their colleagues (see Chapter 23) has led to the inclusion of a V code, "religious or spiritual problem," into the most recent version of the diagnostic and statistical manual for psychiatry (DSM-IV). This V code is not a psychiatric diagnosis of psychopathology but an indication of a normal concern. This provides therapists with a tool to differentiate normal or healthy concerns about spiritual and religious issues from psychopathology. It is hoped that this distinction will help to overcome the historical prejudice among psychotherapists that all religious and spiritual concerns are indications of immaturity or psychopathology.

The context within which most clinicians encounter spirituality, however, is not in the differential diagnosis of spiritual states or spiritual concerns from psychopathology but in trying to understand how spirituality functions within an individual in psychotherapy. The relevant distinction is not between spiritual states and psychopathology but between spiritual practices and beliefs that further the development and transformation of personality and spiritual practices and beliefs that have been incorporated into a psychopathological personality that resists them. Psychotherapeutic practice, therefore, calls for a further refinement of the question of healthy or unhealthy spirituality into a distinction between "true," or transformative, spirituality and "false," or defensive, spirituality.

Psychotherapeutically, *false spirituality* is characterized by spiritual defenses and offensive spirituality. The term *spiritual defenses* refers to spiritual beliefs that keep people from expressing their actual, embodied, emotional self. Such authentic expression would be perceived as incongruent with appropriate "spiritual" behavior. For example, a practitioner of Hinduism, Buddhism, or Christianity may not express anger or assert herself in relationships because she believes that such behavior opposes the precepts of her religion. From the viewpoint of her clinician, however, this inhibition may be a way in which she maintains a self-denying, masochistic stance that is part of an abiding dysphoria about life. Spiritual defenses provide a rationale to disavow parts of one's self. They prolong the suffering of an individual rather than transform it. In the words of Justine McCabe,[5] they allow a person to suffer masochistically rather than transformatively. In this sense, spiritual defenses are masochistic.

Masochistic spiritual defenses are distinguished from *offensive spirituality*, which refers to the assertion of one's self as spiritually developed as a means of constraining another person to be supportive. Such behavior functions narcissistically to bolster a threatened ego. The assertion of a false, spiritual self may thus serve to avoid contact with a disavowed "true" self that may include feelings of need or unworthiness or fears of rejection. Such an assertion serves a defensive function. It is called *offensive* because it is experienced by the other, clinician or not, as an offense. The "offense" is that one is constrained into an uncomfortable role by the subject: the role of a supporting audience for this self-deception. Commonly, if one interrupts such a person to express one's own point of view, hurt feelings, anger, and resentment follow. If one remains quiet and implicitly accepts the other, the experience is often exhausting and anger provoking as well as nontransformative.

The remainder of this chapter provides a series of clinical vignettes to clarify the concepts of spiritual defenses and offensive spirituality. The final section of the chapter distinguishes false spirituality from true spirituality.

DEFENSIVE SPIRITUALITY

The case of Dave illustrates how an inability to stand up for one's self can be disguised as a virtue through a spiritual defense. Dave, a 30-year-old accountant, was employed by the real estate trust of a major church. A devout Christian, he was an active and sincere member of his church. Dave had accepted a significant cut in pay to work for the church as a means of deepening his religious commitment and engaging in spiritual service. It was shocking, therefore, for Dave to find that the church had been neglectful of its tenants and buildings through the inattention of its director. This director reported directly to the minister, who served as chief executive officer of the trust. Dave contacted the minister to inform him of the neglect and misuse of church property, expecting an immediate investigation and a thankful appreciation on behalf of the church for his discoveries. Dave was further shocked when the minister–officer told him that the real estate director was a good man, a cornerstone of the church, who was doing God's will. He stated that there was no wrongdoing and no need to investigate the matter further. Moreover, Dave was instructed not to include his "mistaken allegations" in his financial report to the Board of Directors of the church. When Dave uncovered the same problems 6 months later, he approached the minister again. This time the minister fired Dave for "failing to honor spiritual authority," causing problems for the church, and not being a team player.

Dave became despondent and sought psychotherapy. He blamed himself for his problems and did not consider approaching the board of directors to complain about a cover-up or unfair firing. He felt he had not been sufficiently tactful and understanding of the minister–officer. In his mind, the right thing to do, the Christian thing to do, was to "turn the other cheek," keep his anger to himself, and "rise above" the events as "God's will." Dave failed to acknowledge his minister's misuse of religious authority, and his beliefs supported him in not standing up for himself or challenging another's wrongdoing. Left unchecked, his beliefs would injure his career and the church. Imagine if Jesus had taken this approach in dealing with the moneychangers and hypocrites in the temple!

In therapy, the roots of Dave's masochistic use of religion became clear. His mother was unsympathetic and demanded he submit to her way of doing things, otherwise calling him selfish and unappreciative. She read to him from the Bible, emphasized the need to respect authority, and stated that only submission to God and God's agents on earth would result in his resurrection in the hereafter. Such a problem is religious rather than spiritual. Although Dave was devout in following church teachings, he failed to see authentic spiritual life as the outcome of an internal dialogue with religious tenets. Instead, he perceived "spiritual life" only as submission to an outer authority and failed to affirm inner authority.

A second example concerns Alice, whose orientation was more clearly spiritual than religious. Alice was an experienced meditator, a devotee of a guru, and an active member of a large ashram. She sought psychotherapy as an adjunct to her spiritual practice because she wanted to be fully realized and make as much progress as possible in the shortest period of time. She was a go-getter, not just spiritually but in terms of her outer life, where she functioned as a successful, holistically oriented medical practitioner sincerely devoted and useful to her patients. She was aware that her practice removed her from attending to her own needs. She meditated, engaged in hatha yoga, and attended workshops on "work as spiritual practice" and "the divine nature of giving." She was a sincere, likable, and dedicated spiritual aspirant. She perceived herself as emotionally immature, however, because she found herself exhausted by and, at times, resentful of her patients, rather than selflessly devoted to them (in bliss) as she thought she should be. She hoped that I could help her overcome her "childish needs" and realize her true spiritual self.

In the course of Alice's therapy, a different problem became clear to me. Alice could not depend on anyone emotionally; she could not depend on me to nurture or care for her. Alice disparaged her need for nurturance as infantile and believed it should be either renounced or given over to the guru. Her "spiritual" belief that the guru would meet all her needs, although she did not have a personal relationship with him, obviated the need to ask for or seek nurturance in any personal relationship. In fact, her beliefs obscured her underlying sense that it is bad, shameful, and humiliating to be cared for by another.

Alice's parents had been emotionally unavailable to her while urging her to be successful. Their only disappointment with her was that she had never married and had children. I wondered why she had not done these things. Her answer was that she was not capable of taking care of children and could not form a lasting bond with a man. This dialogue provided the opening for Alice and me to deal with her conflicts about dependency and need and her inability to relate intimately and mutually.

A third example is that of James, who was not a patient of mine but someone who belonged to a meditation group in which I participated. James was a quiet and unassuming man, pleasantly contained and hard to get to know. He would appear as the meditation was about to begin and leave immediately after it was over. Generally he did not participate in any of the social functions that naturally grew from the group. He lived alone with his dog and had no friendships, although he intermittently consulted a teacher about his meditative practice.

Eventually James's teacher suggested he seek psychotherapy, and James consulted me for a referral. James told me he had struggled with depression all his life, which he tried to handle with meditation and spiritual affirmations. Additionally, he struggled with what he called "low-life," homosexual impulses through a vow of celibacy. James had adopted a celibate, hermitlike lifestyle rationalized as ascetic practice, as a means of coping with depression and avoiding homosexual relationships. James can be seen as having taken a "spiritual bypass,"[6] avoiding his emotional conflicts and biological difficulties through adopting a "spirituality" that hid and supported his defensive behavior, redefining it as spiritually valuable. Today he is living testimony to the usefulness of fluoxetine in spiritual practice. He says it helps with his "chi."

OFFENSIVE SPIRITUALITY

Offensive spirituality may be considered the narcissistic use of a spiritual persona or spiritual identification. The narcissistic misuse of spiritual practice has been addressed by cultural critics and the popular press. Many gurus have been dethroned by sexual misuse of the teacher–student relationship or by the destructive misuse of authority (David Koresh, Jim Jones). Cultural critics such as Lasch[1] have portrayed the spiritual aspirant as engaged in narcissistic self-absorption, mistaking spiritualized self-gratification for self-fulfillment. Adherents of New Age spirituality have defended themselves against such attacks by pointing out that a spiritual life is the opposite of narcissism. It involves service to others, service to the world, and overcoming one's attachment to the self. Of course, this defense allows an apologist for "higher consciousness" to avoid looking at the dark side of the New Age movement. Two satires of this problem, *The Life and Teachings of Tofu Roshi*[7] and *The Nirvana Blues*,[8] are must reading for any serious spiritual aspirant.

Commonplace forms of offensive spirituality involve spiritual name dropping or spiritual testing. For example, some "spiritually identified" people appear to test the "spiritual development" of others using a "higher consciousness scorecard" that includes frequency of meditation, depth of experience, status of teacher, adherence to vegetarianism, and spiritual demeanor. Alternatively, some fundamentalist Christians simply insist on acceptance of Christ as one's personal savior as the prerequisite for association. Such standards are thinly disguised forms of narcissism.

Sometimes clinicians are asked by potential clients to pass a spiritual litmus test as a prerequisite for therapy. Such a test may be legitimate (a meditative practitioner wants to know if the therapist meditates as a means of assessing whether the therapist can understand their practice), or it may be defensive (a depressed person wants to know if the therapist is "saved" as a means of making sure the therapist will not look beyond God's will in evaluating the cause of her depression). Such a test can also reflect offensive spirituality. For example, a man whose wife insisted on couples therapy was only willing to go to a therapist who had been "saved" because only a saved person would understand the "God-given" basis for his refusal to have sexual relations with his wife. His wife wondered whether his having sexually molested their teenage daughter 10 years earlier might have something to do with his rejection of sexuality. He insisted, however, that his wife was an "impure purveyor of the flesh" trying to seduce him from the "pure spiritual life" he was leading. She had forgiven him the sins of his past, but he could not associate with her, a woman who had not renounced sexuality as impure. This is offensive spirituality: a righteous assertion of one's spiritual superiority. It insists that others live up to a spiritual standard as a condition for relationship while using the standard to avoid emotional conflicts and problems.

Another case of offensive spirituality is that of Karen, a middle-aged woman who came to me in need of a "spiritually evolved therapist," someone who could understand her "deep meditative practice." She stated that her husband was not supportive of her practice, which "required" not only several hours a day of sitting and reading but also documentation of her "spiritual awakening." Karen was writing a collection of her "prayer-poems" to further others' spiritual development. She knew that many spiritually evolved individuals were "unrecognized in their own country, like saints who were persecuted." She hoped to find a therapist who would affirm her spiritual progress and facilitate publication of her writing "for the service of humanity."

In Karen's view, her unsupportive husband was her "cross to bear." Like her parents, Karen's husband failed to recognize her gifts, her love, and her devotion. In Karen's mind, she was "called" to love him despite his "inability to love me as I deserve." Her love for him, "although he doesn't deserve it," was proof of her "highly evolved" spirituality.

Karen's perception of herself as a saintly, loving wife existed in the face of her refusing to be employed, clean house, or cook meals: all things her husband requested of her. In Karen's view, she should not have to take the "demeaning, menial jobs" available to her just because the "sexist society" did not value and honor the "feminine" talents she possessed. Moreover, her husband should support her after all she had done for him: giving up (the possibility of) "a glorious and successful artistic career" to raise "his" children. Furthermore, she had important "work" to do. She could not be distracted from this work to clean the house. Anyway, it would be good for her "patriarchal husband to get off his throne and do some real work." Finally, she did not "do meals" for her husband because she ate a single, midday meal of grains, fruits, and vegetables. She made sure there were leftovers in the refrigerator for him when he returned home.

I asked Karen to bring in some of her writing and to try to remember some dreams for our next session. Her writing went something like this: "Most holy, infinite spirit, transcendent beyond all mind, beyond all body. Behold here your humble servant devoted to your service and will. Use me to further your grace—your being filled with light and beauty. Radiate through me your eternal presence and drive darkness from the world. May your everlasting love, peace, and harmony guide the world and dwell in the hearts of those who sacrifice their lives for you." Karen was totally unaware of the narcissistic dimensions of her prayers.

Karen's initial dream was surprisingly useful and revealing. In it she was sitting on a toilet having a "most amazing shit." It went on and on, until a gigantic stool stood upright with its top sticking out of the water forcing her to rise off the seat. In the dream, she picked up this gigantic, intact stool and carried it before her with arms outstretched in a kind of religious or spiritual manner as one would carry a large candle to an altar during a religious ceremony.

What was going on here? Karen was identified with being a victim, which entitled her to special rights and understanding. Moreover, her entitlement had been rationalized by her perception of herself as spiritually superior. Her inability to have the love she wanted had been reconstructed as evidence of her saintliness and sanctified as her cross to bear. Her inability to love and her hostility were denied. Her self-centered behavior was justified by her pursuit of "higher spiritual" matters. Because she believed that she was spiritually evolved and served the world, she sought affirmation from a spiritually evolved twin: in this case, her therapist. She hoped I would recognize her and affirm her in her saintliness and not tell her, as her dream tries to, that she is "full of shit" and worships her "shit" as a kind of religious icon.

I eventually confronted Karen with her victim stance and belief that she was an unrecognized saint. These confrontations led to a good deal of hostility about my insensitivity and inaccurate perceptions before Karen could accept that I cared for her and was trying to help her. As a result of empathically confronting Karen with her demands and entitlement in the context of a willingness to care for her disavowed, needful self, Karen did come to see how her spiritualized identity offended others and prevented her from receiving the emotional support she sought. She slowly allowed herself to renounce her rarefied and unappreciated "spiritual" self and accept her human need for nurturance and support. In this way, she found the basis for receiving what she needed and for developing the possibility of a spiritual life.

This case clarifies where the therapist must direct empathy in the treatment of narcissistic spirituality. It is not empathy for the narcissistic "false self" that is needed, but empathy for the "true self," which feels so incapable of being loved and accepted that the spiritually deserving false self is created. Empathizing with the inner, disavowed self does not mean protecting the person from disappointment by supporting the outer, compensatory self. It means helping the person to understand how the false self functions: to protect feelings of worthlessness and to avoid feelings of rejection of bids for nurturance. It means offering to accept and care for such a person in need while confronting her entitlement as an obstacle to the care and acceptance for which she yearns.

A related case further clarifies this type of offensive spirituality. Suzanne and her husband Evan came to see me as a couple at Evan's request. He was angry with Suzanne's impatience with their son, Edward, and her "I can't be bothered" attitude toward both Edward and himself. Suzanne, like Karen, defended herself by saying that she was involved with more important things—spiritual matters—and did not like to spend her time on "trivial" concerns such as hearing about Edward's day in school, taking him to soccer practice, or "having to" get excited about his athletic, artistic, or scholarly accomplishments.

Suzanne was a kind of "spiritual handyperson," teaching meditation and hatha yoga classes at a local yoga center in addition to practicing "healing massage." Suzanne appeared histrionically happy in her New Age lifestyle. She was always having "the most incredible experience." While giving someone a massage, she would suddenly "be bathed in the deep violet light of compassion," which would show her where to "heal the deep wounds" of the person she was working with. For example, she might be "guided" to the liver and "feel their toxins wash through me." It was characteristic of Suzanne to follow this statement with something like, "You know you can't get harmed if you're not attached."

In our sessions Suzanne talked and talked, rarely listened, and had a distinctly hard time understanding what her husband was saying. At any hint of criticism or dissatisfaction from her husband, she felt misunderstood and unfairly treated. She did not experience her husband as a separate person with his own needs and point of view equal in validity to her own. Her spirituality was offensive in that she professed "higher consciousness" without having learned mutuality and giving of herself to another.

CONCLUSION

The emergence of spirituality as a movement in Western society during the last 30 years has allowed an increasing number of people to misuse its ideas and practices to support their own psychological problems. Some people suffer masochistically because they use concepts to disavow their true self and to conceptualize weakness, need, and emotionality as shameful and immature: something to be overcome by spiritual behavior and action. These masochistic, spiritual defenses commonly include (1) submission to the other, or to authority, rationalized as the practice of loving-kindness and spiritual humility; (2) failure to ask for or receive nurturance from another human being, rationalized with statements such as "God is the true source of all bounty and all that I need"; (3) failure to deal with interpersonal or sexual needs, rationalized as ascetic practice; and (4) failure to deal with biological, psychological, or interpersonal dimensions of problems such as depression, rationalized as "spirituality deals with everything—life is a spiritual teaching." Such spiritual defenses are distinguished from offensive spirituality, or narcissistic spirituality, in which a person asserts that he or she is spiritually evolved, hence entitled to special rights and privileges that others should recognize and support. The spiritual narcissist presents himself as evolved or complete, without need of transformation, or as a misunderstood victim who deserves affirmation.

Spiritual defenses and offensive spirituality represent two forms of false or defensive spirituality. They are to be distinguished from true or transformative spirituality. In true spirituality, spiritual beliefs lead a person to perceive and confront the ways in which her personality is defensively or inauthentically constructed. The thrust of authentic spiritual work is to help people give up their false images and concepts of themselves and accept themselves as they are: human, unique, but not better than. Spiritual life is not life beyond the body, the emotions, the mind, and people. It is embodied, ordinary life that transcends the ordinary because the transcendent is found in ordinary life experience. In practice we may know true life, the true nature of who we are, but this task involves accepting and transforming our limited nature. This is something to be embraced, not avoided.

NOTES

1. Lasch, C. (1979). *The culture of narcissism.* New York: Norton.

2. Ferguson, M. (1989). *The Aquarian conspiracy.* Los Angeles: Tarcher.

3. Assagioli, R. (1965). *Psychosynthesis.* New York: Viking.

4. Grof, S., & Grof, C. (Eds.). (1989). *Spiritual emergency: When personal transformation becomes a crisis.* Los Angeles: Tarcher.

5. McCabe, J. (1992). *The role of suffering in the transformation of self.* Unpublished doctoral dissertation, California School of Professional Psychology, Berkeley.

6. Levin, R. (1995). Personal communication.

7. Moon, S. I. (1988). *The life and teachings of Tofu Roshi.* Boston: Shambhala Publications.

8. Nichols, J. (1981). *The nirvana blues.* New York: Ballantine Books.

CHAPTER 25

The Phenomenology and Treatment of Kundalini

BRUCE W. SCOTTON

IN THE HINDU TRADITION, *kundalini* is the name given to the powerful energy that is said to lie dormant at the base of the spine. This energy may arise like a serpent to flow up the spine to the head, awakening energy centers on the way and ultimately leading to spiritual development (see Chapter 11). Many Western people who are not aware of the kundalini concept have reported experiences that parallel the classical descriptions of the kundalini experience, lending support to the objective existence of kundalini phenomena. Furthermore, when such experiences do occur, classical Western psychiatric treatments are often ineffective or produce results so slowly that they may cause acute symptoms to become chronic. Interventions designed to deal with kundalini are often effective and produce the best outcomes. This chapter provides a brief description of the kundalini phenomena and its management so that Western practitioners may recognize and respond to it appropriately.[1,2,3]

THE EXPERIENCE OF KUNDALINI

The sine qua non of the kundalini experience is the strong feeling of energy rising in the spine with accompanying alterations in

261

physiology and awareness. The experience of this energy has been varyingly described as electrical, nuclear, and hot–cold; it also may be experienced synesthetically as light. The rising energy is extremely powerful, and the person typically is awed by the force of it. It may come in waves or appear as a steady flow. The duration may range from hours to months, with the course being either intermittent or continuous.

Kundalini experiences may be brought about by yogic practice or contact with a guru (*shaktipat*), or they may arise spontaneously. In the former cases, particularly when the person has contact with a qualified teacher, the experiences are usually understood and controlled better. The clinician is more likely to see persons who have been experimenting with yoga and breath control on their own or who have spontaneous signs of kundalini with little or no knowledge of it.

THE CHAKRAS

Kundalini experiences are accompanied by alterations in physiology and consciousness that are generally understood in terms of the Hindu chakra system. According to the Hindu tradition, chakras are energy centers located along the spine and in the head. The chakras are connected by *nadis*, or energy channels, which funnel energy throughout the body much like the meridians in acupuncture. The energy itself is termed *prana*. Prana exists throughout the universe and may be concentrated and directed in the body by the breath. *Pranayama*, the study of breath control, uses prana-energy for self-development. In kundalini awakenings, experiences of energy coursing through the nadis or the spontaneous adoption of breathing practices may occur.

The first chakra, *muladhara*, lies at the base of the spine in the perineum. It is the site of the origin of the kundalini. During kundalini arousal, the "opening" of this chakra is associated with feelings of bursting energy or contractions similar to birth pangs. The first chakra is associated with grounding in the physical world, and disturbances of this chakra may manifest as abdominal pains or loss of sphincter control.

Svadisthana, the second chakra, is located at the level of the sacrum. It is the chakra relating to bringing forth in the physical world: procreation and the creation of physical objects. Release of energy in this area often produces disturbances of sexual functioning or episodes of sexual arousal that may last for days.

Manipura, the third chakra, is located at the level of the navel. It is said to relate to the function of the will and use of power. Disturbances here can be associated with physical discomfort in the area and variations in assertiveness. *Anahata,* the fourth chakra, is associated with the heart. Its activation is associated with the experience of unconditional, brotherly love. Disturbances of the heart chakra may manifest as an acute awareness of lack of love and pursuant anguish.

The fifth chakra, *visuddha,* resides in the throat. It relates to communication with the surrounding world through the senses. Disturbances of the senses and reports of paranormal communications appear with release of energy in this area. It should be noted that experiences from this level and those above it are often sufficiently divergent from Western consensual reality that the clinician may find herself ruling out the possibility of psychosis (see Chapter 23).

Ajna, the sixth chakra, is described as located 3 inches behind the eyes. Often called the "third eye" and portrayed as such in Hindu religious art, ajna relates to intuitive vision of the truth, or inward sight, and is the level of consciousness in which the individual can stand in immediate perception of the divine. With the arrival of energy at this level, rapturous experiences of cosmic consciousness or of religious figures may appear. On the other hand, the person may be struck with the inadequacy of his life to date in the face of the grand cosmic scheme and suffer terribly.

Sahasrara is the crown chakra and is seen as the interface of the person with the totality of existence. Consciousness at this level transcends the subject–object dichotomy. Despite earlier attempts to reduce such experience to pathology,[4,5] this is not a state of regression but a highly developed form of consciousness: pure awareness with no object. Persons having experiences at this level may have sharply reduced vital signs for hours with no ill effects. After hundreds of years of reports from India that were dismissed as fancy by Western observers, there are now documented cases of trained yogis who, by withdrawing their consciousness into this chakra, can reduce their respiration and heart rate sufficiently to be sealed in airtight containers for hours and emerge unscathed.[6,7]

MANAGEMENT OF KUNDALINI AWAKENING

Western clinicians who have become aware of the kundalini phenomena have begun to see it clinically. My colleagues and I have treated more than a half dozen cases of difficult kundalini experiences and have found that supportive treatment is best, with the least invasive physiological measures possible. Fear and anxiety are common, particularly amongst persons with no previous knowledge of kundalini. These states respond well to information, reassurance, and advice to take a few days off from other responsibilities. It helps for the clinician to see the person at least weekly during the height of the experience and to be available by phone on an as-needed basis.

The clinician may be called on to intervene by emergency-room personnel or other physicians because of dramatic physiological changes. Among the effects I have seen are persistent bradycardia as low as 40 beats per minute, tachycardia, cool skin, flushed skin, spontaneous trance states, and spontaneous assumption of yogic postures. Here again reassurance, of the clinician as well as the patient, coupled with the least physiological intervention possible, is best.

If the symptoms appear to be too much for the person to handle, "grounding" interventions designed to pull him or her back to ordinary existence may be used. These include a prohibition of any consciousness-altering activity, especially the practices that may have triggered the episode. Regular meals, even in the absence of appetite, are necessary; in particular, meat may serve a grounding function. Hot baths serve to relax and draw the person back to her body. Finally, immersion in routine tasks such as cleaning, mild exercise, laundry, and routine interaction with others serves to refocus attention on the ordinary world. Such interventions are similar to those counseled by Gopi Krishna in what is probably the best-known autobiographical account of a kundalini awakening.[8]

Concerning what may be psychotic symptoms (see the preceding discussion of the visuddha chakra; see also Chapter 26), the best course is to assess for level of functioning and "spread" of the seemingly psychotic symptoms. If the dysfunction seems circumscribed to the kundalini content and experience and the previous psychiatric history is negative for psychosis, the best course is probably supportive with as little drug intervention as possible. If the dysfunction is pervasive and includes psychotic ideation in unrelated areas, appropriate neuroleptic treatment is indicated, with later working through of the spiritual aspect of the experience.

When the person is capable of containing the experience, the clinician should support the sense of significance that accompanies it. If possible, the person should be in touch with a yogic teacher familiar with the phenomena. If the clinician must manage the kundalini episode alone, knowledge of the chakra map will allow understanding of many of the experiences. Naming of phenomena and knowing that they are an expected part of the kundalini experience often helps reassure the person. For clients who wish to read descriptions of kundalini, Gopi Krishna's book is a good first reference.[8]

It is not unusual for kundalini experiences to lead to spontaneous experiences of transcendent states of consciousness. In fact, that is considered the normal outcome of the rising of the kundalini energy along the spine. The clinician should have some knowledge of these states[9] and help the subject integrate them with her life. The subject has been in the realm of the numinous. Failure to recognize and respond accordingly may undo the therapeutic alliance and hinder spiritual growth.

CASE EXAMPLES

Case 1

Renee had been placed in a foster home at an early age and sexually abused by her foster father for years. Her case was complicated by the fact that her foster father at times was loving to her and that caring and abusive attention coexisted and sometimes mingled in the same experience. She came to San Francisco in the 1960s seeking a "purer community of love." She worked as a nurse and, after minor experimentation with psychedelic drugs, began to visit the many different Eastern spiritual teachers who came through the Bay Area. Renee never followed one specific teacher but meditated on her own, read, and sampled bits of what she picked up at various lectures. Although she was not in psychiatric treatment at the time, her descriptions of her life, including the idealizing and denigrating qualities of her relationships, suggested a borderline personality disorder with severe narcissistic wounding.

About 2 years into her experimentation with meditation, yoga, and breath control, Renee had the sudden onset of a flash of burning, blinding energy coursing up her spine to her head. This was followed by a sense of intense pressure in her head and then exhilaration. Following this episode, she believed she had an experience of unitary consciousness. When similar experiences continued daily for a few weeks, Renee went for an interview with a teacher visiting from India. The teacher confirmed Renee's intuition that she was experiencing kundalini and invited Renee to stay at her ashram in India if she could arrange for transportation there.

Renee did not have the resources to travel to India. Furthermore, the experiences of kundalini were so intense that she missed work and earned less. She changed to private duty nursing, which allowed more flexibility in her schedule, but she still missed work because of her kundalini experiences. Finally the episodes began to be painful, involving cardiac palpitations, diaphoresis, transient paralysis, and feelings of intense pressure. She sought treatment with me, saying she had heard I was open to working with kundalini.

The early stages of treatment were marked by Renee's idealization of me as a doctor who knew something about the yogic tradition. She enjoyed telling the details of her story to someone who "understood." She stated she was sure that this was a spiritual opening that had nothing to do with her history of molestation. Her "kundalini crises" continued, however, prompting several visits to the emergency room of a nearby hospital. When all tests were negative, the staff usually managed her with observation and establishment of an intravenous line. Whether she chose not to ask the emergency personnel to call me or did not think of it in her emergent state, I was always informed after the visit. One such visit documented a stable pulse of 40, an unusual event because Renee was obese and did not exercise.

These disturbing physiological phenomena became so frequent that Renee could not work at all. At times she lay on her bed for days at a time in an altered state of consciousness. I helped her obtain Medicare disability, a process greatly hindered by the fact that her symptoms did not constitute a medical diagnosis with a code number.

Despite these disruptive phenomena, Renee remained happy with her experiences, convinced that she was becoming enlightened and wanting to pass on her new understanding to others. I tried to take a balanced approach, confirming her kundalini experiences but also encouraging her to discuss events in her life in which she felt snubbed or belittled. My attempts to focus on and understand these difficult life events were met with anger. Renee began to accuse me of not valuing her spiritual process and of trying to reduce it to pathology. She was willing to try interventions like hot baths and drinking chicken broth to slow the kundalini and bring her back to her body; however, she refused to stop meditating, saying that to stop meditation would be untrue to herself.

With this failure to establish a working therapeutic alliance, a new type of emergency-room visit began. This was marked not by strange physiological or consciousness changes but by destructive rage. Renee would arrive at the emergency room complaining of something like pressure in her head, but the situation would soon escalate to her screaming insults at the staff, throwing objects, and sobbing. The staff, who were familiar with brief decompensations marked by rage in people with borderline diagnoses, were sure to call me.

In this context, Renee's transference changed from idealization to denigration. In Renee's eyes, I failed to teach the emergency-room personnel how to treat someone with kundalini phenomena; I denigrated her by suggesting that other phenomena were at work as well as kundalini; and I failed as a person because I was not open to Renee's teaching me her spiritual knowledge. She saw others as failing her too when several tentative steps to establish connections with other yogis and teachers did not work out. During one of her periods of disappointment with me, Renee quit treatment. She planned to go to India or to an ashram where she could allow her kundalini process to unfold. I saw her briefly on the street 5 years later. She reported that she had had no further treatment, lived in the same residential hotel, and was still angry at me.

Discussion

Renee's case illustrates several important issues. First, it demonstrates the dramatic symptoms that may appear with kundalini phenomena, such as a pulse of 40, hypothermia of 2 to 3 degrees, and great pressure and pain in the head with completely normal laboratory, X-ray, and computerized tomography studies; this state resolved spontaneously only to reappear weeks later and resolve again.

Second, Renee's case illustrates that spiritual or transpersonal phenomena often coexist with psychopathology (see Chapters 10, 23, 24, and 26). With Renee, the kundalini phenomena became obvious at first and were the reason treatment began. When the borderline symptoms appeared, it was clear that neither the borderline disorder nor the kundalini experience was reducible to the other. The "kundalini crises" presented physiological pictures that Western medicine did not recognize and could not help. The borderline rage decompensations were all too familiar to the staff of a city emergency room.

Third, Renee's case illustrates the clinical complexity of the management of such cases. Renee's reluctance to trust me with her psychological problems resulted in her rejection of many of my suggestions for managing her kundalini experience. The uncontrolled nature of the process led to emergency-room visits in which she felt misunderstood and insufficiently protected by me. Her vulnerability and need to see herself as "good" kept her from beginning to work on the borderline problems, which erupted unchecked under the stresses of kundalini phenomena, job loss, and others' lack of understanding of her condition. Ultimately, she terminated treatment and seemed to have stifled her kundalini process by failing to find a helper and a setting safe enough to allow it to unfold. Her spiritual development foundered for want of better treatment for her borderline disorder!

Case 2

I attended a meditation retreat led by a guru who was reputed to be able to impart kundalini experiences by his presence or touch. Three times during the retreat he passed down the rows of meditators and touched them about the head and shoulders as they meditated. I was unaffected and wrote a rather disbelieving question to the guru when we were invited to submit questions.

The fourth time he went down the rows, he pressed my head quite forcibly in the front and back. I felt a sensation of energy moving, bursting from my sixth chakra upward. I was immediately sent into the most profoundly altered state of consciousness I have ever experienced, a place totally beyond subject–object dichotomy. Words are incapable of expressing the experience; the closest I could come would be to say that I or it or all *was*. There was awareness of existence but no pain or pleasure. It was neither hot nor cold. It was black but not dark. After an indeterminate time, there was the sense that differentiation could exist if consciousness moved in that direction. One choice was for me to sit in almost the same state with an awareness of sound that seemed miles away, which was the differentiated world we know. When I chose that, my experience had some qualities. There was an experiencer again, an I. Also, my environment was now warmly black but still without trains of thought other than the awareness of differentiated existence. The other choice was the unitary consciousness I had been experiencing. For a while I went back and forth between the two; then the dualistic choice prevailed. It was as if I were in a giant airplane hangar with the sounds miles away. Gradually the boundaries of the hangar came closer and closer until they became my skin and I was back in my body. The total time of the experience was approximately an hour.

Although I have continued to meditate since that experience, I have attained the state of unitary consciousness only a few times. My personal work continues, and I cannot claim the kundalini experience led to a sudden improvement in my worldly functioning. However, the experience has remained a milestone for me; I know what I am aiming for in my meditation. I have experienced no ill effects and no other symptoms that might be considered hallucinations or delusions in the ensuing 15 years.

CONCLUSION

Kundalini phenomena have been known for a long time in India but are now being noticed more frequently in the West. The experience may present with striking changes in physiology and state of consciousness. Kundalini may occur as a result of meditation, breath control, or shaktipat, or it may occur spontaneously. It may or may not be associated with psychopathology, but it is not reducible to any psychopathology.

Management of the phenomena involves supportive care with "grounding interventions" when it is necessary to slow the process. The least physiological intervention possible is best. Reassurance and education concerning the nature of the process are helpful and may be necessary for caregivers as well as for the subject.

When the kundalini phenomenon coexists with psychopathology, it is necessary to treat the pathology with standard methods. The clinician is first obliged to differentiate between the signs of kundalini and the symptoms of pathology and not to subsume the new and unusual signs of kundalini under some pathological diagnosis. The trick is to differentiate the potential spiritual inflation from the transpersonal experience and to respond appropriately to each (see Chapter 24).

Kundalini release often involves profound experiences of the highest realms of consciousness, realms the clinician herself may not have experienced and of which she may be skeptical. In attempting to treat or assist someone undergoing such an experience, it is essential that the clinician be aware of the power and reality of such altered states of consciousness and be prepared to assist in their unfolding. In all cases the clinician should treat this phenomenon like any transpersonal experience, with appropriate respect for the client's experience of the numinous.

NOTES

1. Sanella, L. (1978). *Kundalini: Transcendence or psychosis.* San Francisco: Dakin.

2. Greyson, B. (1993). Physio-kundalini syndrome and mental illness. *Journal of Transpersonal Psychology, 25,* 1–58.

3. Waldman, M., Lannert, J., Boorstein, S., Scotton, B., Salzman, L., & Jue, R. (1992). The therapeutic alliance, kundalini, and spiritual–religious issues in counseling, *Journal of Transpersonal Psychology, 24,* 2–149.

4. Group for the Advancement of Psychiatry. (1976). *Mysticism: Spiritual quest or psychic disorder?* New York: Author. (To be read together with Deikman's comments.)

5. Deikman, A. (1977). Comments on the GAP report on mysticism. *Journal of Nervous and Mental Disease, 165,* 213–217.

6. Green, E., & Green, A. (1974). On the INS and OUTS of mind body energy. In *Science Year.* Chicago: Field Enterprises.

7. Boyd, D. (1974). *Swami.* New York: Random House.

8. Krishna, G. (1971). *Kundalini: The evolutionary energy in man.* Boulder, CO: Shambhala.

9. Wilber, K., Engler, J., & Brown, D. (1986). *Transformations of consciousness.* Boston: New Science Library.

CHAPTER 26

Transpersonal Psychotherapy With Psychotic Disorders and Spiritual Emergencies With Psychotic Features

DAVID LUKOFF

PSYCHOTIC STATES OF CONSCIOUSNESS hold a special place in transpersonal theory. In Ken Wilber's[1] spectrum model of consciousness, psychosis is neither prepersonal (infantile and regressive) nor transpersonal (transcendent and Absolute) but is depersonal: an admixture of higher and lower elements. He writes that psychosis "carries with it cascading fragments of higher structures that have ruinously disintegrated."[1] He argues, therefore, that psychotic persons often channel profound spiritual insights. Similarly, Carl Jung acknowledged that fragments of archetypal spiritual themes and symbols occur frequently in the experiences of psychotic persons, but he pointed out that "the associations are unsystematic, abrupt, grotesque, absurd and correspondingly difficult if not impossible to understand."[2] However, the Jungian analyst John Perry, who founded an innovative treatment facility for persons in psychotic states, views psychosis more positively as a renewal process in which the psyche is seeking to reorganize itself fundamentally.[3]

271

These differing views within the transpersonal community have led to controversy over the appropriateness of transpersonal therapy for psychotic disorders. Wilber[4] claims that "spiritual therapy" (including transpersonal approaches) is only useful for the "psychotic-like" higher developmental forms of "psychic pathology." For psychoses of lower developmental levels, however, "only intervention at an equally primitive level is effective—namely pharmacological or physiological."[4] Stanislav and Christina Grof also take the stance that "transpersonal counseling is not appropriate for conditions of a clearly psychotic nature."[5] In this chapter, I argue that transpersonal psychotherapy is appropriate and helpful even for serious psychotic disorders as well as for spiritual emergencies that have psychotic features. Differential diagnosis between psychotic disorders and spiritual emergencies is addressed in Chapter 23.

PRINCIPLES OF TRANSPERSONAL THERAPY

Transpersonal therapy can enable persons to realize the transformative aspects of their psychotic episodes. It is based on an alternative perspective of psychosis as potentially "breakthrough rather than breakdown," as R. D. Laing[6] stated it. Transpersonal therapy involves delving into the contents of a patient's hallucinations and delusions to find personal insights and archetypal patterns that play an important role in the patient's existence and personal mythology.[7] It can be conducted during both the acute stage and the postpsychotic integration phase, but it is approached differently in each. Therapy with acutely psychotic individuals is oriented toward getting them safely through their inner journey. In the postpsychotic integration phase, a major part of the work involves helping clients construct a new narrative: a fresh story of their life. James Hillman[8] argued that recovery means recovering the divine from within the disorder, that is, seeing that the contents are authentically religious. If it is well integrated, a psychotic episode can be an initiatory experience that guides a person into a new vocation and passion for life.

These principles of transpersonal psychotherapy are illustrated in the case studies that follow of persons in psychotic states. First, clinical issues that occur with psychotic disorders are presented (divided into acute and postpsychotic phases), followed by a discussion of spiritual emergencies with psychotic features (also divided into acute and postpsychotic phases).

TRANSPERSONAL THERAPY WITH
PSYCHOTIC DISORDERS

Acute Phase

A defining characteristic of the transpersonal clinical approach is sensitivity to spiritual life and experiences. Sally Clay,[9] who is a nationally recognized spokesperson and advocate for former psychiatric patients, in an article entitled "Stigma and Spirituality" gave an account of how the transpersonal dimensions of her psychotic episode were overlooked during her 2-year hospitalization at the Hartford Institute of Living (IOL) when she was diagnosed with schizophrenia. Clay wrote that "not a single aspect of my spiritual experience at the IOL was recognized as legitimate; neither the spiritual difficulties nor the healing that occurred at the end."[9] She does not deny that she had a psychotic disorder at the time, but she makes the case that, in addition to the disabling effects she experienced as part of her illness, there was also a profound spiritual component that was ignored. She highlights how the lack of sensitivity to the religious and spiritual dimensions of psychosis on the part of mental health and religious professionals was detrimental to her recovery.

An Alternative Program

Surveys of psychiatric inpatients have shown that 95% profess a strong belief in God.[10] Mental health professionals have been reluctant to incorporate patients' religious and spiritual belief systems into the therapeutic process even when they are primary to patients' psychopathology.[11] At Camarillo Hospital, a large state psychiatric facility in southern California, I developed a program for carefully diagnosed schizophrenic patients modeled after Perry's Diabysis program for patients with acute psychotic disorders (described later in the chapter).

Most of the patients still had psychotic symptoms when they entered the program. Medication was used, and a token economy focused on everyday independent living skills was part of the unit milieu; in addition, meditation, art therapy, jogging, and exploration of the growth-oriented aspects of patients' psychotic experiences were included in the program. Patients were encouraged to examine the relationship between their own psychotic experiences and Native American vision quests, shamanic initiatory crises, and the perceptual worlds of artists such as Vincent van Gogh.

Many participants in the program reported that expressing their experiences in art and describing them in the group was very moving for them. It was the first time that they could acknowledge the uniqueness and power of their individual experiences. For many, the activities served to reduce the embarrassment that they felt about being or having been "crazy," which was the only perspective that they had been given on their experience. These sessions gave the patients a positive way to reframe their psychotic episodes without diminishing their seriousness. One patient who had hallucinations he believed were from Frankenstein was encouraged to read the book; a productive session dealt with his gaining an understanding of a newly emerging part of his identity (he had been an overly dependent "mama's boy") that was Frankensteinian: primitive, undeveloped, and sexual.

In comparison with patients in a behavioral program that focused on social skills, patients in the transpersonally focused program showed a significantly better pattern on various outcome measures at the end of the 12-week period, including measures of self-esteem. Even scales of hallucinations and delusions, which the behaviorists on the unit predicted would increase because of the "attention" they were being given in these groups, showed reductions.[12] This program demonstrated that treatment in settings such as state hospitals can, and perhaps should, incorporate transpersonal approaches with psychotic patients.

Residential Treatment

Other models for transpersonal treatment of patients in the acute phase of psychotic disorders have been developed in alternative residential settings. The staff at Burch House in New Hampshire has been working with persons diagnosed with psychotic disorders since 1978. David Goldblatt, the cofounder and director, spent 4 years studying with Laing, which profoundly influenced the clinical direction of Burch House.

Hanbleceya is a therapeutic community in Lemon Grove, California, whose name means "quest for vision" in the Sioux language; it was founded by Moira Fitzpatrick, Ph.D., after her psychotic break. Hanbleceya is a long-term (2–4 years) residential program for up to 25 persons. It is based on the therapeutic community model but also incorporates extensive individual therapy, body work, and other transpersonal modalities.

Windhorse is a program providing compassionate care for persons with psychotic disorders developed by the Naropa Institute Buddhist community in Boulder, Colorado; now the program resides in Nova Scotia. It continues to develop innovative methods for home-based treatment that focus on the cultivation of mindfulness to counteract the absence of control over mental states experienced in psychotic states.[13]

Postpsychotic Integration Phase

According to Hillman,[14] in the postpsychotic integration phase the client comes to therapy to be "restoryed." Whereas the role of narrative therapeutic approaches is well recognized with nonpsychotic patients, it has rarely been applied with psychotic patients. In conventional psychiatric practice, the focus with postpsychotic patients is on the mundane aspects of resuming everyday living and acquiring independent living skills. These are important treatment goals; however, Malcom Bowers points out that "to evaluate psychotic experiences with regard to evidence of growth potential is not necessarily to be over-optimistic about the phenomenon . . . [therapists need] to re-examine our therapeutic strategies so that we foster growth whenever possible."[15]

A case example will be used to illustrate outpatient transpersonal psychotherapy conducted at a Veteran's Administration Day Treatment Center with a patient diagnosed with bipolar disorder with psychotic features.[16] Bryan was a 47-year-old artist who had recently undergone a manic psychotic episode that required four hospitalizations over a 2-month period. Following discharge, he complained that he was no longer creative and felt demoralized and depressed despite adequate medication. In the course of our first session, however, I observed that he was intrigued by the fantastic nature of his psychotic experiences. I suggested that he might be able to restore his creativity by writing about these experiences. Over the next 3 months, Bryan proceeded to write six phenomenologically rich essays about various topics, including being controlled by space aliens and feeling alterations in his sense of time. We met in weekly therapy sessions and discussed his essays and the experiences described therein. Bryan referred to our work as "creativity therapy."

Neither the essays nor the events described in them were organized chronologically. There was no story with a beginning, middle, and end: just well-described fantastic experiences and events. With Bryan's assistance, I decided to edit his essays by placing the events in a time sequence. The story that resulted surprised me because neither his hospital intake papers nor discharge notes mentioned that Bryan had a "UFO abduction experience." He reported experiencing a loss of control, sighting an unidentified flying object (UFO), being transported in a space capsule, encountering space aliens, experiencing telepathic communication, being examined by UFO entities, being given a "message," and then being returned. That the narrative of his psychotic experience could be seen as a story with an ancient mythic plot[17] had escaped Bryan's awareness as well as that of the trained mental health professionals who spent 2 months treating him. What was the clinical effect of uncovering and expressing the mythic dimensions of Bryan's psychotic experience? At the end of the 3-month course of individual transpersonal psychotherapy, his depression lifted and his creative energies were engaged. He resumed pursuing an artist's lifestyle, put on an exhibit of his paintings in a neighborhood bar, and reestablished contact with his artist colleagues. After Bryan showed a friend who was a filmmaker his essay entitled "One Manic-Depressive's Sense of Time," the filmmaker decided to make a movie based on it and put Bryan in the starring role. I was pleased to attend its premiere and champagne reception at an art gallery. For Bryan as an artist, the writing and publication of his essays in a professional psychology journal (copies of which he sent to many of his friends) and the production of a film from his writings transformed a psychotic episode into a constructive part of Bryan's personal mythology.

TRANSPERSONAL THERAPY FOR SPIRITUAL EMERGENCIES WITH PSYCHOTIC FEATURES

Acute Phase

Raymond Prince pointed out that "highly similar mental and behavioral states may be designated psychiatric disorders in some cultural settings and religious experiences in others. . . . Within cultures that invest these unusual states with meaning and provide the individual experiencing them with institutional support, at least a proportion of them may be contained and channeled into socially valuable roles"[18] (see Chapter 21). Stanislav and Christina Grof[5] proposed 10 types of spiritual emergency that can appear to be similar to psychotic disorders when viewed cross-sectionally but have the potential for being positively transformative. These include shamanic crises, kundalini awakening, peak experiences, renewal through return to the center, psychic opening, past-life experiences, channeling, near-death experiences, encounters with UFOs, and possession states.

Renewal Through Return to the Center

Perry[3] described his treatment of a 19-year-old male who fit the description of the spiritual emergency called *renewal through return to the center*. He presented with a number of grandiose delusions including that he was an "ace airman" and a second George Washington leading the defense of the country against the Russian Communists who were trying to capture the world. At other times, he was Prince Valiant, emperor of the Germans, and Christ. Perry met with him 3 times a week while he was at the residential treatment center called Diabysis. Perry formulated the presenting problem in terms of a severely damaged self-image that became "compensatorily aggrandized and exalted."[3]

In Perry's view, the psychosis is a renewal process as "components of the psychotic individual's make-up are undergoing change."[3] The psyche withdraws energy from relationships and invests it all in activating the central archetypes. Thus Perry encouraged expression of the psychotic experiences because "therapy should follow the psyche's own spontaneous movements . . . you work with what the psyche presents."[3] He encouraged the patient to draw during his sessions with him; at first, a number of images of death emerged including being cremated, being buried, and clawing his way out of the grave. "I [Perry] interpret these images of death as signifying the dismantling of a certain psychological structure that the psyche finds no longer tenable or favorable to life and growth."[3] What followed was a strengthened Eros principle evidenced by increased connection and affect during the therapy sessions "reach[ing] those affective potentialities thus far existing only in a state of dormancy."[3] Subsequent images in drawing and speech involved rebirth imagery. The whole psychotic renewal process took about 6 weeks, although additional time was spent at the residential treatment center integrating the episode.

Residential Treatment

Kingsley Hall, started in England in the late 1960s by Laing and others who identified themselves as part of an "antipsychiatry" movement, was the first attempt to provide alternative nonmedical-model residential treatment. Diabysis, a Jungian-based treatment center for acutely psychotic patients, was started by Perry and operated in the San Francisco area during the 1970s. Medications were rarely used. Instead, Perry provided art media and encouraged clients to express and explore the symbolic aspects of their psychotic experiences. Perry[3] reported that when clients were treated with this model, most came through their psychosis within 6–10 weeks. Soteria was another residential treatment program that existed in the 1970s and provided a milieu that promoted expression rather than suppression of the contents of the patients' psychotic experiences.[19]

Today, there are still a few functioning treatment programs in which psychosis is viewed as an altered state of consciousness (ASC) that holds the promise for growth. Pocket Ranch in Healdsburg, California, is an eight-bed acute facility on a 440-acre ranch founded by Barbara Findeisen, and its program has a strong connection to the transpersonal perspective, incorporating art therapy, holotropic breathwork, and guided imagery. Medication is used sparingly, and the focus is on the patients' growth as part of their recovery.

Postpsychotic Integration Phase

The postpsychotic integration phase lasts much longer than the psychotic phase, usually many years, but it has not been well documented in the treatment literature. A case example illustrating the transpersonal approach during the postpsychotic integration phase concerns my own hallucinogen-induced psychotic disorder (DSM-IV 292.11) that occurred 25 years ago. For several months following my first ingestion of LSD, I was convinced that I had uncovered the secrets of the cosmos and that I was a reincarnation of both the Buddha and Christ. During the most acute stage, which lasted a week, I slept little and held many conversations with the "spirits" of eminent thinkers in the social sciences and humanities including Laing, Margaret Mead, and Bob Dylan, as well as individuals no longer living, such as Rousseau, Freud, Jung, and of course, the Buddha and Christ. I expected that my 47-page "Holy Book" based on these discussions would unite all the peoples of the world in the project of designing a new society. I sent photocopies of my book to friends and family so that they too could be enlightened.

Now my grand vision reads to me like a typical "sixties" utopian communal proposal for a return to tribal living. Yet I spent months preoccupied with my mission to change the world through the dissemination of my "Holy Book." When it finally became clear to me that others were not receiving me as a new prophet, I went off to live by myself in my parents' summer cottage in Cape Cod. It was the beginning of spring with not many people around. I was no longer in a psychotic state, but I became quite depressed and physically sick, had internal bleeding, and seriously considered suicide. The image of what I took to be my own skeleton spontaneously appeared to me on several sleepless nights.

During the height of these difficulties, while on a walk near the bay, I was startled to hear a voice say, "Become a healer." At that time, lost in self-recrimination and embarrassment over my recent grandiose beliefs and activities, I did not think of myself as having a future. However, this voice—the only disembodied voice I have ever heard emanate from outside of myself—ultimately served as my calling into the profession of clinical psychology. After some training in group encounter and therapy, I worked at a psychiatric hospital and later applied to graduate school in psychology. I also went into Jungian analysis for 4½ years and then studied with many shamans and Native American medicine men and women at the Ojai Foundation in Ojai, California, to integrate my psychotic episode as a transformative transpersonal experience.

I consider my experience a "shamanistic initiatory crisis" for three reasons. First, the ascent to meet the gods, the dismemberment, and the rebirth back into society overlap phenomenologically with traditional shamanic initiatory crises. Second, a psychospiritual crisis called me to become a healer, just as it serves to call shamans to their healing profession. Third, shamans and their practices were involved in the integration of my crisis just as they usually are with novice shamans. My experience was "shamanistic," however, rather than shamanic because I am not part of a shamanic culture and the experience did not render me a shaman. Writing an account of this experience for the magazine *Shaman's Drum*[20] constituted transpersonal narrative therapy, which furthered the integration of this experience.

Having firsthand knowledge of psychosis has contributed greatly to my ability to work with psychotic patients, which I have been doing continuously for the past 20 years. It also greatly influenced my use of transpersonal psychotherapy with psychotic patients, because exploring the transpersonal dimensions of my experience was so important in my own integration.

CONCLUSION

Unfortunately, long-term follow-up studies documenting the effectiveness of transpersonal approaches and the kinds of patients who are more likely to benefit from them have not been conducted. Some criteria have been proposed to make differential diagnoses between serious psychotic disorders and spiritual emergencies and to determine whether hospitalization and medication may be necessary (see Chapter 23). This chapter illustrates beneficial clinical effects of transpersonal treatment with both populations. Simply acknowledging the powerful and often positive transpersonal experiences that occur in psychotic disorders is necessary, if only to develop a therapeutic alliance necessary for ensuring medication compliance.[21] Transpersonal psychiatry also attempts to preserve the transformative potential of psychosis during the acute phase by allowing for expression of symptoms rather than squelching them as is practiced in mainstream medical-model approaches. Transpersonal psychiatry subsequently facilitates the postpsychotic integration of such experiences as a positive influence in a person's ongoing life.

NOTES

1. Wilber, K. (1980). The pre/trans fallacy. *ReVision*, 3, 51–72. Quotation on p. 64.

2. Jung, C. G. (1960). *The psychogenesis of mental disease.* Princeton, NJ: Princeton University Press. Quotation on pp. 262–263.

3. Perry, J. (1974). *The far side of madness.* Englewood Cliffs, NJ: Prentice-Hall.

4. Wilber, K. (1984). The developmental spectrum and psychopathology: Treatment modalities. *Journal of Transpersonal Psychology, 16(2)*, 137–166. Quotation on p. 137.

5. Grof, S., & Grof, C. (Eds.). (1989). *Spiritual emergency: When personal transformation becomes a crisis.* Los Angeles: Tarcher. Quotation on p. xiii.

6. Laing, R. D. (1979). Transcendental experience in relation to religion and psychosis. In J. Fadiman & D. Kewman (Eds.), *Exploring madness* (pp. 113–121). Monterey, CA: Brooks/Cole.

7. Lukoff, D. (in press). The psychologist as mythologist. *Journal of Humanistic Psychology.*

8. Hillman, J. (1980). On the necessity of abnormal psychology: Ananke and Athene. In J. Hillman (Éd.), *Facing the gods* (pp. 1–38). Dallas: Spring.

9. Clay, S. (1987). Stigma and spirituality. *Journal of Contemplative Psychotherapy, 4,* 87–94. Quotation on p. 92.

10. Kroll, J., & Sheehan, W. (1989). Religious beliefs and practices among 52 psychiatric inpatients in Minnesota. *American Journal of Psychiatry, 146,* 67–72.

11. Lukoff, D., Lu, F., & Turner, R. (1992). Toward a more culturally sensitive DSM-IV: Psychoreligious and psychospiritual problems. *Journal of Nervous and Mental Disease, 180,* 673–682.

12. Lukoff, D., Wallace, C. J., Liberman, R. P., & Burke, K. (1986). A holistic health program for chronic schizophrenic patients. *Schizophrenia Bulletin, 12,* 274–282.

13. Podvoll, E. (1990). *The seduction of madness: Revolutionary insights into the world of psychosis and a compassionate approach to recovery at home.* New York: HarperCollins.

14. Hillman, J. (1983). *Healing fiction.* New York: Station Hill Press.

15. Bowers, M. (1979). Psychosis and human growth. In J. Fadiman & D. Kewman (Eds.), *Exploring madness.* Monterey, CA: Brooks/Cole. Quotation on p. 162.

16. Lukoff, D. (1988). Transpersonal therapy with a manic-depressive artist. *Journal of Transpersonal Psychology, 20(1),* 10–20.

17. Jung, C. G. (1978). *Flying saucers: A modern myth of things seen in the skies.* Princeton, NJ: Princeton University Press.

18. Prince, R. H. (1992). Religious experience and psychopathology: Cross-cultural perspectives. In J. F. Schumacher (Ed.), *Religion and mental health* (pp. 281–290). New York: Oxford University Press. Quotation on p. 289.

19. Mosher, L., & Menn, A. (1979). Soteria: An alternative to hospitalization. In H. R. Lamb (Ed.), *Alternatives to acute hospitalization,* (pp. 73–84). San Francisco: Jossey-Bass.

20. Lukoff, D. (1991). Divine madness: Shamanistic initiatory crisis and psychosis. *Shaman's Drum, 22,* 24–29.

21. Schaefer, R. (1983). *The analytic attitude.* New York: Basic Books.

CHAPTER 27

Transpersonal Techniques and Psychotherapy

SEYMOUR BOORSTEIN

FROM FREUD ONWARD, the understanding and practice of psychotherapy grew primarily out of case studies. The same applies to transpersonal psychotherapy. Only case analyses will illuminate the basic principles, indications, and contraindications for various transpersonal techniques as well as interactions with traditional therapy. Toward this end, I offer clinical vignettes of individuals with diagnoses ranging from psychotic and character disorders to neurotic and situational problems.[1] Although spiritual practice is traditionally thought to promote ego transcendence in relatively mature individuals, I find that it also serves to heal and consolidate the ego at more fragile levels of psychological development.[2,6]

A CASE OF PSYCHOSIS

John was a 74-year-old man whom I saw on a once-a-month basis for 32 years. His clinical diagnosis was paranoid schizophrenia, but he was able, with thioridazine, a major tranquilizer, to maintain a solitary existence and, until his retirement, a nonstressful job. When he stopped taking the thioridazine, he became disorganized and confused, and his paranoid ideation became severe enough for him to require hospitalization. His attitude toward people in general was angry and aversive. After he retired, I suggested that he begin reading the text of *A Course in Miracles*,[3] hoping the project might occupy his otherwise empty days. *A Course* includes reflections and daily meditations that are based on Christian tradition but express mystical and ethical principles prominent in many religions, such as Buddhism and Hinduism. *A Course* emphasizes the pleasure and peace of mind that comes from the practice of forgiveness, a quality that I thought would offset his paranoia.

John read *A Course* for several hours each day and reported that his fears and paranoia decreased. He even found himself smiling at strangers in the supermarket: a major behavioral change for him. When he neglected his daily practice of meditating on *A Course*, however, his level of antipathy toward others increased.

Although John had breakthrough experiences of kind, forgiving feelings and experienced less paranoia, his underlying psychosis remained intact. When his neighbor's dog soiled his garden, for instance, John faulted himself for not sending his neighbor enough loving thoughts, believing that this lack had caused the incident. John's paranoid delusions remained, but he no longer raged at his neighbor. The net result was that John felt calmer, less depressed, and more friendly to his family and others.

CHARACTEROLOGICAL ISSUES

Besides psychotic disorders, transpersonal techniques can be effective for characterological problems. Kathleen was a 50-year-old woman who sought therapy for relief from bouts of obsessive worrying. At the time Kathleen came to see me, her recently widowed sister wanted to move in with her. Kathleen and her husband were opposed to the move, but the conflict and guilt Kathleen felt over her "dilemma" were unmanageable. Her other dilemma was her husband's recent retirement and his wish that she accompany him in his pleasurable activities. The more enjoyable the activity, the more anxious Kathleen became.

The source of her problems, Kathleen insisted, was external. If only her sister (or husband) would not present her with dilemmas, Kathleen would be fine. Her general lack of empathic depth, her frequent outbursts of anger and rage at her husband, and her sense of outrage about everyone in her life who had "done her wrong" seemed to reflect elements of a borderline level of ego development. She did not seem to be a candidate for exploratory therapy, because her frenzy about her worries left her unable to reflect on internal, psychological issues. She might have benefited from medication, but she refused to consider it because her aunt had been hospitalized for "mental illness"; to Kathleen, taking medication would mean that she was crazy.

Kathleen wanted relief from her pain immediately. When I suggested that meditation might attenuate her worrying, she was interested, although she felt sure that "sitting down to meditate in the middle of worrying will only make me more agitated!" I therefore suggested a form of moving meditation: walking briskly and repeating to herself (silently or aloud), with each step, "May I be happy! May I be peaceful!" I told her that this was a practice that came from Buddhism, called *metta meditation,* and she agreed to do it in spite of what she called her "bad feelings about religion."

Kathleen was an avid walker and lived conveniently close to many hiking trails. She discovered that if she stayed alert as she walked along, she could note the early onset of a worrisome thought and immediately begin her meditative phrases. This averted a full-scale barrage of obsession, guilt, worry, anger, and rage. The discovery that she had some control over her mental states made them less frightening and led to a general lessening of her anxieties. I think it was important that I suggested the particular meditative phrases to Kathleen. She probably could have developed some measure of concentration simply by saying "one, two," or "Pepsi-Cola, Coca-Cola." However, I think the message of her particular "metta" phrases, that it is permissible (and not selfish) to "pray" for one's own happiness and peacefulness, was specifically valuable for Kathleen. The phrases helped restructure her longstanding beliefs about enjoying herself. I believe the fact that I "prescribed" the phrases made it possible for her to internalize a more nurturing, caring parent image. The interpersonal, transference context of therapy operated here, therefore, in addition to the transpersonal meditation technique.

Paul was another person with a borderline personality disorder. When referred to me, he was suffering from depression and suicidal thoughts. He was unable to take any psychiatric medications because his work involved operating heavy machinery. Paul had little capacity for introspective reflection. Because he was more comfortable with ideas than with feelings, I suggested that he read various spiritual books that I was interested in at that time. Paul particularly enjoyed reading *The Experience of Insight* by Joseph

Goldstein; with my encouragement, he decided to attend a 10-day retreat focused on vipassana meditation. The vipassana technique taught at these retreats involves noting internally and silently what one's experience is, in every moment. According to the Buddhist tradition, the focusing of awareness on the inevitability of change through moment-to-moment consciousness allows the individual to live more calmly with all experiences, pleasant as well as unpleasant. I felt the vipassana training would harness his predilection for thinking to soothe his repressed feelings.

Paul became a skillful meditator, able to note what was happening at every moment. He made no attempt, nor did his teachers encourage him, to use his concentration to reflect more deeply into the nature of his experience. He was pleased with his meditation, and his mood improved, his rage diminished, and his suicidal thoughts disappeared. He felt proud of himself as a "good meditator" in the company of people whose ideals he admired. Paul was able to continue his practice of "noting" after the retreat. He included a regular period of meditative walking in his daily regime and tried to continue the practice of noting throughout all of his activities.

The concentration he developed and maintained by this meditative practice stabilized his improved mood substantially. Although he had previously had difficulties on the job, with frequent outbursts of rage at coworkers, he continued his noting practice and was able to maintain a measure of calm friendliness with colleagues. Probably helped along by the positive feedback from his wife and coworkers, Paul has maintained his meditative practice and psychological well-being for 14 years. Paul considered me to be a much more accomplished meditator than I was and imagined me to be something of a spiritual sage; he experienced a form of idealizing transference. In fact, I was pleased that Paul had such good results from his meditative practice, and I was delighted that his life circumstances seemed to be improving. I am sure that Paul sensed this pleasure. This helped repair aspects of Paul's fragile self system, wounded in childhood by his unempathic, distant parents.

In working with Paul, I suggested specific books he might read, just as I did with John in treating his paranoid disorder. The use of spiritual books in therapy might be called *transpersonal bibliotherapy* and offers an indirect way of introducing transpersonal issues in therapy. With Paul, intense rage and discomfort with emotions made direct therapeutic work on his feelings initially impossible. He was more able to use meditation instructions from an author he did not know than accept "advice" from someone he did. Also, my including him in what he knew to be my interests had a positive effect on Paul's self-esteem. With John, paranoid wariness made it difficult for him to discuss substantive issues or take comments directly from me. A book, in his case *A Course in Miracles*, was less threatening and therefore more effective.

I often use bibliotherapy specifically as a way of introducing the possibility of a spiritual dimension in therapy. When a patient resonates to the idea, I often go on to suggest specific wisdom texts or inspirational stories in the spiritual tradition that has been most meaningful to her or him. I only recommend my own practices when patients specifically want me to do so and when it seems therapeutic to do so.[4]

NEUROTIC DISORDERS

I turn now from characterological disorders to the level of neurotic issues. Frank was a 37-year-old engineer who sought treatment for anxiety and depression that had been increasing since the death of his father 1 year previously. Although he loved his 2 sons, Frank felt stuck in his marriage and was unable to assert himself with his wife, who was harsh and critical. She was, it turned out, just like Frank's mother: beautiful and seductive but narcissistically preoccupied and unable to intuit or respond to the needs of others. Frank's mother had dominated the family in his childhood, and as a child, Frank was ashamed of his father's timidity.

Treatment with Frank was traditional in the sense that I encouraged him to free-associate: to say his thoughts and feelings as they arose. Over the course of 2 years, he spoke often of his difficulties with his wife and indeed began to be more assertive (with my encouragement) about his feelings and needs in that relationship. Although he could intellectually speculate about the roots of his anxiety, I felt that no major unconscious material emerged.

Frank expressed interest in meditation as a way to calm his anxiety, and I suggested to him that he attend a 10-day vipassana retreat. I frequently suggest vipassana meditation for people with neurotic diagnoses; I find that it helps undo defenses and, in particular, allows important memories to surface. Although these retreats are held completely in silence, Frank "fell in love" with the woman sitting next to him in the meditation hall, a woman he did not know at all. He was amazed and dismayed to find his mind constantly preoccupied with intense sexual fantasies of all varieties with this woman as his partner. When her place was vacant the morning before the retreat was to end, he was heartbroken, and when he later saw her in the parking lot leaving with another man, he was furious. In fact, he was aware he had fantasies of killing the man.

When Frank returned from the retreat and came for his next appointment, he was eager to tell me the content of his meditative experiences. As he recounted his story, however, he became increasingly anxious. Suddenly he was convinced that I would be critical of him, that he had been a "bad meditator," had "missed the opportunity to meditate," or had "spent the time entertaining himself with sexual fantasies." Frank and I then spent several months working through the meaning of his triangular (oedipal) experience with the woman and man at the retreat. Many previously unconscious memories arose about his childhood, which reflected his triangular relationship with his parents. At the same time, his reactions to me as an invalidating mother became clear to him. He began to see how he (unconsciously) continued to populate his world with "invalidating mothers" and how his general timidity was a characterological defense against the pain of humiliation. Also, although he had previously been aware only of positive feelings toward his father, he now discovered that he had been angry at his father for not protecting him from his mother. His guilt about his oedipal strivings had prevented him from experiencing or expressing that anger. His father's death had presumably reactivated his guilt about his aggressive feelings toward his father and accounted for his depression.

As Frank's childhood guilt was uncovered and worked through, both his anxiety and his depression subsided. He was more able to communicate effectively with his wife and began to stand up for himself against her criticism. She was initially startled and defensive, but as time passed, Frank reported that his wife noted how he seemed more "manly" now that he was assertive.

Comparing the cases of Paul with borderline personality disorder and Frank with a neurotic depression is highly instructive. I suggested the same type of meditation to both of them, but their experiences were vastly different. For Paul, the meditation served to calm him, controlling his outbursts of rage and his anxiety. For Frank, the meditation uncovered anxiety and anger, revealing repressed, unconscious conflicts. The contrast brings up an important point. In my experience, the psyche of an individual draws what it needs from a spiritual practice. In a sense, the psyche selects what helps most for its healing. This means the clinician need not obsess about which technique to recommend. Rather, he or she must listen to the patient and consistently ask, What will this experience bring out in the patient? From the answer, it will generally be apparent how to proceed.

SPIRITUAL PRACTICE AS A SUBSTITUTE FOR THERAPY

The cases discussed so far demonstrate how a spiritual practice can be used in addition to psychotherapy. The next case illustrates how a spiritual practice can substitute for therapy. Elliott was a 39-year-old computer programmer who had quit his job a year previously when he had been passed over for a promotion. Since that time he had been living on his savings, brooding about the unfair way he had been treated, and struggling in an acrimonious relationship with a woman he had been living with for 6 years. She apparently loved him and wanted to marry him and have a family. He experienced her urging that he get a job as "hassling" and was afraid that marriage would mean he was no longer "free." He had "tried therapy" some years earlier and thought it was "worthless." He came to see me for "just one visit."

Elliot's childhood was difficult. Both of his parents drank excessively, although they managed to maintain their status as university professors. Elliot was physically well cared for (there were always students available to baby-sit), but he felt his parents were remote, enjoying their students more than him. Elliot was bright enough to do well in school with little effort. He often stole money from his parents, went to movies instead of school, and lied about where he had been. He felt he was "smart enough not to have to do what everyone else did." As an adult he began to drink excessively, and his two previous relationships with women had ended because they found him "too selfish."

I felt that Elliot suffered from narcissistic character pathology, which was a defense against the fear and sadness he felt after being emotionally "abandoned" by his parents. When I asked Elliot about the role of religion in his life, he said that his parents had mocked it, considering it "unscientific and childish." The woman he lived with attended church each week, and he sometimes accompanied her there because it pleased her. He admitted that he often felt soothed by being in church but added that he felt "weird" about praying.

I suggested that he buy a copy of *A Course in Miracles* and see if it interested him. I told him that I thought he had psychological problems (no news to him) but that this did not seem the right time for him to work on them. I noted that because he seemed to be expressing concern that his life was passing by, without particular meaning or goal, *A Course in Miracles*, offering a framework of meaning in life, might be appealing. I explained that for people who appreciate its style and are motivated to do the exercises, *A Course* often had a soothing effect.

I chose *A Course* with Elliot because using the book is private and self-controlled. Elliot's narcissistic wounding was so painful, and his shame about stealing, cutting school, and drinking so great, it would have taken him a long time to work with these issues directly. *A Course* also has a built-in soothing mechanism in the form of daily phrases to be repeated to oneself, so that Elliot could titrate the experience of self-discovery and self-acceptance.

I had a note from Elliot 3 months later, thanking me for my suggesting *A Course* and reporting that he was feeling much better. He kept in touch with me at regular intervals, and by 2 years after our single meeting, he had returned to work, married, and had a child. He reported that he was so profoundly moved by the message of forgiveness in *A Course* that he experienced a "change of heart." His former brooding style—finding fault with others in his life for not attending to his needs—had changed, replaced with a consciously cultivated spirit of forgiveness. The immediate positive feedback from his change dramatically increased his energy level and helped him find a job.

My hypothesis about Elliot's dramatic "recovery" is that *A Course* provided him with the sense that he was loved in much the same way that a relationship with an empathic therapist would have done over years of therapy. *A Course*, like many other spiritual traditions, emphasizes that all beings are "at one with God" and loved by God. With this new perspective, Elliot began to accept the "bad" behaviors of his youth that had damaged his self-esteem, forgive himself, and feel compassion for the people he had hurt. As Elliot's self-hatred diminished, so did his self-destructive behavior. As he began to like himself, he was able to identify with Jesus, or the Holy Spirit: compassionate beings concerned about the welfare of others and acting out of kindness. This positive identification replaced the unconscious (and painful) sense he had as a child that he was not worthwhile enough for his parents to pay attention to.

EXISTENTIAL ISSUES

I turn now to a case in which I did not see any major psychological lesions or unconscious conflicts. I felt that the most significant source of emotional pain was an awakening to the existential dilemma of the fragile and changing nature of life, issues more appropriate to the realm of philosophy and religion than traditional psychotherapy. Although therapists may recommend therapy, by reflex, to anyone who consults them, a transpersonal approach must distinguish between purely spiritual or philosophical issues and psychological problems.[5]

Larry came to see me because he had begun to experience catastrophic thoughts and fears about the well-being of his twin sons, freshmen in high school. He knew that his worries had begun suddenly when he had heard about the death of his college roommate's son in a skiing accident. He felt that his worries were "unreasonable," that his sons were as cautious and reliable as he was. He was concerned that his fears, leading him to strictly supervise his sons' activities, would alienate them from him. He noted that every time he saw them leave the house, he wondered if he would ever see them again. He observed that he had never before recognized how fragile life is, and it was terrifying to him. Amazed that his sons and other people did not notice the precarious nature of life as he did, Larry worried that he might be "going crazy."

I met with Larry twice, and my impression was that he was psychologically healthy. His childhood seemed to have been untraumatic, and he liked his parents. He had been married for 16 years, had a warm and loving relationship with his wife, was successful in his career, and until this recent turn of events, had been congratulating himself on constructing a perfect life for himself and his family.

I agreed with Larry that life is indeed fragile and said that I felt that the shock of his friend's son's death had made it impossible for him to avoid confronting this truth. His currently excessive anxiety about his sons and his attempts to control and supervise their behavior, I explained, were his reaction to his discovery. I told Larry I did not think that he needed psychotherapy but that the issues confronting him seemed primarily spiritual ones. He had no interest in religion; the reform Judaism of his youth had seemed like a social club, without spiritual meaning. He was interested in my suggestion that meditation might relax his anxiety and took an introductory course in vipassana meditation at a local junior college. He later tried a weekend retreat, and some months later, a 10-day retreat.

Larry telephoned me a year after our initial visit to thank me for referring him to meditation practice and for reassuring him about his mental health. He reported that his anxiety level had subsided and that his terror about the possibility of something catastrophic happening to one of his loved ones had mellowed into a heightened appreciation of the love he felt for them and gratitude about their current well-being. Larry described having a hard time with vipassana meditation technique because he found it hard to concentrate. He spent the time at retreats thinking about his family and speculating about philosophy. He found he experienced the most support and solace from listening to the teachers explain Buddhist philosophy, which addresses directly the inevitable pain of the human condition. He said, "I never heard so many people talk so much about suffering who seemed so happy!"

I believe it was helpful to Larry to have the support of teachers who validated his intuition about the truth of suffering. The fact that they spoke candidly about the fragility of life, yet seemed able to live relational, committed, enthusiastic lives, was reassuring to him. His fear that his frightening thoughts meant that he was "going crazy" was replaced by the sense that he now saw things clearly and had become more mature. A by-product of his changing awareness was his resolve to lighten his heavy workload and spend more time with his family.

Because Larry initially presented with significant anxiety, it would be tempting for a therapist to recommend therapy. Larry's basic issues, however, revolved around existential and spiritual difficulties rather than significant psychopathology. Traditional psychotherapy alone is not likely to help in situations like Larry's and may lead to interminable analysis. A transpersonal approach, using spiritual techniques, is more effective. Caution is required, however, because many individuals with severe psychopathology present with what is apparently a spiritual problem. Distinguishing between a purely spiritual problem and a psychological issue is clearly crucial (see Chapter 24).

CONCLUSION

The addition of a spiritual dimension to classical psychotherapy may facilitate healing. The vignettes presented in this chapter illustrate work with patients at different levels of ego development to demonstrate how various aspects of spiritual traditions (e.g., reading, study, meditation practice, group support) can be used by the ego in healing. In "prescribing" spiritual practices, I emphasize the aspect of practice that I think will prove most helpful. I choose from a limited list of practices with which I am familiar, believing that in this way I will be able to understand and work with the results of the practice. I have also come to trust that the patient's intuition can be relied on to select practices that will be beneficial and to reject or lose interest in ones that are not. Following the choosing, it remains necessary for the clinician to watch the results. The particular discovery that the patient's intuitive wisdom can be relied on adds additional conviction to my custom of recommending spiritual practice to my patients. It is, perhaps, the root of a transpersonal approach: trust in and appreciation for the power of spiritual experiences. Coupled with the careful attention of a transpersonally oriented clinician, the transpersonal approach becomes transpersonal psychotherapy.

NOTES

1. Erikson, E. (1950). *Childhood and society.* New York: Norton.

2. Boorstein, S. (Ed.). (1996). *Transpersonal psychotherapy.* Albany, NY: SUNY Press.

3. Anonymous. (1995). *A course in miracles.* Tiburon, CA: Foundation for Inner Peace.

4. Boorstein, S. (1983). The use of bibliotherapy and mindfulness meditation in a psychiatric setting. *Journal of Transpersonal Psychology, 15(2),* 173–179.

5. Wilber, K., Engler, J., & Brown, D. (Eds.). (1986). *Transformations of consciousness: Conventional and contemplative perspectives on development.* Boston: New Science Library/Shambhala.

6. Boorstein, S. (in press). *Clinical studies in transpersonal psychotherapy.* Albany, NY: SUNY Press.

CHAPTER 28

Transpersonal Psychotherapy With Religious Persons

DWIGHT H. JUDY

ALTHOUGH TRANSPERSONAL PSYCHIATRY and psychology have addressed the general theme of treating individuals with a spiritual orientation, they have not addressed the issue of treating individuals across the full spectrum of religious orientations one is likely to encounter in an active clinical practice. Among the issues that this chapter addresses are (1) respect for the client's religious orientation, (2) a typology of personal religious orientations, (3) religious orientation and the life cycle, (4) the client's locus of authority, and (5) healing of religious wounds.

RESPECT FOR THE CLIENT'S RELIGIOUS ORIENTATION

As clients discuss the important decisions and issues that bring them to seek assistance, they describe their basic orientation to life. It may be misleading to assume differences where none exist between people who present their life stance in terms of a particular religion and those who do not. Religious fundamentalists invoke God's will and New Age people accede to the wishes of the Universe with virtually identical meanings. Similarly, there may be commonality between traditional religious people who assume that they directly affect every important issue with prayer and atheists who believe their life attitudes determine all that happens to them.

When people use religious language to express their worldview, the results are often both revealing and misleading. Religious language, by its very nature, is metaphoric and does not describe with precision. One person's meaning for the term *God* most likely is not the same as another person's. In the multicultural world in which we live, religious terms take on such a variety of meanings that it is tempting to wonder if we can ever truly communicate with each other regarding deep and essential beliefs. Furthermore, religious language such as "it's God's will" is often difficult for a secular counselor, or even a spiritually oriented counselor, to truly understand. There is a cultural bias in our training against listening to and understanding a broad spectrum of religious language. Often areas unresolved within the therapist become evident in these encounters. What is at stake is nothing less than allowing the client's deepest symbolic system to emerge with its own internal sense of meaning and integrity.

The client's worldview, whether religious or not, must be treated with the utmost respect. Likewise, the therapist must examine each of his own reactions to the client's religious language for countertransference. The task in regard to religious orientation is to allow the client's ultimate questions of meaning or relationship with God to emerge, as well as to explore the connection between his life orientation, his religious history, and the difficulties for which he seeks assistance. Understanding the client's religious orientation is as fundamental to psychotherapy as understanding the client's sexual orientation.

How then can the patient's fundamental orientations to life be perceived so that the therapist can effectively deal with her own projections and countertransference issues, really hear the client's worldview, and penetrate to the essential life questions the client is seeking to discuss? A typology of personal religious orientations can be useful in this endeavor.

TYPOLOGY OF PERSONAL RELIGIOUS ORIENTATIONS

Within Christian spiritual circles, James Fowler's *Stages of Faith*[1] has become fundamental to understanding a person's religious orientation. Through interviews with more than 300 people and a critical analysis of their language forms in addressing matters of deep personal concern, Fowler derived six basic life orientations. He calls these *faith perspectives*. By faith, he does not mean a belief system but rather the substructure of one's whole way of holding reality. *Faith* for Fowler becomes the lens through which all life experiences are perceived and given meaning. Three of Fowler's types are likely to be encountered in clinical practice. I call the three types (1) traditional, (2) individualistic, and (3) symbolic. These three types broadly correspond to Ken Wilber's designation of prepersonal, personal, and transpersonal orientations.[2] Wilber and other stage theorists have been criticized for their hierarchical assumptions; however, Fowler's descriptions can be extremely useful clinically. Clearly each individual will exhibit more complexity than any categorization can indicate.

Traditional

The term *traditional* holds both strong positive and strong negative connotations. I believe this very ambiguity is also reflective of the religious perspective to be described here. Persons of a traditional religious orientation often have some quality of the "true believer" regarding their spiritual beliefs and practices. This viewpoint is often attributed to persons in fundamentalist Christian traditions, but it is broadly applicable across religious traditions. For the person of traditional religious perspective, the "story," or mythic structure, of the religion is taken as a true description of reality. There is a literal interpretation of the religion's sacred texts and traditions. There is also a high degree of reliance on external authority, both of texts and the religion's doctrines and beliefs and also of the authority figures of the tradition. The shared beliefs of the community of believers is extremely important to persons of traditional religious orientation.

The traditional religious perspective is the dominant worldwide religious form, and most religions tend to reinforce this perspective. In its most negative form, this view can lead to a destructive inhibition of personal initiative. In its positive forms, traditional religious communities provide a system of beliefs and methods for personal conduct that gives a sense of security and comfort to their members. When balanced with a view of service to the local community and the world, such religious communities often provide essential support for the poor and others who are "down and out."

This traditional view holds similarities to Wilber's designation of *prepersonal* because it is not so much influenced by rational thought as by the mythic structures of the particular religious system. For this reason, this view is often accompanied by deep faith and profound religious experiences, which may include inner visionary experiences that are interpreted as confirmation of doctrine.

Individualistic

Persons holding an individualistic religious perspective bring a high degree of critical thinking and analytical judgment to their spiritual life. In many cases, they are rebelling from their previous training in a traditional religious structure. They may find themselves looking for a "liberal" church or synagogue, by which they mean one that holds the religious tradition up to critical reflection and in which individual autonomy of belief is encouraged. Authority for personal beliefs clearly resides with the individual and not with the church or other form of religious community. For such persons, matters of belief are to be studied, debated, and left to the individual to resolve. A person of individualistic religious perspective would most likely not enter into a guru–disciple relationship.

The individualistic religious perspective need not be at odds with religious practice. Persons with individualistic religious perspectives may be actively engaged in spiritual life and have their own personal beliefs and practices. They may find communities of like-minded people or practice primarily alone. The negative effects of such a perspective may be a lack of connection with community and an oppositional stance to all organized religion. On the other hand, communities of like-minded individualistic persons may be extremely service-oriented, and the members may give greatly of their time and resources to their community.

This perspective corresponds well to Wilber's designation of *personal*, with its reliance on a rational approach to life. The individualistic person may have little appreciation for the mythic structures of religion, may debunk the miraculous in their tradition, and might have an active antipathy toward persons of a traditional religious orientation. The positive results of the individualistic orientation are that it brings the locus of authority clearly into the individual, and it brings critical reflection and sound scholarship into the religious domain.

Symbolic

Persons with a symbolic religious orientation possess a mature openness toward the symbolic world. They may be alive in their own inner world to archetypal presences. They may have an active interior prayer or meditation life. They may be open to voices of the "deeper self." As such, they may have a profound appreciation for the miraculous elements in religious traditions, both as manifestations of numinous events and as metaphoric representations of personal transformational experiences. In distinction from persons of traditional religious practice, however, they hold the locus of authority within themselves. Although they have an appreciation of external authority as an example and guide, they also bring critical reflection to their religious practice; however, they do not hold the domain of reason to be the final arbiter in religious matters.

Such individuals correspond well to Wilber's designation of *transpersonal*. They are mature individuals who experience a variety of interior states yet honor the wisdom of religious traditions. They may be active within a religious community or envision themselves as contributing members of their larger community apart from a formal religious affiliation. In either case, there is a belief in the importance of contributing to the larger human community through acts of charity and attention to social structures that promote a society of kindness to all of its members.

RELIGIOUS ORIENTATION AND THE LIFE CYCLE

As Robert Coles's[3] work with children suggests, every person is a theologian, beginning from childhood. All of us seek to create a pattern of ultimate meaning in the universe. We do so by giving form to God or an equivalent construct for that description of the final force holding together all of the multiple energies of the universe.

Through the course of a lifetime, people tend to move from traditional to individualistic to symbolic religious orientations. The traditional religious perspective is the natural perspective of childhood; the individualistic perspective is natural to early adulthood; and the symbolic perspective is natural to midlife and beyond. Although such a progression is common, an individual's way of articulating his faith stance may make it difficult to "locate" people on this typology.

This is not to imply that a mature adult cannot hold to a traditional religious perspective with integrity. Such a stance is actually normative in many ways, and persons commonly live their entire lives quite satisfactorily within that basic orientation. However, the normal tendency in early adulthood in Western culture is toward high rational development. This change may result in rejection of a traditional religious upbringing or paying it only token observance. Such a person may develop an individualistic religious perspective. In treatment, when a client looks deeply into factors limiting personal creativity, it is common to find a primitive God image, introjected in childhood, within the psyche. To connect with that image and reform it may be the pivotal point of therapy.

Arrested development can also occur when there has been a seemingly natural progression of religious development from traditional to individual perspectives. Many rationally educated religious people have lost a living, personal connection to God. On a retreat, one such person reported going again and again to a stream to play in the mud. Finally, after several days of doing so, he remembered being about 8 years old, playing in the same way, and feeling very close to God. The recovery of that memory enabled him to reconnect affectively with a positive source of divine creative energy and to shift into the symbolic religious perspective, through which he found greatly renewed personal creativity.

SHIFT OR CONFLICT IN LOCUS OF AUTHORITY

Persons seeking treatment are frequently making the first, tentative steps toward shifting their locus of authority from external sources to their own internal source of authority. Indeed, the act of seeking help itself is often an enormously courageous act, bringing individuals into conflict with their family and social milieu. One such circumstance emerged in my practice concerning a minister with a traditional religious orientation who was involved in a long-term relationship outside his marriage. For several years he had been able to tolerate the inherent conflict between the external center of authority in his religious tradition and his own center of personal authority. In the course of treatment, however, the tension of this contradiction had to be directly faced, and a choice had to be made. The final choice somehow had to make room for both his traditional religious stance and his emerging personal autonomy.

Another arena in which this type of conflict can emerge is within couple counseling, where it is quite possible to have a disjuncture between basic religious orientations. The resulting differences in attitude about the locus of authority may manifest as conflicts about child rearing and the decision-making process. For example, if one member of the couple holds strong authoritarian views in the context of a traditional religious orientation and the other member holds an individualistic orientation, which seeks to grant internal authority to oneself and one's children, marital and child-rearing conflict will inevitably result. The therapeutic relationship will bring forth the unresolved conflicts of these two styles in the process of trying to find a solution to the marital problems.

HEALING RELIGIOUS WOUNDS

An area of therapeutic work that has historically belonged in the realms of spiritual direction and pastoral counseling is that of healing religious wounds. As spiritual issues are dealt with more commonly in psychotherapy, this issue is more likely to surface. The phrase *religious wounds* is used to distinguish the negative impact of a religious structure from the negative impact of the family. Although religious wounds may be correlated with family wounds, they may come forth in a less virulent form if the family structure was essentially healthy. There are three critical factors that may interact to determine the impact of childhood experience on adult life. One factor is the degree of punitive family structure. The second is the degree of punitive God image that is proclaimed through the religious structure. The third is the degree of personal autonomy that is allowed in the developing child.

One of the most intriguing aspects of religious belief that can emerge within psychotherapy is the way in which people use God in relation to their personal experience and their religious upbringing. In this process, God may take the form of the punitive parent, the nurturing parent, the moral judge, or a wellspring of creativity.

If there is a punitive family structure but a benevolent God image from religious instruction, the child may find a way to maintain a strong level of internal comfort and may develop internal transpersonal support at an early age. On the other hand, if there is a punitive family situation and a punitive God image, reinforced by a traditional religious community, extreme damage to self-esteem may develop and movement toward autonomy may be impaired. In that case, there is nowhere to turn for comfort and escape. Under these conditions, some individuals find a positive God image for themselves in childhood, sometimes through spending time alone in nature. In these cases, the positive God image serves virtually as a surrogate parent, providing the internal comfort needed.

My experience is that when the internal God image is nurturing, a high degree of psychological health is possible for the individual, even for victims of abuse. It is intriguing to speculate that one of the most significant aspects of Twelve-Step recovery programs is the creation of God as a positive object for the psyche. By postulating this positive image, Twelve-Step recovery begins a process of remaking oneself in a positive image, regardless of the earlier negative introjections.

The seriousness of the abusive religious situation is that, when coupled with the abusive family situation, the child is put in the untenable position of having the broader community, under the sanction of the Holy, reinforce the home abuse. In many cases of sexual abuse, this circumstance creates further internal shaming within an already shamed child. In such situations, the individual has no choice but to seek distance from or reject outright the abusing environment, both family and religious. The rejection of the religious community, although perhaps not as laden with difficulty as the rejection of the abusive family, is an extremely difficult challenge to face. In many cases, individuals have been thoroughly indoctrinated to believe that their sole avenue to God is through the religious structure of their childhood. To make a conscious choice to leave it, therefore, brings many of the same internal conflicts an individual faces when taking psychological distance from an abusive family. In these circumstances, the counselor's role is one of support, encouragement, and assistance. It may well be appropriate in inner vision work to invite clients to bring forth a transpersonal helper, such as their own inner Christ, Mary, Buddha, or other wisdom figure, to assist in the inner healing process.

Frequently, religious wounding is hidden or covered over. Many adults have experienced religious environments in childhood, particularly Christian ones, that seemed abusive to them. The forms of this abuse range from the proclamation of an abusive God, to severely restrictive views of sexuality, to simply the discrepancy the child observed between the great moral teaching of the religion and the day-to-day lives of the people who espoused it. Many years ago, they turned away from this religious tradition, perhaps looking into other forms of religious expression; however, the wound was not addressed. It was hidden or covered over.

What is missing in these cases is a reconnection with a living spirituality within the religious tradition of their childhood. Although there may not be an arrested God image, there is an arrested linguistic development of thinking about and imaging life experience in the language of their childhood religion. Often there is a deep and unspoken longing for "coming home," with no perceived way to do so.

Just as we need to make peace with our family of origin, we also need to make peace with our religion of origin, because it was the first window into the vastness of the universe, as declared by a broader community of people than our family. Making peace does not mean embracing again, but it does mean recognizing the gifts that it gave us, receiving those afresh, and perhaps grieving the loss that we experienced. It may mean finding the living strain of spiritual nature that exists within that tradition and reconnecting with it through reading and more trustworthy guides.

CONCLUSION

Transpersonal theory has made room for religious experience as a component of the human psyche. It has brought psychological discourse back to that place where American psychology began, to those concerns so eloquently addressed by the father of American psychology, William James, in his lectures, *The Varieties of Religious Experience.*[4] Transpersonal psychology invites us to continue the dialogue between religious conceptualization and the day-to-day psychological experience with which we give meaning to our lives.

NOTES

1. Fowler, J. W. (1981). *Stages of faith: The psychology of human development and the quest for meaning.* San Francisco: Harper.

2. Wilber, K. (1980). *The atman project: A transpersonal view of human evolution.* Wheaton, IL: Theosophical Publishing House/Quest.

3. Coles, R. (1990). *The spiritual life of children.* New York: Houghton Mifflin.

4. James, W. (1982). *The varieties of religious experience: A study in human nature.* New York: Viking/Penguin.

CHAPTER 29

The Near-Death Experience as a Transpersonal Crisis

BRUCE GREYSON

WHEN PEOPLE COME CLOSE to death, they may go through a profound experience in which they appear to leave their body and enter some other realm or dimension, transcending the boundaries of the ego and the ordinary confines of time and space. Raymond Moody,[1] the psychiatrist who named this phenomenon the "near-death experience," described it as an ineffable experience that may include feelings of peace, unusual noises, being out of the physical body, movement through a dark tunnel, meeting other spiritual beings, a life review, a border or point of no return, a return to the physical body, and profound changes in attitudes and values. Subsequently, Kenneth Ring[2] proposed a model of the near-death experience unfolding in sequential stages of peace and contentment, detachment from the physical body, entering a darkness, seeing a brilliant light, and entering a supernal realm of existence.

The near-death experience (NDE), once regarded as a meaningless hallucination, has become the subject of serious study by medical and other researchers in recent years. To some extent, this growing professional concern is due to the inescapability of the NDE. The accounts of experiences that many of these patients attempt to relate to medical personnel are so consistent and so real to the patients that the medical community has found it increasingly difficult to ignore them.

Once thought to be rare, the NDE is now acknowledged to be reported by at least one-third of people who come close to death.[2,3] A Gallup Poll[4] estimated that about 5% of the American population, or about 13.6 million Americans in 1995, have had NDEs.

Researchers have yet to find personal traits or variables that can predict who will have an NDE or what kind of NDE a person may have. Retrospective studies of near-death experiencers (NDErs) have shown them to be psychologically healthy individuals who do not differ from other people in age, gender, race, religion, religiosity, or mental health.[2,3,5,6,7,8]

Several neurochemical models have been proposed for the NDE, invoking the role of endorphins or various neurotransmitters, and neuroanatomical models have linked the NDE to specific sites in the brain.[9,10,11] At this point, such models are not testable, but they offer the hope that scientists may someday bridge the gap between mystical experience and physiological events. Although correlating the NDE with physical structures or chemicals in the brain would not necessarily tell us what causes the NDE, it could provide new tools and techniques for investigating the mechanisms and aftereffects of these experiences.

Regardless of their cause, these transcendent NDEs can permanently and dramatically alter the individual experiencer's attitudes, beliefs, and values, and they are often the seeds that eventually flower into profound spiritual growth. The progressive sophistication of biomedical advances has allowed increasing numbers of patients to be resuscitated who otherwise might have died. Thanks to this medical technology, the NDE may become the most common doorway to spiritual development. It is unusual among doorways, however, in that it opens regardless of whether or not the experiencer is seeking enlightenment, and precisely because it often occurs to people who are not looking or prepared for spiritual growth, it is particularly likely to lead to a psychospiritual crisis.

The growing literature on the aftereffects of the NDE has focused on the beneficial personal and spiritual transformations that often follow. Typical aftereffects, reported by many independent researchers, include increases in spirituality, concern for others, and appreciation of life, and decreases in fear of death, materialism, and competitiveness.[3,12,13,14,15,16,17,18] NDErs tend to see themselves as integral parts of a benevolent and purposeful universe, in which personal gain, particularly at another's expense, is no longer relevant. These profound changes in attitudes and in behavior have been corroborated in long-term studies of NDErs, in interviews with their significant others, and in research comparing NDErs with survivors of close brushes with death who do not recall NDEs.[16,18]

Despite the prevalence of NDEs and considerable research into their positive aftereffects, little is known about the psychosocial and psychospiritual problems NDErs often face. Although NDErs might naturally feel distress if the NDE conflicts with their previously held beliefs and attitudes, the emphasis in the popular press on the positive benefits of NDEs inhibits NDErs who are having problems from seeking help. Sometimes people who were totally unprepared to face a spiritual awakening, as in an NDE, may doubt their sanity; yet they are often afraid that rejection or ridicule will follow if they discuss this fear with friends or professionals. Too often, NDErs receive negative reactions from professionals when they describe their experiences, which naturally discourages them even further from seeking help in understanding the experience.

Many NDErs gradually adjust on their own to their experience and its effects. However, that adjustment often requires them to adopt new values, attitudes, and interests. Family and friends may find it difficult to understand the NDEr's new beliefs and behavior. On the one hand, family and friends may avoid the NDEr, who they feel has come under the influence of some evil force. On the other hand, family and friends who have seen the popular publicity about the positive effects of NDEs may place the NDEr on a pedestal and expect unrealistic changes. Sometimes, friends expect superhuman patience and forgiveness from the NDEr or miraculous healing and prophetic powers. They may become bitter and reject the NDEr who does not live up to the new role as a living saint.

Common emotional problems following NDEs include anger and depression at having been returned, perhaps against one's will, to this physical dimension. NDErs may find it difficult to accept that return, and experience "reentry problems" analogous to those of astronauts returning to Earth. They often have problems fitting the NDE into their traditional religious beliefs or into their traditional values and lifestyle. Because the experience seems so central to their "core," and seems to set them apart from the people around them, NDErs may identify too strongly with the experience and think of themselves first and foremost as an NDEr.

Because many of their new attitudes and beliefs are so different from those of the people around them, NDErs can overcome the worry that they are somehow abnormal only by redefining for themselves what is normal.

The NDE can also bring about interpersonal problems. NDErs may feel a sense of distance or separation from people who have not had similar experiences, and they may fear being ridiculed or rejected by others, sometimes with good reason. It can be difficult for the NDEr to reconcile the new attitudes and beliefs with the expectations of family and friends; as a result, it can be hard to maintain the old roles and lifestyle, which no longer have the same meaning. NDErs may find it impossible to communicate to others the meaning and impact of the NDE on their lives. Having experienced a sense of unconditional love in the NDE, the NDEr frequently cannot accept the conditions and limitations of human relationships. Above and beyond these problems, which all NDErs may face to some degree, people who have had unpleasant or frightening NDEs have additional concerns about why they had that kind of experience, and they may be troubled by terrifying flashbacks of the experience itself. Similarly, additional problems may follow NDEs arising out of a suicide attempt or in young children.

The way a psychiatrist or psychotherapist—or a friend or family member—responds to an NDEr can have a tremendous influence on whether the NDE is accepted and becomes a stimulus for psychospiritual growth or is hidden away—but not forgotten—as a bizarre experience that must not be shared for fear of the experiencer being labeled mentally ill. One focus of transpersonal psychiatry is to help individuals recognize and realize a presumed ultimate state that transcends our usual state of functioning, a state of mystical illumination or cosmic unity. To the extent that the NDE exposes the experiencer to that transcendent state of mystical union, it can be thought of as accomplishing that major focus of transpersonal psychiatry.

A second goal of transpersonal psychiatry is to help individuals understand and overcome the psychodynamic processes and mental–emotional conditions that interfere with transpersonal realization; quite often, NDErs have difficulty in integrating that illumination into their daily lives, a difficulty that transpersonal psychiatrists can address. Transpersonal therapists, in addition to being committed to helping their clients in their impulses toward emotional growth in the direction of an ultimate state, must also be aware of psychodynamic processes that may impede that growth, including their own. Transpersonal therapists must therefore know and use traditional therapeutic techniques when appropriate, adding to them practices that facilitate growth and awareness beyond traditionally recognized levels of health.

Some of the techniques developed to assist individuals on a spiritual path toward enlightenment may not be applicable to the NDEr, who has not been prepared for and sometimes does not want these changes. The approaches outlined in this chapter have been developed by a consensus panel of clinicians and NDErs specifically for working with the NDEr.[19] Whereas some of these therapeutic strategies reflect good traditional psychiatric care for anyone in distress and others are commonly applied transpersonal psychiatric practices that would be helpful in any psychospiritual crisis, still others apply uniquely to helping the NDEr.

APPROACHES DURING OR IMMEDIATELY AFTER THE NDE

A key to working with patients immediately after an NDE is the therapist's appreciation of the unexpectedness of the experience. Whether or not the NDE and its insights are welcomed, they were in most cases unanticipated. In contrast to many other individuals in psychospiritual crisis, the NDEr rarely has had any preparation or conditioning for a paradigm-shattering experience.

During the near-death event itself, professional staff involved in resuscitating a patient should be alert for insensitive comments and behavior. Patients who appear unconscious may be aware of their surroundings and may later remember callous or offensive actions or statements. When resuscitation staff say or do things that may be misinterpreted, an explanation to the apparently unconscious patient at the time may prevent having to untangle frightening memories at a later point.

During and immediately after periods of apparent unconsciousness, human contact may be critical in reorienting a patient. Simultaneous verbal and tactile orientation, manually outlining the patient's body boundaries while talking to him, may speed the return of bodily consciousness following an NDE. When interviewing patients immediately after a close brush with death, therapists should be alert for clues that the individual may have had an NDE. Such patients may drop subtle hints to test the interviewer's openness to listening before they risk sharing the experience. The therapist should not push for the details of an NDE but wait for clues that the individual wants to talk further. NDErs may be reluctant to share the details until they trust the interviewer. One should permit them to describe their experiences at their own pace while watching for those subtle hints—tests of one's receptivity—that they want to tell more.

Before approaching an NDEr, therapists should explore their own attitudes toward the NDE. One should be aware of one's own prejudices, both positive and negative, about what NDEs mean and about the people who have such experiences. Therapists should avoid imposing their own beliefs or interpretation of the experience on the NDEr. The interview should be guided by the individual's own account and understanding of her NDE, rather than by the therapist's preconceptions or judgments. One should listen for clues concerning how the patient makes sense of the experience and help the NDEr clarify that interpretation by reflecting her words. Each interviewer must develop his own personal ways of encouraging talk about the NDE. Using one's own personal style of verbal and nonverbal communicating is the best way to express a willingness to listen openly.

Regardless of what the therapist believes about the ultimate meaning or cause of the NDE, it must be respected as an extremely powerful catalyst for transformation. To neglect the profound potential of the experience to initiate both positive and negative changes in personality, beliefs, and physiological function is to discredit what is often the patient's most pressing concern. One must respect not only the experience but the experiencer as well. NDEs happen to all types of persons, and the experiencer's personal, cultural, and spiritual background should not be ignored by focusing exclusively on his role as an NDEr.

Labeling the NDE or giving the NDEr a clinical diagnosis on the basis of the NDE is more likely to hinder understanding and alienate the individual than to help. When an individual NDEr does meet diagnostic criteria for a treatable disorder, it must be clear to both therapist and patient that the diagnosis is independent of and unrelated to the NDE. Attempts to classify the experience as a pathological entity are neither accurate nor helpful.

Honesty is critical in establishing a therapeutic rapport with an NDEr. When appropriate, the therapist may respectfully share her reactions to the experience without discounting or contradicting the patient's perceptions and interpretation. The NDEr must be assured of confidentiality; he must be able to trust that the therapist will not divulge the existence or contents of the NDE without permission. Patients may be cautious about sharing an event as anomalous or as intimate as an NDE until they feel that the interviewer will respect it, and they may justifiably have concerns about the respect or attitudes of others with whom the interviewer might share that information.

The most helpful intervention following an NDE is to listen attentively to whatever the patient wants to say. Individuals who appear agitated by an experience often feel great pressure to understand it. They usually become more frustrated if they are told not to talk about it or are sedated into silence. Allowing NDErs to talk permits them to share and thereby diffuse any negative emotions. Unlike delirious patients, who may become more agitated by verbalizing their confusion, NDErs usually are relieved if allowed to struggle until they find the correct words to describe their experiences.

NDErs should be encouraged to express whatever emotions were precipitated by the experience. Most NDEs are characterized by intense emotions, and the individual may still have those unusually intense feelings afterward, which need to be shared, vented, or explored. The therapist should take a reflective rather than analytical stance. Feeding back to NDErs their own descriptions and emotions helps them clarify seemingly ineffable experiences, whereas premature interpretations may heighten the NDEr's fear of being misunderstood or ridiculed.

In hospital units or other settings in which close brushes with death are common, it may be helpful to rotate interviewers to prevent burnout. NDErs who are excited about their extraordinary experiences might need fresh listeners periodically who have the time and patience to hear them out.

One of the most helpful interventions is education about NDEs in general. Straightforward factual information shared in a nonjudgmental way often alleviates concern about the implications and consequences of the NDE. Near-death experiencers should be educated about the universality of the experience but granted the uniqueness of their particular NDEs. Although patients are usually relieved to learn how common NDEs are, therapists must guard against using the prevalence of NDEs to trivialize an individual's experience or its unique impact on her life.

When NDErs appear distressed immediately following an NDE, they should be helped to identify the specific problems related to the experience. Therapists should explore possible intrapsychic and interpersonal difficulties, using the patient's understanding of and fantasies about his individual situation and personality. Once the specific problem is identified, therapists should tailor their interventions to the specific problem needing attention. No two individuals will have the same NDE, the same previous personality, or the same life situation to which they return.

Finally, NDErs may need guidance immediately after the experience in dealing with the physiological crisis that brought them close to death. Focusing on the NDE itself and its meaning, they may find it hard to arrange necessary medical and psychosocial care. For concerns centered on the experience itself, they may be referred to other NDErs or to local professionals who have worked with other NDErs. Many cities have near-death support groups, in which NDErs and their significant others regularly discuss issues concerning the experience; a list of such support groups is available from the International Association for Near-Death Studies (IANDS), P.O. Box 502, East Windsor Hill, CT 06028.

LONG-TERM APPROACHES AFTER THE NEAR-DEATH EXPERIENCE

The therapist who attempts to work with an NDEr after the initial contacts should realize that the NDE raises issues about existence and purpose that are not necessarily addressed in other therapeutic relationships. The profound aftereffects of an NDE may influence the therapist's psychospiritual growth as well as the NDEr's. Therapists should decide whether they wish to accept that challenge before entering into an ongoing relationship focused on the NDE. Having decided to continue working with an NDEr, a therapist should clarify her expectations and those of the NDEr. The therapist must ensure that she understands what help the NDEr wants from the relationship and what outcomes the NDEr desires; furthermore, she should ensure that the NDEr understands the therapist's expectations of the relationship and its outcomes. Particular caution must be exercised with patients known to the therapist before their NDE. It should not be assumed that therapy begun before an NDE will continue along the same course after the experience. Even though the patient's underlying problems and personality may be unchanged, his life goals and priorities may be dramatically altered by the NDE.

Areas to be addressed in the therapeutic relationship may need to be limited. Taking into consideration the NDEr's personality, situation, and level of functioning before the NDE, one must clarify what problems result from the NDE as distinct from some other source. Attempting to help an individual with NDE-related problems and to counsel him regarding other problems, or to treat any coexisting psychopathology, may lead to conflicting interests or objectives. For example, some types of long-standing psychopathology may be alleviated by helping the patient adapt to societal norms, whereas the same individual's NDE-related distress may be exacerbated by an attempt to adapt to values no longer seen as meaningful. Therapists working with issues precipitated by an NDE may need to refer the patient to another therapist to work on problems that are unrelated to the NDE.

Both participants in the therapeutic relationship must continually work toward mutual trust. Because of the striking contrast between everyday reality and that of the NDE, it may take longer than usual for an NDEr to trust even the most sensitive therapist with some features of the experience and its aftereffects. The otherworldly reality of the NDE may also make it difficult for even the most open-minded helper to trust some of the NDEr's memories or interpretations of the experience.

Rigid adherence to traditional forms and appearances of clinical roles may undermine a therapist's rapport with the NDEr. Because many labels and definitions lose their meaning after an NDE, the therapist must rely more on direct experience with the NDEr and less on her formal training and knowledge of clinical techniques. Labeling the NDEr's problems and distancing oneself from the patient for the sake of analytic objectivity may interfere with, rather than foster, the therapist's understanding of the NDEr's problems. Therapists should be flexible in regard to length and frequency of sessions. Because the NDE may differ radically from the individual's other experiences and be extremely difficult to describe in words, its exploration may take unusually long sessions and may unmask overwhelming emotions and thought patterns that require frequent sessions.

The therapist should avoid any appearance of abandoning the NDEr. Frustration is common in trying to communicate information about the NDE and its aftereffects, and individuals may give up trying if they see the therapist as giving up. Furthermore, NDErs who feel they were "sent back" to life against their will may feel rejected in their wish to remain in the alternative reality of the NDE, may feel judged unworthy of remaining in that state, and may be particularly sensitive to further rejection.

Regarding the NDEr as a victim of the experience is countertherapeutic. Conversely, helping the patient to appreciate her active role in the creation or unfolding of the NDE may help the individual to understand and resolve problems arising from the experience.

The therapist should encourage grief work for those parts of the ego that may have died. Even unwanted parts of the ego that were abandoned or transcended in the NDE may need to be grieved for. The therapist should explore prominent features of the NDE for clues regarding sources of continuing problems after the experience. Whatever components of the NDE appeared most prominent in the experience itself or in its recollection, such as the life review, precognitive visions, or particular strong feelings, may yield critical insights into the meaning of continuing problems. Investigation of those features may help elucidate these problems. Therapists should also pursue anomalous details of the NDE and the NDEr's free associations to those details. Encouraging the patient to interpret NDE imagery on multiple levels, as one might interpret dream imagery, may yield valuable insights into subsequent difficulties.

Techniques for inducing altered states of consciousness may aid in recall of further details of the NDE and may help train the NDEr to shift voluntarily between different states of consciousness. Techniques for integrating the left and right hemispheres, in particular, may facilitate the NDEr's ability to use practically the insights gained in the experience. Guided imagery, projective techniques, and nonverbal modes of expression such as art and music may be helpful in uncovering and expressing changes that are difficult to describe verbally.

Therapists should also explore the patient's sense of having a specific purpose or mission after surviving the NDE. If he identifies a definite reason for having been "sent back" to life, that "unfinished business" may be related critically to continuing problems. With NDErs who report having chosen to return to life, that decision should be explored. Continuing problems may be related to regrets or ambivalence over having returned. Likewise, NDErs who report having chosen not to return to life or having wished not to return may feel ongoing guilt about their reluctance to return or anger at having been sent or brought back. Therapists should also investigate the NDEr's sense of having been manipulated by a higher power. A sense of being used, either positively or negatively, may contribute to ongoing problems following an NDE.

The therapist should explore fully the NDEr's fears about unwanted aftereffects. Whether or not fears about the consequences of an NDE are realistic, they can cause continuing problems. The NDE itself should be distinguished clearly from its aftereffects. The NDEr must feel free to reject, resist, or moderate unwanted aftereffects without having to devalue the NDE itself. Although the NDE and its recollection are permanent facts in the individual's subsequent life, various aftereffects may wax and wane in a natural course or may be moderated by therapy.

The therapist should also explore family dynamics as they relate to the NDE. Subtle changes in values, beliefs, or attitudes following an NDE may require changes in family interactions that, in turn, may contribute to ongoing problems. Home visits may be useful in assessing the NDEr's interactions and the reactions of family and friends to the NDEr. The therapist should offer family therapy or refer the patient to a family therapist if family dynamics have been disrupted sufficiently.

The therapist should avoid glorifying or idealizing the NDE and its aftereffects. The newness and uniqueness of the experience may lead both the NDEr and the therapist to regard it, or the NDEr, in romanticized terms. Likewise, remarkable physical, emotional, or mental aftereffects may be endowed with undue importance simply because they are so different from aspects of the individual's prior functioning. The NDEr must learn to balance her perspective toward the more striking aftereffects within the context of the entire NDE. Apparent paranormal effects are particularly liable by their novelty to capture the interest of both therapist and NDEr, leading to neglect of more important aspects of the experience that may hold greater potential for fostering the individual's psychospiritual growth.

In the same way, the patient must learn to balance his perspective toward the NDE within the context of his entire life. The NDE and its aftereffects cannot be ignored, but neither should they be focused on to the neglect of other aspects of the patient's life. The overwhelming need to understand the meaning or message of an NDE can lead the experiencer to overvalue its content or its aftereffects. Therapists should be alert for what Carl Jung[20] called "inflation": If the NDEr overidentifies with the uniqueness of the experience and subsequent changes, she may develop a distorted perspective of the experience within the context of her entire being. Jung cautioned: "The danger of wanting to understand the meaning is overvaluation of the content."[20] Although talking to other NDErs is helpful in normalizing the experience, identification only with a cohort of NDErs may lead to alienation from others who have not had similar experiences, to a conviction that worldly matters are not meaningful or important, and to consequent neglect of basic problems not directly related to the NDE. The therapist may help individuals who are "addicted" to the NDE or its aftereffects to withdraw from it gradually or to moderate their focus on the experience.

In withdrawing an individual from the awesome reality of the NDE, it may help to remind the NDEr that problems may be insoluble on the level that generated them. NDErs often report that certain problems generated in daily interactions were resolved only with the help of insights afforded by the NDE. Similarly, problems generated in the NDE may be resolvable only in the arena of daily existence and not by reverting to the alternative reality of the NDE. Psychosocial rehabilitation may help the NDEr relearn to adapt to mundane demands that may no longer seem relevant but are still necessary. For example, the timeless quality of the NDE may make it difficult for some survivors to remain grounded in the present once they return. Some individuals may become preoccupied with the past after a profound life review, whereas others may fixate on the future as a result of profound precognitive visions in the NDE. In extreme cases, a firm here-and-now therapeutic focus may be necessary to permit the NDEr to function effectively in the present.

On the other hand, the therapist should not expect NDErs to be able to resume life as usual after an NDE; their external reality may have to be altered to reflect their internal changes. If the NDEr's new attitudes, beliefs, and values are irreconcilable with old roles and lifestyle, those lifestyle issues may need to be altered to conform to the NDEr's new goals and priorities. In extreme cases, therapy may need to address the dissolution of careers and major relationships. Finally, the therapist's ultimate usefulness to the NDEr may be in helping to channel insights and values gained during the experience into constructive action. The same altered attitudes, beliefs, and life goals that can create conflicts in the NDEr's environment can also be instrumental in altering that environment for the better. Having internalized new values, beliefs, and attitudes, the NDEr may feel compelled to externalize them. The best way for many NDErs to validate and reconcile internally the experience and its aftereffects is to use what they have learned to help others. The therapeutic work is complete when the NDEr has found a way to actualize in daily life the sense of unconditional love he received in the NDE.

These approaches will allow the transpersonal psychiatrist to help patients accept the NDE and integrate it more fully into their worldview, decrease their sense of alienation from significant others who have not shared the experience, integrate the insights gained from the experience, and reconstruct a purposeful life in which the NDE and its aftereffects can be balanced with the demands of the individual's daily life, realizing the promise of psychospiritual growth from the confrontation with death and an alternative reality.

NOTES

1. Moody, R. A., Jr. (1975). *Life after life.* Covington, GA: Mockingbird.

2. Ring, K. (1980). *Life at death: A scientific investigation of the near-death experience.* New York: Coward, McCann & Geoghegan.

3. Sabom, M. B. (1982). *Recollections of death: A medical investigation.* New York: Harper & Row.

4. Gallup, G., Jr., with Proctor, W. (1982). *Adventures in immortality: A look beyond the threshold of death.* New York: McGraw-Hill.

5. Gabbard, G. O., & Twemlow, S. W. (1984). *With the eyes of the mind: An empirical analysis of out-of-body states.* New York: Praeger.

6. Greyson, B. (1991). Near-death experiences precipitated by suicide attempt: Lack of influence of psychopathology, religion, and expectations. *Journal of Near-Death Studies, 9,* 183–188.

7. Irwin, H. J. (1985). *Flight of mind: A psychological study of the out-of-body experience.* Metuchen, NJ: Scarecrow Press.

8. Locke, T. P., & Shontz, F. C. (1983). Personality correlates of the near-death experience: A preliminary study. *Journal of the American Society for Psychical Research, 77,* 311–318.

9. Jansen, K. L. R. (1990). Neuroscience and the near-death experience: Role for the NMDA-PCP receptor, the sigma receptor and the endopsychosins. *Medical Hypotheses, 31,* 25–29.

10. Morse, M. L., Venecia, D., & Milstein, J. (1989). Near-death experiences: A neurophysiological explanatory model. *Journal of Near-Death Studies, 8,* 45–53.

11. Saavedra-Aguilar, J. C., & Gómez-Jeria, J. S. (1989). A neurobiological model for near-death experiences. *Journal of Near-Death Studies, 7,* 205–222.

12. Atwater, P. M. H. (1988). *Coming back to life: The after-effects of the near-death experience.* New York: Dodd, Mead.

13. Bauer, M. (1985). Near-death experiences and attitude change. *Anabiosis: The Journal of Near-Death Studies, 5(1)*, 39–47.

14. Flynn, C. P. (1986). *After the beyond: Human transformation and the near-death experience.* Englewood Cliffs, NJ: Prentice-Hall.

15. Grey, M. (1985). *Return from death: An exploration of the near-death experience.* London: Arkana.

16. Greyson, B. (1983). Near-death experiences and personal values. *American Journal of Psychiatry, 140,* 618–620.

17. Noyes, R., Jr. (1980). Attitude change following near-death experience. *Psychiatry, 43,* 234–242.

18. Ring, K. (1984). *Heading toward omega: In search of the meaning of the near-death experience.* New York: Morrow.

19. Greyson, B., & Harris, B. (1987). Clinical approaches to the near-death experiencer. *Journal of Near-Death Studies, 6,* 41–52.

20. Jung, C. G. (1969). The transcendent function. In *The structure and dynamics of the psyche* (2nd ed.) (R. C. F. Hull, Trans.). Princeton, NJ: Princeton University Press.

CHAPTER 30

Treating Former Members of Cults

ARTHUR J. DEIKMAN

FROM TIME TO TIME, a psychotherapist receives a request for help from someone who has recently left a cult.[1] These patients may present symptoms of anxiety and depression, as do many others, but they constitute a group with special problems that require special knowledge on the part of the therapist.

The story these patients recount is remarkably similar from one to the next, regardless of differing educational, social, or financial backgrounds. They usually tell of joining the cult when they were at a transition point in their lives. Dissatisfied with their ordinary pursuits and relationships and hungry for a meaningful life that would satisfy their spiritual longings, they encountered an attractive, smiling young man or woman who enthusiastically described the happiness to be found in his or her dedicated, loving group and its wonderful, enlightened leader. They were invited to visit the group and did so. At that first meeting, they were impressed, if not overwhelmed, by the warm attention they received. In addition, they may have been emotionally stirred by singing, meditation, or other activities and may even have entered an altered state of consciousness under the influence of the group's leader. Such impressive experiences were interpreted as proof of both the leaders' advanced spiritual state and the newcomer's readiness to receive initiation. After one or two more meetings, they decided to join.

Having joined, the new convert's life was immediately filled with work, meetings, and exercises that left little time or energy for the life he or she left behind. Even if the convert was married and had a family, the partner and the children were regarded as less important than the avowed mission of the group to benefit all of humanity: to save the world. The conflict between group demands and outside commitments grew steadily sharper until the convert relinquished all relationships with those outside the group or the family broke up as the spouse reached the limit of tolerance. The convert was now totally dependent on the group and the leader for emotional and financial support.

The group that initially was warm and loving revealed its cold, punitive side whenever a convert questioned the group's beliefs or criticized the behavior of the leader. Such dissent was labeled "selfish" or "evil," and group approval was withdrawn and the dissenter isolated. Members were taught, therefore, that what the group had given, the group could take away. Out of fear of such punishment by the group and of humiliation and censure by the leader, converts found themselves engaging in the intimidation and coercion of fellow converts, the deception and seduction of new recruits, and other behaviors that violated ethical standards held before joining the cult. Such actions were rationalized by reference to the overriding importance of the group's purpose and to the leader's superior wisdom.

Eventually, the strain of conforming to the demands of the group became too much, especially if children were involved. The convert protested, refused to comply with the latest demands, and was dealt with severely. Finally, in desperation, he (or she) left the cult. Immediately, the leader branded him as damned, possessed by Satan, and having lost his soul. At the very least, he had failed the test and lost his chance at enlightenment. Just as painful, people with whom he had shared his most intimate secrets and felt the greatest acceptance and love now turned their backs and refused to communicate. Feeling totally alone, the ex–cult member experienced a turmoil of feelings: rage at the betrayal, fear of retaliation, horror at the possibility of perpetual damnation, grief at the loss of group support and affection, and shame at having been duped. At this point, he may turn to a therapist for help.

The anxiety and depression such patients feel usually is secondary to a bigger problem: a loss of trust in others and, especially, a loss of trust in their own judgment and spiritual perceptions.

Additionally, they may feel guilt over unethical actions they engaged in to please the group and despair at the loss of time, money, and relationships. To recover from the trauma of their cult experience, these patients need to understand what happened and why, and so does the psychotherapist who treats them.

MOTIVATIONS FOR JOINING

People who join cults do so for two principal reasons: (1) They want to lead a meaningful, spiritual life and (2) they want to feel protected, cared for, and guided by someone who knows what to do in a confusing world. The first motive is conscious and laudable; the second is unconscious or not recognized for what it is. Therein lies the problem: The wish to have a perfect parent and a loving, supportive group lies concealed in the psyche of even the most outwardly independent person. When the opportunity arises to gratify that wish, it powerfully influences judgment and perception and paves the way for exploitation by a cult.

There is good reason for cults to be associated primarily with religious–spiritual organizations. Religions are based on the belief in a transcendent, supreme power usually characterized along parental lines: God is all-powerful and all-knowing, meting out rewards and punishments according to how well a person has carried out the commandments He has issued. The doctrines vary, but even in nonmonotheistic Eastern traditions, Heaven and Hell in some form are designated as the consequences of good and bad behavior.

Although mystics are unanimous in defining God as incomprehensible and not of this world, human dependency needs require something more approachable and personal. Even in Buddhism, therefore, whose founder declared that concepts of gods and heaven were an illusion, many followers bow to a Buddha idol to invoke Buddha's protection and blessing. But even more satisfying to the wish for a superparent is an actual human with divine, enlightened, or messianic status. The powerful wish to be guided and protected by a superior being can propel a seeker into the arms of a leader who is given that status by his or her followers. Such a surrender to the fantasy of the perfect parent may be accompanied by a feeling of great joy at "coming home."

This analysis does not imply that the intimations of a larger reality and a larger purpose, sensed by human beings for thousands of years, are only a fantasy. The problem is that the spiritual dimen-sion and dependency wishes can get badly confused. The patient needs to disentangle the perception of a spiritual dimension from the less-than-divine longings that have infiltrated, taken over, and distorted what is valid. It is important that the psychiatrist treating an ex–cult member keep this distinction in mind.

One way to clarify the confusion is to help the patient see clearly the problems that she had hoped "enlightenment" and member-ship in the group would solve. These problems may include lone-liness, low self-esteem, the wish for the admiration of others, fear of intimacy, fear of death, and the wish for invulnerability. Indeed, membership in the group may assuage loneliness and provide the support and closeness that the patient had not experienced previ-ously. Memories of such good experiences may occasion acute feel-ings of loss in the ex–cult member and give rise to doubts concern-ing whether or not leaving was the best thing to do.

JUDGING THE CULT LEADER

To look objectively and critically at the cult experience, the ex-member needs to gain freedom from the "superior leader trap." As indicated earlier, this trap is sprung if there is criticism or ques-tioning of the leader's actions and directives. Basically, it takes the following form: The Leader operates on a higher plane than you or I. Because of that, we are not able to judge the rightness or wrong-ness of his or her actions. Ordinary, conventional standards do not apply here.

Although this conclusion may sound reasonable, the leader in fact can be judged by criteria established in the mystical literature. There is a striking consensus in these writings concerning the nature of the spiritual path and the duties of a genuine teacher. That consensus permits one to make judgments of whether the teacher's actions advance spiritual development or hinder it.

It is important to realize that the basic activity of the spiritual traditions is to assist spiritual students to "forget the self." The self referred to is what is usually termed the *ego* but is better under-stood as being the psychological processes dedicated to biological survival. That primitive aim is expressed in greed, fear, lust, hatred, and jealousy: the traditional vices. These vices are functional for the intention of survival. The mode of consciousness one experi-ences is functional also, and it is adapted to one's intentions. For example, building a bookcase calls forth a particular form of consciousness—the instrumental—featuring an emphasis on the object characteristics of the world, a reliance on abstract concepts, and a focus on past and future and on differences and boundaries. This mode of consciousness is needed to fulfill the intention of making a useful object. When one wants to receive something from one's surroundings, however, as in relaxing in a tub of steaming hot water or having a massage, one needs a different mode of consciousness—the receptive—featuring an emphasis on sensual experience, a blurring of boundaries, a focus on *now*, and a sense of connectedness with the environment.

Ordinary survival aims, therefore, call forth instrumental consciousness. But if it is desired to experience the world in its wholeness, unity, and interconnection—the essence of spiritual consciousness—a different intention must be operative, along with a lessening of control by the survival self.[2]

Keeping in mind this functional relationship of motivation and self to consciousness, one can see that the spiritual traditions use a variety of means to transform the seeker's initial motivations, which are heavily weighted toward greed, dependency, and power, into motivations of service and contemplation. Meditation, teaching stories, service, and the example set by the teacher can be understood as tools for accomplishing a deep shift in basic intention, permitting access to spiritual consciousness.

This framework provides a means for making a preliminary judgment about people who declare themselves to be spiritual teachers. All one needs to do is observe their behavior and notice the intentions and type of self that is being reinforced. If there is considerable emphasis on what the convert will gain from following the teacher, such as "bliss," psychic abilities, or the joy of enlightenment, these promises will arouse greed and acquisitive strategies. After all, the desire for bliss is not fundamentally different from the desire for money. If the teacher warns that rejecting the teaching will result in damnation, loss of one's soul, and loss of all hopes of spiritual advancement, fear is aroused and the survival self is activated. Likewise, if the leader makes use of flattery by bestowing attention or praise, this can arouse vanity in the convert and competition in the group members. In all these instances, the teacher is intensifying the operation of the survival self and the form of consciousness it generates. These activities are antispiritual, and leaders that employ them are not genuine spiritual teachers; they are not entitled to any special deference or trust.[3]

Of course, exploitation of followers for sexual pleasure or financial gain cannot be justified in any manner and testifies to the unenlightened, self-centered state of the teacher. Such exploitation is not to be found in the lives of the great mystics. They operated by even more rigorous standards than those that are imposed by conventional society. This is not to say that mystics are examples of perfect human beings. Perfection is not part of earthly existence for anyone or anything. But financial or sexual exploitation represents a drastic failure of responsibility that disqualifies a teacher from any special consideration. Psychotherapists are well aware of how harmful such violations of trust can be.

The behavior of most cult leaders departs widely from the path laid down in the mystical literature and can be seen to be harmful to spiritual development. By employing this functional framework, ex–cult members can judge for themselves the presumed sanctity of the leader and the appropriateness of the leader's behavior.

CULT BEHAVIOR IN NORMAL SOCIETY

Just as it is important to have a means of judging a spiritual teacher, it also is important for the ex–cult member and the therapist to be able to answer the more general question: "Is this group a cult?" Patients need to be able to answer that question to avoid making the same mistake again, and therapists are likely to be asked that question by a worried parent or spouse. Usually, the group in question has obvious cult trappings, but society abounds with groups and organizations that appear normal but have the potential for cultlike behavior: large corporations, political groups, professional organizations, government bodies, and established religions. These sectors of normal society seldom are thought to share characteristics with The People's Temple or the less dramatic groups such as the Moonies and the Krishna devotees collecting money in airports; however, careful study of cults reveals four basic cult behaviors that occur to varying degrees in almost all groups, including those that do not have a strange appearance or engage in bizarre behavior.[4] Identifying these basic behaviors permits one to replace the question, "Is this group a cult?" with the more practical one, "To what extent is cult behavior present?" The latter question is more useful because in the field of the transpersonal, as elsewhere, there is a continuum of groups ranging from the most benign and least cultlike to the most malignant and destructive.

THE FOUR BASIC CULT BEHAVIORS

Compliance With the Group

Everybody is concerned with how he or she is viewed by the people whose opinions matter to us: our "reference group." No matter how outwardly independent and nonconformist we may be, there is usually a group of people who share our values and whose approval we want. Membership in this group is signaled by conformity in dress, behavior, and speech. People outside of cults may suppress deviant thoughts also, although less obviously, if they believe that their expression could result in loss of status with the people important to them.

The power of groups has been noted by psychologists beginning with Gustav Le Bon and Sigmund Freud, and analyzed in detail by Wilfred Bion, who proposed that members of groups tend to adopt one of three primitive emotional states: dependency, pairing, or fight–flight. His description of the dependency state is an apt description of cults, but he saw the process taking place in varying degrees in all groups:

> The essential aim ... is to attain security through and have its members protected by one individual. It assumes that this is why the group has met. The members act as if they know nothing, as if they are inadequate and immature creatures. Their behavior implies that the leader, by contrast, is omnipotent and omniscient.[5]

It is plausible that natural selection favored individuals who were good at discerning what the group wanted because preservation of their membership in the group gave them the best chance of survival. As a consequence, it is likely that human beings have evolved to be exquisitely sensitive to what the group wants. "Political correctness" probably has a long history.

Dependence on a Leader

Leaders draw power from their followers' wish for an ideal parent, a wish that is latent in all adults no matter what kind of parent they had. Although cult leaders may be charismatic, they need not be as long as they are believed by the group members to possess superior powers and secrets. Cult leaders are authoritarian, encouraging dependence and discouraging autonomy. Obedience and loyalty are rewarded, and critical thinking is punished. Furthermore, to enhance dependency on the leader, pair bonding is discouraged. The leader must come first; family and lovers come last. The disruption of intimate relationships is accomplished by a variety of means: enforced chastity, separation of parents from children, arranged marriages, long separations, promiscuity, or sexual relations with the leader. All these aspects are counter to healthy leadership, which fosters growth, independence, and mature relationships and has as its aim that the followers will eventually achieve an eye-level relationship with the leader.

Avoiding Dissent

Dissent threatens the group fantasy that the members are being protected and rewarded by a perfect, enlightened leader who can do no wrong. The security provided by that fantasy is the basic attraction that keeps members in the cult despite highly questionable actions by the leader. Questioning the fantasy threatens that security, and for this reason, active dissent is seldom encouraged. To the contrary, dissenters are often declared to be in the grip of Satan. Sometimes they are scapegoated, and hidden, unconscious anger toward the leader is released against the dissenter. Almost all groups derive security from their shared beliefs and readily regard dissenters as irritations, to be gotten rid of. Nevertheless, the mark of a healthy group is a tolerance for dissent and a recognition of its vital role in keeping the group sane. Paranoia develops and grandiosity flourishes when dissent is eliminated and a group isolates itself from outside influence. As recent cult disasters have shown us, grandiose and paranoid cult leaders often self-destruct, taking their group with them.

Devaluing the Outsider

What good is being in a group if membership does not convey some special advantage? In spiritual groups, the members are likely to believe that they have the inside track to enlightenment, to being "saved," or to finding God because of the special sanctity and spiritual power of the leader. It follows that they must be superior to people outside the group: It is they, the converts, who have the leader's blessing and approval. Devaluation can be detected in the pity or "compassion" they may feel for those outside. This devaluation becomes most marked in the case of someone who elects to leave the group and is thereby considered "lost," if not damned. The more such devaluation takes place, and the more the group separates itself from the outside world, the greater the danger of cult pathology.

Devaluing of the outsider is part and parcel of everyday life. Depending on which group we designate as the outsider, our scorn may be directed at "liberals," "Republicans," "blacks," "Jews," "yuppies," or "welfare bums": however the outsider is designated. Such disidentification can authorize unethical, mean, and destructive behavior against the outsider, behavior that otherwise would cause guilt for violating ethical norms. Devaluation of the outsider is tribal behavior and so universal as to suggest a "basic law of groups": Be one of us and we will love you; leave us and we will kill you.

Devaluing the outsider reassures the insider that he or she is good, special, and deserving, unlike the outsider. Such a belief is a distortion of reality; if one considers the different circumstances of each person's development and life context, one is hard put to judge another person to be intrinsically inferior to oneself. Certainly, actions can be judged, but human beings are one species, at eye level with each other.

CULT BEHAVIOR IN THE PSYCHOTHERAPIST

The psychotherapist treating an ex–cult member may be tempted to devalue the patient for being duped and exploited and for believing weird doctrines. Especially in the role of expert in human psychology, we therapists wish to be reassured that nothing like that would happen to us because we are too discerning, mature, and sophisticated. As a matter of fact, we are not immune by virtue of our profession; psychotherapists with the best credentials have participated directly in cults. There have even been psychotherapeutic cults led by fully trained and accredited psychoanalysts,[6] and noted psychoanalysts have commented on the cult aspects of psychoanalytic training institutes.[7,8]

Furthermore, cult behavior is evident within the psychiatric profession as a whole. Perusal of the psychiatric literature indicates a remarkable absence of dissent from the current enthusiasm for biological psychiatry, an enthusiasm not different from the overcommitment to environmental influences that characterized the 1950s, 1960s, and 1970s. Indeed, research that challenges the biological perspective is ignored.⁴ The biological–medical consensus is reinforced by economic factors; those working in academic environments experience pressure to shape their research focus and strategy so that they will be funded. Being awarded a research grant usually depends on the approval of the "leading experts" in the field, the very persons who have established, and are committed to, the prevailing theoretical perspective. Furthermore, the same authorities are asked to judge articles submitted for publication to psychiatric journals. Avoidance of dissent and devaluation of the outsider can take place unnoticed, therefore, through rejection of submitted papers and denial of research funds. To this may be added informal devaluation through unsupported derogatory comments made at professional gatherings.

THE VALUE OF AWARENESS

It is important that both the therapist and the ex–cult member be able to see that cult behaviors are endemic in our society. Such awareness can protect the therapist from the influence of such behaviors and allow ex–cult members to realize that they are not freaks, weak and dependent persons, or fools. Rather, they were led astray by unconscious wishes that they share with all human beings. These wishes were stimulated at a time when they were especially vulnerable and under circumstances that any person might have found difficult to combat.

CONCLUSION

Cult behavior reflects the wish for a loving, accepting sibling group that is protected and cherished by a powerful, omnipotent parent. The problem with such a wish and its accompanying fantasy is that no human being can fill the role of the superparent, and adults can never again be children. To preserve the fantasy, reality must be distorted; because of this distortion, cult behavior results in a loss of realism. In the more extreme cases, the consequences can be drastic. Diminished realism is a problem in any situation, however, and for this reason, cult behavior is costly no matter where it takes place: affecting business decisions, governmental deliberations, day-to-day relationships in the community, or the practice of psychotherapy. Fortunately, awareness of these cult behaviors offers protection from their influence. Psychotherapists can foster that awareness, benefiting patients, themselves, and society.

NOTES

1. By *cult*, I mean a group headed by a charismatic leader who has spiritual, messianic, or therapeutic pretensions and indoctrinates the followers into an idiosyncratic belief system.

2. Deikman, A. (1982). *The observing self: Mysticism and psychotherapy*. Boston: Beacon Press.

3. Deikman, A. (1983). The evaluation of spiritual and utopian groups. *Journal of Humanistic Psychology, 23(3)*, 8–19.

4. Deikman, A. (1990). *The wrong way home: Uncovering the patterns of cult behavior in American society*. Boston: Beacon Press.

5. Rioch, M. (1975). The work of Wilfred Bion on groups. In A. D. Colman & H. D. Bexton (Eds.), *Group relations reader*. Sausalito, CA: GREX. Quotation on p. 24.

6. Temerlin, M., & Temerlin, J. (1982). Psychotherapy cults: An iatrogenic perversion. *Psychotherapy: Theory, Research and Practice, 19(2)*, 131–141.

7. Arlow, J. (1972). Some dilemmas in psychoanalytic education. *Journal of the American Psychoanalytic Association, 20*, 556–566.

8. Kernberg, O. (1986). Institutional problems of psychoanalytic education. *Journal of the American Psychoanalytic Association, 34*, 799–834.

CHAPTER 31

Psychopharmacology and Transpersonal Psychology

BRUCE S. VICTOR

PSYCHOPHARMACOLOGY and transpersonal psychology are commonly perceived as antithetical to one another, a fact that reflects a culture-wide mind–body split. The only area in which these two fields have found common ground has been in clinical and research work with psychedelic drugs. Unfortunately, governmental sanctions have all but stopped the use of psychedelics in the clinical context and as tools to investigate the physiology and cartography of the human psyche. The development of a transpersonal psychiatry requires, however, that the biological and the spiritual are not viewed as inherently inimical. This chapter points out the traditional linkage between spirituality and biological intervention and discusses the potential role of psychopharmacology in transpersonal psychotherapy. It also seeks to clarify the mistaken metapsychological assumptions that have kept these disciplines apart.

Historically, the biological and the spiritual were not considered separate, particularly in the realm of healing. Many traditional societies frequently employed psychotropic substances, not only as medicinal products, but also as a necessary part of the "pre-shamanic" curriculum, to assist the healer in expanding his psychological and spiritual healing powers. These substances were also employed by the nonshamanic members of traditional societies for worship and problem solving, for example, the peyote ritual among some Native American tribes.[1]

At least four factors have contributed to the current conceptual and clinical separation of the biological from the spiritual. First, this separation is an extension of the traditional Western religious distinction between body and soul, with a decided denigration of the former in favor of the spiritual significance of the latter. Because many spiritual traditions do not denigrate the physical world or see it as less spiritual, the split between body and spirit may be seen as a Western cultural bias.

Second, psychoanalytic psychology was based on a dualistic conceptualization of mind and body. The psychoanalytic concept of psychic energy is incompatible with the concept of physical energy used in biological psychiatry. This has resulted in a split between biological and psychodynamic psychiatry, a split that has widened as humanistic and transpersonal psychology differentiated themselves from psychodynamic psychology. Both biological and psychodynamic schools have participated in this split. For example, although the theories of Carl Jung are often seen as forming a conceptual bridge from the psychoanalytic to the transpersonal, they did little to include neurochemistry or neurophysiology as mediators of mental change. In fact, Jungian analysts often appear to subtly denigrate the biological and physiological factors as though they are lower and less significant matters than the archetypal and transcendent reality.[2]

Transpersonalists are often "top-downers" and minimize or disregard the significance and importance of the biological base in development. Correspondingly, biological theorists have been dismissive of the significance of the psychological and spiritual. The historical context of the latter view can be appreciated in considering the words of Benjamin Rush, the only physician signatory of the Declaration of Independence, who hypothesized that all psychological distress could be explained by abnormalities in cerebral blood flow and recommended various schedules of leechings to correct them. In contemporary biological psychiatry, the "dopamine theory of schizophrenia," although seductively parsimonious, cannot explain the myriad manifestations of this bewildering disease nor how the variations of symptoms might be expressed.[3] As later work demonstrated, the course of schizophrenia is profoundly influenced by the immediate environment of the person suffering from the disease, which would seem to argue against the notion that the neurochemicals are the sole causative agents of the disease. Today, the biopsychosocial model is commonly espoused but frequently not used in practice.

A third factor contributing to the divorce of the biological from the transpersonal or spiritual is rooted in the crass and undifferentiated nature of early biological interventions. Indeed, the earliest biological interventions in psychiatry such as "insulin therapy" or electroconvulsive therapy appear to be antithetical to spiritual development, because they produced coma, convulsions, and immediate amnesia. It is not surprising, therefore, that spiritual and biological clinical interventions came to be seen as disparate. Despite today's major advances in psychopharmacology, side effects such as acute dystonic reactions, akathisia, and the potentially fatal neuroleptic malignant syndrome continue to make biological interventions less palatable to those of an avowed transpersonal bent.

The final factor is one that could be termed a "trivialization of the biological." Traditional societies had clear and established rules regarding the use of mind-altering substances. There were specifications regarding who among the population were permitted to use them, when they could be used, what specific substances might be used, and why they were to be used on certain occasions. In contrast to these societies, Western cultures in the twentieth century have emphasized the notion of "recreational drug use." Faculty at prominent universities in this country indiscriminately handed out psychedelic drugs to their students, oblivious to the necessity of considering both "setting" (the environmental context of the proposed ingestion) and "set" (broadly, the internal preparedness of the user) in their use (see Chapter 18). Because of this casual treatment of what might be considered sacramental substances, psychotropic chemicals came to be feared for their consequences and denigrated concerning their potential transpersonal significance.

These factors led to a profound reaction on the part of those charged with enforcing social regulation of these substances, with unfortunate clinical consequences. As a result, marijuana is rarely available even for such patient groups as terminal cancer patients, who would benefit from its use in conjunction with chemotherapy. Similarly, clinical research using LSD and other psychedelics has been all but completely forbidden.[4] The result has been the separation of psychedelic psychotherapy from psychoanalytic "depth work" as well as from transpersonal therapies, which are often portrayed as transcending the biochemical level.

At the time of this writing, the core of the treatment of most of the major (DSM-IV Axis I) psychiatric disorders is psychopharmacological.[5] Indeed, psychotherapy unaided by psychopharmacological intervention is notoriously ineffective for the treatment of bipolar disorder, major depressive disorder, panic disorder, obsessive–compulsive disorder, schizophrenia, and other psychotic disorders, as well as disturbances of mental status that are thought to be due to "medical conditions." Furthermore, there is an increasing appreciation of the biochemical contributions to what are referred to as *character disorders* (DSM-IV, Axis II). Whereas personality disorders were once conceptualized, almost by definition, as the component of a person that remained unaffected by neurochemical considerations, there is increasing evidence of dysregulation of serotonergic systems, for example, in patients with borderline personality disorder, that are similar to those in patients with more classical-appearing affective disorders. Clinicians such as Peter Kramer, in his book *Listening to Prozac,* have reviewed the evidence that developmental trauma leads to biochemical imbalance of which the chief manifestation appears to be dysfunctional character "traits" (e.g., rejection–sensitivity, obsessiveness, decreased self-esteem). Furthermore, these traits seem amenable to improvement by psychopharmacological intervention.[6]

These clinical observations are finding increasing substantiation in the clinical literature, such as in the effectiveness of serotonin reuptake inhibitors in the treatment of borderline personality disorder as well as more characterological-appearing syndromes such as dysthymic disorder. Within such a context, it is no longer a viable position for a psychotherapist of any theoretical persuasion to take a stand against medications in the treatment of potentially disabling psychiatric syndromes. Only after integration of neurochemistry and psychopharmacology with transpersonal psychological theory and psychotherapy can a transpersonal psychiatry be achieved.

TRANSPERSONAL MISPERCEPTIONS OF PSYCHOPHARMACOLOGY

It is important to clear up some of the misperceptions of psychopharmacological intervention frequently found among transpersonalists. First, psychopharmacology in no way obviates the need for psychotherapy. The goal of pharmacotherapy, symptom relief, is consistent with the goals of psychotherapy, which involve symptom relief in the context of personality development. Although pharmacotherapy may be more effective than psychotherapy in the relief of symptoms in many major psychiatric disorders, medication cannot provide the vessel for the process of character transformations (the Jungian *temenos*); this can be provided only in the context of a safe dyadic relationship that provides intimacy without boundary infraction and generates some measure of insight or self-reflection. It is possible to distinguish between the eradication of debilitating symptoms and the enhancement of personal growth. A therapeutic relationship can do the latter more effectively than medication.

There is a misperception on the part of some transpersonally oriented psychotherapists that symptom eradication, particularly the diminution of severe disabling anxiety and depression, will somehow remove the impetus for insight and personal growth. This belief is an extension of one first espoused by Sigmund Freud, who contended that the heightening of anxiety ultimately increased the access to unconscious material and thus to the development of insight through the psychoanalytic process.[7] Even though Freud seemed to repudiate this position in his later writings, and despite the lack of research or even clinical substantiation for this position, this tenet has persisted in the writings of later psychoanalysts. In fact, recent empirically conducted psychotherapy research seems to substantiate the opposite: that insight appears to develop proportionately to the reduction of subjectively experienced anxiety. This research, detailed in Joseph Weiss's book *How Psychotherapy Works,* strongly suggests that insight and, by implication, personal growth become possible only when the patient perceives it is safe to take the next psychodevelopmental step.[8]

Some transpersonally oriented therapists legitimately point out that psychotic episodes and physical suffering often seem to be required parts of the "preshamanic curriculum"; Jung contended that only those who have been wounded themselves can heal others. The notion of the "spiritual emergency" propounded by Stanislav and Christina Grof suggests that psychotic-appearing experiences may be part of the development of a broadened "transpersonal" perspective and that mental health professionals, especially psychiatrists with an attachment to the conventional "medical model," may risk interrupting an important developmental process in the name of symptom eradication. The same authors have also noted that depressive episodes can be a signal that there is something in the sufferer's life that needs to change and that the episodes can present the opportunity for meaningful growth by forcing a new perspective.[9]

The resolution of this seeming contradiction lies in the assessment of whether the presence of the debilitating state serves the function of psychological growth. Although the experience of pain, whether psychological or physical, can be a powerful motivator for personal change, its persistence beyond a certain point can retard it. Additionally, painful states can become a part of a debilitating, unconscious attachment much the same way that pleasurable states can. It becomes a challenge to the transpersonally oriented clinician to determine whether the level of pain induced by an experience of altered consciousness represents such an attachment or whether the person can actively work with the pain therapeutically toward further psychological growth.

Indeed, even in traditional societies, where altered states of consciousness are more meaningfully woven into the fabric of social and cultural functioning, the experience of these states is not open to anyone; what is part of the "preshamanic curriculum" for one person would not necessarily be a suitable experience for another.[10] Traditional cultures, therefore, have notions of psychopathology. Transpersonal practitioners from Western culture bear the same responsibility as traditional healers to differentiate growth-producing experiences from those that are likely to be debilitating. One important role of pharmacotherapy is to titrate the level of symptoms, whether they be pain, depression, anxiety, or psychotic states, so that they can be integrated by the person in the service of growth.

PRINCIPLES OF TRANSPERSONAL PSYCHOPHARMACOLOGY

The first principle is that of arriving at an appropriate differential diagnosis, separating transcendent experience from psychopathology. Ken Wilber has addressed this problem in his essay addressing the "pre/trans" distinction: that is, differentiating between experiences that represent the failure to achieve necessary ego functions and those that represent moving beyond them[11] (see Chapter 23). The decision to medicate or not needs to be based on just such a clinical assessment.

The second principle of transpersonal psychopharmacology is the appreciation of what psychopharmacological intervention can and cannot do. Psychotropic medications can be particularly effective for reducing the anxiety and agitation associated with an altered state of consciousness and thus make the process more amenable to psychotherapeutic intervention. They cannot substitute for the container of a psychotherapeutic relationship, however, and to try to use them in that way would prevent the search for the meaning of the experience. Psychiatric medications should be used as an aid for helping the patient tolerate his own experience rather than as a substitute for the therapist that communicates to the patient that the therapist cannot tolerate that patient.

Third, the transpersonal psychopharmacologist must have the capacity for the integration of spiritual disciplines with meaningful psychopharmacological intervention. This task clearly requires the knowledge of when each would be helpful. It would be harmful to treat an actively manic patient without aggressive pharmacotherapy; however, many of the same manic patients desire an educational and therapeutic context in which to understand some of the spiritual experiences in their state of altered consciousness. The transpersonally oriented therapist can be particularly helpful in providing the requisite education or introduction to spiritual discipline after the patient has become sufficiently clinically grounded.

Finally, the transpersonal psychopharmacologist must be able to choose the least potentially troublesome alternative amidst an increasingly bewildering array of psychotropic agents. Although this task is required of any therapist choosing a medication, it is especially true for one who is transpersonally oriented and therefore focused on the broad context of meaning of the patient's experience and on promoting the highest level of function. There is no psychopharmacological intervention without side effects; it is important, therefore, that these be minimized at all costs to provide the patient with the appropriate combination of mental stability and agility. Such a model of prescribing bridges Cartesian dualism.

This chapter may serve as an introduction regarding the use of psychotropic medications in the context of transpersonal psychotherapy. I hope these preliminary thoughts invite further consideration and commentary as the perspectives of psychobiology and transpersonal psychology are seen as less and less antithetical.

NOTES

1. Dobkin, D. D. (1984). *Hallucinogens: Cross cultural perspectives.* Albuquerque: University of New Mexico Press.

2. Steele, F. B. (1994, March). The chemical in the alchemical and vice versa. Paper presented at the Chemical in the Alchemical Conference, C. G. Jung Institute, San Francisco, CA.

3. Davis, K. L., Kahn, R. S., Ko, G., et al. (1991). Dopamine in schizophrenia: A review and reconceptualization. *American Journal of Psychiatry, 148,* 1474–1486.

4. Grinspoon, L., & Bakalar, J. (1979). *Psychedelic drugs reconsidered.* New York: Basic Books.

5. American Psychiatric Association. (1994). *Diagnostic and statistical manual of mental disorders* (4th ed., rev.). Washington, DC: Author.

6. Kramer, P. (1993). *Listening to Prozac.* New York: Viking Press.

7. Freud, S. (1911–1915). Papers on technique. In J. Strachey (Ed. and Trans.), *The standard edition of the complete psychological works of Sigmund Freud* (Vol. 7, pp. 255–568). London: Hogarth Press.

8. Weiss, J. (1993). *How psychotherapy works.* New York: Guilford Press.

9. Grof, S., & Grof, C. (1989). *Spiritual emergency.* Los Angeles: Tarcher.

10. Halifax, J. (1979). *Shamanic voices: A survey of visionary narratives.* New York: E. P. Dutton.

11. Wilber, K. (1980). The pre/trans fallacy. *ReVision, 3,* 51–72.

CHAPTER 32

Psychedelic Psychotherapy

GARY BRAVO AND
CHARLES GROB

THE USE OF PSYCHEDELIC PLANTS for healing purposes is a
shamanic tradition that stretches back thousands of years. In modern industrial cultures, the use of psychedelic drugs for healing
began approximately in 1950 and was banned in the late 1960s.
Now, after 2 decades of virtual neglect, there has been a call for
renewed clinical research with psychedelics.[1,2] This chapter discusses the three major paradigms for the use of psychedelics in clinical psychiatric research and psychotherapy: the psychotomimetic,
the psycholytic, and the psychedelic.

THE PSYCHOTOMIMETIC PARADIGM

Initial work with psychedelics centered around the "model psychosis." This paradigm, the psychotomimetic, asserted that admin-
istering psychedelics was equivalent to introducing a "toxin" to the
brain that produced a breakdown in ego function and loss of reality testing: a temporary psychosis. After systematic comparisons of
psychedelic experiences with natural psychoses, however, emphasizing the contrast between the auditory hallucinations, emotional
flatness, withdrawal, and frequent delusions of the schizophrenic

335

patient with the visual illusions, emotional lability, preference for companionship, and infrequent delusions of the psychedelic-intoxicated person, it was determined that "there are many superficial resemblances, but the total clinical syndrome is considerably different."[3] This finding, along with the fact that the attempt to discover a naturally occurring schizophrenia-inducing "psychotoxin" proved unsuccessful, led to the abandonment of the psychotomimetic paradigm. More recently, however, researchers again have become interested in exploring the relationship between the psychedelic state and the acute psychotic state[4] and in the use of psychedelics as a tool to study psychopathological symptoms in humans.[5]

THE PSYCHOLYTIC PARADIGM

The psycholytic model makes use of the capacity of psychedelics to bring the unconscious contents of the mind to conscious awareness. Low doses of the drugs are carefully titrated over many sessions to produce unconscious material without overwhelming the patient's ability to reflect and verbalize. The therapist works within the patient's personal psychodynamic psychology and avoids going into archetypal or transpersonal layers of the psyche. This approach, which was most popular in Europe,[6] seemed to work best with character-disordered patients, patients with psychosomatic problems, and victims of severe trauma. An articulate example of psycholytic psychotherapy is provided by the book *Shivitti: A Vision*, in which a Jewish writer using the pseudonym *Ka-tzetnik 135633*[7] describes a series of five LSD-assisted sessions under the guidance of Jan Bastiaans in the Netherlands. Under the influence of LSD, and with the gentle prompting of Bastiaans, the author emotionally relives and catharts his experiences in a Nazi concentration camp. Eventually the treatment helped to alleviate 30 years of depression, "survivor guilt," and posttraumatic stress disorder. Bastiaans[8] found that only a powerful substance such as LSD could break through the resistance to reexperiencing severe trauma such as that found in holocaust survivors.

THE PSYCHEDELIC PARADIGM

When higher doses of psychedelic drugs were given, patients began to describe spiritual and mystical experiences that did not fit the personal psychology framework of psychoanalysis but appeared to have therapeutic effects. A new technique of psychedelic therapy evolved that had as its goal the production of an ego-dissolving mystical experience. This method, which generally encompassed one or several sessions, was favored by centers in the United States and Canada. Early on, there were successes claimed for such intractable disorders as chronic alcoholism, antisocial behavior, and autism, as well as in alleviating the pain and anguish of those suffering from terminal illness.[9] Most of the early studies did not use rigorous scientific methods and thus were discounted by later reviewers. The successes were impressive, however, and the adverse effects minimal.[10] Most of this clinical work was banned by the mid–1960s; however, the Maryland Psychiatric Research Institute, which included Stanislav Grof, continued to investigate the psychedelic paradigm well into the 1970s, treating more than 750 patients with diagnoses of substance abuse, terminal illness, and neurosis and experimenting with novel psychotropics, such as dipropyltryptamine (DPT) and methylenedioxyamphetamine (MDA).[11]

Grof[12] developed the most comprehensive theory of LSD psychotherapy. He believed that LSD, when used with a therapeutic focus, allowed people to work through deep traumatic fixations in their psyche. He devised a way to enhance this process, using music to stimulate a range of emotional states and body work to resolve energetic blocks (see Chapters 8 and 35). Another psychoanalytically trained psychiatrist, Salvador Roquet, had his worldview transformed after participating in the recently rediscovered magic mushroom healing rituals with the Mexican *curandera* Maria Sabina. Roquet later devised a group-therapy technique using high doses of a variety of psychedelics, sensory overload, and somatic exercises to weaken psychological defenses and promote ego-shattering experiences in patients undergoing psychedelic psychotherapy.[13]

There is no standardized technique of psychedelic psychotherapy. Most theorists agree, however, that the psychedelic drugs themselves are not the healing agents; rather, they are adjuncts to the psychotherapeutic process, and their therapeutic value is determined by the structure of the therapy and the quality of the therapist. Nevertheless, the technique of psychedelic therapy should be viewed as a specialized procedure within psychotherapy, and it is essential that the therapist have extensive training in psychedelic psychotherapy, part of which consists of firsthand experience with the psychedelic "terrain" of the different substances. Early reviews of psychedelic therapy suggested that therapists who had experienced the drugs obtained better results than those who had not.

A subject's report from the Spring Grove Research Center in Baltimore illustrates many of the aspects of psychedelic psychotherapy. A woman in her 40s discovered she had metastatic cancer with a terminal prognosis and underwent an LSD session. Her description of the experience follows:

The day prior to LSD, I was fearful and anxious. I would at that point have gratefully withdrawn. By the end of the preparatory session practically all anxiety was gone, the instructions were understood, the procedure clear. . . .

At about this time, it seems, I fused with the music and was transported on it. So completely was I one with the sound that when the particular melody or record stopped, however momentarily, I was alive to the pause, eagerly awaiting the next lap of the journey. A delightful game was being played. What was coming next? Would it be powerful, tender, dancing, or somber? . . .

Mainly I remember two experiences. I was alone in a timeless world with no boundaries. There was no atmosphere; there was no color, no imagery, but there may have been light. Suddenly I recognized that I was a moment in time, created by those before me and in turn the creator of others. This was my moment, and my major function had been completed. By being born, I had given meaning to my parents' existence.

Again in the void, alone without the time–space boundaries. Life reduced itself over and over again to the least common denominator. I cannot remember the logic of the experience, but I became poignantly aware that the core of life is love. At this moment I felt that I was reaching out to the world—to all people—but especially to those closest to me. I wept long for the wasted years, the search for identity in false places, the neglected opportunities, the emotional energy lost in basically meaningless pursuits. Many times, after respites, I went back, but always to variations on the same themes. The music carried and sustained me. . . .

Later, as members of my family came, there was a closeness that seemed new. That night, at home, my parents came, too. All noticed a change in me. I was radiant, and I seemed at peace, they said. I felt that way too. What has changed for me? I am living now, and being. I can take it as it comes. Some of my physical symptoms are gone. The excessive fatigue, some of the pains. I still get irritated occasionally and yell. I am still me, but more at peace. My family senses this and we are closer. All who know me well say that this has been a good experience.[14]

The question of psychedelic-assisted psychotherapy reemerged in the 1980s with the rediscovery of a long-forgotten drug: 3,4-methylenedioxy-methamphetamine (MDMA). Not strictly a psychedelic but rather a representative of a related group sometimes termed *empathogens,* MDMA is less likely to release experience in the higher spiritual or archetypal realms. Psychotherapists found that MDMA facilitated the relaxation of defense mechanisms, enhanced access to the emotions, and allowed a feeling of safety, thus increasing trust in the therapeutic alliance. This "opening" occurred without the perceptual and cognitive distortions that were often a concern with the traditional psychedelics.[15] Surveys of MDMA users indicated that MDMA's main subjective effect was a unique capacity to provide the user with decreased defensiveness and an increased ability to interact empathically with others.[16] Before the outlawing of MDMA in 1985, it was estimated that thousands of psychotherapy sessions with MDMA had been conducted.[17]

Theoretical information and abundant anecdotal material exist suggesting that MDMA's action on the serotonergic system might in fact prove relevant for helping such conditions as depression, obsessive–compulsive disorder, and posttraumatic stress disorder.[18] In addition, MDMA has been reported to relieve unremitting pain and anxiety in cancer patients and interpersonal defensiveness within marital and group therapy.[15] MDMA's potential as a psychotherapeutic adjunct has not been developed because of governmental concerns about widespread abuse and the potential neurotoxicity of the drug.

The psychedelic ibogaine, contained in the root of a plant from central Africa, has a long tradition of use in tribal initiation rites and has recently been promoted as a potent interrupter of heroin and cocaine addiction. Ibogaine is claimed to attenuate opiate withdrawal greatly, leaving a long-lasting lack of craving. Studies in opioid-addicted animals support this contention. Ibogaine can induce powerful spiritual experiences and life reviews in addicts, which may motivate them to make changes in their lives.[19]

CAUTIONS

What are the dangers of transpersonal psychedelic psychotherapy? First, because the aim is to weaken a person's ego resistances until a breakthrough occurs, patients with weak egos and boundaries, such as psychotics or prepsychotics, should be excluded.

The most common adverse reaction to psychedelics is the "bad trip," which is a panic or depressive reaction to the perceived loss of mental control caused by the psychedelic or from the flooding of previously repressed or unconscious material. These mind states are magnified and can seem endless to a person in an altered state of consciousness. In addition, psychotic and paranoid states can emerge under the acute psychedelic intoxication. Acute adverse reactions occurring during therapy are generally seen as part of the uncovering process; the goal is for them to be contained in the therapy session and worked through. Prolonged psychoses are a rare complication in clinical contexts.[20]

Chronic adverse reactions to psychedelics include the phenomenon of *flashbacks*, called "hallucinogen persisting perception disorder" in DSM-IV; these are spontaneous, transient, and intermittent occurrences of perceptions and emotions that were originally experienced during a psychedelic intoxication. They can be extremely frightening or annoying to the experiencer, or they can be well tolerated or even pleasurable. The flashback phenomenon is not well defined, and incidence data range from 15 to 75% of psychedelic users.[25] The incidence after therapeutic use has not been well studied.

The problem of physical damage to the body from psychedelics, especially of the nervous system, has long been a cause of concern and controversy. Reports of chromosome damage from LSD proved to be unfounded.[12] More recently, large doses of MDMA have been shown to cause damage to serotonin neurons in laboratory animals,[21] but the meaning of this finding is unclear.[22] Similarly, the indoleamine ibogaine may induce neurotoxicity in the Purkinje cells of the cerebellum in rats, but again the relevance of this finding to therapeutic use in humans is unknown. The question of long-term impairment in psychedelic users has been controversial; some studies of heavy psychedelic users suggest mental pathology, such as eccentric thinking, lack of motivation, and passivity. Prospective studies are nonexistent, leaving open the question of cause and effect.[1]

As it is with all psychotherapies, assessing outcome in psychedelic psychotherapy is problematic. Psychedelics are not used as chemotherapeutic agents in the allopathic mode to reduce a symptom or correct a biochemical defect. New paradigms for psychedelic drug use must be developed, perhaps with help from shamanic models, in which the substances are given in elaborate spiritual healing rituals that integrate religion and therapy[23] (see Chapter 21). Although much has been written about the importance of "set and setting" in the evaluation of drug effects, this aspect has largely been ignored in psychopharmacological research. *Set* refers to the personality, intention, mood, and preparation of the individual ingesting a drug, whereas *setting* refers to the environment in which the drug is taken, including physical, interpersonal, and cultural aspects. Shamanic healers are aware of these factors and use ritual, mythology, singing, and the powerful effects of expectation to provide their communities access to shared transpersonal experiences, thus enhancing social cohesion[24] (see Chapters 10 and 21).

CONCLUSION

Psychedelic psychotherapy, like transpersonal psychiatry in general, stretches the paradigms of current psychiatric theory and practice. To open up the field and prevent another overreaction by society and its regulators, investigators will need to demonstrate that research and clinical work with psychedelics can be conducted in a careful and responsible manner. Only in this way can the potential for healing and for increasing the understanding of consciousness from this class of chemicals be realized.

NOTES

1. Grinspoon, L., & Bakalar, J. B. (1986). Can drugs be used to enhance the psychotherapeutic process? *American Journal of Psychotherapy, 40,* 393–404.

2. Strassman, R. J. (1995). Hallucinogenic drugs in psychiatric research and treatment: Perspectives and prospects. *Journal of Nervous and Mental Disease, 183,* 127–138.

3. Hollister, L. E. (1968). *Chemical psychoses* (p. 122). Springfield, IL: Thomas.

4. Fischman, L. G. (1983). Dreams, hallucinogenic drug states, and schizophrenia: A psychological and biological comparison. *Schizophrenia Bulletin, 9,* 73–94.

5. Hermle, L., Funfgeld, M., Oepen, G., Botsch, H., Borchardt, D., Gouzoulis, E., Fehrenbach, R. A., & Spitzer, M. (1992). Mescaline-

induced psychopathological, neuropsychological and neurometabolic effects in normal subjects: Experimental psychosis as a tool for psychiatric research. *Biological Psychiatry, 32,* 976–991.

6. Leuner, H. (1983). Psycholytic therapy: Hallucinogenics as an aid in psychodynamically oriented psychotherapy. In L. Grinspoon & J. B. Bakalar (Eds.), *Psychedelic reflections.* New York: Human Sciences Press.

7. Ka-tzetnik 135633. (1989). *Shivitti: A vision.* San Francisco: Harper & Row.

8. Bastiaans, J. (1983). Mental liberation facilitated by the use of hallucinogenic drugs. In L. Grinspoon & J. B. Bakalar (Eds.), *Psychedelic reflections.* New York: Human Sciences Press.

9. Abramson, H. A. (Ed.). (1967). *The use of LSD in psychotherapy and alcoholism.* New York: Bobbs-Merrill.

10. Yensen, R. (1985). LSD and psychotherapy. *Journal of Psychoactive Drugs, 17(4),* 267–277.

11. Yensen, R., & Dryer, D. (1992, September). *Thirty years of psychedelic research: The Spring Grove experiment and its sequels.* Talk presented at the European College of Consciousness International Congress, Göttingen, Germany. (Available from the Orenda Institute, 2403 Talbot Road, Baltimore, MD 21216.)

12. Grof, S. (1980). *LSD psychotherapy.* Pomona, CA: Hunter House.

13. Clark, W. H. (1983). Life begins at sixty. In L. Grinspoon & J. B. Bakalar (Eds.), *Psychedelic reflections.* New York: Human Sciences Press.

14. Pahnke, W. N., Kurland, A. A., Unger, S., Savage, C., Wolf, S., & Goodman, L. E. (1970). Psychedelic therapy (utilizing LSD) with cancer patients. *Journal of Psychedelic Drugs, 3,* 63–75. Quotation on pp. 63–64.

15. Greer, G., & Tolbert, R. (1990). The therapeutic use of MDMA. In S. J. Peroutka (Ed.), *Ecstasy: The clinical, pharmacological and neurotoxicological effects of the drug MDMA.* Norwell, MA: Kluwer Academic.

16. Liester, M. B., Grob, C. S., Bravo, G. L., & Walsh, R. N. (1992). Phenomenology and sequelae of 3,4-methylenedioxy-methamphetamine use. *Journal of Nervous and Mental Disease, 180(6),* 345–352.

17. Beck, J., & Rosenbaum, M. (1994). *Pursuit of ecstasy: The MDMA experience.* Albany: SUNY Press.

18. Riedlinger, T. J., & Riedlinger, J. E. (1994). Psychedelic and entactogenic drugs in the treatment of depression. *Journal of Psychoactive Drugs, 26,* 41–55.

19. Goutarel, R., Golinhofer, O., & Sillans, R. (1993). Pharmaco-dynamics and therapeutic applications of iboga and ibogaine. In T. Lyttle (Ed.), *Psychedelic monographs and essays* (Vol. 6). Boynton Beach, FL: PM & E Publishing Group.

20. Cohen, S. (1960). Lysergic acid diethylamide: Side effects and complications. *Journal of Nervous and Mental Disease, 130,* 30–40.

21. McKenna, D., & Peroutka, S. (1990). Neurochemistry and neurotoxicity of 3,4-methylenedioxymethamphetamine (MDMA, "Ecstasy"). *Journal of Neurochemistry, 54,* 14–22.

22. Grob, C. S., Bravo, G. L., Walsh, R. N., & Liester, M. B. (1992). Commentary: The MDMA–neurotoxicity controversy: Implications for clinical research with novel psychoactive drugs. *Journal of Nervous and Mental Disease, 180(6),* 355–356.

23. Bravo, G., & Grob, C. (1989). Shamans, sacraments, and psychiatrists. *Journal of Psychoactive Drugs, 21,* 123–128.

24. Andritzky, W. (1989). Sociopsychotherapeutic functions of ayahuasca healing in Amazonia. *Journal of Psychoactive Drugs, 21,* 77–89.

25. Abraham, H. D. (1983). Visual phenomenology of the LSD flashback. *Archives of General Psychiatry, 40,* 884–889.

CHAPTER 33

Clinical Aspects of Meditation

SYLVIA BOORSTEIN

THIS CHAPTER DISCUSSES the clinical aspects of meditation, particularly focusing on its use as an adjunct to psychotherapy and the negative effects that can arise from intensive practice.[1] There are two major categories of meditation practices, *concentration* and *awareness*. The two types of meditation have distinctive features, uses, and results (see Chapter 17).

CONCENTRATION MEDITATION

In concentration practices, the meditator's attention is focused on a single object. The focus might be a bodily sensation such as the experience of breathing or feeling one's feet touch the ground in walking. The object of meditation could also be the repetition, silently or aloud, of a word or phrase. Sometimes a visual object is used, such as a candle flame, or a sacred image like a mandala. Sometimes the image is a visual recollection. In all these practices, the meditator keeps attention focused on the chosen object, and whenever attention wavers, it is returned to the focus.

Concentration practice promotes composure, a sense of well-being, and an overall feeling of relaxation. Practitioners usually report that they feel refreshed following a period of meditation. Concentration meditations also reduce reactivity to other stimuli;

for instance, they may raise the pain threshold. Because these techniques are generally relaxing, they are often helpful to people experiencing situational stress and anxiety disorders.

The following experience illustrates the value of meditation practice for attenuating psychological and somatic symptoms of situational stress. Patricia, a 40-year-old psychotherapist, sought my advice about additional psychotherapy for herself. She had completed 3 years of psychotherapy 10 years previously and felt it had been successful. She recalled that what she had experienced as genuine, positive regard by her therapist had healed the wounds of constant belittling she had received from her cold and critical father. She felt that her therapist's validation of her self-worth had been integral to her evolution as an effective therapist.

Her consideration of further therapy appeared to begin subsequent to two stressful developments. Her husband had recently expressed unhappiness about their relationship, so that her marriage was in question. Also, she had been cited, unjustly, by a client for unethical conduct. Although she was innocent of the violation, the necessary responses (involving lawyers, letters, and so on) were stressful. She had begun to experience insomnia, nausea, and headaches. Her most troubling symptom was a sudden and complete loss of self-confidence as a therapist, so that each working day was both depressing and alarming.

Because Patricia had had previous experience with vipassana (mindfulness) meditation, I urged her to attend a 20-day retreat scheduled for the next month before embarking on further depth psychotherapy. To provide interim support, I met with her weekly during the 1-month preretreat period. Primarily, I hoped to offer collegial support while the investigations of alleged malfeasance continued.

Patricia began the retreat with both her marital and her legal status unresolved. Because mindfulness meditation practice could have intensified her physical symptoms and anxiety, Patricia decided to work with concentration techniques only, focusing on awareness of the breath as a means of calming the mind. She reported that after 1 week she was sleeping soundly and her nausea and headaches had disappeared. Periodically, she would recall her "two problems," but she was able to recognize them as dilemmas of her life that needed attention rather than feeling victimized or frightened by them. She reported that she had resisted the impulse to figure out solutions to these problems during the retreat. Instead, she made the decision to use the time to attempt to regain her emotional and physical health. At the end of 3 weeks, she left the retreat prepared to address both situations, feeling confident that in both areas she had behaved with integrity and that the outcome of each, although beyond her control, was manageable. Her marriage ended 6 months later; she was exonerated of any professional wrongdoing; her symptoms did not reappear; and she continued her professional career.

The following case illustrates the use of a concentration technique to counteract anxiety and obsessive worrying. Anita was a 50-year-old woman who sought psychotherapy for periodic bouts of worrying about family problems. Her discomfort was considerable, although not constant, but she steadfastly refused to consider drug therapy. Her brother, who was a major problem for her, had been treated for many years for manic-depressive illness with lithium and was marginally functional. Anita felt that taking a drug would be admitting to a similar illness. Apart from her bouts of worrying, however, Anita functioned well in her job and with her family.

I suggested a form of concentration meditation to Anita. I specifically told her that I did not think her symptoms had significant unconscious derivatives. Her brother was a source of anxiety to her (phoning her at work, making constant demands); I told her that she probably had inherited her mother's tendency to fret and had internalized her mother's demand that she "ought" to take care of her brother. I supposed, although I did not tell this to Anita, that she was also furious at her brother and mother for their ongoing demands: I did not think this insight would be useful to her at the beginning of therapy, because her self-esteem was largely related to her sense that she was the family's mainstay.

The meditation I suggested to Anita was the recitation of *metta*, or "loving kindness" phrases. The phrases are variations of a simple formula: "May I be peaceful. May I be happy. May all beings be peaceful. May all beings be happy." I instructed Anita to set aside 10 minutes 3 times a day to sit quietly and repeat these phrases silently to herself, saying each phrase on either the inhalation or the exhalation. Four phrases required two complete breaths. A variation of the practice was saying the phrases to herself while walking. Anita liked to leave her workplace at lunchtime and walk, so that this meditation fit into her routine easily. She said each phrase on two steps as she walked and found she enjoyed her walks more. Her phrases gave her walking a rhythmic cadence, and she was delighted to find that if she practiced diligently, she did not get involved in ruminative worry.

I saw Anita weekly for a month, then biweekly for 2 months, and after that only occasionally when she felt a need to meet. She experienced sufficient symptom relief to feel less frightened and victimized by her occasional periods of worry. We used the analogy that her "fits of worrying" were like migraines, an unpleasant symptom that she was predisposed to but that she could treat with the "analgesic" of meditation.

AWARENESS MEDITATION

The second major category of meditation practices is awareness meditation. Here the meditator attempts to cultivate composure with a wide focus of attention on all current experience, internal and external. An attempt is made to be aware of all changing physical sensations, mental states, thoughts, and perceptions while maintaining a nonreactive attitude to them. An example of this form of meditation would be mindfulness meditation, a practice central to Buddhist tradition.[2,3,4]

Awareness, or mindfulness, meditation differs from concentration practices in that the techniques bring people into more immediate awareness of painful emotions and psychological dilemmas. In awareness practice there is no place to hide. People with healthy ego structures are usually able to use the insights gained constructively. Indeed, memories that were too painful to bear often become tolerable with awareness meditation. These painful recollections can then be integrated and the trauma healed. On the other hand, awareness practice may be difficult for individuals with a fragile ego structure. Even with a minimal daily practice, direct confrontation with strong emotions may be stressful and destabilizing.

The case of Alice illustrates how intensive meditation practice can uncover traumatic memories that are best dealt with in psychotherapy. Alice was 32 years old and a college graduate; after 1 year of teaching high school, she traveled to India and lived in ashrams, practicing meditation with several teachers over a period of 7 years. She had a series of romantic involvements during this time, but none developed into an enduring relationship. She returned to the United States and began a 3-month intensive mindfulness meditation retreat, during which time she began to have memories of sexual abuse and incest that she had never recalled previously. She became distraught and frightened about what she felt were valid memories.

I met with Alice several times to help her evaluate her situation. Her memories of her childhood were vague and limited, which seemed consistent with someone who had suffered major trauma. I referred her to a Jungian therapist, with whom Alice worked for several years. Alice last wrote to me to let me know that she had ended therapy and was about to marry a man who taught at her school. She said that she was continuing a daily period of meditation every morning, that it helped her prepare for the day ahead, but that she felt extended retreat practice was not appropriate for her at this time. She assured me that she was not afraid of practicing and was confident that she could face whatever memories came up, but she felt that at this time she needed to put effort into building her relationship.

Harriet provides another example of how awareness meditation can bring up important psychodynamic material. Harriet was 60 years old and taking early retirement from her college teaching position for medical reasons. She sought therapy at the advice of her internist, who felt it might be helpful in lowering her elevated blood pressure. Harriet was pleasant and agreeable but somewhat tense and stiff at our first meeting. She seemed interested in exploring the potential of therapy, but she was uncomfortable with talking about feelings. During our once-weekly sessions, she began to talk about her disappointment with her life: the fact that her two marriages had not worked out well and that her children were estranged from her. She was interested in the fact that I was a Buddhist meditation teacher, and after hearing a talk I gave at a local church, decided to try a 7-day meditation retreat.

The isolation and silence of the meditation retreat were not a problem for Harriet; her parents had been Quakers and she was accustomed to being in groups where people sat quietly. In fact, it was reassuring to her that she did not need to interact socially because she was, by nature, somewhat shy. What did surprise her, after some days of silent meditation practice, was the flood of emotions that she began to experience. Memories of her childhood surfaced, and although they were not memories of traumatic events, she was surprised at how emotional she became over them. This is not unusual; many people who do intensive meditation report that their memory seems to become clearer and more vivid, giving them access to even mundane memories of the distant past.

The retreat experience, particularly the flood of heartfelt feelings, brought about an important shift in Harriet's demeanor. She seemed more open, relaxed, and sentimental. She talked more openly about her disappointments in life and felt relaxed enough to cry about the sadness she felt over things that had not worked out well. She left therapy after several months, feeling more at ease and less depressed, with plans to continue with her meditation practice.

Although it often brings up disturbing material, awareness meditation can also be used to counteract situational stresses, as the next case illustrates. Paula was 35 when she came to see me for therapy. Her husband had left her, apparently after years of discontent. He had filed for divorce and was planning to marry a woman he had been involved with for some time.

Paula was stunned. Although her relationship with her husband was periodically stormy, she had assumed that their marriage was intact. They had two young children. Because Paula's parents had endured years of stormy relations, Paula had assumed such a state was normal and that things would eventually become more mellow, just as they had with her parents. The biggest blow was the thought that her husband had left her for another woman, because Paula prided herself on being attractive and vivacious.

I taught Paula a simple awareness meditation. I asked her to review with me the "uncontrollable crying" she had reported having the night before. She said, "I started to cry and I didn't think I could stop." I asked, "What happened next?" She replied, "I decided to take a bath to see if that would be relaxing."

"Then what happened?"

"I cried and cried in the tub, and I couldn't stop."

"Then what happened?"

"The water in the tub got cold so I got out."

"Then what?"

"Then I was hungry, so I made a sandwich."

At that point, Paula looked at me and smiled. What had become clear was that her grief, although intense, was replaced by other feelings: Her grief was not and would not be perpetual. This is the goal of this particular type of meditation: a focus on the constantly changing content of consciousness and the fact that no state will last forever. The experience of the meditation and its insight were reassuring to Paula. She felt less tense about allowing herself to cry and more confident that her sense of deep shame would also eventually pass. I met with Paula weekly for 6 months. By the end, she was feeling secure enough to continue on her own and has kept in touch with me over the years to let me know that she and her children are doing well.

SIDE-EFFECTS AND NEGATIVE RESULTS
OF MEDITATION

Both concentration and awareness meditations may produce unusual alterations of both mind and body states (see Chapter 17). Most often, these alterations are benign and even pleasant. Meditators report feeling tingling or vibration throughout the body, feelings of lightness or warmth, and often enhanced feelings of benevolence. These effects are much more common in intensive meditation retreats, but they can also occur with simple daily practice.

Both concentration and awareness meditations can produce distressing consequences as well. In evaluating these distressing reactions, it is important to distinguish between what is psychopathology and what is simply a well-known, benign sequela of meditation.

The case of Jane illustrates a dramatic but benign consequence of meditation. A 30-year-old woman, Jane was referred to me by her physician, as a therapist and meditation teacher. She had read a book about meditation, started a simple concentration practice, and found that as soon as she focused her attention on just a few breaths, her body began to move spontaneously. Mostly, her arms would jerk around in what looked like random movements. Jane became frightened that she had suffered a stroke or otherwise damaged her nervous system by her meditation. She seemed basically healthy psychologically. She taught second grade, was in a stable marriage, and was not particularly interested in a spiritual path. She had started meditation because it was a popular topic in magazines at the time. Her main fear was that the jerking motions would start while she was in a public place and that she would be embarrassed.

I reassured Jane that although her jerking body movements were not a frequent occurrence with meditators, they sometimes happen to people who have a strong facility for focusing intently on one object. The movements are called *kryas* in Sanskrit, and some yogic traditions even regard them as signs of spiritual advancement. Jane was relieved to find that I recognized what she was describing and left feeling more relaxed. I told her that her fears about her situation were probably intensifying her focus, because she was always on high alert waiting for the movements to start; I suggested she assume that if she did not pay much attention to the movements and did not try to focus, they would subside. I also told her to stop meditating temporarily.

Several weeks later, Jane sent a note explaining that her symptoms were subsiding. She added that she had been evaluated by the neurology department at a prestigious medical school. The neurologists were polite and respectful about her "odd" condition. They took a videotape of her and reported they had never seen anything like it. However, they reassured Jane that she was neurologically normal.

Meditation can also cause temporary states of excitation, as another case illustrates. Fifty years old, Olivia came to see me at the suggestion of the psychiatrist at the local acute psychiatric facility who had treated her for an overnight stay just a few days previously. Olivia and her husband had been happily married for 25 years; had full-time, stable jobs; and shared many interests. They had no children. Two years before I met Olivia, her husband was diagnosed with pancreatic cancer, and the next 20 months until his death had been a time of intense preparation between the two of them for his inevitable death. They had joined a support group for people facing life-threatening illness and had meditated together. Olivia cared for her husband directly and continuously until the time he died. After his death, Olivia felt strongly that she could feel his presence with her. Indeed, she sensed she could feel other people's moods and thoughts to a much greater degree than before. She felt exhilarated by this intensified capacity for intuition, even though she was profoundly sad that her husband had died. She stopped feeling hungry or sleepy. Days passed without her sleeping, and her sense of extended perception increased.

She began to feel that she had a special understanding of the dying process and could help other people on the verge of death. A casual acquaintance of hers was, at that moment, dying in the local hospital, and Olivia burst into the family group at the bedside and began to explain how they should relate to the dying person. They reacted negatively and demanded that she leave the room. Olivia became distraught. She consulted her family doctor because she began to feel confused about people's reactions. Later that day, she became so agitated she was brought to the local psychiatric facility where she was admitted for the night and treated with haloperidol (Haldol), a tranquilizer. She woke the following morning, entirely calm and clear-minded, terribly embarrassed about her impetuous behavior in bursting into the deathbed scene and quite concerned about whether she had lost her mind completely.

When I met Olivia a few days after her hospitalization, she was clear and alert, fully appropriate in affect, concerned about her mental health, and somewhat incredulous about what she had been doing. I assured her that I thought her strange behavior was the result of the heightened focus of attention she had been practicing for almost 2 years, coupled with the extremely strong feelings she was having about her husband's death. I explained that people doing concentration practices often begin to feel that they have extrasensory perception and that sometimes they truly do. Because her sleeplessness and periods of not eating had contributed to the unusual feelings she was having, I suggested that she try to maintain a normal lifestyle: Eating, exercising, and sleeping as regularly as she could.

Five years afterward, Olivia had continued to meditate, although she made sure she ate and slept regularly during retreats, avoiding extended periods of focused practice and checking with her meditation teachers as her practice became more concentrated. Her symptoms never returned. She recently remarried happily.

Not every consequence of meditation is benign, as the case of Emily illustrates. A 55-year-old woman with no significant psychiatric history, she was one of 90 meditators at a 2-week retreat at which the meditations focused on cultivating intensified feelings of good will and compassion toward others. The technique of the practice is the steadfast repetition in the mind of phrases wishing others well, a kind of ongoing prayer of good intention. Except for interviews with teachers, the retreat was held in silence, as is the usual practice. Emily met with a meditation teacher and other students every other day. She reported that she was pleased with her experience, and she did not seem to be unbalanced in her affect to any of the teachers. Sometime during the second week of the retreat, Emily sought out one of the teachers privately to report her ecstatic state of mind. She described being flooded with love for all beings.

In most cases, students feel pleasantly relaxed by loving-kindness meditation, and often they experience mild rapture in the body and mind. The level of rapture is related to the steadiness of concentration, and for most people, the ecstatic state is just enough to dispel feelings of antipathy. Some students experience radically altered states of consciousness, involving overwhelming feelings of benevolence and love. These students usually revel in the experience and remember it long afterward. They often feel they are more genuinely loving, although perhaps not constantly ecstatic, in their ongoing lives.

In retrospect, the teacher who met with Emily recalled that her mood seemed somewhat manic but not inconsistent with the behavior of many other meditation students experiencing ecstatic meditative states. Two days later, Emily was clearly disoriented, talked in disconnected and irrational sentences, and exhibited behavior that seemed driven and incomprehensible. Various staff members and teachers spent time with her taking walks, having meals, attempting to help her to reintegrate her experience.

Emily was finally referred to a psychiatric facility and spent a night there, after being treated with a phenothiazine. Her daughter was contacted and took Emily home with her. Follow-up a week later revealed that Emily was continuing treatment with a local psychiatrist; although she was less agitated, she was still somewhat confused.

Emily's case is both puzzling and sobering. Most major meditation retreats require that students provide a full disclosure of any significant physical or emotional conditions. Emily had done so, and she had no preexisting problems. She had also successfully completed two retreats previously without apparent problems, although both had been only 5-day retreats. Her psychiatric decompensation is thus a puzzling reminder that meditation is a powerful technique with potentially serious negative consequences.

CONCLUSION

Apart from the case of Emily, which is anomalous, both concentration and awareness meditations generally have salubrious effects. They promote relaxation and a sense of well being, which most often allow meditators to address the difficulties in their lives with clearer vision and an enlarged perspective. Intensive meditation practice may become problematic for people with less stable ego boundaries. The altered perceptions of body sensations and mind states that often accompany intense meditation may be frightening to people who are borderline psychotic. For them, hatha yoga, a focusing and calming practice that maintains a sense of groundedness in the body, probably would be more suitable. When people with fragile ego structure arrive as participants in long retreats, I suggest that they do walking practice in place of sitting meditation as a way of maintaining ego boundaries.

Sometimes, benign, albeit unusual, sequelae of intensive practice occur in people who are otherwise psychologically healthy. As always, a careful diagnostic history and a broad view of the patient's entire range of current life functioning can allow one to make the differential diagnosis between a temporary odd alteration of perception and more serious psychopathology. When confronted with unusual symptomatology in an otherwise psychologically mature person who is also a meditation practitioner, therapists might want to confer with meditation teachers or read further in meditation literature before making a diagnostic formulation and treatment plan.

NOTES

1. Bogart, G. (1991). The use of meditation in psychotherapy: A review of the literature. *American Journal of Psychotherapy, 45,* 383–412.

2. Kabat-Zinn, J. (1994). *Wherever you go, there you are: Mindfulness meditation in everyday life.* New York: Hyperion.

3. Boorstein, S. (1995). *It's easier than you think: The Buddhist way to happiness.* San Francisco: HarperSanFrancisco.

4. Boorstein, S. (in press). *Don't just do something, sit there.* San Francisco: HarperSanFrancisco.

CHAPTER 34

Guided-Imagery Therapy

*

WILLIAM W. FOOTE

GUIDED-IMAGERY THERAPY is a psychotherapeutic method employing a client's own internal imagery to uncover and resolve emotional conflicts. As the name implies, guided imagery requires the therapist to take an active role in guiding the client through an exploration of fantasies, dreams, meditations, drawings, and other creations of the imagination. The use of guided imagery as a therapeutic tool is far from new. Both yoga and tantric Buddhism use an elaborate system of internal imagery (see Chapters 11 and 12). Similarly, Native American vision quests and sand paintings involve images (see Chapter 15), as do techniques of the Australian aborigines.

Poetry, literature, music, and conversational language are replete with imagery expressing deep emotions; however, the therapeutic use of imagery has often been considered unscientific in the West. Fortunately, many psychotherapists, including Sigmund Freud, Carl Jung, Roberto Assagioli, and Milton Erickson, as well as those employing past-life regression (see Chapter 36), have experimented with imagery as a useful therapeutic tool.

Jung offered a poignant testimony: "The years when I was pursuing my inner images were the most important in my life—in them everything essential was decided."[2]

BASIC OUTLINE

According to Jung, emotions translate directly into images. Exploring these images, therefore, provides an effective means for dealing with their underlying emotions. Unlike psychoanalytic dream analysis, which views dream imagery as a facade that intentionally hides its meaning, guided-imagery therapy sees images as direct manifestations of emotion; that is, images are not deceptive but indicative of the individual's true self. A therapist may find it helpful, therefore, to ask his clients to express and attend to their internal images. Various writers have described different techniques.[1-7] The approach I use has evolved through trial and error over many years of experience.

Identifying Good Candidates

Not all clients are well suited for guided-imagery therapy. Clients must exhibit an interest in an experiential and alternative form of therapy. Otherwise, the client will be too skeptical and distrustful to benefit from this approach. Many clients have participated in some form of conventional, verbal psychotherapy before seeking guided imagery. The majority benefited from traditional therapy but eventually reached an impasse in their progress, probably owing to an overreliance on intellectual understanding. If a client is receptive to developing and discussing her internal images, I proceed quickly to guided-imagery therapy.

There are certainly contraindications to the use of this therapy. Sound ego structure is imperative. Even if a client appears motivated to use an alternative approach, attention must be given to a well-formulated diagnosis. Clients with borderline personality disorders or psychoses are not appropriate. Any client with boundary issues must be evaluated closely because of the intensified closeness and intimacy with the therapist involved in guided imagery. Clients with posttraumatic stress disorder could be appropriate, depending on the severity of the flashbacks and the time and skill the therapist has available.

The Role of the Therapist

From the outset, the therapist must be aware of her role and explain it to the client. I make it clear that I will only suggest interpretations of and interactions with images. With the exception of the induction of the relaxation state, I do not demand that the client picture a particular image. Imposing an image in that way often results in the client being "good" and "pleasing" the therapist. This gives a distorted experience. An extremely suggestible client may adopt the imposed image, interpreting it as a true memory. This phenomenon has created many problems for therapists who deal with issues of childhood sexual abuse.

Maintaining neutrality while offering gentle guidance is a rule. When discussing the client's images, it is helpful to frame one's observations as questions: Is it possible for you to see any light in the darkness? What feelings are evoked here? Your body appears frightened. Could you tell me what's happening?

Establishing Trust and Dealing With Fears

The therapist can build trust with the client by explaining that everyone, including the therapist, experiences internal images and that everyone's imagery is unique. This shared experience with images promotes a safe and encouraging environment in which the client can explore his imagery. It is also extremely important for the client to have a clear understanding that there are no right or wrong images. This point cannot be overstated. Most clients harbor considerable fear about what they might (or actually do) uncover. These anxieties include the fear of having negative emotions, the fear of losing control, the fear of being perceived as foolish, and the fear of regressing to a point of no return. I emphasize to my clients that I will not think they are immoral if they experience negative, even violent, internal images. Everyone has a "dark side." Hinduism and Buddhism regularly portray even the most compassionate deities with wrathful forms.

Relaxation and Initial Guided Imagery

After the preliminary discussion, a guided-imagery session may be begun with relaxation exercises. I place the client in a comfortable position, ensure that he feels physically safe, and ask him to close his eyes and breathe deeply. I then ask the client to focus on his breath and the steady, gentle rising and falling of his stomach. As the client relaxes and focuses on the breathing, I ask him to picture a goblet above his head. If there is difficulty picturing the goblet, I ask that he imagine it in any way: through thought, feeling, or sensation. I suggest that the goblet fills with bright, crystalline energy that flows over the body. My leading here is important. The image of energy slowly flowing over the body allows further relaxation as well as entrance to an altered state of consciousness, which can be experienced in a variety of ways. After the body is engulfed with the energy, I invite the client to allow the energy to flow through the body from the base of the tailbone to the top of the head. Once the energy is seen, felt, heard, and sensed, visualizing the body and energy becoming one is the next step.

After checking with the client about how he is experiencing the process, I ask the client to deal with a scene that is troubling, for instance, to picture himself at work, with his coworkers busily working around him. From this image, the client will experience an emotional response and further images. The therapist must ask as many questions as necessary to develop her own inner picture of the client's imagery and the dilemma that those images create for the client. The therapist needs to be able to guide the client to try to resolve the dilemma, for example, suggesting, "Can you put tape over the mouths of your coworkers, seat them, and ask them to listen to what you need?"

Ending the Session: Grounding the Client in the Present and Providing Encouragement

The goal of the initial session is simply to introduce the client to guided imagery and to reestablish hope in therapy. Most clients feel a sense of accomplishment and optimism after their initial experience of working with images. It is important not to leave the client in a state of altered consciousness at the end of a session. Sufficient time to bring him back to the present reality must be planned as part of the therapeutic session. I have found double sessions to be advantageous for the first few sessions, provided the material is fruitful, and they are usually welcomed by the client.

A technique for ending the session includes the following comments: "It is time now to balance your right and left side, your back and your front. It is time to send a taproot of energy from the base of the spine to the center of the earth, wrapping it around something strong. Send energy from your toes and fingers to the earth as rootlets. Experience the energy from your feet on the earth." After these statements, I ask the client to come into his body, into the room, and into the present moment, finally opening his eyes. Even then the client often has not fully returned to everyday consciousness. It is helpful in ascertaining the client's consciousness of present time to ask questions such as the following: Where are you? What day is it? What is your age? How old are you? I usually insist that a short walk concentrating on the feet hitting the sidewalk is necessary before driving or doing anything that requires concentration on practical matters.

During the last portion of the session, I affirm the wonderful work that has just been done, complimenting the client on his courage in exploring the self in a new way. Such encouragement is rewarding for the client, who usually becomes more fully motivated for future sessions.

ADVANCED GUIDED IMAGERY: WORKING WITH ENERGY POINTS

When the client has developed a basic understanding of guided-imagery therapy, he is ready to experience more advanced levels. In my practice, I have found that the internal imagery developed by yoga and tantric Buddhism is an extremely powerful therapeutic tool (see Chapters 11, 12, and 25). I therefore introduce the client to the use of chakra centers. *Chakra* is a Sanskrit word that literally means "wheel." Yoga and tantric Buddhism use the word to refer to several points in the human body that are said to be centers of psychic or spiritual "energy." The number of chakra centers varies among the different Eastern traditions. In my practice, I use seven chakra centers, namely, the crown of the head, the middle of the forehead (also referred to as the "mind's eye"), the throat, the heart, the navel, the area above the pubic region, and the base of the spine. Each of these centers has particular psychological significance, as described in Chapter 25.

In Eastern philosophy, each chakra center is endowed with rich imagery, which has been discovered and described by early practitioners. Using the basic schematic of "energy" centers, however, I allow my clients to develop their own imagery but interpret the imagery according to the location of the chakra. Because different chakras involve various experiences from the biological to the sexual, interpersonal, and transpersonal, exploring the images of all seven chakras allows the therapist to guide the client systematically through virtually all his emotional dilemmas.

To illustrate the use of chakra centers in guided-imagery therapy, I present the following case vignettes.

Brad

Brad, a 35-year-old married executive with three children, sought therapy for depression. He recognized that his depression came from the stress of his job and, perhaps, stress involving his marriage and children. Brad was losing sleep and overeating, and although he was not suicidal, he felt that he was at the end of his rope and wanted to give up on everything. Brad had been in psychotherapy several years prior to seeing me, and he was frustrated by how slow and temporary his progress seemed. Consequently, he was prepared to try anything that might restore his hope and give him rapid, recognizable results.

At our second session, I prepared Brad for guided imagery. Brad had never heard of chakra centers, and I sensed that explaining them to him would prompt him to engage in an internal intellectual debate and cause him to be too skeptical to proceed; therefore, I referred to the chakra centers simply as points of energy. After a brief relaxation exercise, I asked Brad to be aware of feelings in his body: how he was positioned; how his limbs, back, and buttocks felt against the couch; how warm and secure he felt. I suggested he visualize a goblet overflowing with energy surrounding his body, as described earlier. When Brad had no difficulty with this process, I asked him to concentrate on the first chakra, seeing from within it as if it were an entire world of its own. Brad described what he saw: "It seems very dark in here. I don't like it. It's cold." I worked with this imagery to explore his emotions. "Is there any light whatsoever, Brad?" I inquired. He said that there was, and the light grew as he focused on it. Soon Brad saw a gray tunnel high above his head with light at the end of it. He felt frustrated because the tunnel was out of reach, so I suggested that Brad picture a ladder that he could use to climb up. Brad did so and walked to the end of the tunnel. There he found a window, went through, and instantly felt like he was floating in the open air, free from fears and worries.

With the first chakra "cleared," that is, resolved of obstructive images, I guided Brad to his other energy points with similar results. His experience with the third chakra, associated with emotions and his own power, is noteworthy. After focusing on the third chakra, Brad was able to visualize it to be free from obstruction. He saw nothing that bothered him and felt a vast capacity to love. Brad then began to cry. Explaining that when he thought of love, he saw an image of his mother, Brad said that he had last seen his mother on her deathbed and deeply regretted that he had never told her how much he loved her. I asked Brad if he could tell his mother now, visualizing her standing before him in his third chakra. He did so, and almost at once, Brad's image of his mother was replaced by empty, soothing space. Brad's wife then began to appear and disappear in Brad's imagery. I suggested that this might be because he felt the same type of guilt toward his wife that he had for his mother, because his job was forcing him to neglect his wife. He found this insight emotionally liberating. After this brief work in guided imagery, Brad's depression lifted. He continued in a positive, forceful manner in his business and personal life.

It is helpful to notice the suggestions I made to Brad in his imagery. When Brad was working with imagery associated with the first and fourth chakras, he often did not know what to do. My suggestions allowed movement to occur and helped guide Brad to find resolutions to some of his conflicts. In general, suggestions are often needed initially, but as the client becomes more familiar with image work, the therapist is able to observe more and suggest less.

James

James sought therapy for depression. He was distrustful and offered little information on his own. He purposely steered clear of any negative emotions and made certain topics off-limits. Eventually, James revealed that he had seen a psychiatrist some years before with traumatic results. James distrusted psychiatrists, therefore, but he was willing to try alternative approaches.

In our initial session, I told James about my work with internal images and chakras and spent the next session teaching him relaxation techniques and developing basic images. By our third session together, James was able to explore his own spontaneous internal images and to express his emotional reactions to those images.

A major breakthrough in James's therapy came during his work on fourth-chakra images. He initially saw a serene lake, but the image quickly became heavy and frightening. James felt compelled to find out what was in the lake, so he pictured himself jumping into the water and swimming toward the other side. Then James encountered five large black boulders. The rocks were labeled *ugliness, pain, sex, rejection,* and *offending my mother.* Noting these labels and the importance of returning to those topics, I encouraged James to muster superhuman strength and lift the boulders. James visualized himself hurling the great rocks one by one out of the lake, far beyond sight.

For a number of sessions that followed, James and I did not engage in guided-imagery therapy; instead, he discussed childhood experiences that he was able to reveal to another person for the first time in his life. Following this, James began making changes in his behavior toward his family, his mother, and women in general. He felt more effective in life and progressively less dysfunctional. James maintained this improvement, which I have found to be the usual case: The positive effects gained from guided imagery are maintained for the long term, in contrast to those gained from direct hypnotic suggestions.

Marie

Marie sought therapy feeling frustrated by her apparent inability to express herself creatively. She had been in several different types of therapy before, but she found that their usefulness was short-lived. As an artist, Marie was open to creative approaches to her problems, and she readily welcomed the concept of guided-imagery therapy. She was intrigued by the chakra centers and had little problem seeing her internal images.

In one session, Marie had an image of an enormous pyramid in her heart chakra. She later wrote:

> Dr. Foote suggested that I go inside and see what was inside the pyramid. I found a small door, and inside a narrow path leading to a light bulb that hung low from the center of the building. It was a giant storage area, full of old things like bent pipes, wheelbarrows and a tricycle. I could see only the objects close to the source of light. Dr. Foote then suggested that I raise the light higher so that I could see the full interior. Reluctantly, I raised the light, sensing that I would see more of the clutter and complications. I was right. In the full light I saw old bedsprings, more bent pipes, farm tools, and a pile of weeds and straw. In another part of the pyramid were statues of people in a Giacometti style, familiar but too distorted to be recognizable. The very top of the pyramid was filled with milkweed pods which were releasing their seeds.
>
> Dr. Foote asked me to consider whether this pyramid might house the clutter of my life, and if so, if it might be distracting me from the things which are really important in my life. I thought of my initial reluctance to look at all the contents of the pyramid, and I knew that Dr. Foote was once more onto something impor-

tant. He suggested that I look at the pyramid from above, which made it look much smaller than before. I watched the top of the structure and saw the fluffy tops of the milkweed appear. I considered it closely, and I touched the fluffy heads of the weeds. I took the seeds and placed them back into the pyramid. Instantly and inexplicably, I felt calm and satisfied by my actions. Dr. Foote suggested that perhaps I had inherited a lot of emotional clutter in my life, and rearranging the clutter by my own hand was therefore satisfying. Since that day, I have found the pyramid to be a valuable inner tool—an image that I can bring to my consciousness whenever I feel I am getting an overload of material and emotions requiring my attention.

The results of this work have sustained the client for many years. She has become more creative and no longer "takes on" others' emotional states or belief systems.

REFLECTIONS

The use of images is helpful in any form of therapy. Images facilitate understanding of issues by offering a metaphor for the experience or conflict at hand. The ego can integrate the image without becoming trapped in intellectual debates. Using altered states of consciousness to access imagery allows the ego to reach even deeper, more carefully hidden conflicts.

As the vignettes describe, guided imagery is useful in short-term therapy, during which a single problem can be dealt with. Once the client states a problem in short-term therapy, however, the focus must remain on that issue. It is the role of the therapist to prevent extended associations or images that reveal further issues from interfering with the goal.

When the client is thoroughly briefed on working with imagery, resistance is usually not a severe problem. Gentle suggestion with the emphasis on a trial experience usually is sufficient. For example, one client, a "born-again Christian," was resistant to the idea of guided imagery, but he agreed to a trial experience. Throughout the process, I continually asked him whether any of the material conflicted with his religious beliefs. He was delightfully surprised at how well guided imagery blended with his beliefs, allowing us to continue deeper work.

I have found attachment to the intellect to be the major obstacle to imagery work. Many clients are too afraid initially to allow the intellect to be overruled by an experience. Not being able to control or explain images can be difficult and painful at first. Traditional verbal therapy is best for such a client, to be followed later by guided imagery.

The imagery process can also be too appealing at times. One client felt peaceful, happy, and content when working with her images in an altered state of consciousness. She had to stop her imagery, however, because the realities in her private and professional life were too problematic and intense. She feared she might not want to return to the real world.

Guided imagery can promote negative responses. Early on, when I was experimenting with the technique, my excitement and exuberance took over, and my judgment and discernment took a back seat, leading to countertherapeutic results. Proceeding cautiously and taking the client into consideration at all times are essential.

CONCLUSION

Guided-imagery therapy offers a number of benefits over traditional psychotherapeutic approaches, as illustrated by the vignettes presented in this chapter. After only one session, Brad felt his sense of overwhelming frustration begin to lift and experienced a renewed sense of hope that he could overcome his problems. James was able to experience and express his negative emotions and uncover past events that continued to hinder his present happiness. Marie felt a transformation in her approach to life and developed lasting images that she continues to use to maintain her emotional well-being and creative work.

These accomplishments may have been possible with other forms of therapy. The fact remains, however, that each of these individuals had experience with other therapeutic modalities and each found guided-imagery therapy to be much more direct and rapid. In many ways, guided-imagery therapy transforms clients into their own therapists, and with guidance, they are able to deal with problems effectively as new difficulties arise on life's winding path.

NOTES

1. Achterberg, J. (1985). *Imagery in healing: Shamanism and modern medicine.* Boston: New Science Library/Shambhala.

2. Jung, C. G. (1989). *Memories, dreams, reflections* (A. Jaffe, Ed.; R. & C. Winston, Trans.; p. 199). New York: Vintage Books.

3. Leuner, H. (1984). *Guided affective imagery—the basic course: Mental imagery in short-term psychotherapy* (E. Lachman, Trans.). New York: Thieme-Stratton.

4. Middelkoop, P. (1989). *The wise old man: Healing through inner images* (A. Dixon, Trans.). Boston: Shambhala Publications.

5. Sheikh, A. A. (Ed.). (1984). *Imagination and healing.* Farmingdale, NY: Baywood Publishing.

6. Shorr, J. E. (Ed.). (1989). *Imagery: Current perspectives.* New York: Plenum Press.

7. Zeig, J. (Ed.). (1994). *Ericksonian methods: The essence of the story.* New York: Brunner/Mazel.

CHAPTER 35

Breathwork: Theory and Technique

KATHRYN J. LEE AND PATRICIA L. SPEIER

HISTORY

Breathwork is a general term for techniques that primarily involve breathing or manipulation of the breath. These techniques have been developed to access nonordinary states of consciousness and promote healing of the psyche. The connection of breath to psyche and spirit is reflected in the common Greek and Latin roots *phren* (mind) and *spiritus* (breath), found in modern words such as phrenic, diaphragm, schizophrenia, inspire, expire, and spirit. The book of Genesis speaks of "the breath of the spirit of life," also suggesting this connection.

Use of the breath to enter states of nonordinary consciousness spans many cultures and dates back thousands of years. Many cultures have used breathing techniques in some form of religious initiation. The ancient Essenes, for example, used a form of near suffocation through submersion in water to baptize and transform their initiates.[1,2] Shamans of various cultures, including North and

South American natives and African tribes, use alterations in breathing to guide them in diagnosis and healing of illness. Members of cultural groups also use breath for healing; among these groups are the Kalahari !Kung Bushmen, who use rapid, shallow breathing[3] to attain !kia through their "healing dance." Around a fire the !Kung women sing while the men dance until this altered state of consciousness, !kia, occurs. During !kia, the !Kung are able to perform extraordinary activities, especially to heal others. !Kia itself is an intense physical and emotional state that may be accompanied by convulsion-like tremors and heavy breathing.[4]

There is also an extensive tradition of exploration of the use of the breath in spiritual development. Spiritual paths often include some form of altered breathing as a part of their system of increasing mind–body integration. In the sitting meditation practiced in Zen and other Buddhist traditions, one attends to the natural flow of breath, thereby increasing mindfulness in each moment. Taoist traditions of breathing meditation (qigong and tai chi chuan) date back more than 4,000 years.[5] These practices involve special breathing exercises intended to increase and balance the flow of *chi*, which is the life force and connecting link between body, mind, and spirit.[6] *Pranayama*, in the yogic tradition, involves both hyperventilation and the prolonged holding of the breath.[7] *Prana*, or "absolute energy," is understood as the source of vitality, which is taken in primarily through breathing. Prana both enlivens and heals the body. In these and other spiritual practices, the breath is used as a vehicle to enhance or create a greater mind–body connection and to promote growth and the attainment of higher spiritual states.

This ancient knowledge about the mind–body connection and its relation to the breath has been rediscovered by Western explorers of human psychology. Wilhelm Reich observed that restriction of the breath serves as a primary mechanism of psychological defense and resistance. The common tendency of individuals to hold their breath and inhibit exhalation was recognized by Reich as a powerful way of controlling feeling and decreasing anxiety.[8] From these insights he developed a form of therapy he called *character analysis vegetotherapy*; its aim was to mobilize feeling through deeper, freer breathing, which involved developing the capacity to give in fully to the spontaneous movements involved in the respiratory process. Reich later added the technique of using physical pressure to facilitate the breakthrough of emotional feelings and repressed memories.

Alexander Lowen, the best known of Reich's students, developed basic body positions and exercises as an extension of Reich's work. These are fundamental to the system now called *Bioenergetics*. Breathing is "as crucial to bioenergetics as it is to Reichian therapy" because "only through breathing deeply and fully can one summon the energy for a more spirited and spiritual life."[9] The relationship of breath to bodily tension has also received attention in the short-term dynamic therapy of Habib Davanloo, who recognizes somatic signals, such as sighs and changes in body tension, as signs of breaking through resistance to unconscious impulses and feelings.[10]

The movement toward what is currently called *breathwork* began during the 1960s when Leonard Orr made some remarkable self-discoveries. While experimenting in a hot tub, he triggered powerful experiences that he believed were relived aspects of his birth. He gradually developed the technique that he named *rebirthing* to help others attain what he had discovered.[11] Orr believes that

> the purpose of rebirthing is to remember and re-experience one's birth: to relive physiologically, psychologically, and spiritually the moments of one's first breath and release the trauma of it. . . . In addition to healing the damage done by the birth trauma to the individual consciousness it has been found that rebirthing repairs the damage done to the breathing mechanism at birth and removes the blocks where inner and outer breath meet . . . rebirthing merges the inner and outer breath which creates a bridge between the physical and spiritual dimensions.[11]

Orr's theory and technique are based on rebirthings originally performed in hot tubs. He eventually concluded that the breathing, rather than the water, was most critical to the process that he called the "breathing release." He therefore developed a "dry" form of rebirthing. Essential components of rebirthing, according to Orr, include a safe setting and the presence of a "rebirther," a person who has been successfully rebirthed and is able to coach the neophyte. Orr's work includes a psychological, philosophical, and spiritual basis for his theory and practice.

A substantial advancement of breathwork as a healing modality has been brought about by Stanislav and Christina Grof. Their development of *Holotropic Breathwork* has its seeds in Stanislav Grof's early LSD research and bears many similarities to both Reich's and Orr's techniques.[12] Grof noted that nonordinary states of consciousness triggered by LSD doses could be intensified or reactivated by hyperventilation. From the observation that alterations in breathing lead to alterations in consciousness, and from their studies of the use of breath in other cultures and in spiritual disciplines, the Grofs developed their techniques of Holotropic Breathwork and holonomic integration.[13] Since its inception in the late 1970s, Holotropic Breathwork and other forms of breathwork continue to grow in popularity and attract international interest and participation.

PROCEDURE

In this chapter Holotropic Breathwork is elaborated in detail, and all clinical examples refer specifically to this technique, which is the basis of our breathwork training and practice. The work requires a trained facilitator who has sufficient experience with the technique and familiarity with nonordinary states of consciousness. Breathwork is best done in a safe and conducive setting with appropriate physical and time boundaries to allow for the process to develop optimally. This usually involves open floor space to accommodate possible movement of the "breather" (the person undergoing the technique) and sufficient time to allow the breather to experience fully and integrate the breathwork session. The breather is usually paired with a sitter, who is not the facilitator but acts to provide support and safety for the breather's process.

A typical setting might be a large, pleasant, empty room that allows the individuals to feel buffered from intrusions from the outside world. The room must be large enough to accommodate the participants in a lying position. Body-sized mats, pillows, tissues, towels, and bathroom facilities are made available to meet the physical needs of the participants, who may cry, cough, vomit, and so on, in the course of a breathing session. Typically, the technique and the theory of breathwork are discussed before the session begins to familiarize the participants with what may happen to them during nonordinary states; painful, frightening, pleasant, or blissful experiences are frequently an important part of the breathwork process.

The breather begins by lying supine on a mat. The intention is to allow the breather to let go of practical concerns so that she may more easily enter a nonordinary state of consciousness. Usually the facilitator begins the session with an induction, which includes suggestions for relaxation and suspension of conventional judgments about internal processes.

The breather is then encouraged to increase the depth and frequency of her breathing, which is the primary mechanism leading to nonordinary states. Music is generally used to help optimize the rhythm of the breath. Initially, the music has a "driving" energy and beat to encourage rapid breathing and activate the shift from a normal to an altered state of consciousness. Music that is "popular," has lyrics, or is familiar to the individual is avoided, because such music might keep the breather in usual patterns of thinking. As the session progresses, the music slowly changes in character, becoming emotionally more evocative and, at the end, more ethereal.

Throughout the session, the breather is asked to remain supine, although this may be difficult for her. Some individuals are extremely active during the process and may thrash about, dance, cry, or yell as the internal process develops. Others remain still. Movements may need to be attended to by the facilitator to guarantee the physical safety of the breather or others in the vicinity. At the end of the session, breathers often require the intervention of the facilitator to resolve and integrate the process. Bodily tension or other indications of held energy may be worked with by focused body or energy work in conjunction with short bursts of hyperventilation. Focused body work is a manipulative technique dependent on skillful touch by the facilitator to intensify or relieve somatic symptoms that arise during the session.[14] Although it is extremely important for the facilitator to allow the process to develop without undue intrusion, skillful intervention by the facilitator is often necessary for the fruitful outcome of the process. This aspect of breathwork is quite dependent on the experience and intuitive ability of the facilitator.

Each session may be self-contained and complete, or it may be part of an ongoing process. Ideally, at the conclusion of each breathwork session, the breather feels a sense of completeness. She may choose to draw a mandala as an extension of the process, trying to suspend any analysis of the session until after this drawing or other artwork is completed. The process of the nonordinary state, however, sometimes continues beyond the boundaries of the session. It is helpful, therefore, for breathers to be aware of this fact and to allow a buffer of space and time for themselves after a breathwork session.

POTENTIAL BENEFITS

The usefulness of breathwork is multifaceted. At the most basic level, this technique lets one experience oneself and the world in a different or nonordinary way. This expansion of consciousness may impact individuals in a subtle or dramatic way depending on their previous mind-set and experience with nonordinary states of consciousness. From a therapeutic standpoint, breathwork may help access repressed memories and experiences. It may also provide physical release of psychogenic and psychosomatic symptoms. The experience of breathwork may lead to understanding of perinatal imprinting, or patterning of one's personal experience. It may also lead to increased awareness and understanding of archetypal imprinting, or patterning of personal or universal experience.

These uses suggest a role for breathwork in an individual's personal development, especially as an adjunct to ongoing therapy or spiritual practice. In our opinion, breathwork is not a replacement for psychotherapy; it can be most healing when integrated with psychotherapy, other forms of therapy (such as various forms of bodywork, movement/dance therapy, and so on), or an ongoing spiritual discipline or practice.

The contraindications for breathwork range from physical to psychological and need to be assessed by a qualified professional. Use of antipsychotic medication is a definite contraindication, whereas use of other psychoactive medications may constitute a relative contraindication. Physical conditions including cardiovascular disease, epilepsy, recent bone fractures, and pregnancy are probable contraindications that require the judgment of a physician. Chronic psychotic states or lack of an intact ego are definite contraindications. Fragile ego states, severe personality disorders, and cyclic mood disturbances are relative contraindications, and assessment by a psychiatrist or psychologist is necessary before breathwork is undertaken.

CASE EXAMPLES

The breathwork examples used here for the purposes of illustration come from a number of different sources. In the first example, Case A, the experience was described by the breather as a transpersonal opening for her. Besides this opening, the case demonstrates the potential power of a single breathwork experience.

The breather was a 42-year-old woman whose lover had recently died. She denied significant psychological problems and was interested in breathwork as a curiosity. She described her breathwork experience as "incredible" and "unexpected." During the session she experienced "flying up" and meeting her deceased lover. She reported feeling warmly reunited and that they had an important conversation during which she was able to say all the things she longed to tell him, including a final good-bye (she had not been present at the time of her lover's death). After the session she felt "completely at peace" with her lover. She felt no further need to engage in the breathwork process, stating that what happened was a "once-in-a-lifetime" experience and that she did not wish to lessen the impact she felt it had for her by engaging in further breathwork sessions.

The following, Case B, provides an example of how breathwork can be useful in building an internal sense of security and in the resolution of psychosomatic symptoms. These symptoms were likely related to infant attachment problems, which involved maternal emotional deprivation.

The breather was a 28-year-old man with a long-standing history of anxiety and depression with intermittent suicidal ideation and a history of a suicide attempt. He also complained of multiple somatic symptoms including headaches, intestinal cramping, and diarrhea. He craved attention and companionship but felt separate from and unable to trust others. In his first breathwork session, he experienced a "warm and wonderful presence," which he identified as his mother who then "moved away from him." This led to the feeling of extreme sadness. He sobbed inconsolably, with a sense of "total abandonment," until these feelings suddenly changed to a feeling of wonderment as he found himself alone in an enormous cave. He felt very warm and protected and had a strong sense that "everything was okay."

The breather continued intermittent breathwork combined with psychotherapy and noted a decrease in his anxiety, depression, and sense of isolation following each breathwork session. During the breathwork sessions, he was allowed to regress and experience helplessness and abandonment. A sense of security was gradually increased and internalized with concomitant decrease in his somatic symptoms. He now reports an absence of headaches and only occasional diarrhea when he feels "very stressed." He subsequently developed his first "truly intimate" relationships with both men and women and later married.

Next is an example of how physical symptoms might be exacerbated, rather than resolved, by the breathwork process. Case C was a 38-year-old man who denied any psychological symptoms but complained of a mild cold. Despite this, he insisted that he felt well enough to participate in breathwork. He appeared to be quite distressed throughout the session, thrashing and moaning as if in pain, and at the end of the session, he complained of feeling warm and seemed somewhat irritable and agitated. Despite the persistent urgings of the facilitators, the breather refused all body work or suggestions that the process might not be complete. He remembered nothing of the session itself, and did not want to explore what had happened to him through mandalas or other artwork. The man left the session and developed a significant fever and flulike illness. The facilitators contacted him in follow-up and again recommended further breathwork, but he felt that the process had exacerbated his illness and did not want to explore the work further.

This example points to the importance of working with the process until there is a sense of resolution. Ideally any "leftover" symptoms should be attended to by intensifying the process through specific energy work or further breathing. If a person is resistant and refuses to cooperate, one can expect that there may be symptomatic exacerbation, as this example demonstrates.

The following example, Case D, demonstrates another relative contraindication and difficulty inherent in the use of breathwork. The breather was a 36-year-old man with a lifelong history of depression. During his breathwork session he experienced feeling enclosed, "suffocated," and hopeless. He emerged from the session feeling more deeply depressed with a great sense of futility. The details of his session are unknown, but the man reported that attempts to work with these feelings were unsuccessful, and he left the session. He later developed suicidal ideation, which frightened him sufficiently that he presented himself to an emergency room, where he was admitted for surveillance.

Case D demonstrates that serious depression may be quite resistant to and even exacerbated by the process. Depression that is labile, however, can frequently be helped by the process of breathwork.

Psychosomatic conditions have proved to be particularly responsive to breathwork. Migraine headaches, Raynaud's disease, some musculoskeletal symptoms, and asthma (as Case E shows) have all been observed to be greatly relieved in some people by this process.

A 60-year-old woman with a history of childhood asthma, who continued to be dependent on bronchoinhalers as an adult, experienced shortness of breath and the feeling that an asthmatic attack was imminent in her first breathwork session. She found this extremely frightening and was unable to continue the session. Subsequent sessions had a similar pattern, but she was dogged in her conviction to continue the work in spite of her panic around these occurrences. Finally, the facilitators convinced her to do focused body work around her difficult breathing. With this body work, she experienced a full-blown asthmatic attack accompanied by feelings of loss and terror. Through continued careful "holding" of the process by the facilitators, the symptoms abruptly abated and she felt a peaceful sense of relief. Her breathing came easily. Since those initial sessions, she has continued to do breathwork to work on other issues. She has had no further symptoms of asthma either in her sessions or in her daily life, and she no longer needs asthma medications. She feels confident that her asthma is resolved.

This case points out the importance of body or energy work in the completion of many breathwork sessions. The nonordinary state reached by changes in the breathing pattern can create an opportunity for body work to move beyond old somatic resistances. In this way healing, not just relief, of psychosomatic symptoms occurs.

POSSIBLE CRITICISMS

As demonstrated in these examples, breathwork may be useful under some conditions but has potential hazards as well. Traditional psychiatry might argue that this technique brings up unconscious material too quickly, and some people may not be able to deal with this material, leading to uncontained emotional or even psychotic states. The defiance of natural homeostasis, it could be argued, may have destructive implications. Some spiritual practitioners may also criticize this technique for facilitating individuals in the experience of potentially overwhelming forces from the unconscious without the structure of a spiritual practice. Grof has replied to such criticism that the process has its own intelligence and time in which it works. We believe that there are significant risks in using Holotropic Breathwork as the sole treatment modality, because there may not be adequate containment for serious symptoms and disorders. In conjunction with ongoing psychotherapy or spiritual practice, however, breathwork can be a useful addition to the healing process.

Some practitioners may be critical of this technique because of its capacity to exacerbate rather than relieve symptoms. Conventional views of healing frequently look askance at treatments that intensify or worsen conditions they are intended to treat. However, psychiatry has long accepted the concept that conditions may intensify or seemingly become "worse" in the process of healing, for example in the concept of regression in the service of the ego. Similarly, Grof perceives symptoms as part of the healing process and therefore encourages the intensification of these symptoms in working through an illness. In our experience, a transient exacerbation of symptoms is often a necessary part of the process of healing. By focusing on the somatic as well as the mental–emotional aspects, more rapid and complete healing can take place.

CONCLUSION

Modern breathwork practitioners have developed techniques for exploring and healing the psyche based on ancient traditions of working with the breath. These techniques have become widespread throughout the United States and Europe, and there is a growing acceptance of their usefulness. Breathwork is a powerful technique for inner growth, exploration, and potential healing. It is best done with an experienced practitioner in the context of ongoing psychotherapy or practice of a spiritual discipline.

NOTES

1. Larson, M. A. (1967). *The Essene heritage.* New York: Philosophical Library.
2. Grof, S. (1994). Personal communication.
3. Katz, R. (1973). Education for transcendence: Lessons from the !Kung Zhu/twasi. *Journal of Transpersonal Psychology, 5(2),* 136–155.
4. Katz, R. (1982). *Boiling energy: Community healing among the Kalahari !Kung.* Cambridge, MA: Harvard University Press.
5. Shin, T. (1994). *Qi gong therapy.* Barrytown, NY: Station Hill Press.

6. Wu, Z., & Mao, L. (1992). *Ancient way to keep fit* (S. Luzeng, L. Beijian, & L. Zhenkai, Trans.). Bolinas, CA: Shelter Publications.

7. Ramacharaka, Yogi (1904). *Science of breath.* Chicago: Yogi Publication Society.

8. Reich, W. (1942). *The function of the orgasm.* New York: Orgone Institute Press.

9. Lowen, A. (1975). *Bioenergetics.* New York: Coward, McCann & Geoghegan. Quotations on pp. 40, 66.

10. Davanloo, H. (1990). *Unlocking the unconscious.* Chichester, England: Wiley.

11. Orr, L., & Ray, S. (1977). *Rebirthing in the New Age.* Millbrae, CA: Celestial Arts. Quotation on p. 69.

12. Grof, S. (1985). *Beyond the brain: Birth, death, and transcendence in psychotherapy.* Albany, NY: SUNY Press.

13. Grof, S. (1988). *The adventure of self-discovery.* Albany: SUNY Press.

14. Juhan, D. (1987). *Job's body.* Barrytown, NY: Station Hill Press.

CHAPTER 36

Past-Life Therapy

RONALD W. JUE

ALTHOUGH EXPLORATIONS into the psychological phenomena of "past-life experiences" began in the 1960s, past-life regression therapy is still controversial. It is often misunderstood and rejected because of its metaphysical overtones and the sensational claims sometimes made for the technique. But research into psychedelic, hypnotic, and near-death experiences (see Chapters 18, 29) suggests that experiences of past lives can provide clients with valuable insights and healing, whether or not the experiences are objectively true.

Past-life experiences can be conceptualized in terms of recent theories of the mind, such as Rupert Sheldrake's[1] notion of "morphic resonance," David Bohm's[2] theory of "implicate order," or Karl Pribram's[3] holographic model of the mind. These theories suggest that the whole of the psyche is embedded within each of its parts. For example, a theme of "succeeding in spite of all obstacles" may be prominent within an individual's work life. This theme is also likely to appear in the individual's intimate relationships, dreams, and childhood memories, and it may take psychosomatic form. The motif may also appear in past-life scenarios through deep, vivid images that allow the individual to work with the problem in transformative ways. Through trance techniques, past-life regression gives access to levels of the psyche not usually reached by conventional therapeutic techniques.

INDICATIONS

Most practitioners of past-life therapy agree that the technique is primarily useful with clients who are ready to assume greater responsibility for their lives and who are open to exploring how repressed emotional response patterns are related to current difficulties.[4] One can also undertake past-life therapy with patients whose primary motivation is symptom alleviation.

Some individuals seek past-life experiences for inspiring or ego-enhancing purposes. In reality, such experiences are rare. In her series of cases, Helen Wambach[5] found that few past-life scenarios are pleasant or uplifting. Most images involved war, violence, hunger, and various forms of deprivation. Considerable ego strength is a prerequisite for past-life therapy. This approach is not recommended for persons who have psychoses or borderline personality disorder or individuals unable to integrate symbolic material adequately. Past-life therapy does not appear to be effective for individuals who are obsessional about guilt or shame and who seem to need to play out the role of victim. Clinical indications include unexplained phobias, psychosomatic problems lacking any known cause, and anomalous experiences; these problems are often resistant to traditional talk therapy but can respond dramatically to past-life techniques.

PREPARATION AND INDUCTION

The first step is to obtain a complete psychological history. This is necessary to understand the relationship between the pattern of problems that appears in past-life scenarios and current life difficulties. A knowledge of the individual's childhood and current attitudes toward love, sex, money, power, and spiritual matters is essential. A medical history may help to elucidate underlying psychological and psychosomatic issues.

Understanding the patient's philosophical assumptions is important, because the ease of induction is influenced by these beliefs. Individuals who do not believe in reincarnation or are not interested in metaphysical issues are usually more comfortable when the language and metaphors used in therapy are drawn from their own world perspective. A wide range of inductions may be used by the therapist.[4] Techniques include dreamwork, breathwork, active imagination, and guided imagery. The goal is a deeply relaxed, hypnotic state. Many techniques use catalytic visual elements such as doors, passageways, vehicles, stairs, or tunnels that lead the patient into another lifetime. The art of induction is to find an approach that is congruent with the disposition and ideology of the patient. The induction itself becomes a doorway by which the individual can enter an altered state, which then allows primary-process material to emerge.

Not all individuals are able to enter a trance and experience past-life imagery. Weiss[6] noted that about 60% of his subjects experience past-life scenarios. Forced induction is not recommended because it often leads to confabulation with limited depth or self-realization. When a client successfully and voluntarily enters an altered state, however, he usually begins to experience vivid images involving several sensory levels—sight, sound, touch, and smell—and the experience often takes on a life of its own without external direction.

DISIDENTIFICATION

The second stage of past-life regression is *disidentification*. This process involves learning to identify and disidentify with the various characters and personalities in the scenarios. This stage is like going into the "green room" backstage of a theater, where the actors put on and remove the accouterments of their roles.

Past-life scenarios foster the process of disidentification by highlighting roles that are polar opposites to the individual's real-life identity. For example, a person who sees herself as a victim in real life often has past-life scenarios of being a persecutor. By experiencing life as a victimizer instead of a victim in the past-life scenario, the individual is forced to disidentify from a familiar role. Other common compensatory polarities include male–female, power–powerlessness, worthiness–unworthiness, sexual abuse–impotency, and arrogance–humbleness.

In the process of playing different roles in past-life scenarios, the individual begins to see how historical, social, and cultural factors shape his roles in current life. Most individuals realize that what they took to be their true identity is really a social role, distinct from their core self. Indeed, many individuals gain a sense of a "witnessing consciousness": an awareness that transcends ordinary consciousness and is not a part of the individual's personality.

Clients often describe this witnessing consciousness as their "core essence" and frequently identify it as their soul. By playing the part of many characters in past-life scenarios, most individuals also begin to develop a much more empathic relationship with other people in real life, from parents and family members to coworkers.

As in any psychotherapy, resistances often arise in past-life regressions. These resistances usually defend the script that a person plays out in real life. For example, when an individual is caught up in real life with a script focused on being angry with other people, there often is resistance in past-life scenarios to experiencing forgiveness or compassion. Selective awareness—and resistance—occurs on all levels and in both ordinary and altered states of consciousness.

INTEGRATION AND TRANSFORMATION

The third stage of past-life regression therapy involves integrating past-life scenarios with current life patterns. One way in which this occurs is through the individual's discovery of hidden, unconscious motivations governing the various characters in the scenarios. For instance, an individual may discover the implicit "covenants" or "contracts" between two characters in a past-life scenario, so that one person is the victim and the other the victimizer. The patient may also discover how characters in past-life scenarios "set up" situations so that they always fail. These insights are often readily applied to the client in everyday life and facilitate the clients' becoming aware of their unconscious motivation. An individual may see, for example, how he also uses implicit "covenants" in relationships and how these covenants lead to real-life problems. Clients begin to realize that they make many decisions on an unconscious level, following implicit scripts. The insight usually motivates the individual to start changing those scripts. Past-life scenarios thus lead to insight and transformation.

With an increased awareness of the unconscious factors that shape their lives, most patients also begin to have faith in an inherent sense of meaning in their lives, which needs to be trusted and honored. This sense often takes the form of finding an inner wisdom that proposes solutions to long-standing problems. Indeed, many past-life regression practitioners, including myself, became involved with past-life memories when asking a patient in an altered state to "go to the situation that created the problem you find yourself in at the present time." Such a spontaneous regression is often about events in the distant past. The material is usually surprisingly relevant, cathartic, and transformative, as if an inner intelligence were at work seeking the cause of an individual's symptoms, the underlying dynamics, and a resolution. Other authors have called this spontaneous problem-solving phenomenon the *Higher Self*.[4]

Ultimately, the therapist's task is to assist the patient in dismantling or "deconstructing" past-life scenarios to understand their relevance to present-day problems. Without this work, regression therapy becomes nothing more than a parlor game. The result is paradoxical: As patients integrate their past-life imagery with their real-life situations, they learn to appreciate and live more in the present.

A CASE STUDY

To illustrate the process of past-life therapy, a transcript from an actual regression session is presented. The names have been changed to protect the identity of the patient.

Dawn, a professional woman in her 40s, was concerned because she had never had a loving and supportive relationship with a man. Her experiences with men had turned out to be toxic and frustrating. Five years before, Dawn chose to have a baby as a single mother. Although her experience as a mother was satisfying and fulfilling, she longed for someone with whom to share the child, and she retained a nagging feeling that somehow she had failed as a woman. She also came under criticism because of her extremely close bonding with her son.

The following session is part of a series and is typical of the imagery Dawn experienced. The session began with an induction that involved one of Dawn's favorite places: a garden. After using the garden imagery to evoke a state of deep relaxation, Dawn visualized moving through a gate into a past-life experience.

THERAPIST: Your unconscious mind is now allowing you to go beyond this garden, to know that beyond this garden is a place, a time, that you were once familiar with. Why is it that you have not made any significant relationships with the opposite sex during this lifetime? Where is the energy coming from? Why has that energy been reinforced throughout this lifetime? Go on back now.

PATIENT: The only place I'm getting to is sort of autumn, almost winter, by a forest, not in a forest but alongside one. That's all I see at the moment, not me but the place and the time of year and the wind is blowing.

THERAPIST: Is this a forest you are familiar with?

PATIENT: No. I think it's some place in the past: Europe or farther East.

THERAPIST: I want you to focus on that. As you begin to focus on the forest, you can allow the nature of the forest to deepen your experience. Allow your mind to open up and develop the context of this forest scene and whether this is the place that you should look at in terms of understanding the lack of positive and loving experiences. Allow yourself to move either forward or backward in time in the scene, into significant events connected with this lifetime.

Dawn then described walking in the woods with a little pony. She was overcome with grief at this point and explained that she was an orphan, living with a rather silent and uncommunicative man and woman. The only relationship she had was with her little horse.

THERAPIST: What's the special relationship you have with the horse?

PATIENT: It's just that it's my friend. My only friend.

THERAPIST: What do you do with this horse?

PATIENT: Go into the woods, walk with it. It's more like a dog—no saddle or bridle.

THERAPIST: How are you experiencing yourself in that family context? I want you to look. Just be in touch with your feelings and the relationship between yourself and this family and yourself and this horse. See yourself as moving into scenes that will help you illuminate the nature of this relationship.

Dawn described her feeling of isolation. She felt no love and no hate. She did her share of chores so she was not a burden. She was extremely connected with nature, with the woods and hills and seasons as well as with the horse. One day, the man went out in the woods and did not return. Soon afterward, while Dawn was out, the woman sold Dawn's horse, and Dawn later found the horse dead in the forest, overworked and abused. A few days later, Dawn went swimming in a river and was caught in a bad current. She made no effort to save herself and was drowned.

PATIENT: I gave up. I didn't do it thoughtfully. I was just swimming in the river. I knew that the middle was very dangerous and I didn't really care that it was. It was sort of like Russian roulette. I had to see what happened and it was too strong for me and carried me over some rocks. I guess I hit my head.

THERAPIST: And when you see yourself in that river and hit on the head, what are your feelings and the last thoughts prior to your becoming unconscious?

PATIENT: Maybe next time it will be clearer. My purpose.

THERAPIST: Maybe next time it will become clearer. Any other feelings here?

PATIENT: Just sadness.

THERAPIST: What does the sadness say?

PATIENT: It's as though I lost so much but I did okay as long as I had the horse. Even though I'd lost my parents. But that was too much. And even loving nature wasn't enough to sustain me.

Dawn related the pattern she had uncovered to her current life and her difficulties finding nurturing relationships. The focus then shifted to where the pattern came from. Dawn moved to a vivid scenario from Egypt, where she had been betrothed to a cousin almost from birth. They grew up together and developed strong feelings of attachment and love. When Dawn was 16, however, she was abruptly sent away to become a priestess in a temple. She was given no explanation and felt the young man she loved had betrayed her. In continuing with the scenario, Dawn realized that her father owed a great debt and had been given the choice between giving her, his daughter, to the temple or having his entire family killed.

PATIENT: Someone had to accompany whoever it was who had just died. Either our whole family went with the person who died or I went as a priestess.

THERAPIST: You then became the sacrificial one?

PATIENT: Yes. And I never saw or heard from this boy or his family again. I knew nothing about them. But now I'm seeing that he killed himself. [Deep crying.]

THERAPIST: Because he really loved you, too, didn't he? He felt the loss.

PATIENT: [Crying.] He took poison.

THERAPIST: Uh huh. It seems almost as though both of you became victims of filial duty here.

PATIENT: [Deep crying.] I don't know why I felt his family had done it, because I see now it wasn't so.

THERAPIST: Seeing it now, where is that energy, that anger? Do you feel that you're releasing it, now that you've seen that there was no one who really wanted to reject you?

PATIENT: I feel the anger at the religious power that things could be done like that.

Continuing the scene, Dawn saw that she grieved for several years and then took up her duties as a priestess. She became the wise woman of the temple, one to whom people came for knowledge. When she was quite old, she just stopped eating and let herself die.

THERAPIST: What are your last thoughts and feelings just before your spirit passes from your body?

PATIENT: They're sort of double. One is that I've done a good job at what I was supposed to do. And another was that something was totally unfinished. With the relationship, I feel the pain a little bit again that I had felt on that last night of the year when I was 16.

THERAPIST: So that on your departure, there's really the feeling on one level of satisfaction but on another level there are unresolved feelings.

PATIENT: Yes. I both succeeded and didn't succeed. I succeeded in that I allowed myself to bend to the purpose that they gave me and flowed with the wind.

THERAPIST: I have a feeling that there's more here. Take this life now and see yourself moving out of it and into a space where you can look and view that entire life and compare it to where you are now and see how the energies and the unresolved relationship had an effect upon the decisions you have made in this lifetime. What do you see?

PATIENT: Somehow it seems, I don't know, that I had some reparative work to do in having my son, that I cannot have my son and have a relationship too. That's the feeling that I have, that I've chosen in this lifetime to do something with my son.

THERAPIST: With your son? Do you feel any of your son's energy from that lifetime?

PATIENT: [Voice breaking.] Well, I'm almost thinking he was the man [crying].

THERAPIST: You feel that?

PATIENT: I think . . . at least from my sadness . . . this time it was safer to have him as a son.

THERAPIST: Because in this way you could protect him, love him, love him in a way that would not have any intrusive factors coming in.

PATIENT: It seems that he won't hurt me this way.

THERAPIST: He can't hurt you as your son.

PATIENT: I have to look at my relationship with my son. I'm making it so there wouldn't be room for a man.

THERAPIST: That's right. There wouldn't be room for a man. It's almost as though you have created a very sacred space and that's part of your decision, and that space between you and him is not to be violated.

PATIENT: Yes. Well, I get that feedback from people, too, and I don't know what's right and what's wrong. I don't know.

THERAPIST: I think it will be more clear to you as he grows up.

In these regressions, Dawn experienced scenarios reiterating her chronic, real-life feelings of aloneness, abandonment, and rejection. The scenarios helped her reframe her problems, however. The trance involving a life in Egypt helped Dawn discover a pattern she had in real life, that she was often mistaken when she believed no one cared for her. That scenario also underscored how she had no room in her life for a loving man because her son was a replacement: a situation that now caused her other emotional conflicts. With these insights and with much hard work over several years, Dawn was gradually able to change her outlook and life situation.

CONCLUSION

Past-life regression provides vivid scenarios that reveal powerful, underlying emotional patterns in a person's life, offering intense catharsis, insight, and reframing. The term *past-life therapy*, however, is a misnomer because scenarios of "past lives" are only a small part of the therapeutic process and the illumination of the past is not the central focus. Some past-life therapists regard the patient's images as true, but this is not necessary: The scenarios can be regarded as metaphors. The goal is to use these images to bring about resolution of present-day conflicts. The ability to find meaning in present relationships, to gain a deepened sense of empathy with others, and to have a sense of the interrelatedness of all parts of life are core aims of past-life therapy. The true validity of past-life scenarios lies in how the process moves an individual toward understanding the subtle dimensions of projection, the emotional consequences of his behaviors, the "decision-making" process that occurs on different levels of consciousness, and the attitudinal and perceptual framework underlying his belief system. In short, past-life experiences become a metalanguage by which individuals can understand more deeply the nature of their own psyche and life's meaning.

NOTES

1. Sheldrake, R. (1988). *The presence of the past.* New York: Random House.

2. Bohm, D. (1980). *Wholeness and the implicate order.* London: Routledge & Kegan Paul.

3. Pribram, K. (1971). *Languages of the brain.* Englewood Cliffs, NJ: Prentice-Hall.

4. Lucas, W. (Ed.). (1993). *Regression therapy: A handbook for professionals* (Vols. 1 & 2). Crest Park, CA: Deep Forest Press.

5. Wambach, H. S. (1978). *Reliving past lives: The psychology of past-life regression.* New York: Ballantine Books.

6. Weiss, B. L. (1988). *Many lives, many masters.* New York: Simon & Schuster.

CHAPTER 37

Transpersonal Psychiatry in Psychiatry Residency Training Programs

FRANCIS G. LU

FOR THE FIRST TIME, the Accreditation Council for Graduate Medical Education has acknowledged the importance of religious–spiritual issues in psychiatry residency training programs; the council has mandated that all residency training programs in psychiatry address religious–spiritual factors that influence development and educate residents about religious–spiritual cultural factors relevant to understanding and relating to patients.[1] This innovation should stimulate the development of model curricula in transpersonal psychiatry.

In contrast, a study by Randy Sansome[2] showed that few residency training programs had didactic course work on any aspect of religion and that supervision infrequently addressed religious issues. The authors stated that "an academic approach to role of religion in psychiatry warrants consideration."[2]

This chapter is partially based on a monograph by Larson, D., Lu, F., et al. (1996). Model curriculum for psychiatry residency training programs: Religion and spirituality in clinical practice. Rockville, MD: National Institute for Healthcare Research.

This gap in training reflects the gap between religiousness of mental health professionals and of the general public.[3] M. Scott Peck characterized this gap in graphic terms in a standing-room-only lecture he gave at the 1992 Annual Meeting of the American Psychiatric Association, which was subsequently published:

> American psychiatry is, I believe, currently in a predicament. I call it a predicament because its traditional neglect of the issue of spirituality has led to five broad areas of failure: occasional, devastating misdiagnosis; not infrequent mistreatment; an increasingly poor reputation; inadequate research and theory; and a limitation of psychiatrists' own personal development. Taken further, these failures are so destructive to psychiatry that the predicament can properly be called grave.[4]

Hopeful signs for change include recent official American Psychiatric Association actions. In 1989, the Trustees approved a document subsequently published in the *American Journal of Psychiatry* entitled "Guidelines Regarding Possible Conflict Between Psychiatrists' Religious Commitments and Psychiatric Practice."[5] These guidelines called for psychiatrists to maintain respect for their patients' beliefs. Second, the DSM-IV[6] acknowledged for the first time a nonpsychopathological category entitled "Religious or Spiritual Problem" in the section entitled "Other Conditions That May Be a Focus of Clinical Attention." Furthermore, a section on "age, gender, and cultural considerations" was added to 92 narrative sections describing mental disorders as well as an outline for cultural formulation. In general, religion has been treated more respectfully in DSM-IV.

This expectation of respect for cultural diversity can also be applied to patients with religious, spiritual, and transpersonal beliefs. Although this chapter focuses on psychiatric residency training, the suggestions contained in it are readily applied to psychology graduate training, clinical social work training, and medical school education.

OBJECTIVES

The set of criteria entitled Special Requirements for Residency Training in Psychiatry lists knowledge, skill, and attitudinal objectives. These objectives as applied to the transpersonal area would include those listed in the following headings. The subjects of the chapters of this textbook that are applicable to the training goals are also indicated.

A. Knowledge

The Resident should demonstrate competence in the following:

I. Defining the transpersonal including these phenomenal aspects: experiences/attitudes/practices/beliefs (from here on these items are called simply "experiences").
   A. Relevant chapters in this textbook include the introduction (Scotton) and the chapters on shamanism (Walsh), meditation (Walsh), psychedelics (Bravo & Grob), near-death experience (Greyson), parapsychology (Tart), and consciousness (Battista). See also the chapters on William James (Taylor), Ken Wilber (Walsh & Vaughan), and Stanislav Grof (Yensen & Dryer).
II. Understanding the unique impact of transpersonal experiences on physical and psychological development in infancy, childhood, adolescence, and adulthood.
   A. Relevant chapters include those on aging and adult spiritual development (Chinen), psychotherapy with the religious (Judy), Ken Wilber (Walsh & Vaughan), Carl Jung (Scotton), and cults (Deikman)
III. Understanding a differential diagnosis for transpersonal phenomena at both the individual and religious/spiritual-system levels.
   A. Relevant chapters include those on diagnosis (Lukoff, Lu, & Turner), anthropology (Peters), kundalini (Scotton), transpersonal psychotherapy (S. Boorstein), offensive spirituality (Battista), transpersonal therapy in psychotic disorders (Lukoff), and psychedelics and psychotherapy (Bravo & Grob).
IV. Understanding the transpersonal factors that affect the course and treatment of psychiatric disorders.
   A. Relevant chapters are the same as for Item 3.
V. Understanding the impact of transpersonal experiences on the relationship between psychiatrist and patient, including transference and countertransference.
   A. Relevant chapters include those on transpersonal psychotherapy (S. Boorstein), offensive spirituality (Battista), psychotherapy with the religious (Judy), kundalini (Scotton), near-death experiences (Greyson), and clinical aspects of meditation (S. Boorstein).

VI. Understanding how transpersonal issues affect medical ethics as applied to psychiatric practice.
   A. Relevant chapters include those on offensive spirituality (Battista), cults (Deikman), and near-death experiences (Greyson).

VII. Understanding the variety of transpersonal experiences and traditions, each with its unique perspective on transpersonal issues.
   A. Relevant chapters include those on yoga (Scotton & Hiatt), Buddhism (Scotton), Kabbalah (Schachter-Shalomi), kundalini (Scotton), American Indian spirituality (Sandner), Christian mysticism (Judy), history of transpersonal psychology (Chinen), philosophy (Chinen), anthropology (Peters), Freud (Epstein), Jung (Scotton), William James (Taylor), Assagioli and Maslow (Battista), Grof (Yensen & Dryer), and Ken Wilber (Walsh & Vaughan).

B. Skills

The resident should demonstrate competence in the following:

I. Interviewing transpersonally committed patients with sensitivity to communication styles, vulnerabilities, and strengths.
   A. Relevant chapters include those listed in Item A5 as well as those on anthropology (Peters), past-life therapy (Jue), and breathwork (Lee & Speier).

II. Listening for, eliciting, and understanding accurate and complete histories, including the importance of the transpersonal in the patient's life.
   A. Relevant chapters include those listed in Items A5 and B1.

III. Diagnosing, assessing, and formulating treatment plans for patients, with an understanding of their transpersonal experience.
   A. Relevant chapters include those listed in Items A3, A4, and B1.

IV. Recognizing the differential diagnosis of transpersonal phenomena.
   A. Relevant chapters include those listed in Item A3.

V. Providing appropriate psychotherapeutic interventions with an understanding of the patient's transpersonal experience.
   A. Relevant chapters include those on transpersonal psychotherapy (S. Boorstein), transpersonal psychotherapy in psychosis (Lukoff), offensive spirituality (Battista), psychotherapy with the religious (Judy), psychedelics and psychotherapy (Bravo & Grob), near-death experience (Greyson), past-life regression (Jue), visualization and guided imagery (Foote), and breathwork (Lee & Speier).
VI. Recognizing and using specific transference and countertransference reactions. Negative reactions may indicate unresolved therapist issues in this area.
   A. Relevant chapters include those listed in Item A5.
VII. Knowing when to obtain consultation and how to work with transpersonally oriented professionals.
   A. Relevant chapters include those listed in Items A5 and B5.
VIII. Recognizing possible biases against the transpersonal found in the psychiatric literature and understanding their origins.
   A. Relevant chapters include the introduction (Scotton) and those on differential diagnosis (Lukoff, Lu, & Turner), near-death experiences (Greyson), and parapsychology (Tart).

C. Attitudes

Residents should demonstrate the following in their behavior and demeanor:

I. An awareness of their own transpersonal experiences and the impact of these experiences on their identity and worldview.
II. An awareness of their own attitudes toward various transpersonal experiences and the possible biases that could influence their assessment and treatment of patients with these experiences.
III. Empathy and respect for patients from a variety of transpersonal backgrounds.

LEARNING FORMATS

Several learning formats are needed to fulfill the objectives. Given the existing full schedules of residents, residency training programs can best achieve incorporation of transpersonal material through integration with existing learning formats whenever possible. To help achieve the attitudinal objectives, it is suggested that training programs use an experiential small-group training format patterned after the work of Elaine Pinderhughes.[7] She has successfully led small groups of mental health professionals in the exploration of issues of race, ethnicity, and power. Transpersonal issues could be included as one aspect of the training.

Didactic material can be incorporated into essential courses that are already taught. For example, material on transpersonal issues concerning development could be integrated into courses on human development. Material on differential diagnosis of transpersonal phenomena could be incorporated into courses on psychopathology or differential diagnosis. Material on treatment could be integrated into courses on psychotherapy and psychopharmacology. Transpersonal ethical issues could be included in ethics courses. Information on the variety of transpersonal experiences and traditions could be selectively incorporated into a cultural psychiatry course that included religious–spiritual aspects. Elective tutorials could review more of this material in greater depth.

Experiential learning during residency clerkships affords many opportunities for learning about transpersonal issues. For example, in emergency and inpatient psychiatry rotations, issues related to differential diagnosis are likely to arise. In the consultation–liaison and geriatric psychiatry rotations, death, dying, and suffering potentially evoke transpersonal experiences as well as call on the appropriate use of transpersonal interventions. Addiction psychiatry rotations would allow residents to understand and use transpersonally oriented treatment methods such as attending meetings of Alcoholics Anonymous and other self-help groups.

SUPERVISION

Supervision must be sensitive to the transpersonal. The importance of upgrading faculty skills and knowledge in this area is critical. A way to begin might be to identify a small group of faculty who have interest and expertise in the transpersonal and for them to identify themselves to potential supervisees. They could be available also for consultation and as case-conference discussants. Other learning formats include Grand Rounds, Case Conferences, Journal Clubs, and Films.

A basic list of requirements for the transpersonal supervisor would include an openness to the transpersonal dimension of development, the ability to sense a transpersonal experience, some knowledge of a variety of spiritual paths, the active pursuit of her own spiritual development, a firm grounding in psychotherapy, and a tolerance for both patients and supervisees working in different styles and traditions from her own.

Transpersonal psychotherapy can be conceptualized and practiced as the balance of two seemingly opposing efforts: reductive psychotherapeutic work and spiritual development. The reductive work focuses on understanding current difficulties in terms of failures in development or failures to master certain situations. It traces problems to their first appearances, develops understanding of the maladaptive pattern that is repeating, and fosters the development of better responses. The spiritual work focuses on development that is still ongoing and states of being that may be realized in the future. At any juncture in the therapeutic work, the therapist can look backward to analyze the genesis of the current resistance to growth or can look forward to foster the growth that is needed. The art and science of the discipline consists in using both modes of work appropriately with each person.

Both therapist and supervisor must carefully avoid the danger of the spiritual Procrustean bed. Although it is essential that each transpersonal practitioner have his own spiritual work, it is equally essential that he understand that his theory, religion, and practices are only some of many valid ways. Each clinician must be guided by his own development and yet allow his patients and students to grow along different paths.

Finally, a brief warning about the pull to be a guru seems necessary. The power and unfamiliarity of transpersonal experience and the human discomfort with uncertainty often combine to create a strong pull for a therapist or supervisor to be seen as a guru. Knowledge of this propensity and time spent thinking about its presentation and its clinical management form an essential aspect of transpersonal training.

Space limitations prevent a detailed examination of transpersonal supervision. For further details, see Bruce Scotton's article.[8]

CONCLUSION

Because of the increasingly multicultural and transpersonally oriented population in the United States, psychiatry residents are more and more likely to encounter patients with transpersonal experiences and commitments wherever they see patients. It is hoped that this chapter will help them to be better prepared to assess and work with these patients both in training and in practice.

NOTES

1. Accreditation Council for Graduate Medical Education. (1995, January). *Special requirements for residency training in psychiatry.* Chicago: Author.

2. Sansome, R. A., Khatain, K., & Rodenhauser, P. (1990). The role of religion in psychiatric education: A national survey. *Academic Psychiatry, 14,* 34–38. Quotation on p. 37.

3. Bergin, A. E., & Payne, I. R. (1990). Religiosity of psychotherapists: A national survey. *Psychotherapy, 27,* 3–7.

4. Peck, S. (1993). *Further along the road less traveled.* New York: Simon & Schuster. Quotation on p. 233.

5. American Psychiatric Association. (1990). Guidelines regarding possible conflict between psychiatrists' religious commitments and psychiatric practice. *American Journal of Psychiatry, 147,* 542.

6. American Psychiatric Association. (1994). *Diagnostic and Statistical Manual* (4th ed.). Washington, DC: Author.

7. Pinderhughes, E. (1988). *Understanding race, ethnicity and power.* New York: Free Press.

8. Scotton, B. (1985). Observations on the teaching and supervision of transpersonal psychotherapy. *Journal of Transpersonal Psychology, 17(1),* 57–75.

CHAPTER 38

Toward a Psychology of Human and Ecological Survival: Psychological Approaches to Contemporary Global Threats

ROGER WALSH

NUCLEAR WEAPONS, population explosion, resource and food-supply depletion, and environmental deterioration pose increasing threats to human survival. Moreover, all these major global threats are human-caused and therefore can be traced in large part to psychological origins. This chapter suggests a transpersonal psychology for human survival and global preservation and identifies ways in which mental health professionals may contribute to resolving global problems. The transpersonal movement emphasizes the importance of an inclusive, integrative framework that acknowledges the value and complementarity of apparently divergent approaches: behavioral and dynamic, individual and social, cognitive and existential, Eastern and Western. Transpersonal

This chapter is based in part on a paper that appeared in the *American Journal of Psychotherapy*.

approaches thus model at the psychological level what they counsel at the cultural and international level, namely, the setting aside
of traditional boundaries, conflicts, and claims for exclusivity and
the welcoming for objective appraisal of contributions of all cultures and ideologies.

COGNITIVE PERSPECTIVES

Within recent years there has been a growing recognition of the
potent yet frequently unrecognized power of beliefs to shape experience and behavior. Beliefs tend to modify what we look for, what
we recognize, how we interpret, and how we respond to these
interpretations. What is absolutely crucial is that these largely
unconscious processes tend to become self-fulfilling prophecies.[1,2]
For this reason, it is crucial to identify the beliefs shaping our contemporary crises.

The following are some of the beliefs that may be particularly
dangerous: *There's nothing I can do,* or *it's not my responsibility. My
beliefs/views/ideology are the truth and the only truth. It's their fault, not
ours, that they're hungry, that there is an arms race, and so on. You can't
trust them.* Worst of all, *They're not really human.*

Beliefs such as *it's hopeless* and *there's nothing that can be done,*
although understandable in light of the enormity of our difficulties, may exacerbate feelings of apathy and despair and prove dan-
gerously self-fulfilling. Likewise, beliefs that *there's not enough food
to go around* or that *there's no way of getting the food to people* are not
only patently incorrect, they are dangerous.[3]

DEFENSE MECHANISMS

"Humankind cannot bear very much reality," according to T. S.
Eliot, and defense mechanisms are the crutches we use to help us
avoid reality. Defense mechanisms particularly relevant to this discussion are repression, denial, projection, rationalization, and intellectualization. Repression and denial play major roles in this difficulty and spawn statements such as *I'd rather not think about it,* or
it's not really so bad. We wish to deny not only the state of the world
but also our role in producing it. Hence we use projection to
attribute to others the unacknowledged facets of our own self-
image and motives and thus create the image of the enemy.

The strain to consistency then demands that this image of the enemy be maintained through selective perception and further defenses.[4] The result is a classical paranoid relationship. What was initiated by the defense mechanisms of repression and projection is now aggravated and perpetuated by self-fulfilling negative expectations and a vicious feedback cycle of escalating mutual suspicion, defensiveness, and hostility.

When the suffering we produce must be discussed, its emotional impact can be reduced by the mechanism of intellectualization. Thus, the language of military science has always avoided reference to killing people or creating suffering.[5] This mechanism has reached new heights of sophistication among nuclear strategists, whose "nuke speak" is a strange and bloodless language by which the planners of nuclear war drain the reality from their actions.[6] Abstract discussions of reentry vehicles (missile warheads), countervalue (destroying cities), and collateral damage (killing civilians) facilitate planning for what are, in stark reality, strategic methods of producing more deaths and destruction than ever have occurred in the history of human conflict.

When these defenses are examined, it can be seen that they represent unskillful attempts to deal with fear. Indeed, from this perspective many international and nuclear threats can be seen as expressions of fear: fear of attack, for our survival, of losing our comforts, of alien lifestyles, of foreign ideologies, and of depletion of economic supplies.

REINFORCERS

Our individual, national, and international behaviors represent choices based on expected reinforcement. These patterns are extremely complex, but we can recognize several broad and dangerous trends. One clear-cut problem involves a focus on immediate rather than delayed gratification. This has become increasingly important because we are now dealing with problems whose effects become identifiable only after long periods of time. Pollution, for example, can take years to accumulate to toxic levels. Yet we are simultaneously reinforcing ourselves, our political leaders, and our military for ensuring short-term gratification. For example, few politicians have been willing to support legislation to reduce consumption of nonrenewable fossil fuels.

In addition, decision makers are now often spatially and emotionally distanced from the consequences of their decisions. For example, leaders can merely push buttons rather than engage in hand-to-hand combat; can allow millions to starve without ever setting eyes on a hungry person; or can pass legislation allowing massive pollution or ecological disturbance while living in far-removed air-conditioned comfort.

These factors are also closely linked to citizens' lifestyles. For example, our choice to drive our cars rather than use public transportation results in greater gasoline demands. These demands, in turn, reinforce suppliers and politicians for increasing immediate supplies even at the cost of greater pollution and more rapid depletion.

MECHANISMS CITED BY EASTERN PSYCHOLOGIES

Eastern psychologies suggest a wide range of mechanisms relevant to global threats.[7] Buddhist psychology, for example, offers sophisticated analyses of many causes of individual and social pathology (see Chapter 12). Buddhist psychology traces all these factors to the so-called three poisons: addiction, aversion, and delusion. Asian psychologies extend the scope of addiction beyond objects such as drugs and food, to which Western psychologists usually limit it. Rather, they suggest that addiction can occur to practically any thing or experience, including material possessions, relationships, beliefs, ideologies, affects, and self-image. Addiction is said to fuel greed, possessiveness, anger, and frustration; to reduce flexibility and choices; and to be a basis of fear and defensiveness. "The world has enough for everyone's need," Gandhi is quoted as saying, "but not enough for everyone's greed."

The second poison, aversion, is the desire to avoid or attack unpleasant stimuli; it can be regarded as addiction's mirror image and also as a source of anger, attack, fear, and defensiveness.

The third of the three poisons is delusion. Our usual state of mind, according to Eastern psychologies, is neither clear, optimal, nor wholly rational. Our addictions, aversions, and faulty beliefs filter and distort our perception, motivation, and sense of identity in such powerful yet unrecognized ways as to constitute a form of delusion or psychosis, a form that is rarely appreciated because it is culturally shared. Such a claim is consistent with the thinking of a number of Western psychologists, such as Erich Fromm,[8] Willis Harman,[9] Fritz Perls,[10] and Charles Tart.[11] "If we had to offer the briefest explanation of all the evil that men have wreaked upon themselves and upon their world since the beginning of time . . . it would be simply in the toll that his pretense of sanity takes as he tries to deny his true condition," said Ernest Becker.[12]

PSYCHOLOGICAL AND SOCIAL IMMATURITY

Fear, greed, aversion, ignorance, unwillingness to delay gratification, defensiveness, and unconsciousness are marks of psychological immaturity. They point to the fact that global crises reflect, not only the gross pathology of a Hitler or a Stalin, but even more so the myriad forms of "normal" psychological immaturity, inauthenticity, and failed actualization. In daily life, such individual immaturities are usually regarded as unexceptional. According to Abraham Maslow: "What we call 'normal' in psychology is really a psychopathology of the average, so undramatic and widely spread that we don't even recognize it ordinarily,"[13] From this perspective, culture can be seen, not only as a force for education and evolution, but also as a shared conspiracy against self-knowledge and psychological growth in which people collude to protect one another's defenses and illusions.

APPROPRIATE RESPONSES

Education

As described earlier in the chapter, many faulty beliefs and behaviors can be traced to ignorance or defenses against recognizing the true nature of our situation. It therefore follows that corrective education is essential. For long-term survival, main reliance must be placed on the education and training of future generations. Yet how many schools and universities offer adequate courses on global problems and human survival and how many psychology or psychiatry departments offer courses on the psychological roots of these problems? Here is a vital role for mental health professionals. To be most effective, education should include information about both the state of the world around us and the psychological forces within us that create it. We need to educate ourselves and others. As always, the ignorance of others is obvious; our own is less so. Yet, as many people have pointed out, self-education is a critical first step in becoming an effective activist.

Changing Reinforcers

It will be important to provide greater reinforcement for decisions that take long-term consequences into account. This requires increased information, for example, environmental impact reports and feedback on the costs and benefits, particularly long-term ones, of economic, industrial, and legislative decisions. Ecological choices could be selectively reinforced by modifying economic and social incentives and taxes, such as by raising the price of non-renewable resources and reducing those of renewable ones. Lifestyles emphasizing voluntary simplicity not only may be essential but also may prove inherently more satisfying[15] than lifestyles that emphasize high consumption. Of course this has long been a central claim of religious sages and social activists such as Gandhi. "The fewer the necessities the greater the happiness" is the theme they echo.

Social Learning Theory and the Media

Given the awesome psychological and social power of the media, it may be crucial to encourage its representatives to offer more socially relevant programming and prosocial models.[16] Mental health professionals have a great deal to contribute here. Research has already demonstrated the multiple and frequently deleterious effects of current media programming. These contributions can be expanded by extending research and using the findings to educate the public, the media, and legislators about the psychological, social, and global implications of media content. In doing so, mental health professionals have the opportunity of becoming an invaluable advocacy group, unique in offering unbiased, experimentally based information coupled with nonpartisan concern for social and global welfare.

Search for Areas of Commonality and Shared Purpose

Family therapists and organizational psychologists know that one of their first tasks is to help their clients recognize areas of shared purpose and commonality. As global therapists for our deeply interconnected and interdependent "global village," we would want to do the same. Many of our contemporary difficulties are not respecters of traditional boundaries. Ecological imbalances, pollution, and radioactive contamination do not halt politely at international borders. Increasingly, what we do unto others we also do unto ourselves. It may well be that, as Martin Luther King said, we will live together as brothers or die together as fools.

POSSIBLE BENEFICIAL EFFECTS

Unprecedented challenges such as those described might strip away our defenses and call us to examine our individual and collective lives with new urgency and depth. There is even the possibility of using our current dilemma to consciously cultivate our sensitivity to these existential issues. Existential and Eastern psychologies, in particular, emphasize using the awareness of death as a spur to fuller, more conscious, and more choice-based living. In the words of Sigmund Freud, "If you want to endure life, prepare yourself for death."[17]

To open ourselves fully to the existential givens of life is not only one of the hallmarks of psychological maturity, but also one of its causes. Because in the light of our own mortality and of the enormity of preventable suffering in the world; of the rampant inhumanity, greed, hatred, delusion, and defensiveness; and of our precarious existence, we are forced to question anew the meaning, purpose, and appropriateness of our lifestyles, work, values, and goals. It is to the extent that we confront these questions authentically and fully that we are likely to choose to respond in helpful ways that also foster maturity and adaptation. The consequence of nonmaturity and noncooperation may be nonexistence.

THE CALL TO SERVICE

Inasmuch as we respond to our current dilemma with maturing responses, service and contribution may increase. Both research and theory indicate that psychological maturity is associated with a greater orientation toward service.[18,22] Whether significant degrees of psychological maturation occur or not, it may well be that increasing numbers of people will be moved to contribute, and one of today's more hopeful signs is the rapidly growing number of people, including psychiatrists and psychologists, addressing global concerns.

Certainly activists are needed, but especially needed are people who not only are effective activists but also understand the underlying psychological issues. Because many of the causes of our crises stem from normative cultural beliefs and values, the effectiveness of the people will depend on the degree to which they can extract themselves from limiting and distorting cultural biases. This is the process of "detribalization," by which a person matures from an ethnocentric to a global worldview.[19] Such a person no longer looks through, but rather looks at, the cultural filters and hence can work on them.[20,22]

In short, we need people of wisdom and maturity who work not only to relieve suffering, but also to awaken themselves and others. This process of "service learning" is of course a form of the ancient tradition of karma yoga, the discipline in which service and work are viewed as opportunities for learning and awakening. The aim is impeccable service that optimally relieves suffering and awakens both self and others. In doing so, it aims at inclusive treatment of both symptom and cause, self and other, psyche and world. Mental health professionals may be in particularly strategic positions to make significant contributions. Individuals can provide public and professional education through lecturing, writing, use of the media, or establishing relevant courses; they can offer consultation to individuals and groups working on these issues; they can do background research and study; and they can counsel the growing numbers of people who are psychologically distressed by current events. Groups and organizations of mental health professionals can meet for discussion, self-education, and mutual empowerment; create task forces and resource groups; organize conferences and courses; support and lobby for relevant education and research; and disseminate their conclusions.

It may be that it is time for us to create new disciplines such as transpersonal ecology,[14,22] "a psychology of human survival": a discipline drawing on the insights of all schools of psychology, linking and facilitating people from all nations, races, and groups who wish to apply their expertise to these, the most urgent issues of our time; unveiling the psychological forces that have brought us to this turning point in history; working to transform them into forces for our collective survival, well-being, and fulfillment; and thereby pointing beyond itself to a psychology, not just of survival, but of human survival and well-being. Such a discipline might provide not only a catalyst for work in this area, but also a context and vision for psychology as a whole. It might also serve as a model for other fields, which might in their turn create, for example, an eco-logically oriented sociology, economics, or philosophy.[23,24] Perhaps Abraham Maslow was not entirely hyperbolic when he said of psy-chologists that "the future of the human species rests more upon their shoulders than upon any groups of people now living."[21] Never in the course of human history have the needs and oppor-tunities for contribution in general, and psychological contribution in particular, been greater.

NOTES

1. Bandura, A. (1977). Self efficacy: Toward a unifying theory of behavioral change. *Psychological Review, 84,* 191–215.

2. Merton, R. (1957). *Social theory and social structure.* Glencoe, IL: Free Press.

3. Brown, L. (1981). *Building a sustainable society.* New York: Norton.

4. Frank, J. (1982). *Sanity and survival in the nuclear age: Psycholog-ical aspects of war and peace.* New York: Random House.

5. Schell, J. (1982). *The fate of the earth.* New York: Knopf.

6. Barash, D., & Lipton, J. (1982). *Stop nuclear war: A handbook* (p. 227). New York: Grove.

7. Walsh, R. (1988). Two Asian psychologies and their implica-tions for Western psychotherapists. *American Journal of Psychother-apy, 42,* 543–560.

8. Fromm, E. (1970). *Zen Buddhism and psychoanalysis.* New York: Harper & Row.

9. Harman, W. (1962). Old wine in new wineskins. In J. Bugental (Ed.), *Challenges of humanistic psychology.* New York: McGraw-Hill.

10. Perls, F. (1969). *Gestalt therapy verbatim.* Lafayette, CA: Real People Press.

11. Tart, C. (Ed.). (1992). *Transpersonal psychologies.* New York: HarperCollins.

12. Becker, E. (1973). *The denial of death* (pp. 29–30). New York: Free Press.

13. Maslow, A. H. (1968). *Toward a psychology of being* (p. 16). Princeton, NJ: Van Nostrand.

14. Fox, W. (1991). *Toward a transpersonal ecology.* Boston: Shambhala.

15. Elgin, D. (1981). *Voluntary simplicity.* New York: Morrow.

16. Singer, J., & Singer, D. (1983). Psychologists look at television: Cognitive, developmental, personality, and social policy implications. *American Psychologist, 38,* 826–834.

17. Freud, S. (1955). Thoughts for the times. In J. Strachey (Ed. and Trans.), *The standard edition of the complete psychological works of Sigmund Freud* (Vol. 14, p. 299). London: Hogarth Press.

18. Walsh, R., & Vaughan, F. (1983). Towards an integrative psychology of wellbeing. In R. Walsh & D. H. Shapiro (Eds.), *Beyond health and normality: Explorations of exceptional psychological wellbeing* (pp. 388–431). New York: Van Nostrand Reinhold.

19. Levinson, D. J. (1978). *The seasons of a man's life.* New York: Knopf.

20. Wilber, K. (1977). *The spectrum of consciousness.* Wheaton, IL: Quest.

21. Maslow, A. H. (1956). *A philosophy of management.* Lecture presented to Cooper Union, New York.

22. Walsh, R., & Vaughan, F. (Eds.). (1993). *Paths beyond ego: The transpersonal vision.* Los Angeles: Tarcher.

23. Wilber, K. (1995). *Sex, ecology, spirituality.* Boston: Shambhala.

24. Wilber, K. (1996). *A brief history of everything.* Boston: Shambhala.

PART IV

Conclusion

CHAPTER 39

Integration and Conclusion

BRUCE W. SCOTTON,
ALLAN B. CHINEN, AND
JOHN R. BATTISTA

THE AUTHORS AND CLINICIANS represented in this textbook have set forth a multifaceted approach to spirituality and psychiatry. Taken together, these interdisciplinary perspectives provide an understanding of the human psyche that is more comprehensive than current psychiatric and psychological approaches. The result is a true science of body, mind, soul, and spirit, honoring the biopsychosociospiritual continuum that is the human condition. From the many diverse viewpoints presented in these chapters, several common, basic principles emerge that help define the field of transpersonal psychiatry and psychology. The principles can be divided into two groups: those dealing with theory and basic science and those involving clinical applications.

TRANSPERSONAL THEORY AND SCIENCE

1. The field requires methodological pluralism, including the use of quantitative and qualitative approaches, affirming both "subjective" self-reports and "objective" physical phenomena. The model is no longer that of the natural sciences, committed to studying

only "physical" objects, but rather an openness to all experience, no matter how odd in appearance or rare, as well as to the structures of consciousness. This method is William James's "radical empiricism," which is surely the true, deep motivation of science. Ken Wilber emphasizes this methodological pluralism with his metaphor of the three eyes of knowledge—sensory, intellectual, and contemplative—each with its own distinctive standards of rigor. Such pluralism reflects the postmodern condition, and a truly scientific approach to the psyche must involve such multiple perspectives.

2. As a result of the preceding characteristics, transpersonal psychiatry must be multidisciplinary, relying on the methods, findings, and traditions of various fields including biology, anthropology, literature, criminology, theology, and sociology. Artists, writers, and poets have as much to contribute in their way as neurochemists and statisticians. Each discipline represents a different psychic perspective. The crucial question here is not whether a claim made by a particular discipline is true or false but in what sense it is true and how it helps transpersonal psychiatry alleviate human suffering.

3. A cross-cultural approach is essential to transpersonal psychiatry and psychology. Insight, wisdom, and knowledge are certainly not limited to modern Western science but are spread throughout humanity. Different cultures create divergent realities and promote development of diverse aspects of human potential. The field simply cannot afford the Western ethnocentrism that has pervaded much of modern psychiatry and psychology. As ready as we are to check different gene pools for resistance to a disease or to assay various ligands for activity at specific binding sites, so must we be willing to explore different cultures for solutions to problems of aggression or for methods of facilitating spiritual qualities that we may not even have a name for in Western culture.

4. Spiritual experience is universal across cultures and history. It is not a strange, inexplicable variant but a normal result of human development. In fact, even in a materialistic, secular culture such as ours, transpersonal concerns pervade the works of great thinkers and artists and are characteristic of more mature, better adjusted individuals.

5. Human development, generally speaking, proceeds from prepersonal, or preegoic, stages to personal, or egoic, phases and on to transpersonal, or transegoic, levels. Pathologies and develop-

mental arrests may arise at each point. This is the biopsychoso-ciospiritual developmental continuum, which anchors and integrates transpersonal psychiatry, providing both a clinical and a theoretical framework.

6. Well-tried systems exist to facilitate spiritual development and to address pathologies at all levels. Western studies of the mind have focused particularly on prepersonal and personal levels, whereas Eastern traditions have emphasized understanding the transpersonal. The connection between transpersonal and everyday consciousness is conceptualized in different ways, for example in the theories of Carl Jung, Roberto Assagioli, Ken Wilber, Michael Washburn, and John Battista, among others, drawing on anthropology, psychoanalysis, philosophy, and cybernetics. Spiritual traditions, of course, have their own accounts of the interconnections between transpersonal states and everyday events; examples include Buddhist Abhidharma, yogic metaphysics, and the theology of Jewish, Christian, and Islamic mysticism.

7. Transpersonal states take different forms at different stages of human development. In adolescence, for example, there is often an upsurge in transpersonal inspirations, which many tribal cultures channel into initiation ceremonies such as Native American vision quests. Spiritual concerns return with aging and most religious traditions, including Hinduism, Confucianism, Judaism, and Christianity, teach that aging is a spiritual journey. Several transpersonal theories emphasize the incremental, linear nature of spiritual development, holding that transpersonal states add on to previous psychological structures. These additive theories include the works of Lawrence Kohlberg, James Fowler, Wilber, and Battista. Another group of theories emphasize the dialectic nature of the development, holding that regression often precedes progression. These theories include those of Jung, Washburn, and Stanislav Grof.

8. Finally, given the vast multiplicity of human experience and of the avenues to its study and understanding, the appropriate stance toward this work—clinical, theoretical, and research—must include a significant component of awe, curiosity, and openness to the mystery that is the human psyche. We need to continue to acknowledge that all our theories and spiritual traditions are only attempts to articulate complex phenomena that can never be fully captured in a concrete form. This is surely the original aim and sentiment of science: to further awareness and understanding in an attitude of humility and wonder.

CLINICAL PRINCIPLES

1. The practice of transpersonal psychiatry and psychology requires a holistic approach, because the significance and effect of spiritual experiences depend on the individual as a whole. This larger context helps determine whether a particular experience is prepersonal, personal, or transpersonal. An ecstatic vision of Christ or Buddha, for example, is likely to be overwhelming to a person with schizophrenia, producing further disorganization in his life. Such an experience is prepersonal. A similar vision may be an unexpected opening to personal growth for someone functioning at a higher level, inspiring that individual to make major changes in her relationships without embracing an explicit spiritual path. The experience would be personal rather than transpersonal. Finally, an ecstatic vision may lead an individual to change a successful career into one with a new emphasis on public service and spiritual illumination. This would be an explicitly transpersonal experience.

2. Transpersonal development in a single individual may involve different lines of development and sometimes leads to "lacunae" of lower functioning. Just as a person may be intellectually gifted but emotionally immature or socially awkward, an individual may also be highly developed spiritually with respect to contemplative practice but poorly evolved in relationships or with sensual experience. This contrast is clear in cases of spiritual leaders who have gone astray, succumbing to alcoholism or sexual misconduct. Spiritual illumination in one area of personal development can coexist with relative spiritual ignorance in another. The transpersonal lessons gained in retreats or monastic settings do not always generalize to everyday experience in human relationships. In traditional spiritual terms, this is the problem of "returning to the marketplace" and bringing transcendent insight to everyday life.

3. Clinical interventions in transpersonal psychiatry must be aimed at the individual's developmental level and the particular presenting problem. With individuals at a prepersonal level of development, for example, the goal is generally the establishment of a competent ego, with stable internalized structures. Examples of phenomena at this level include psychoses, borderline personality disorders, panic attacks, and severe depressions. Clinical interventions usually emphasize biological measures such as medication as well as social support. With individuals at a personal level of development, the goal is usually to remedy isolated problems in

ego functioning, for example, resolving intrapsychic conflicts and improving interpersonal relationships through reductive, psychodynamic work. A spiritual focus can be a distraction or a defense in this case, in which the individual may prefer to dwell in numinous experiences rather than deal with real, everyday interpersonal difficulties. Spiritual practices can be misused in narcissistic ways. Alternatively, individuals may be advanced, skillful meditators and still suffer problematic interpersonal patterns with which they need assistance. The focus here would be on practical relationship issues.

3.1. Finally, an individual may have relatively minor difficulties functioning in life but major concerns about the ultimate meaning of existence. Or a well-adjusted individual may have unusual experiences, such as spiritual emergence, kundalini arousal, or ecstatic visions. These issues are transpersonal and require an explicitly spiritual approach. Psychopathology as traditionally defined in psychiatry would not be involved. Clinicians may need to refer these high-functioning individuals in a transpersonal crisis to practitioners experienced in spiritual guidance. The choice of which spiritual traditions to embrace is complex and depends on the individual's background and interests. Ethical issues arise here, because clinicians must be sensitive about imposing their own spiritual or philosophical views, even unconsciously.

4. Regardless of an individual's developmental level, transpersonal interventions can be used therapeutically. Meditation offers a clear example. Meditative practices can be used as a self-soothing exercise for some individuals with anxiety or borderline personality disorders; that is, a transpersonal technique can offer help for prepersonal difficulties. For someone with good ego functioning, meditation can be used to encourage unconscious material to emerge for the purpose of enriching and deepening psychotherapy. Beyond these psychological, therapeutic uses, meditation has its own explicitly transpersonal function for individuals on a spiritual path. For example, meditation is used in Buddhism to experience the ultimate transitoriness of the world and, in Jewish or Christian mysticism, to commune with God. Even in psychosis, spiritual experiences can be useful, providing meaning to an individual, particularly in the postpsychotic integration phase. The importance and role of transpersonal approaches for prepersonal difficulties is most dramatic with addiction work. Many Twelve-Step programs explicitly rely on spiritual approaches; in these instances, transpersonal inspiration helps with biologically based problems.

5. Spiritual techniques are not innocuous and can have negative effects, again depending on the individual's level of development. Awareness meditation, which brings up powerful unconscious material, can overwhelm someone with a vulnerability to psychosis or with borderline personality disorder. Perhaps the most dramatic example of the risk involving powerful transpersonal techniques involves the use of psychedelics: Persons with schizophrenia using psychedelics suffer psychotic breaks lasting weeks, whereas normal individuals experience uncontrolled altered consciousness and hallucinations for several hours. By contrast, experienced shamans, who generally have sturdy egos, typically control their altered states for use in healing and tribal ceremonies.

6. Our emphasis on a developmental model for transpersonal psychiatry must not obscure the principle that each person will trace her own unique path through life and cannot be expected to fit perfectly any single map of development. Theory and practice must be tailored to the individual, not vice versa. For example, there may be significant differences between the developmental forms and experiences of the genders that are not yet appreciated. Similarly, further cross-cultural studies may reveal new developmental pathways not yet envisioned in Western psychology.

An example may help summarize these clinical principles. Dreams represent an altered state of consciousness that is normal and essential for human life. Clinical work with dreams depends on the individual and his overall situation. For a person with schizophrenia, the clinical focus is less likely to be on deep, archetypal meanings and more likely on improving everyday functioning by reconstituting acceptable social roles. For someone with intact ego functioning who is well defended psychologically, the emphasis is usually on the unconscious conflicts represented in the dreams, which may be threatening to the person. Finally, some dreams are "big" and transcend individual concerns. These dreams often reveal insights and images of value to a whole tribe or society and may contain paranormal perceptions. Explicitly spiritual, these dreams are truly transpersonal. Dreams therefore illustrate the biopsychosociospiritual continuum: They have a definite biological substrate and function, often offer significant psychological and interpersonal insights, and sometimes contain profound spiritual meaning. The same considerations apply to transpersonal experiences in general.

Because of the many uses of transpersonal experiences, clinical experience and judgment are essential in transpersonal psychiatry for two major issues: (1) defining the therapeutic goals for a particular individual and (2) matching transpersonal interventions to him, choosing from biological, psychological, social, and spiritual techniques. This pragmatic judgment is surely the heart of transpersonal psychiatry, just as curiosity and awe for all of human experience is its soul.

CHAPTER 40

An Annotated Guide to the Transpersonal Literature

JOHN R. BATTISTA

THIS CHAPTER WAS DEVELOPED from recommendations of the authors of the volume to provide a guide to the classical and essential readings in transpersonal psychology and psychiatry, spiritual studies, and spiritual traditions.

TRANSPERSONAL PSYCHOLOGY AND PSYCHIATRY

Overview and Introduction to the Field

Walsh, R., & Vaughan, F. (Eds.). (1993). *Paths beyond ego.* New York: Putnam. This fine book contains excerpts from many of the classical works by influential writers in the field. It is an excellent introduction and the easiest way to become acquainted with the full breadth of transpersonal psychology and psychiatry.

The Transpersonal Worldview

Wilber, K. (1995). *Sex, ecology, spirituality.* Boston: Shambhala Publications. This major, synthesizing work by the most influential writer in the transpersonal field provides an excellent overview and perspective on transpersonal thought and its relationship to other disciplines and intellectual traditions. Although it is not a place to start, it is essential reading for the committed student.

Consciousness Studies

Wilber, K. (1977). *The spectrum of consciousness.* Wheaton, IL: Theosophical Publishing. This classical book in the transpersonal field presents Wilber's spectrum theory of consciousness. It is essential reading and the best place to start reading Wilber.

Neumann, E. (1970). *The origins and history of consciousness.* Princeton, NJ: Princeton University Press. This thought-provoking, classical text by an influential Jungian analyst argues that individual consciousness passes through the same archetypal stages of development that marked the history of human consciousness. A rich introduction to symbolism and the evolution of human consciousness, it is challenging reading but well worth it.

Grof, S. (1976). *Realms of the human unconscious.* New York: Dutton. The result of the thousands of sessions of psychedelic psychotherapy conducted by Grof, this book maps the levels of consciousness uncovered, from intense personal suffering to cosmic communion.

Bucke, R. (1969). *Cosmic consciousness.* New York: Dutton. Using biographies and quotations from the works of great men and women of history, Bucke demonstrates different types of spiritual experience. This book provides solid evidence for the fact that, even in our materialistic culture, the idea of transpersonal development lies hidden in our estimate of greatness of achievement and being.

James, W. (1929). *Varieties of religious experience.* New York: Modern Library. The pioneering transpersonal work in modern Western psychiatry and psychology. James collected and analyzed examples of different levels of spiritual consciousness.

Human Development from a Transpersonal Perspective

Wilber, K. (1980). *The atman project.* Wheaton, IL: Theosophical Publishing. This book contains an extension of Wilber's spectrum theory of consciousness showing how it provides a means of understanding the stages of human development over the course of life. Essential reading.

Psychopathology from a Transpersonal Perspective

Grof, S., & Grof, C. (Eds.). (1989). *Spiritual emergency.* Los Angeles: Tarcher. This fine collection of essays covers the problems involved with spiritual awakening and how they may be misconceptualized from the perspective of traditional psychology and psychiatry.

Wilber, K., Engler, J., & Brown, D. (1986). *Transformations of consciousness.* Boston: Shambhala Publications. This excellent series of articles covers the developmental stages in spiritual growth. It is included in the psychopathology section because the articles on psychopathology and psychotherapy are essential reading, covering the extension of Wilber's spectrum model to these domains.

Transpersonal Psychotherapy

Vaughan, F. (1995). *The inward arc: Healing in psychotherapy and spirituality* (2nd ed.). Nevada City, CA: Blue Dolphin Press. A book of practical wisdom for integrating psychology and spirituality. This book was listed as a classic by the transpersonal interest group of the American Psychological Association.

Deikman, A. (1982). *The observing self: Mysticism and psychotherapy.* Boston: Beacon. Presents a dynamic, contemporary, functional framework for unifying psychotherapy and spirituality.

Epstein, M. (1995). *Thoughts without a thinker.* New York: Basic Books. This fine book presents a well-written, sensible, and well-grounded approach to psychotherapy from a Buddhist perspective.

Reynolds, D. (1980). *The quiet therapies.* Honolulu: University of Hawaii Press. This outstanding little book reviews Japanese approaches to psychotherapy. The very act of reading it brings a sense of balance.

Jungian Psychology

Jung, C. (1965). *Memories, dreams, reflections.* New York: Vintage Press. Jung's autobiography is essential reading for anyone interested in transpersonal psychology from a Jungian perspective.

Whitmont, E. (1969). *The symbolic quest.* Princeton, NJ: Princeton University Press. A very readable and sound introduction to Jungian psychology and psychotherapy that complements the fine and more commonly recommended *Boundaries of the Soul* by June Singer.

Edinger, E. (1973). *Ego and archetype*. Baltimore: Penguin Books. This outstanding book discusses the dialectic between ego and self throughout the life cycle and how it can be used to understand psychological problems and psychotherapy. In addition, it gives an excellent description of Christ as the archetype of the individuating ego. Essential for transpersonal Jungian psychology.

Jacobi, J. (1965). *The way of individuation*. New York: Harcourt, Brace & World. This beautiful book gives a wonderful introduction to Jungian concepts of development through the life cycle: what Jung called the process of individuation.

Meditation

Shapiro, D., & Walsh, R. (Eds.). (1984). *Meditation: Classic and contemporary perspectives*. New York: Aldine. A collection of outstanding papers on meditation theory and research.

Kabat-Zinn, J. (1991). *Full catastrophe living: Using the wisdom of your body and mind to face stress, pain, and illness*. New York: Delta. A careful, well-documented guide to using meditative awareness for healing.

Journals and Magazines

Journal of Transpersonal Psychology, P.O. Box 3049, Stanford, CA 04309. This is the major journal in the transpersonal field and is essential reading for anyone who wishes to stay current in the field.

ReVision, Heldref Publications, 1319 Eighteenth Street NW, Washington, DC 20036–1802. This interesting journal of consciousness and transformation was initially edited by Ken Wilber. Each issue now has a guest editor who focuses the issue on a particular topic, such as gender or evolution, and presents a series of articles showing the relationship of this topic to the transpersonal inquiry. Overall, a thought-provoking, broadening, and useful journal. Highly recommended.

Noetic Sciences Review, P.O. Box 909, Sausalito, CA 94966–0909. This magazine is an extension of the work of The Institute of Noetic Studies, a remarkable organization that supports research, holds conferences, publishes books, and disseminates information related to the general field of consciousness studies and its interface with traditional science.

Common Boundary, 5272 River Road, Suite 650, Bethesda, MD 20816. This popular magazine exploring spirituality, psychotherapy, and creativity is a useful means to stay in touch with the impact of spirituality on psychotherapy and the culture in general. Highly recommended.

Transpersonal Review, 4893 Escobedo Dr., Woodland Hills, CA 91364. A new journal that attempts to make at least some mention of all new books in the field and in many related fields. A distinguished board of editors is polled for their ratings of the books. Several in-depth reviews are also featured. The most exciting journalistic development in the field in many years.

SPIRITUAL STUDIES

This section emphasizes books that will assist readers in their own spiritual development.

Biographies

Neihardt, J. (1972). *Black Elk speaks*. New York: Simon & Schuster. This moving story of Black Elk, a holy man of the Oglala Sioux who lived during the period of the westward spread of the white man, is a great classic of spiritual biography. In addition, it is a superb introduction to Native American spirituality and the role of visions in spiritual life. A must read.

Ram Dass. (1974). *The only dance there is*. New York: Anchor Books. Ram Dass is one of the authentic spiritual teachers in the West and certainly the best storyteller. These talks, originally delivered at the Menninger Foundation, entertain while teaching and enlightening. The reader will be inspired to move on to Ram Dass's other books, *Be Here Now* and *Grist for the Mill*.

Paramahansa Yogananda. (1969). *Autobiography of a Yogi*. Los Angeles: Self Realization Fellowship. This classical story of the life and awakening of Paramahansa Yogananda, the leader of the Self Realization Fellowship, has amazed and moved countless individuals through innumerable editions.

Roberts, B. (1982). *The experience of no-self*. Boulder, CO: Shambhala Publications. A former Catholic nun provides a moving account of her spiritual odyssey to the land beyond the self. A fine book.

O'Halloran, M. ("Soshin" Pure Heart). (1994). *Enlightened mind.* Boston: Tuttle. These letters and diary entries chronicle the rigors, frustrations, and enlightenment of this Irish-American woman during her years of Zen training in Japan. A very human, readable, moving, and educational tale of this young woman who is identified with the bodhisattva Kannon, the Buddhist saint of compassion, by those who knew her in Japan.

Matthiessen, P. (1978). *The snow leopard.* New York: Bantam Books. This is a remarkable spiritual travelogue of a journey across Nepal and Tibet taken by Peter Matthiessen, a Buddhist practitioner–seeker, and George Schaller, a zoologist, searching for the elusive and seemingly mythic snow leopard. Also try Matthiessen's funny, tragic, and profound spiritual novel, *At Play in the Fields of the Lord.*

Novels

Nichols, J. (1981). *The nirvana blues.* New York: Ballantine Books. This irreverent, outrageous spoof of the fallout of pursuing higher consciousness will have you falling off your chair laughing in the middle of the night, because you won't be able to put it down.

Castaneda, C. (1968). *The teachings of Don Juan.* Berkeley, CA: University of California Press. This is the first of a highly influential series of books detailing the teachings of Don Juan, a Yaqui shaman, to the rational, everyman of Carlos Castenada. Studying the transpersonal field without having read these books is like being a science fiction fan who has never seen the *Star Wars* trilogy.

Moon, I. (1988). *The life and letters of Tofu Roshi.* Boston: Shambhala Publications. Tofu Roshi, an imaginary spiritual teacher, answers Ann Landers–type questions from spiritual aspirants in a style that is up and down in the funny department. The appendix to the book, however, "How to Give Up Self-Improvement," must be both the funniest and most profound teaching around.

Matarasso, P. (1977). The *quest of the Holy Grail.* New York: Penguin Books. This most beautifully written translation of the French version of the quest of the Holy Grail is one of the great epic stories in the spiritual literature; it is complete with Bible-based, spiritual dream interpretation. If you can relate to the Judeo–Christian tradition or to Jungian archetypal psychology, this is for you.

Levin, M. (1975). *Classic Hassidic tales.* New York: Penguin Books. These classic teaching stories of the Rabbi Bal Shem Tov and his great grandson Rabbi Nachman have long been revered for their ability to reveal the living spirit of Judaism and a personal relationship with God.

Poetry

Mitchell, S. (1993). *The enlightened heart.* New York: Harper-Collins. This remarkable anthology of sacred poetry from all traditions and ages by this gifted translator will expose you to the best of a wide assortment of poets and guide you for the future. A gem.

Rexroth, K. (1976). *One hundred poems from the Japanese.* New York: New Directions. Rexroth's translations of Japanese and Chinese poems collected as *One Hundred Poems from the Japanese* and *One Hundred Poems from the Chinese* are simply the best collections of spiritually evocative poems ever published. Some of the poems have been reprinted as *Love Poems from the Japanese* by Shambhala Publications in 1994.

Rumi. (1986). *Unseen rain.* New York: Threshold Books. Rumi is probably the most popular poet among transpersonalists. All of Rumi's works are well worth reading. These short quatrains are my personal favorites and will appeal to people who like the imagery of traditional Japanese and Chinese poetry.

Eliot, T. S. (1943). *The four quartets.* New York: Harcourt, Brace. The classical and profound paradoxical poetry of Eliot is must reading, again and again, out loud.

Spiritual Guidance by Contemporary Practitioners

There are many wonderful books in this area. The following are only a few of many, many possibilities selected because of their significance or the importance of being exposed to their author.

Kornfield, J. (1993). *A path with heart.* New York: Bantam Books. This Buddhist-based guide through the perils of spiritual life by this well-known and well-respected psychologist and meditation teacher is a humane, humorous, open, and useful source for the spiritual aspirant.

Moore, T. (1994). *Care of the soul.* New York: HarperCollins. This best-selling book, influenced by the work of Jungian analyst James Hillman, provides a moving and practical guide for cultivating depth and sacredness in everyday life.

Welwood, J. (1990). *Journey of the heart.* New York: HarperCollins.

A fine exploration of relationship as a spiritual practice and path. A balancing and much needed perspective.

Levine, S. (1982). *Who dies?* Garden City, NY: Doubleday. This powerful and influential book discusses conscious living and conscious dying as a result of the author's experience working with dying people. A fine book by a fine teacher.

Nh'at Hanh, T. (1987). *Being peace.* Berkeley, CA: Parallax. This lovely book by a highly influential Vietnamese Zen Buddhist emphasizes the importance of "being peace" to make peace in the world. It is a good introduction to his work, which emphasizes being conscious and loving in the moment and serving others through community.

SPIRITUAL TRADITIONS

General Introduction and Overview

Mitchell, S. (1991). *The enlightened mind.* New York: Harper-Collins. This lovely collection of sacred prose across all traditions and all times provides a wonderful introduction to the heart and wisdom of most spiritual traditions.

Hixon, L. (1989). *Coming home: The experience of enlightenment in sacred traditions.* Los Angeles: Tarcher. An excellent introduction to different spiritual paths.

Huxley, A. (1970). *The perennial philosophy.* New York: Harper/Colophon. Reviewed by the *New York Times* as the greatest anthology in the field of religion, it is even more than that. Huxley notes the parallels and connections among religious traditions and convincingly supports his conclusions with quotations.

Hinduism and Yoga

Sri Aurobindo. (1973). *Essays on the Gita.* Pondicherry, India: Sri Aurobindo Ashram. A fine introduction to the Gita and the awesome mind and being of Sri Aurobindo, the great integrating sage of the twentieth century. Sri Aurobindo's masterpieces, *The Life Divine* and *The Synthesis of Yoga*, are two of the great transpersonal classics of this century. However, they are advanced and challenging reading.

Swami Prabhavananda. (1969). *The spiritual heritage of India.* Hollywood, CA: Vedanta Press. This comprehensive overview of

Indian philosophy and religion by this well-known Vedanta teacher is especially valuable because it contains many useful selected quotes from the great Indian spiritual texts. Also try his quite lucid and inspiring *Sermon on the Mount According to Vedanta*.

Taimini, I. K. (1972). *The science of yoga*. Wheaton, IL: Theosophical Publishing House. This remarkable commentary on the even more remarkable *Yoga-Sutras* of Patanjali is must reading for the student who wants to understand and practice yoga.

Zimmer, H. (1956). *Philosophies of India*. New York: Meridian Books. This fine book was prepared by Joseph Campbell from notes left by the Indian scholar Heinrich Zimmer. It presents a clear exposition of Buddhism, Brahmanism, Jainism, yoga, and tantra within a clear historical and cultural understanding of India. A well-respected classic.

Buddhism

Rahula, W. (1974). *What the Buddha taught*. New York: Grove Press. This clear and lucid introduction to the essential teachings of the Buddha is a time-honored classic that has survived the literal flood of texts giving an overview of Buddhism. Essential reading.

Suzuki Roshi, S. (1985). *Zen mind, beginner's mind* (20th ed.). New York: Weatherhill. To my mind this is the most precious gem of the entire spiritual literature. Its great gift is that the way Suzuki Roshi expresses himself is consonant with what he says. This Soto Zen masterpiece emphasizes being and suchness in each moment.

Sogyal, Rinpoche. (1992). *The Tibetan book of living and dying*. San Francisco: Harper San Francisco. Sogyal communicates the warmth of the Tibetan people with stories and spiritual exercises as well as didactic material. A book that rewards rereading.

Taoism and Chinese Philosophy

Lao Tsu. (1972). *Tao Te ching* (G.-F. Feng and J. English, Trans.). New York: Random House. A wonderful translation and rendition of this most profound teaching. A book to be read and reread.

Wilhelm, R., & Baynes, C. (Trans.). (1971). *The I Ching* (8th ed.). Princeton, NJ: Princeton University Press. This is a fantastic translation of one of the greatest books of all time, a venerable storehouse of wisdom. It is a book of divination that is meant to be used by asking it questions. The philosophy and life approach that it presents are profoundly moving and corrective. An essential classical work.

Christianity

Merton, T. (1962). *New seeds of contemplation.* New York: New Directions. A fine introduction to the spiritual teachings of the most influential contemporary Christian contemplative who thoroughly explored Eastern wisdom. After reading this one, try his book *The Wisdom of the Desert* and his autobiography, *The Seven Storey Mountain.* An important and essential voice, well worth studying.

Underhill, E. (1974). *Mysticism.* New York: New American Library. This classical work on Christian mysticism introduces the essential literature in the field and inspires one to read some of it. Highly recommended.

Griffiths, B. (1982). *The marriage of East and West.* Springfield, IL: Templegate Publishers. Bede Griffiths, a highly revered Christian monk who lived in a Christian ashram in India that followed Hindu and Christian customs and practices, presents his valuable synthesis of Christianity, Judaism, and the teachings of the Vedas. A wonderful example of contemporary contemplative Christianity.

Levi. (1969). *The Aquarian gospel of Jesus the Christ* (36th printing). Santa Monica, CA: De Vorss. This remarkable book, said to be read off the Akashic Records, presents Christ as an avatar who forged the path to Christ consciousness, which we are all to follow. It answers many of the questions and resolves problems of persons raised in the Judeo-Christian tradition but alienated from it.

Fox, M. (1991). *Creation spirituality.* San Francisco: HarperCollins. An excellent introduction to the work of the controversial Matthew Fox, who has tried to reintroduce the natural, embodied living God, the feminine, and the creative into Christian theology.

Sufism

Shah, I. (1964). *The Sufis.* London: Octagon Press. Shah presents a tough-minded, unifying view from a tradition that is relatively unknown and unappreciated in the West. It is immensely clarifying of the whole transpersonal enterprise.

Index

427

Individuation, 42, 47

Infancy, as source of merger fantasy, 32–33

Inflation of ego, 93, 182–83, 312–13

Information theory of consciousness, 85–94, 203

Instrumental vs. receptive consciousness, 320

Intellect, attachment to, 363–64

Interior Castle (Avila), 142

Internalized object relations. *See* Complexes

Interpersonal problems: and near-death experience, 305, 312; in past-life therapy, 382–86

Intersubjective self, 88

Intrauterine existence, and oceanic feeling, 80

Introverted perspective, in Indian wisdom tradition, 105

Intuition, 88, 351

I–Thou relationship, 124

James, Henry, Sr., 22

James, William, 5, 9, 21–27, 177, 222

Jesus Christ, 134–35

Jnana yoga, 110

John, E. Roy, 85

Journal of Transpersonal Psychology (JTP), 10–11

Judaism, Kabbalah mysticism, 123–30

Jung, Carl G.: active imagination vs. vision quest, 152; archetypal themes in psychosis, 271; contributions to TP&P, 39–50; on imagery as therapy, 355; on importance of spiritual experience, 5; on inflation of ego, 312; spiritual

dimension of alcohol abuse, 241

Jungian psychology vs. other theories, 59–60

Kabbalah mysticism, 123–30

Kant, Immanuel, 220–21

Karma, 106, 110, 116, 403

Keleman, Stanley, 87

Kingsley Hall program, 278

Kirsch, James, 42

Knowledge: information as, 86; theory of, 67–68, 197–98, 217–27

Kramer, Peter, 330

Kundalini yoga, 111, 261–70

Laing, R. D., 272, 274, 278

Lasch, Christopher, 250

Leadership, cult vs. normal, 316–17, 319–23

LeShan, L., 189

Leuner, Hanscarl, 76

Lévi-Strauss, Claude, 209

Libido, Jung vs. Freud, 46

Life and Teachings of Tofu Roshi, The (Moon), 255

Life cycle: fairy tales as symbolic of development, 155–64; religious orientation role, 297–98

Light, properties of, 196–97

Liminality, 209–10

Linear vs. cyclical view of time, 106

Listening to Prozac (Kramer), 330

Logical positivism, 219

Love: and Bhakti yoga, 109; as goal of Christian mysticism, 140, 142; as mystical experience, 32

Lowen, Alexander, 368

LSD, 75–82, 177–79, 278–79, 340, 368–69